A COMPENDIUM OF
SPOKEN WORDS

Everyday Vocab • Essential Word Power
Techniques of Correct Pronunciation

A COMPENDIUM OF SPOKEN WORDS

Everyday Vocab • Essential Word Power
Techniques of Correct Pronunciation

KUMKUM GUPTA

ARIHANT PUBLICATIONS (INDIA) LTD

ARIHANT PUBLICATIONS (INDIA) LTD

卐 ***Administrative & Production Offices***

Regd. Office 'Ramchhaya' 4577/15, Agarwal Road, Darya Ganj, New Delhi -110002
Tele: 011- 47630600, 43518550; Fax: 011- 23280316

Head Office Kalindi, TP Nagar, Meerut (UP) - 250002
Tel: 0121-2401479, 2512970, 4004199; Fax: 0121-2401648

卐 ***Sales & Support Offices***

Agra, Ahmedabad, Bengaluru, Bhubaneswar, Bareilly, Chennai, Delhi, Guwahati, Haldwani, Hyderabad, Jaipur, Jhansi, Kolkata, Kota, Lucknow, Meerut, Nagpur & Pune

卐 ***ISBN*** 978-93-5094-483-7

卐 ***Price*** ₹ 115.00

PO No. : TXT-59-T059452-5-24

Typeset by Arihant DTP Unit at Meerut
Printed & Bound by Arihant Publications (I) Ltd. (Press Unit)

For further information about the products from Arihant,
log on to www.arihantbooks.com or email to info@arihantbooks.com

PREFACE

आपके हाथों में यह किताब आपको अंग्रेजी बोलने हेतु आवश्यक सभी प्रकार के Spoken Words की जरूरत को पूरा करने वाली एक अनूठी किताब है। एक हिन्दीभाषी व्यक्ति को अपने विचारों को अंग्रेजी में करने हेतु अर्थात् अंग्रेजी बोलने हेतु सर्वप्रथम आवश्यकता पड़ती है हिन्दी के शब्दों के समरूप अंग्रेजी शब्दों की अर्थात् ऐसे अंग्रेजी के शब्द जो अंग्रेजी बोलने में काम आते हैं। यह माना जाता है कि अंग्रेजी बोलने की शुरूआत करने के लिए करीब 2000 अंग्रेजी शब्दों (Spoken Words) की ही आवश्यकता पड़ती है। लेकिन जैसे–जैसे व्यक्ति अंग्रेजी बोलने में प्रवीण होता जाता है उसे अधिक Spoken Words की आवश्यकता होती है।

इस किताब में लगभग 9000 विभिन्न प्रकार के अंग्रेजी शब्दों का समावेश है। इस किताब में अंग्रेजी बोलने में प्रयुक्त शब्दों को दिया गया है जिनके हिन्दी उच्चारण एवं शब्दार्थ को देते हुए वाक्यों में प्रयोग भी दिए गए हैं, जो आपको उस शब्द का सही सन्दर्भ में प्रयोग करने में सहायक होंगे।

इसके अतिरिक्त अपने आस–पास दैनिक जीवन में प्रयुक्त वस्तुओं एवं विभिन्न क्षेत्रों में प्रयुक्त अंग्रेजी शब्दों को भी इस किताब में समाहित किया गया है।

इसके अतिरिक्त इस किताब में निम्न का समावेश किया गया है, जो इस किताब को बाजार में उपलब्ध इस तरह की अन्य सभी किताबों से अलग एवं श्रेष्ठ साबित करता है।

Important Word Power for Effective Spoken English

1. Important Synonyms
2. Important Antonyms
3. Homonyms
4. Paronyms
5. Contronyms
6. Heteronyms
7. Palindromes

हिन्दीभाषी लोगों को अंग्रेजी शब्दों के उच्चारण में होने वाली परेशानियों को ध्यान में रखते हुए, इस किताब में उच्चारण से सम्बन्धित एक अध्याय का अलग से समावेश किया है जो आपको अंग्रेजी के शब्दों का सही उच्चारण करने में सहायक होगा।

Spoken Words की यह किताब एक बहोपयोगी किताब है, जो आपको न केवल अंग्रेजी बोलना सीखने में सहायक होगी बल्कि यह हर प्रतियोगी परीक्षा में Word Power से सम्बन्धित प्रश्नों को हल करने में भी सहायक होगी।

शुभकामनाओं सहित

लेखिका

CONTENTS

How to Pronounce a Word Correctly?

अच्छे English Pronunciation से आशय है कि आप जो कुछ भी बोल रहे हैं वह सम्बद्ध व्यक्ति सरलतापूर्वक समझ सके एवं वह standard pronunciation के काफी नजदीक हो और उच्चारण में unpleasantness या rudeness कतई भी न हो। English ऐसी भाषा है जिसमें आप word को केवल-मात्र देखकर उसके उच्चारण का पता नहीं लगा सकते हैं ? देखने में But (बट) एवं Put (पुट) एक ही प्रकार से उच्चरित होने वाले शब्द लगते हैं। इसी तरह No (नो) एवं Do (डू) भी एक जैसे शब्द प्रतीत होते हैं, परन्तु उनके उच्चारण में भिन्नता है। इसका अर्थ है कि आपको हर शब्द के उच्चारण को अलग से सीखना होगा।

Importance of Correct Pronunciation

सही उच्चारण (Correct Pronunciation) को समझना आवश्यक तथा महत्त्वपूर्ण है। इसका कारण हम ऐसे समझ सकते हैं–

A. First Impression आप जब किसी व्यक्ति से मिलते हैं तथा बातचीत शुरू करते हैं तो वह व्यक्ति न तो आपकी grammar पर ध्यान देगा और न ही आपकी vocabulary पर। तब आपका pronunciation ही आपके first impression का निर्धारक होगा।

B. Communication आपकी English grammar यदि बहुत अच्छी नहीं है तो आप simple grammatical structures का उपयोग करके काम चला सकते हैं। यदि आपकी vocabulary बहुत अच्छी नहीं हैं तो आप simple words का उपयोग कर सकते हैं लेकिन यदि आपका pronunciation ही सही नहीं है यानि faulty है तो आपको communication में बहुत परेशानी आ सकती है। एक स्थिति देखें–

कुछ दिन पूर्व मेरा एक मित्र अमेरिका गया। उसने बताया कि जब भी वह किसी स्थानीय नागरिक से बात करता था तो वह व्यक्ति बार-बार What? What? या Pardon .. Pardon... करता रहता था। मुझे पुनः अपने बोले वाक्य को repeat करना पड़ता था। फिर वह उसी वाक्य को खुद बोलकर मुझसे पूछता था कि क्या आप यह कहना चाहते थे?

इस तरह अपने faulty pronunciation के कारण वह व्यक्ति अपने अमेरिका प्रवास की तमाम अवधि में काफी परेशान रहा।

Is Your Pronunciation OK?

आप शायद यह समझते हैं कि यदि मैं कक्षा में ठीक बोल सकता हूँ या सहपाठियों से अथवा अध्यापकों से निःसंकोच बात कर सकता हूँ तो मेरा उच्चारण ठीक है। यह आपका भ्रम है। English एक विदेशी भाषा है।

हमारा उच्चारण स्थानीय दृष्टि से तो ठीक हो सकता है लेकिन वास्तविक रूप में हमारा उच्चारण ठीक नहीं होता है। अतः हमें इसको भली-भाँति समझना होगा और इसमें पर्याप्त सुधार करना होगा तथा परिवेश के अनुरूप pronunciation में सुधार को प्रयास करना होगा।

Standard English Pronunciation

अच्छा व Standard English pronunciation वह है जिससे कि सम्बद्ध व्यक्ति सरलतापूर्वक समझ सके और आपको अपनी बात सुविधापूर्वक समझा सके। समझने और समझाने की तमाम प्रक्रिया standard pronunciation पर ही निर्भर करती है। आपका pronunciation standard होने पर unpleasantness और rudeness की स्थिति पैदा नहीं होती।

यह आवश्यक नहीं है कि आपका उच्चारण अमेरिका के राष्ट्रपति या ब्रिटेन के प्रधानमन्त्री जैसा ही हो। ब्रिटेन में भी कई प्रकार से क्षेत्रीय अंग्रेजी भाषा बोली जाती है। उनका उच्चारण अपने क्षेत्र के अनुसार आपस में काफी भिन्न है लेकिन फिर भी वह उच्चारण Standard English pronunciation के काफी निकट है।

Standard English pronunciation को समझने हेतु आपको CNN और BBC जैसे विदेशी Channels TV पर अवश्य देखने चाहिए। इससे आप स्पष्टतया समझ पाएँगे कि Standard English pronunciation क्या है।

Learning the Correct Pronunciation

English एक ऐसी भाषा है जिसमें word को केवलमात्र देखकर उसके उच्चारण का आभास नहीं किया जा सकता है। आपको हर शब्द के उच्चारण को अलग से सीखना होगा। सब शब्दों का उच्चारण सीखने हेतु Phonetic Transcription का प्रयोग किया जाता है। विभिन्न Dictionaries में शब्दों को Phonetic Alphabet में ही लिखा जाता है जिससे आप उस शब्द की सही स्थिति जानने के साथ-साथ उसका सटीक उच्चारण भी सीख सकते हैं। उच्चारण में syllables की विशेष महती भूमिका होती है।

What are Syllables?

English भाषा का प्रत्येक word, syllables से बना होता है। एक word में एक, दो, तीन या उससे भी अधिक syllables हो सकते हैं। निम्न table को ध्यानपूर्वक देखें–

Word	Syllables	Number of Syllables
pen	pen	1
house	house	1
table	ta-ble	2
photo	pho-to	2
expensive	ex-pen-sive	3
interesting	in-ter-est-ing	4
exceptional	ex-cep-tion-al	4

ध्यान से देखने पर ज्ञात होगा कि प्रत्येक syllable में कम-से-कम एक स्वर (*Vowel*) *a,e,i,o,u* या vowel sound अवश्य है।

English में सही उच्चारण हेतु word stress की जानकारी होना बहुत महत्त्वपूर्ण है। हर भाषा में word stress का प्रयोग नहीं किया जाता है; जैसे Japanese व French में सभी syllable समान रूप से उच्चरित किए जाते हैं जबकि English भाषा में words के सही उच्चारण हेतु word stress पर ध्यान देना आवश्यक होता है।

English में हमें किसी syllable को धीरे तो किसी पर जोर देकर बोलना होता है। उदाहरण के लिए निम्न तीन शब्दों का उच्चारण देखिए–

1. PHO-TO-GRAPH — इसमें तीन syllables हैं एवं इसके उच्चारण में हमें प्रथम syllable PHO पर stress डालना होगा।
2. PHO-TO-GRAPH-ER — इसमें चार syllables हैं तथा इसको उच्चरित करते समय हमें syllable TO पर अधिक stress डालना होगा।
3. PHO- TO-GRAPH-IC — इसमें भी चार syllables हैं तथा इसका उच्चारण करते समय syllable GRAPH पर अधिक stress डालना होगा।

किसी word में जब एक से अधिक syllables होते हैं तब यह स्थिति आती है। नीचे लिखे अन्य शब्द भी देखिए–

1. TEACHer
2. jaPAN
3. aBOVE
4. converSATION
5. imPORtant
6. deMAND

उक्त words में CAPITAL letters में मुद्रित syllable को stress के साथ उच्चरित करने पर ही शब्दों का सही उच्चारण होगा। यदि आपने stress गलत syllable पर डाल दिया तो आपका उच्चारण भी गलत हो जायेगा। England एवं America के नागरिक, stressed syllable का बहुत ध्यान रखते हैं। आप भी यदि English बोलते समय word stress का ध्यान रखें तो आपका उच्चारण उच्चकोटि का हो जाएगा।

What's Word Stress?

एक शब्द में जब कई syllables होते हैं तो आवश्यकता व स्थिति के अनुसार किसी syllable पर अधिक तो किसी पर कम stress देकर उनका उच्चारण किया जाता है।

Rules of Word Stress in English

Rule 1. सर्वप्रथम यह ध्यान रखें कि एक word में केवल एक ही stress हो सकता है। यदि आप दो stress सुन रहे हैं तो इसका अर्थ है कि आप दो words सुन रहे हैं।

Rule 2. केवल vowels को ही stress किया जा सकता है consonants को नहीं।

निम्न बिन्दुओं को भी ध्यान में अवश्य रखें–

(i) सामान्यतया दो syllables वाले nouns या adjectives में stress पहले syllable पर होता है; जैसे–
AMErica, IMport, TAble (Nouns)
HAPpy, SLENder, CLEver (Adjectives)

(ii) दो syllables वाली verbs में stress अन्तिम syllable पर रहता है; जैसे–
to deCIDE, to imPORT, to rePEAT (Verbs)

(iii) सामान्यतया जिन words के अन्त में 'ic' या 'sion' अथवा 'tion' आता है, उन words में stress (penultimate syllable = second from end) अन्तिम syllable से पहले वाले syllable पर रहता है; जैसे–
photoGRAPHic, geoLOGic, geoGRAPHic, teleVIsion, reveLAtion.

(iv) जिन शब्दों के अन्त में 'cy', 'ty', 'phy', 'gy' या 'al' आता है उनमें ante-penultimate syllable अर्थात् third from end (अन्तिम syllable से तीसरा वाला) पर stress रहता है; जैसे–
deMOcracy, phoTOgraphy, CRItical, geoLOgical.

(v) Compound words में यदि वह Compound noun है तो stress पहले part में रहता है, यदि वह Compound adjective या Compound verb है तो stress दूसरे part पर रहता है; जैसे–

(a) BLACK bird, WHITE house (Compound noun)

(b) bad TEMpered, old FASHioned (Compound adjective)

(c) to underSTAND, to overDRAW (Compound verb)

ध्यान रखें उक्त नियमों के बहुत से अपवाद भी हैं। Pronunciation को सिर्फ नियमों द्वारा ही नहीं सीखा जा सकता है। आप अंग्रेजी शब्दों को बोलने की जितनी अधिक Practice करेंगे आप उतना ही शीघ्र English का correct pronunciation सीख सकेंगे।

Learn the Correct Pronunciation!

अंग्रेजी phonetic language नहीं है। इसका अर्थ है कि हम शब्द की केवल spelling देखकर उसका उच्चारण नहीं कर सकते हैं। कुछ शब्द ऐसे हैं जिनकी spellings में समानता होने के बावजूद अलग-अलग स्थिति में उच्चारण में भिन्नता है; जैसे–

I like to read (रीड) this book. I have read (रेड) that novel.

इसके अलावा कुछ शब्द ऐसे भी हैं जिनकी spellings अलग होने के बावजूद उनके उच्चारण समान हैं; जैसे–

I have read (रेड) that novel. His favourite colour is red (रेड).

अंग्रेजी भाषा में अधिकांश गलतियाँ प्राय: उच्चारण सम्बन्धी ही होती हैं। अंग्रेजी भाषा में कुल 26 अक्षर हैं जिनमें से 5 स्वर (Vowels A, E, I, O, U) तथा शेष 21 व्यंजन (Consonants) हैं। कुछ vowels व्यंजन की ध्वनि देते हैं तो कुछ consonants स्वर की ध्वनि देने हेतु प्रयुक्त होते हैं। English भाषा में शब्दों के उच्चारण में शुद्धता हेतु निम्न नियमों का गम्भीरतापूर्वक पालन करें।

Pronunciation of Vowels (स्वर)

1. Vowel A के उच्चारण के नियम

Vowel A के प्रमुख उच्चारण निम्नलिखित हैं–आ (ऑ), ऐ, एअ, ए।

(a) A = आ (ऑ)

All	ऑल	सब	Wall	वॉल	दीवार
Call	कॉल	बुलाना	Small	स्मॉल	छोटा
Stall	स्टॉल	अस्थायी विक्रय स्थल	Car	कार	गाड़ी
Far	फार	दूर	Are	आर	है, हो

(b) A = ऐ (ै)

An	ऐन	एक	Can	कैन	बाल्टी
Fan	फैन	पंखा	Cat	कैट	बिल्ली
Dad	डैड	पिता	Band	बैण्ड	बाजा

(c) A = एअ

Care	केअर	परवाह	Mare	मेअर	घोड़ी
Fare	फेअर	किराया	Dare	डेअर	साहस करना
Ware	वेअर	बर्तन	Share	शेअर	हिस्सा बाँटना

(d) A = ए ····· लम्बा उच्चारण

A के आगे यदि Y या I का प्रयोग हो, तो A का उच्चारण ए के समान हो जाता है, परन्तु यह कुछ लम्बा उच्चारण देता है; जैसे–

Bay	बे	खाड़ी	Day	डे	दिन
Say	से	कहना	Stay	स्टे	ठहरना
Main	मेन	मुख्य	Brain	ब्रेन	दिमाग
Fay	फे	परी	Gay	गे	प्रसन्न
Lay	ले	रखना	Maid	मेड	कन्या
Ray	रे	किरण	Pain	पेन	दर्द
Nail	नेल	नाखून	Plain	प्लेन	सादा

A के आगे यदि कोई consonant और फिर e रखा हो, तो A का उच्चारण ए के समान हो जाता है, परन्तु यह ए भी कुछ लम्बा उच्चारण देता है; जैसे–

Cage	केज	पिंजरा	Race	रेस	दौड़
Base	बेस	आधार	Tape	टेप	फीता
Sale	सेल	बिक्री	Tale	टेल	कहानी
Tame	टेम	पालतू	Face	फेस	चेहरा
Make	मेक	बनाना	Sage	सेज	साधू
Bake	बेक	पकाना (तन्दूर में)	Trade	ट्रेड	व्यापार

2. Vowel E के उच्चारण के नियम

Vowel E के प्रमुख उच्चारण निम्नलिखित हैं–ए (`), इ, ई।

(a) E = ए (`) ····· छोटा उच्चारण

Net	नेट्	जाली	Beg	बेग	भीख माँगना
Cent	सेन्ट्	सौ, एक सिक्का	Fend	फेन्ड्	रोकना
Keck	केक	जी मिचलाना	Less	लेस	कम
Bell	बेल	घण्टी	Hell	हेल	नर्क
Pet	पेट	पालतू	Sell	सेल	बेचना
Met	मेट	मिला	Fell	फेल	गिरा

(b) E = इ

Be	बी	होना	We	वी	हम
He	ही	वह	She	शी	वह
Ear	ईअर	कान	Seal	सील	मुहर
Me	मी	मुझे	Meal	मील	भोजन
Real	रीअल	वास्तविक	Feel	फील	अनुभव करना

(c) Ee = ई ····· लम्बा उच्चारण

See	सी	देखना	Bee	बी	मधुमक्खी
Weep	वीप	रोना	Sleep	स्लीप	सोना
Deep	डीप	गहरा	Sweep	स्वीप	झाड़ू लगाना

(d) Ea = इ ····· छोटा उच्चारण

Sea	सी	समुद्र	Pea	पी	मटर
Beat	बीट	पीटना	Meat	मीट	मांस
Mean	मीन	अर्थ देना	Cheat	चीट	धोखा देना
Before	बिफोर	पहले	Heroic	हिरोइक	साहसी

Eleven -	इलेवन -	ग्यारह	Near -	निअर -	पास
Eclipse-	इक्लिप्स -	ग्रहण	Pear -	पिअर -	नाशपाती
Effect -	इफेक्ट -	प्रभाव	Rear -	रिअर -	पिछला भाग

(e) E = अपनी कोई ध्वनि नहीं है।

किसी शब्द के अन्त में यदि 'e' आता है तो उसका अपना कोई उच्चारण नहीं होता, परन्तु उससे पहले आए एक या एक से अधिक व्यंजनों (Consonants) को छोड़कर जो अन्य स्वर (Vowel) होता है, उसका उच्चारण लम्बा हो जाता है।

(i) पूर्ववर्ती स्वर यदि a हो तो 'a' का उच्चारण ए होता है और 'e' का अपना कोई उच्चारण नहीं होता है; जैसे–

Shame -	शेम -	लज्जा	Name -	नेम -	नाम
Lame -	लेम -	लंगड़ा	Same -	सेम -	वही
Bale -	बेल -	गड्डा	Late -	लेट -	देरी
Came -	केम -	आया	Tame -	टेम -	पालतू
Rate -	रेट -	दर	Fame -	फेम -	प्रसिद्ध

Some more examples

Rat -	रैट -	चूहा	परन्तु	Rate -	रेट -	दर
Man -	मैन -	मनुष्य	परन्तु	Mane -	मेन -	गर्दन के लम्बे बाल
Mat -	मैट -	चटाई	परन्तु	Mate -	मेट -	मित्र/संगी
Pan -	पैन -	कड़ाही	परन्तु	Pane -	पेन -	शीशे का टुकड़ा

(ii) पूर्ववर्ती स्वर यदि 'i' हो तो 'i' का उच्चारण आई होता है और अन्तिम 'e' का अपना कोई उच्चारण नहीं होता है; जैसे–

Line -	लाइन -	रेखा	Nine -	नाइन -	नौ
File -	फाइल -	रेती	Lime -	लाइम -	नींबू (खट्टा)
Five -	फाइव -	पाँच	Hive -	हाइव -	मधुमक्खी का छत्ता
Ripe -	राइप -	पका हुआ	Fine -	फाइन -	दण्ड
Bide -	बाइड -	ठहरना	Bike -	बाइक -	बाइसिकल

Some more examples

Bit -	बिट -	टुकड़ा	परन्तु	Bite -	बाइट -	काटना
Sit -	सिट -	बैठना	परन्तु	Site -	साइट -	स्थान
Kit -	किट -	सारंगी, थैला	परन्तु	Kite -	काइट -	पतंग
Pip -	पिप -	फलों के छोटे बीज	परन्तु	Pipe -	पाइप -	बाँसुरी

(iii) पूर्ववर्ती स्वर यदि 'o' हो तो 'o' का उच्चारण ओ होता है और अन्तिम 'e' का अपना कोई उच्चारण नहीं होता है; जैसे–

Hope -	होप -	आशा	Joke -	जोक -	मजाक
Nose -	नोज -	नाक	Rose -	रोज -	गुलाब का फूल
Lone -	लोन -	अकेला	Bone -	बोन -	हड्डी
Code -	कोड -	संहिता	Coke -	कोक -	पत्थर का कोयला
Dome -	डोम -	गुम्बद	Home -	होम -	घर

Some more examples

Rob - रॉब - लूटना	परन्तु	Robe - रोब - घाघरा
Hop - हॉप - फुदकना	परन्तु	Hope - होप - आशा करना
Not - नॉट - नहीं	परन्तु	Note - नोट - लिखा हुआ संकेत
Dot - डॉट - बिन्दु	परन्तु	Dote - डोट - मूर्ख होना

(iv) पूर्ववर्ती स्वर यदि 'u' हो तो 'u' का उच्चारण ऊ और यू होता है और अन्तिम 'e' का अपना कोई उच्चारण नहीं होता है; जैसे–

'u' का ऊ के रूप में उच्चारण

Rule - रूल - नियम June - जून - जून मास
Jute - जूट - पटुआ, पटसन Rude - रूड - असभ्य, अशिष्ट

'u' का यू के रूप में उच्चारण

Tube - ट्यूब - नली Cube - क्यूब - घन
Mute - म्यूट - मूक Nude - न्यूड - नंगा
Cute - क्यूट - सुन्दर Jute - जूट - पटसन
Tune - ट्यून - सुर Yule - यूल - क्रिसमस

(f) Ew = इयू

'e' के आगे यदि 'w' हो तो 'ew' का उच्चारण इयू से होता है, परन्तु 'e' से पूर्व का consonant ह्रस्व उच्चरित होता है; जैसे–

Dew - ड्यू - ओस Sew - स्यू - सीना
New - न्यू - नया Few - फ्यू - कुछ
Blew - ब्ल्यू - बजाया Drew - ड्रियू - खींचा
Mew - न्यू - म्याऊँ Crew - क्रयू - जत्था

3. Vowel I के उच्चारण के नियम

Vowel I के प्रमुख उच्चारण निम्नलिखित हैं–इ और आई, परन्तु कभी-कभी यह अ जैसा उच्चारण भी देता है; जैसे–

(a) I = इ ह्रस्व उच्चारण

Pin - पिन - सुई Big - बिग - बड़ा
Ship - शिप - जहाज Trick - ट्रिक - चाल
Kill - किल - मारना Shrink - श्रिंक - सिकुड़ना
City - सिटी - शहर Mill - मिल - चक्की
Hill - हिल - पहाड़ी Bit - बिट - टुकड़ा
Dim - डिम - धुँधला Fill - फिल - भरना

(b) I = आइ

Kind - काइण्ड - दयालु Hind - हाइन्ड - पिछला
Bind - बाइण्ड - बाँधना Blind - ब्लाइण्ड - अन्धा
Mild - माइल्ड - कोमल Child - चाइल्ड - बच्चा
Kite - काइट - पतंग Lime - लाइम - चूना
Pile - पाइल - ढ़ेर Wild - वाइल्ड - जंगली

(c) I = अ

Birth	बर्थ	जन्म	Firm	फर्म	संस्था
First	फर्स्ट	पहला	Dirt	डर्ट	मिट्टी
Bird	बर्ड	पक्षी	Girl	गर्ल	लड़की
Gird	गर्ड	बाँधना			

(d) I = आय

Fire	फायर	आग	Admire	एडमायर	प्रशंसा करना
Sire	सायर	महाशय	Hire	हायर	किराये पर लेना
Direct	डायरेक्ट	सीधा	Dire	डायर	भयानक
Wire	वायर	तार	Tire	टायर	थकना

(e) Ie, ei = ई

Receive	रिसीव	लेना	Deceive	डिसीव	धोखा करना
Sieve	सीव	छलनी	Siege	सीज	घेरा
Tie	टाइ	बाँधना	Shield	शील्ड	ढ़ाल
Diet	डाइट	खुराक	Field	फील्ड	खेत
Grieve	ग्रीव	शोक करना/दुःख	Friend	फ्रेन्ड	मित्र
Lie	लाइ	झूठ			

4. Vowel O के उच्चारण के नियम

Vowel O के प्रमुख उच्चारण निम्नलिखित हैं-अ, ऑ, ओ, आउ, उ, ऊ, वॉय।

(a) O = अ ह्रस्व उच्चारण

Son	सन	पुत्र	Come	कम	आना
Done	डन	किया हुआ	Some	सम	कुछ
None	नन	कोई नहीं			

(b) O = ऑ

Ox	ऑक्स	बैल	Box	बॉक्स	सन्दूक
Hot	हॉट	गर्म	Dot	डॉट	बिन्दु
God	गॉड	ईश्वर	Dog	डॉग	कुत्ता
Conduct	कन्डक्ट	आचरण	Doctor	डॉक्टर	चिकित्सक
Form	फॉर्म	आकार	Hog	हॉग	सूअर
Log	लॉग	लकड़ी का लट्ठा			

(c) O = ओ

Old	ओल्ड	पुराना	Gold	गोल्ड	सोना
Post	पोस्ट	डाक	Ghost	घोस्ट	प्रेत
Bold	बोल्ड	साहसी	Cold	कोल्ड	ठण्डा
Fold	फोल्ड	तह	Rotate	रोटेट	घुमाना
Port	पोर्ट	बन्दरगाह			

(d) Ow—ओ-आउ

ओ :	Row	रो	पंक्ति	Bow	बो	झुकना
	Show	शो	दिखाना	Grow	ग्रो	उगना

आउ : How	-	हाउ	-	कैसे	Cow	- काउ	-	गाय
Now	-	नाउ	-	अब				

(e) O = उ, ऊ

उ : Look	-	लुक	-	देखना	Cook	- कुक	-	पकाना
Good	-	गुड	-	अच्छा	Book	- बुक	-	पुस्तक
ऊ : Moon	-	मून	-	चाँद	Boot	- बूट	-	जूता
Room	-	रूम	-	कमरा	Broom	- ब्रूम	-	झाडू

(f) Oy = वॉय

Boy	-	बॉय	-	लड़का	Toy	- टॉय	-	खिलौना
Joy	-	जॉय	-	प्रसन्नता	Foyer	- फॉयर	-	सिनेमा या होटल में विशाल छतदार स्थान
Hoyden	-	हॉयडन	-	जोशीली लड़की	Coy	- कॉय	-	शर्मीला

(g) Ou = ऑव

Hour	-	ऑवर	-	घण्टा	Sour	- सॉवर	-	खट्टा

5. Vowel U के उच्चारण के नियम

Vowel U के प्रमुख उच्चारण निम्नलिखित हैं– अ, उ, यू, यो।

(a) U = अ

Cup	-	कप	-	प्याला	Tub	- टब	-	नांद
Hut	-	हट	-	झोंपड़ी	Sun	- सन	-	सूर्य
Mud	-	मड	-	कीचड़	Curd	- कर्ड	-	दही
Bus	-	बस	-	बस	Mug	- मग	-	जलपात्र
But	-	बट	-	लेकिन	Bulk	- बल्क	-	भार
Fun	-	फन	-	मजाक	Fur	- फर	-	पशुओं के घने बाल
Up	-	अप	-	ऊपर	Nut	- नट	-	पेंच, अखरोट

(b) U = उ

Put	-	पुट	-	रखना	Push	- पुश	-	दबाना, धकेलना
Pull	-	पुल	-	खींचना	Hurrah	- हुर्रा	-	हर्षनाद
Bull	-	बुल	-	बैल	Bush	- बुश	-	झाड़ी
Full	-	फुल	-	भरा हुआ	Jubilee	- जुबिली	-	महोत्सव

(c) U = यू, यो

यू: Duty	-	ड्यूटी	-	कर्त्तव्य	Durable	- ड्यूरेबल	-	टिकाऊ
यो: Cure	-	क्योर	-	आराम होना	Pure	- प्योर	-	शुद्ध

6. (Consonant और semi-vowel के रूप में प्रयुक्त) Y के उच्चारण के नियम

Y एक व्यंजन है परन्तु कहीं-कहीं यह semi-vowel का काम भी करता है।

Y के प्रमुख उच्चारण निम्नलिखित हैं–ई, आय, आई।

(a) Y = ई

Policy	-	पॉलिसी	-	नीति	Icy	- आइसी	-	बर्फीला
Greedy	-	ग्रीडी	-	लालची	Hearty	- हार्टी	-	हार्दिक

(b) Y = आय

Tyre	टायर	टायर	Pyre	पायर	चिता
Tyrant	टायरैन्ट	क्रूर	Typhoid	टायफॉइड	मियादी बुखार

(c) Y = आई

Dyke	डाइक	खाड़ी	Type	टाइप	प्रकार
Dynasty	डाइनेस्टी	वंश	Tycoon	टाइकून	लब्धप्रतिष्ठ व्यापारी

Pronunciation of Consonants (व्यंजन)

B ब	C स	D ड	F फ	G ज	H ह
J ज	K क	L ल	M म	N न	P प
Q क	R र	S स	T ट	V व	X क्स
Y य	Z ज				

I. 'C' के उच्चारण के नियम

1. 'C' के आगे यदि 'e, i, y' आदि कोई वर्ण दिया हुआ हो, तो 'c' का उच्चारण स होता है; जैसे–

(a)	Rice	राइस	चावल	Pice	पाइस	पैसा
	Niece	नीस	भतीजा	Cease	सीज	रुकना
(b)	Citizen	सिटिजन	नागरिक	Cigar	सिगार	बीड़ी, सिगरेट
	Circle	सर्कल	घेरा	Cinema	सिनेमा	चलचित्र
	City	सिटी	शहर	Civil	सिविल	नगर का
	Cistern	सिस्टर्न	हौज	Cinder	सिन्ड्र	अंगारा
(c)	Cyclone	साइक्लोन	तूफान	Icy	आइसी	बर्फीला
	Cycle	साइकिल	साइकिल	Cypher	सिफर	शून्य

2. 'C' के आगे यदि a, o, u, k, r, l आदि में से कोई एक वर्ण दिया हुआ हो, तो c का उच्चारण 'क' होता है; जैसे–

(a)	Cat	कैट	बिल्ली	Cattle	कैटल	पशु
	Cavity	कैविटि	छेद	Catalogue	कैटेलॉग	सूची-पत्र
	Cave	केव	गुफा	Cage	केज	पिंजरा
	Car	कार	कार	Cane	केन	छड़ी, बेंत
(b)	Cot	कॉट	चारपाई	Colour	कलर	रंग
	Collar	कॉलर	कालर	Cottage	कॉटेज	झोपड़ी
	Cog	कॉग	दाँता	Coke	कोक	पत्थर का कोयला
	Coin	कॉइन	सिक्का	Cobra	कोबरा	साँप
(c)	Curse	कर्स	कोसना	Custom	कस्टम	रिवाज
	Cut	कट	काटना	Curtain	कर्टेन	पर्दा
(d)	Lock	लॉक	ताला	Duck	डक	बत्तख
	Dock	डॉक	बन्दरगाह	Rock	रॉक	चट्टान
(e)	Crow	क्रो	कौआ	Cruel	क्रुअल	क्रूर
	Cradle	क्रेडल	पासना	Crass	क्रास	अनाड़ी
(f)	Clock	क्लॉक	दीवार घड़ी	Clatter	क्लैटर	बकबक करना
	Clerk	क्लर्क	लिपिक	Clean	क्लीन	स्वच्छ

3. 'C' के आगे यदि 'ia' दिया हुआ है तो 'c' का उच्चारण श होता है; जैसे–

Social	सोशल	सामाजिक	Musician	म्यूजिशियन	संगीतकार
Racial	रेश्यल	वंश सम्बन्धी	Facial	फेश्यल	मुख सम्बन्धी

4. 'C' के आगे यदि 'h' दिया हुआ हो, तो 'c' का प्रायः उच्चारण च, क और श भी होता है; जैसे–

(a)	Cheat	चीट	धोखा देना	Chess	चेस	शतरंज
	Cheer	चीयर	ताला-चाभी	Chair	चेयर	कुर्सी
	Bench	बेन्च	बेन्च	Reach	रीच	पहुँचना
(b)	Chemist	केमिस्ट	दवा बेचने वाला	Character	कैरैक्टर	चरित्र
	Cholera	कॉलेरा	हैजा	Chorus	कोरस	गायक समूह
(c)	Chemise	शिमीज	शमीज	Chiffon	शिफॉन	बारीक कपड़ा
	Machine	मशीन	मशीन	Chicane	शिकेन	छलना

II. 'G' के उच्चारण

'G' के उच्चारण निम्नलिखित हैं–ग और ज।

'G' का प्रमुख उच्चारण तो ग है, परन्तु यदि 'g' के आगे 'e' आ जाए तो इसे ज से उच्चरित किया जाता है; जैसे–

1.	Gun	गन	बन्दूक	Bag	बैग	थैला
	Gate	गेट	बड़ा दरवाजा	Pig	पिग	सूअर
	Fog	फॉग	कुहरा	Gag	गैग	मुँह बन्द करना
2.	Page	पेज	पृष्ठ	General	जनरल	साधारण
	Pigeon	पिजन	कबूतर	Germ	जर्म	कीटाणु
	Gist	जिस्ट	सारांश	Magistrate	मैजिस्ट्रेट	जज
	Ginger	जिन्जर	अदरक	Giant	जायन्ट	दानव

III. 'S' के उच्चारण के नियम

'S' के प्रमुख उच्चारण निम्नलिखित हैं–ज, स, श।

1. किसी शब्द के अन्त में यदि 'be, g, gg, ge, oe, ie, ee, y' आदि में से कोई एक वर्ण आए तो इनके आगे लगे s का उच्चारण ज होता है; जैसे–

Tribes	ट्राइब्ज	कबीले	Bags	बैग्ज	थैले
Eggs	ऐग्ज	अण्डे	Ages	एजिज	युग
Heroes	हीरोज	नायक	Armies	आर्मीज	सेनाएँ
Rupees	रुपीज	रुपये	Boys	ब्वॉयज	लड़के
Bribes	ब्राइब्ज	रिश्वतें	Scribes	स्क्राइब्ज	पेशेवर पत्र-लेखक
Trees	ट्रीज	पेड़	Fees	फीस	शुल्क
Flags	फ्लैग्ज	झण्डे	Rugs	रग्ज	कम्बल
Cages	कैजिज	पिंजरे	Wages	वेजिज	मजदूरी
Mugs	मग्ज	प्याले	Pages	पेजिज	पृष्ठ
Nigroes	नीग्रोज	हब्शी	Mangoes	मैंगोज	आम
Cities	सिटीज	शहर	Potatoes	पोटैटोज	आलू

2. किसी शब्द के अन्त में यदि 'f, p, pe, te' आदि में से कोई एक वर्ण दिया हुआ हो, तो ध्वनि श होती है; जैसे–

Russia	रशिया	रूस	Passion	पैशन	भावना
Asia	एशिया	एशिया	Admission	एडमिशन	प्रवेश

3. किसी शब्द में यदि 's' या 'ss' के आगे 'ia, ion' आदि में से कोई एक वर्ण आया हो तो s का उच्चारण स होता है; जैसे–

Roofs	रूफ्स	छत	Caps	कैप्स	टोपियाँ
Ropes	रोप्स	रस्से	Kites	काइट्स	पतंगें

IV. 'T' के उच्चारण के नियम

1. 'T' का प्रमुख उच्चारण ट है; जैसे–स्थितिवश 'T' के उच्चारण निम्नलिखित हैं–श, च, थ, द।

Tea	टी	चाय	Teat	टीट	थन
Cat	कैट	बिल्ली	Dirty	डर्टी	गन्दा
Team	टीम	खिलाड़ियों का दल	Try	ट्राइ	कोशिश करना
Treat	ट्रीट	बर्ताव करना	Tear	टीयर	फाड़ना
Task	टास्क	कार्य	Bat	बैट	बल्ला

2. किसी शब्द में यदि 't' के बाद 'ia, ie, io' आदि में से कोई एक वर्ण दे रखा हो, तो 'T' की ध्वनि श हो जाती है; जैसे–

Initials	इनिशियल्ज	हस्ताक्षर	Partial	पार्शल	पक्षपाती
Patient	पेशेन्ट	रोगी	Ratio	रेशो	अनुपात
Portion	पोर्शन	भाग	Promotion	प्रमोशन	पदोन्नति
Attention	अटेन्शन	ध्यान	Station	स्टेशन	स्टेशन

3. किसी शब्द में यदि 's' के आगे 'tion' आए या 't' के आगे 'ure' आए तो 'T' का उच्चारण च होता है; जैसे–

Question	क्वैस्चन	प्रश्न	Culture	कल्चर	सभ्यता
Nature	नेचर	प्रकृति	Picture	पिक्चर	तस्वीर

4. किसी शब्द में यदि 'T के बाद 'H' आए तो इसकी ध्वनि द, थ होती है; जैसे–

This	दिस	यह	Thick	थिक	घना, मोटा
That	दैट	वह	Thin	थिन	पतला
There	देअर	वहाँ	Thread	थ्रेड	धागा
Then	देन	तब	Three	थ्री	तीन
These	दीज	ये	Theme	थीम	प्रसंग

परन्तु कभी-कभी 'Th' ट की ध्वनि भी देता है; जैसे–

Thames	टेम्स	टेम्स नदी	Thomas	टामस	व्यक्ति का नाम

Silent Letters (अनुच्चरित अक्षर) in Various Words

अंग्रेजी भाषा में कुछ मूक (silent) वर्ण भी होते हैं, परन्तु विदेशी भाषा होने के कारण ये इसके लिए एक समस्या बन जाते हैं। विद्यार्थियों की सुविधा के लिए यहाँ कुछ ऐसे शब्दों को प्रस्तुत किया गया है। आपको निरन्तर अध्ययन और अभ्यास के द्वारा ऐसे शब्दों पर command प्राप्त करनी है।

When

'B' is silent : 'm' के बाद तथा 't' से पूर्व का 'b' प्राय: silent रहता है; जैसे–

Bomb	बॉम	बम	Tomb	टॉम	समाधि
Comb	कॉम	कंघा	Lamb	लैम	मेमना
Dumb	डम	गूँगा	Debt	डैट	ऋण
Thumb	थम	अँगूठा	Doubt	डाउट	सन्देह

'P' is silent : / **'M' is silent :**

'n' तथा 's' से पूर्व आया 'p' प्राय: silent रहता है और 'm' के पश्चात् 'n' silent रहता है; जैसे–

Pneumonia	न्यूमोनिया	निमोनिया	Autumn	ऑटम	पतझड़
Pneumatics	न्यूमैटिक्स	वायुशास्त्र	Column	कॉलम	पृष्ठ
Psalm	साम	भजन	Condemn	कन्डेम	निन्दा करना
Psychology	साइकोलोजी	मनोविज्ञान	Hymn	हिम	स्तुति गान

'L' is silent : 'm, f, k' एवं 'd' से पूर्व 'l' silent रहता है; जैसे–

Palm	पाम	हथेली	Calm	काम	शान्त
Psalm	साम	भजन	Balm	बाम	मरहम
Half	हाफ	आधा	Calf	काफ	बछड़ा
Talk	टॉक	बातें करना	Folk	फॉक	जनसमूह
Would	वुड	will का past tense			
Could	कुड	can का past tense			

'K' is silent : / **'G' is silent :**

'n' से पूर्व आया 'k' silent रहता है; और— 'n' से पूर्व आया 'G' silent रहता है; जैसे–

Know	नो	जानना	Gnat	नैट	मच्छर
Knife	नाइफ	चाकू	Sign	साइन	चिह्न
Knot	नॉट	गाँठ	Resign	रिजाइन	त्याग-पत्र देना
Knock	नॉक	खटखटाना	Reign	रैन	शासन
			Design	डिजाइन	रचना

'C' is silent : / **'H' is silent :**

Scent	सेन्ट	इत्र	Hour	आवर	घण्टा
Science	साइन्स	विज्ञान	Honour	ऑनर	इज्जत
Scene	सीन	दृश्य	Heir	एअर	उत्तराधिकारी

'U' is silent : / **'W' is silent :**

Guard	गार्ड	चौकीदार	Wrap	रैप	लपेटना
Guess	गैस	अनुमान लगाना	Wrong	रॉन्ग	गलत
Guest	गेस्ट	अतिथि	Answer	आन्सर	उत्तर
Churn	चर्न	मथना	Sword	सोर्ड	तलवार

'Gh' is silent : किसी शब्द के अन्त में यदि 'gh, ght' हो तो 'gh' प्रायः silent रहता है; जैसे–

High -	हाई -	ऊँचा	Fought -	फॉट -	लड़ा
Sigh -	साई -	आहें भरना	Taught -	टाट -	पढ़ाया
Thigh -	थाई -	जाँघ	Fight -	फाइट -	युद्ध
Though -	दो -	यद्यपि	Bright -	ब्राइट -	चमकीला
Through -	थ्रू -	से	Delight -	डिलाइट -	आनन्द
Bought -	बॉट -	खरीदा	Slight -	स्लाइट -	तनिक-सा
Caught -	कॉट -	पकड़ा	Might -	माइट -	शक्ति
Brought -	ब्रॉट -	लाया	Knight -	नाइट -	योद्धा
Laugh -	लाफ -	हँसना	Thought -	थॉट -	विचार

'D' is silent : 'g' से पूर्व यदि 'd' दिया हुआ हो तो 'd' प्रायः silent हो जाता है; जैसे–

Edge -	ऐज -	किनारा	Grudge -	ग्रज -	ईर्ष्या
Hedge -	हैज -	झाड़ी	Budget -	बजट -	लेखा-जोखा
Ledger -	लेजर -	बहीखाता	Bridge -	ब्रिज -	पुल

'T' is silent : किसी शब्द के अन्त में यदि 'ten' दिया हुआ हो तो 't' प्रायः silent रहता है; जैसे–

Hasten -	हेसन -	जल्दी करना	Listen -	लिसन -	ध्यान से सुनना
Often -	ऑफन -	अक्सर, प्रायः	Soften -	सॉफन -	कोमल होना

'Q' कभी अकेला नहीं आता। 'Q + u' सदैव क्व की ध्वनि देता है; जैसे–

Quick -	*क्विक -*	*शीघ्र*	*Quill -*	*क्विल -*	*काँटा*
Queen -	*क्वीन -*	*रानी*	*Quilt -*	*क्विल्ट -*	*रजाई*

UNIT 1

Words in Frequent Use... @ Alphabet

A

- **Abandon** *(अबैण्डन)* – त्यागना Government has *abandoned* that site quite a long time back.
- **Abode** *(अबोड)* –आवास, घर Heaven is considered to be God's *abode*.
- **Abound** *(एबाउन्ड)* –बड़ी संख्या में India *abounds* with rich flora and fauna.
- **About** *(अबाउट)* – के बारे में This book talks *about* the freedom struggle of India.
- **Abroad** *(एब्रोड)* –विदेश में His eldest son is living *abroad*.
- **Absent-minded** *(एबसेन्ट-माइण्डेड)* – विकृत मस्तिष्क वाला His *absent-mindedness* will land him into trouble one day.
- **Absorb** *(अब्जॉर्ब)* –सोख लेना, समाहित कर लेना Western Culture is *absorbing* the youth's mind day-by-day.
- **Accept** *(अक्सेप्ट)* – स्वीकार करना The bridegroom was not ready to *accept* the bride at all.
- **Access** *(अक्सेस)* – प्रयोग करने का तरीका There are many villages in India which don't have *access* to electricity.
- **Accompany** *(अकम्पनी)* – साथ जाना Sudeep *accompanied* while I was going home.
- **Accomplish** *(एकम्पलिश)* – पूरा करना I had *accomplished* half of the job before the end of the day.
- **According to** *(अकॉर्डिंग टू)* – के अनुसार *According to* Gandhiji, Honesty is the best policy.
- **Accurate** *(एक्यूरेट)* – सही Meteorological department was not able to give the *accurate* predictions about the cyclone.
- **Accused** *(एक्यूज्ड)* – अपराधी He is *accused* of spreading false rumour in order to defame her.
- **Ached** *(ऐक्ड्)* – दर्द होना My leg *ached* a lot after playing two consecutive matches of badminton.
- **Achieved** *(एचीव्ड)* –प्राप्त किया He *achieved* the pinnacle of his career at a very young age.

- **Acknowledged** *(ॲकनॉलिज्ड)* –मानना, स्वीकार करना He *acknowledged* the receipt of fax.
- **Acquaintance** *(एक्वान्टैन्स)* –परिचित, ज्ञान, जानकारी I made him an *acquaintance* within two days.
- **A bit** *(ए बिट)* –थोड़ा सा Please lower the volume *a bit.*
- **A day off** *(ए डे ऑफ)* –एक दिन की छुट्टी Please take *a day off* from your busy schedule.
- **A loaf of bread** *(ए लोफ ऑफ ब्रेड)* – रोटी का एक टुकड़ा With rising inflation, it's very difficult for poor to manage even with *a loaf of bread.*
- **Acquire** *(एक्वायर)* –प्राप्त करना Kingfisher Airlines has recently *acquired* a 26% stake in Air Deccan.
- **Adage** *(एडेज)* –सूक्ति, कहावत Every old *adage* doesn't hold true today's age.
- **Adapt** *(अडैप्ट)* –अनुकूल बनना, परिस्थितियों के अनुसार कार्य करना One must always be ready to *adapt* to the changing times.
- **Add** *(एड)* – जोड़ना, सम्मिलित करना Please *add* some sugar to the tea.
- **Addition** *(एडीशन)* –अतिरिक्त There was an addition to property taxes this year.
- **Address** *(एड्रेस)* –पता The President *addressed* the students at the convocation.
- **Adequate** *(एडिक्वेट)* –पर्याप्त India does not have *adequate* energy resources to meet the requirements.
- **Adjoining** *(एड्ज्वाइनिंग)* –साथ वाला There is an empty tract of land *adjoining* my house.
- **Adjusted** *(एड्जस्टेड)* –ठीक किया He can get *adjusted* to any surroundings.
- **Administration** *(एड्मिनिस्ट्रेशन)* –प्रशासन He claims that the present *administration* is corrupt.
- **Admire** *(एड्मायर)*–प्रशंसा करना We should *admire* his leadership skills.
- **Admit** *(एड्मिट)* – स्वीकार करना I *admit* my mistake.
- **Adopt** *(अडॉप्ट)* – अनुकूलित करना, स्वीकार करना RBI will have to *adopt* some new strategy to tackle inflation.
- **Advance** *(अडवान्स)* – आगे बढ़ना, पेशगी I gave him the money in *advance.*
- **Advanced** *(अडवांस्ड)* – प्रगतिशील Government needs to provide *advanced* equipments to ramp up the agricultural output.
- **Adventurous** *(अडवेन्चरस)* – साहसिक The safari through Amazon forests is quite *adventurous.*
- **Advised** *(एड्वाइज्ड)* –सलाह दी Doctor has advised a month's bed rest.
- **Advocate** *(एड्वोकेट)* – अधिवक्ता, पक्षधर He *advocates* honesty in all his actions.
- **Affairs** *(अफेयर्स)*–बातें, मामले, घटनाएँ *International affairs of India are handled by foreign ministry.*
- **Affect** *(अफेक्ट)*–प्रभावित करना The poor monsoon can *affect* the agricultural yield.

- **Affection** *(अफेक्शन)*–स्नेह, प्यार Pandit Jasraj has a great *affection* for music.
- **Afford** *(अफोर्ड)*–प्रदान करना Poor can't *afford* even two meals a day conveniently.
- **Afraid** *(अफ्रेड)*–भयभीत We should never be *afraid* of failures.
- **After a while** *(आफ्टर ए ह्वाइल)*–कुछ समय पश्चात् I'll catch you in the restaurant *after a while.*
- **Afterwards** *(आफ्टरवार्ड्स)*–बाद में The Seven-Eleven incident had a terrible impact *afterwards.*
- **Again** *(अगेन)*–फिर से, दोबारा Please don't do it *again.*
- **Against** *(अगेन्स्ट)*–विरुद्ध, खिलाफ Cruelty on animals is *against* natural justice.
- **Agencies** *(एजेन्सीज)*–अभिकरण Many non-profit *agencies* are working for the upliftment of poor.
- **Aggressively** *(एग्रेसिवली)*–गुस्से से, क्रोध से The crowd was marching *aggressively* to protest price-hike.
- **Agitated** *(एजिटेटेड)*–विरोध किया The crowd got *agitated* by bomb blast.
- **Agitation** *(एजिटेशन)*–आन्दोलन It is very easy to incite a religious *agitation* in India.
- **Agree** *(एग्री)*–सहमत I completely *agree* with your proposal.
- **Agreeable** *(एग्रीएबल)*–सहमति योग्य The solution was *agreeable* to the board of directors.
- **Agreed** *(एग्रीड)*–सहमत हो गए The council *agreed* to my point unanimously.
- **Agriculture** *(एग्रिकल्चर)*–खेती, कृषि The *agriculture* is the main source of income in the villages.
- **Ahead** *(अहैड)*–आगे, सामने India is moving *ahead* of many countries in the field of IT.
- **Aim** *(ऐम)*–निशाना, लक्ष्य Always *aim* for the Moon, so that at least stars will be yours.
- **Algebra** *(अलजेब्रा)*–बीजगणित *Algebra* is both easy and difficult at the same time.
- **Alien** *(एलियन)*–विदेशी Jealousy is *alien* to her nature.
- **Alive** *(अलाइव)*–जीवित, जीवन्त The values propounded by Gandhiji are still *alive.*
- **All the same** *(ऑल द सेम)*–एक समान Granted that the place is risely, *all the same* I want to go there.
- **All** *(ऑल)*–सभी We *all* are proud of India.
- **Allot** *(अलॉट)* – देना You should *allot* equal time to all the subjects while writing CAT.
- **Alloted** *(एलॉटेड)* – आवंटित The fund *alloted* for agricultural upliftment is not adequate.

- **Allowance** *(अलाउन्स)* – भत्ता Daily *allowance* forms a part of the salary structure of all the organizations.
- **Allowed** *(एलाउड्)* – अनुमति दी We are not *allowed* to smoke in public places.
- **Almonds** *(ऑमन्ड्स)* – बादाम *Almond* oil is good for hair.
- **Alms** *(ऑम्स)* – भीख Giving *alms* to needy people is a service to God.
- **Alone** *(अलोन)* – अकेला Living *alone* has become her second nature.
- **Also** *(ऑल्सो)* – भी He *also* wants to go abroad for higher education.
- **Altar** *(आल्टर)* – वेदी Devotees were offering their prayers on the *altar* in the church.
- **Alter** *(आल्टर)* – परिवर्तित करना You'll have to *alter* the lengths of your trousers.
- **Although** *(ऑलदो)* – हालाँकि *Although* all should be offended but you could be spared.
- **Always** *(ऑलवेज)* – हमेशा I would *always* like to be your friend.
- **Amaze** *(अमेज)* – आश्चर्य करना I was *amazed* to see the poor perfomance of Indian team in Asia Cup.
- **Amazing** *(अमेजिंग)* – आश्चर्यजनक It's really *amazing* to see the change in his accent.
- **Ambassador** *(एम्बेसेडर)*– राजदूत, उच्च पदस्थ प्रतिनिधि Today companies are in hunt of celebrities to make them their brand *ambassadors.*
- **Ambition** *(एम्बिशन)* – महत्त्वाकांक्षा My *ambition* is to become an entrepreneur.
- **Ambitious** *(एम्बीशियस)* – महत्त्वाकांक्षी I like his *ambitious* attitude.
- **Amount** *(अमाउन्ट)* – धन, पैसा, राशि Recently large *amounts* of foreign funds are flowing in the Indian market.
- **Anaesthetist** *(ऐनेस्थेटिस्ट)*–चेतना शून्य करने वाला His father is an *anaesthetist* specialist in a Government hospital.
- **Analyse** *(एनालाइज)*– विश्लेषण *Analyse* the problem before finding the solution.
- **Ancestors** *(एनसेस्टर्स)* – पूर्वज The huge mass of land belongs to his *ancestors.*
- **Ancient** *(एन्सियेन्ट)*– प्राचीन This *ancient* monument is a symbol of Mughal art.
- **Angry** *(एंग्री)* – क्रोधित He sent a letter to his boss *angrily.*
- **Announce** *(अनाउन्स)* – बोलना, घोषणा करना The principal is going to *announce* the name of school topper in the morning assembly.
- **Annoyed** *(एनॉयड)* – चिढ़ाना, तंग करना He got *annoyed* at his behaviour in the party.
- **Answer** *(आन्सर)* – उत्तर *Answer* the questions to the point?
- **Antarctica** *(अन्टार्कटिका)*– दक्षिणी ध्रुव प्रदेश *Antarctica* is considered to be one of the coldest regions on earth.
- **Antelope** *(एन्टीलोप)* – बारहसींगा *Antelope* can also prove to be ferocious if provoked.

- **Anthill** *(आन्टहिल)*– बाम्बी A lot of *anthills* can be found on the ground after a rainfall.
- **Anticipation** *(एण्टीसिपेशन)*– पूर्व ज्ञान There were many *anticipations* of Darwinian Theory.
- **Antidote** *(एन्टीडोट)* – प्रतिकारक, दूषित प्रभाव को दूर करने वाली वस्तु There is no *antidote* to AIDS.
- **Antagonist** *(एन्टागोनिस्ट)* – विरोधी *Antagonist* Communists decided to withdraw their support from UPA governments.
- **Ants** *(आन्टस्)* – चींटी *Ants* are considered as hard working insects.
- **Anxiety** *(एन्जाइटी)* – बेचैनी I couldn't sleep for the whole night out of *anxiety* for examination result.
- **Anxious** *(एंक्शस)*–व्याकुल, चिन्तित I am *anxious* about your health.
- **Anyhow** *(एनीहाउ)*–किसी भी हालत में *Anyhow,* I have to reach Delhi by 6 o'clock.
- **Anyone** *(एनीवन)*– किसी से *Anyone* of you can help him by crossing the road.
- **Apart from** *(अपार्ट फ्रॉम)* – को अलग करके *Apart from* general knowledge, what else is asked in the interview?
- **Apologized** *(अपोलोजाइज्ड)*-क्षमा माँगी He *apologized* for his rude behaviour.
- **Apostle** *(एपोस्टल)* – प्रचारक, नई दिशा देने वाला
  1. Bhagat Singh was an *apostle* of independence struggle of India.
  2. Kotwal Dhan Singh was an *apostle* of First War of Independence in 1857.
- **Appear** *(एपीयर)* – प्रकट होना Praveen Kumar *appears* as a class all rounder.
- **Appearance** *(एपीयरेन्स)* – आकृति, प्रकट होना His cheerful *appearance* pleases everyone.
- **Appeared** *(एपीयर्ड)* – उपस्थित हुआ The news *appeared* to be stratagem to defame him.
- **Applause** *(एप्लॉज)* – प्रशंसा He was welcomed by a huge round of *applause.*
- **Appointment** *(अपॉइन्टमेन्ट)* – नियुक्ति I have an *appointment* with my manager post lunch.
- **Appreciated** *(एप्रिशियेटेड)* – सराहा गया APJ Abdul Kalam will always be *appreciated* for his efforts in transforming India.
- **Apprenticeship** *(एप्रेन्टिसशिप)* – प्रशिक्षुता I had my *apprenticeship* under renowned professor of IIT.
- **Approached** *(अप्रोच्ड)* – नजदीक आया A problem should always be *approached* with a cool mind.
- **Apricot** *(एप्रिकॉट)* – खुबानी *Apricot* is good for skin.
- **Architecture** *(आर्किटेक्चर)*–शिल्पकला, वास्तुशास्त्र The *architecture* of Infosys Campus is envied by many companies.
- **Area** *(एरिया)*–क्षेत्र The house spans an *area* of 2,000 square feet.
- **Argue** *(आरग्यू)*–तर्क देना Never *argue* with your elders.

- **Argument** *(आरग्यूमेन्ट)*–तर्क The *argument* was not supported by any evidence.
- **Arise** *(एराइज)*–उत्पन्न The question of helping him can't even *arise* in my mind.
- **Armed** *(आर्म्ड)*–शस्त्रों से लैस The forces were *armed* with lethal weapons.
- **Arms** *(आर्म्स)*–भुजाएँ, बाँहें I threw my *arms* around her and hugged her.
- **Around** *(अराउण्ड)*–चारों ओर Is there any grocery *around*?
- **Arrange** *(अरेन्ज)*–व्यवस्था करना (1) He will *arrange* the sources for the company. (2) Lets *arrange* for a luxury bus to go for the tour.
- **Arrangement** *(अरेन्जमेन्ट)*–प्रबन्ध The internal *arrangement* of the house is very cozy.
- **Arrest** *(अरेस्ट)*–गिरफ्तार करना Police has *arrested* a woman trying to steal ornaments.
- **Arrive** *(अराइव)*–पहुँचना Rajdhani Express always *arrives* in time.
- **Arrived** *(अराइव्ड)*–आ पहुँचा He *arrived* last Monday.
- **Arrogance** *(एरोगैन्स)*–घमण्ड His *arrogance* reflects in his attitude and behaviour towards his colleagues.
- **Art** *(आर्ट)*–कला Translation is an *art*.
- **Articles** *(आर्टिकल्स)*–भाग, सामग्री I need some stationery *articles* and office equipments.
- **Artistic** *(आर्टिस्टिक)*–कलात्मक We witnessed an *artistic* flower arrangement.
- **As usual** *(एज यूजवल)*–हमेशा की तरह She went to the church on Sunday *as usual*.
- **Aside** *(असाइड)*–पृथक्, एक ओर She has started setting *aside* money to buy a car.
- **Aspect** *(ऐसपेक्ट)*–पहलू I try to see the positive *aspect* of every happening.
- **Assault** *(एसॉल्ट)*–हमला The mugger *assaulted* the housewife with a knife.
- **Assignment** *(असाइनमेन्ट)*–निर्धारित कार्य This *assignment* is a difficult one.
- **Assistant** *(असिस्टैन्ट)*–सहायक He has joined the firm as an *assistant*.
- **Associate** *(एसोसियेट)*–मिलना, समागम करना He can *associate* with strange people well.
- **Association** *(एसोसियेशन)*–संगठन The traders have formed an *association*.
- **Assured** *(एश्योर्ड)*–विश्वास दिलाया, आश्वस्त किया She *assured* me to consider the case sympathetically.
- **Astonished** *(एस्टोनिश्ड)*–आश्चर्यचकित His behaviour *astonished* me.
- **Astrologer** *(एस्ट्रोलॉजर)*–ज्योतिषशास्त्री Some *astrologers* have forecasted about the Third World War.
- **Astronomy** *(एस्ट्रोनॉमी)*–ज्योतिषशास्त्र We are on the threshold of a new era in *astronomy*.
- **Attain** *(अटेन)*–उपलब्धि प्राप्त करना If you like to *attain* success, work hard.
- **Attempted** *(अटेम्पटेड)*–प्रयास किया He *attempted* again but failed.

- **Attended** *(अटेन्डेड)*–उपस्थित हुआ He *attended* the coaching institutes twice but failed.
- **Attention** *(अटेन्शन)*–ध्यान Police *attention* shows the seriousness of serial blasts.
- **Attitude** *(एटीट्यूड)*–व्यवहार A man with positive *attitude* only can get success.
- **Attract** *(अट्रैक्ट)*–आकर्षित करना Sushmita's good looks *attract* many men to stare at her beauty.
- **Attraction** *(अट्रैक्शन)*–आकर्षण Aishwarya was the centre of attraction there.
- **Attributed** *(एट्रिब्यूटेड)*–श्रेय दिया He *attributed* that quotation to Shakespeare.
- **Audible** *(ऑडिबल)*–सुनने योग्य She spoke in an *audible* voice.
- **Audience** *(ऑडियेन्स)*–श्रोता The broadcast reached an *audience* of millions.
- **Auspicious** *(ऑस्पीशियस)*–शुभ, मंगल It is an *auspicious* beginning for the campaign.
- **Authoritative** *(ऑथोरिटेटिव)*–आधिकारिक, प्रामाणिक She commanded the troops in an *authoritative* manner.
- **Authorities** *(ऑथोरिटीज)*–अधिकारीगण He requested the *authorities* to help him.
- **Available** *(अवेलेबल)*–प्राप्य, उपलब्ध Not a single room is *available* here.
- **Avert** *(एवर्ट)*–होने से रोकना Talks with the union over the weekend have *averted* a sure strike.
- **Avid** *(एविड़)*–उत्सुक She misses not having enough books because she's an *avid* reader.
- **Avoided** *(अवॉयडेड)*–उपेक्षा की He *avoided* the conflict tactfully.
- **Awake** *(अवेक)*–चेतन He was now *awake* to the reality of his predicament.
- **Award** *(अवार्ड)*–इनाम He was given gallantry *award* for the bravery.
- **Aware** *(अवेअर)*–सावधान Indian Government is *aware* of every development in Kashmir.
- **Away** *(अवे)*–दूर Keep yourself *away* from the bad company.
- **Awe** *(ऑव)*–भय She stared over the edge with a feeling of *awe.*
- **Awkward** *(ऑक्वर्ड)*–भद्दा He made an awkward gesture.
- **Axis** *(ऐक्सिस)*–धुरी, कक्षा The Earth rotates on its *axis.*

B

- **Back** *(बैक)*–वापस, पीठ I called him up just a few minutes *back.*
- **Backyard** *(बैकयार्ड)*–घर के पीछे का आँगन In the *backyard*, there is a beautiful garden.
- **Bad tempered** *(बैड टेम्पर्ड)*–गुस्से में, गुस्सैल His *bad tempered* attitude is not liked by anyone.
- **Bade** *(बेड़)*–कहना I *bade* him farwell by throwing a small party.

- **Balance** *(बैलेन्स)*–सन्तुलन Pollution is disturbing the ecological *balance.*
- **Banned** *(बैन्ड)*–प्रतिबन्ध लगा दिया गया, पाबन्दी लागू कर दी गई Liquor is *banned* in Gujarat.
- **Barrier** *(बैरियर)*–अवरोधक, रोक Politics is great *barrier* in the path of development of India.
- **Barrister** *(बैरिस्टर)*–वकील, अधिवक्ता He is a *barrister* in London.
- **Baseness** *(बेसनेस)*–कमीनापन Everyone in the office is aware of his *baseness.*
- **Beak** *(बीक)*–चोंच Woodpecker can dig hole in a tree using its *beak.*
- **Bear** *(बीअर)*–सहन करना I had to *bear* the brunt of his mistake.
- **Beast** *(बीस्ट)*–जानवर Tiger is a ferocious *beast.*
- **Became** *(बिकेम)*–बना Her former friend *became* her worst enemy.
- **Bed cover** *(बैड कवर)*–चादर The *bed covers* available in the market are of various qualities.
- **Bedding** *(बेडिंग)*–बिस्तर People carry *bedding* with them on long journeys.
- **Befitting** *(बेफिटिंग)*–योग्य, अनुरूप The role was *befitting* his personality.
- **Before** *(बिफोर)*–सामने The train had left *before* I reached station.
- **Began** *(बिगेन)*–प्रारम्भ किया Tears *began* to flow from my eyes after hearing the story.
- **Begged** *(बैग्ड)*–निवेदन किया We *begged* before him but he didn't budge an inch.
- **Beggar** *(बैगर)*–भिखारी In India, you will find a large number of *beggars* around temples.
- **Behind bars** *(बिहाइन्ड बार्स)*–सलाखों के पीछे He has been put *behind bars* for three years.
- **Belief** *(बिलीफ)*–विश्वास The incident strengthened my *belief* in God.
- **Belonged** *(बिलॉंग्ड)*–स्वामित्व था The packet *belonged* to that man in black shirt.
- **Below** *(बिलो)*–नीचे There is a cat sleeping *below* the table.
- **Benefit** *(बेनेफिट)*–लाभ There are many *benefits* of living in a metropolitan city.
- **Bereave** *(बिरीव)*–विलाप करना/दुःखी होना Government offered a compensation of 5 lacs to the *bereaved* families.
- **Beside** *(बिसाइड)*–पास में He was sitting *beside* me in the meeting.
- **Besides** *(बिसाइड्स)*–इसके अलावा *Besides* industrialization, there are many other factors resposible for global warming.
- **Best-known** *(बेस्ट-नोन)*–सर्वाधिक प्रसिद्ध People are sceptical about the Nuke deal for the reason *best-known* to them.
- **Bestowed** *(बेस्टोव्ड)*–प्रतिपादित की गई, दी गई May almighty *bestow* all the bliss on the lucky couple.
- **Betrayal** *(बिट्रायल)*–विश्वासघात I cannot tolerate *betrayal* of trust at any cost.

- **Better off** *(बेटर ऑफ)*–धनी, सम्पन्न Even small countries like Poland are *better off* than India on Human Development Index.
- **Bidding** *(बिडिंग)*–बोली लगाते हुए The *bidding* process went on for the whole day.
- **Biggest** *(बिगेस्ट)*–सबसे बड़ा Madhya Pradesh is the *biggest* state of India.
- **Biography** *(बायोग्राफी)*–जीवनी I would like to read the *biography* of Mahatma Gandhi.
- **Bit** *(बिट)*–अंश He got a *bit* depressed on seeing his result.
- **Bite** *(बाइट)*–दंश The *bite* of a honey bee is very poisonous.
- **Bitter** *(बिटर)*–कड़वा The curry tastes *bitter.*
- **Blame** *(ब्लेम)*–दोष Don't *blame* me for his follies.
- **Blessing** *(ब्लेसिंग)*–आशीर्वाद देना, धन्य-धन्य कहना My termination from my previous company proved to be a *blessing* in disguise for me.
- **Blind** *(ब्लाइन्ड)*–अन्धा He is *blind* by one eye.
- **Blocked** *(ब्लॉक्ड)*–अवरुद्ध या बन्द The pipe got *blocked* by the sewage inside.
- **Blossom** *(ब्लॉसम)*–विकसित होना, खिलना *Blossoming* flowers in the rainy season are very soothing to see.
- **Blow** *(ब्लो)*–आघात The death of Gandhiji was a great *blow* to the nation.
- **Bodyguard** *(बॉडी-गार्ड)*–अंगरक्षक Her father appointed a *bodyguard* for her safety.
- **Bones** *(बोन्स)*–हड्डियाँ Human body has 206 *bones.*
- **Booked** *(बुक्ड)*–आरक्षित किया We have *booked* the movie tickets in advance.
- **Boring** *(बोरिंग)*–कष्ट देना, परेशान करना The weekends are very *boring* here.
- **Borrow** *(बॉरो)*–उधार लेना You can *borrow* some money from Deepesh Ji.
- **Boasting** *(बोस्टिंग)*–डींग हाँकते हुए His *boasting* habit had made him unpopular among his friends.
- **Bother** *(बॉदर)*–परेशान करना Don't *bother* me please.
- **Bottom** *(बॉटम)*–पैंदा They started at the *bottom* of the hill.
- **Bounced** *(बाउन्स्ड)*–उछलना He *bounced* back with full energy.
- **Bound** *(बाउण्ड)*–बाँधा I am *bound* to fulfil my promise.
- **Boundless** *(बाउण्डलेस)*–सीमाहीन, अनन्त He has a *boundless* enthusiasm to win the race.
- **Bounds** *(बाउण्ड्स)*–बन्धन What he did was beyond the *bounds* of acceptable behaviour.
- **Bowing** *(बोइंग)*–झुकते हुए Servants were *bowing* before their master.
- **Bow** *(बो)*–झुककर अभिवादन करना The government will have to *bow* to the opposition pressure.
- **Brain** *(ब्रेन)*–मस्तिष्क Human *brain* is very complex in structure.
- **Branches** *(ब्रान्चेज)*–शाखाएँ The banyan tree has numerous *branches.*

- **Branded** *(ब्राण्डेड)*—व्यापारिक चिह्न, दागा हुआ Lets purchase a *branded* shirt for him.
- **Brave** *(ब्रेव)*—बहादुर Kiran Bedi is a *brave* woman.
- **Bravo** *(ब्रेवो)*—वाह ! वाह !, शाबाश *Bravo!* We won the match.
- **Break** *(ब्रेक)*—अवकाश Rupneet eats some snacks in his school *break*.
- **Breathe** *(ब्रीद)*—श्वास लेना We should try to *breathe* in clean air.
- **Brick** *(ब्रिक)*—ईंट A *brick* is made in a kiln.
- **Bride** *(ब्राइड)*—दुल्हन The *bride* was looking like an angel in the wedding.
- **Bright** *(ब्राइट)*—चमकीला, होशियार He is a *bright* student of his school.
- **Bring** *(ब्रिंग)*—लाना I *bring* vegetables from the market daily in the morning.
- **Briskly** *(ब्रिस्कली)*—तेजी से She walked *briskly* in the cold air.
- **Broad** *(ब्रॉड)*—चौड़ा The carpet is as *broad* as long.
- **Broke down** *(ब्रोक डाउन)*—रुक गई, खराब होना The car *broke down* midway.
- **Broke the news** *(ब्रोक दि न्यूज)*—समाचार दिए Aaj Tak was the first channel which *broke the news* of Arushi's murder.
- **Broom** *(ब्रूम)*—झाड़ू Use a *broom* to clean the floor.
- **Brought** *(ब्रॉट)*—लाया His actions have *brought* disgrace to his family.
- **Brushed** *(ब्रश्ड)*—सहलाया The kidnap of the celebrity's son has *brushed* aside the main issues of the country.
- **Buck** *(बक)*—नर हिरण Killing *buck* is banned all over India and is a punishable crime.
- **Built high hopes** *(बिल्ट हाइ होप्स)*—बड़ी उम्मीद रखी He has *built high hopes* for his career.
- **Built** *(बिल्ट)*—बनाया The Taj Mahal was *built* in the 18th century.
- **Bullock** *(बुलक)*—बैल *Bullocks* are tied to a cart to plough the field.
- **Burden** *(बरडन)*—भार (बोझा) A girl is still considered as a great *burden* on the family.
- **Burst** *(बर्स्ट)*—फूटना I *burst* into a huge laugh at his joke.
- **Business** *(बिजनेस)*—व्यापार, व्यवसाय The aim of government is not to do business just to earn but to uplift the society.
- **Buyer** *(बायर)*—क्रेता In the 18th century there were not too many *buyers* of the Indian textile.
- **By all means** *(बाइ ऑल मीन्स)*—हर तरह से *By all means*, I have to defeat him.

C

- **Calculation** *(कैलकुलेशन)*—गणना His *calculation* went wrong and he lost the game.
- **Call** *(कॉल)*—बुलाना Opposition's *call* for strike got mixed response from public.

- **Calm** *(काम)*–शान्त करना The audience went *calm* after a heart touching performance by the actor.
- **Calves** *(कॉव्ज)*–बछड़े Students followed the cunning leader's instructions like *calves.*
- **Came down** *(केम डाउन)*–नीचे उतरा The prices of petrol have *came down* substantially.
- **Came out** *(केम आउट)*–बाहर आए He *came out* with flying colours despite all the struggles he did.
- **Candidate** *(कैन्डीडेट)*–उम्मीदवार, प्रत्याशी Three lac *candidates* appear this year in the examinations for IAS.
- **Candy** *(कैण्डी)*–मिश्री-मावा The batsman hit the ball straight to the fielder giving a *candy* of a catch.
- **Cantonment** *(कैन्टोन्मेन्ट)*–छावनी The *cantonment* was filled with soldiers who had come to attend the military games.
- **Capital** *(कैपिटल)*–राजधानी, पूँजी, सख्त The accused was convicted of the crime and was awarded *capital* punishment by the court of law.
- **Care** *(केअर)*–देखभाल One should always take *care* of one's parents.
- **Career** *(कैरियर)*–भविष्य, व्यवसाय You must be sincere towards your *career* and goal.
- **Carefree** *(केयरफ्री)*–चिन्तारहित His *carefree* attitude made him loose his goodwill.
- **Careful** *(केयरफुल)*–सचेत Be *careful* about your *health.*
- **Careless** *(केयरलेस)*–लापरवाह Diana's records show her *carelessness.*
- **Cargo** *(कार्गो)*–सामान The ship sunk with the *cargo* on board.
- **Carpet** *(कारपेट)*–गलीचा I need two *carpets* for my drawing room.
- **Carried** *(कैरीड)*–ले गई He got *carried* away with his initial success.
- **Case** *(केस)*–मुकदमा, मामला He filed a *case* against his neighbour.
- **Caste** *(कास्ट)*–वर्ण, जाति *Caste* is always misused in our country.
- **Casually** *(कैजुअली)*–आकस्मिक रूप से He *casually* asked her about her plan of getting married.
- **Caught** *(कॉट)*–पकड़ा He was *caught* red handed while making a theft.
- **Cause** *(कॉज)*–कारण His absence from the meeting is a *cause* of concern in political circles.
- **Cave** *(केव)*–गुफा That *cave* was more than 150 feet deep.
- **Cavity** *(कैविटी)*–छेद, गुहिका Sugar canned drinks have rotten your tooth and created *cavity* therein.
- **Cease** *(सीज)*–रुकना, बन्द होना A small number of firms had *ceased* trading in shares.
- **Ceiling** *(सीलिंग)*–छत (भीतरी) He got the *ceiling* painted in red colour.

- **Celebration** *(सेलिब्रेशन)*–उत्सव There was birthday *celebration* in my house on the day of robbery.
- **Cells** *(सेल्स)*–कोशिकाएँ Soap destroyed the *cell* walls of bacteria.
- **Centred** *(सेन्टर्ड)*–केन्द्रित All the discussions were *centred* to the use of atomic energy for peaceful purpose.
- **Ceremony** *(सेरेमनी)*–उत्सव I shall try to attend the marriage *ceremony* positively.
- **Certainly** *(सर्टेनली)*–निश्चित रूप से I will *certainly* attend the meeting.
- **Challenging** *(चैलेन्जिंग)*–चुनौतीपूर्ण Passing CAT examinations is indeed a *challenging* task.
- **Chamber** *(चैम्बर)*–प्रकोष्ठ He got a *chamber* built for his office.
- **Chance** *(चान्स)*–अवसर This is your second *chance* to appear in this examination.
- **Changed** *(चेन्ज्ड)*–बदल गया The new Chairman has *changed* all the policies of promotions and transfers.
- **Character** *(कैरैक्टर)*–चरित्र Dr Manmohan Singh is a man of *character*.
- **Charm** *(चार्म)*–मन मोह लेना, जादू कर देना She *charmed* him into giving her all his money.
- **Chase** *(चेज)*–पीछा करना The police *chased* the thief and caught him.
- **Cheap** *(चीप)*–सस्ता Don't buy *cheap* goods.
- **Cheated** *(चीटिड़)*–ठगा जाना We were *cheated* by their clever-sounding scheme.
- **Cheeks** *(चीक्स)*–गाल Tears were running down her *cheeks*.
- **Cheer** *(चीयर)*–खुशी Everybody *cheered* the birthday girl.
- **Cheerful** *(चीयरफुल)*–प्रसन्न She was in a *cheerful* mood.
- **Cherished** *(चेरिश्ड)*–संजोए हुए She has the *cherished* her goal to become an IAS officer.
- **China** *(चाइना)*–चीनी मिट्टी These utensils are made of *china* clay.
- **Chirp** *(चिर्प)*–चहकना Birds were *chirping* in the bushes.
- **Chivalry** *(शिवैलरी)*–वीरता The Rajputs are known for their *chivalry*.
- **Choice** *(चॉइस)*–इच्छा His *choice* of colours was indeed very nice.
- **Cholera** *(कॉलेरा)*–हैजा He is suffering from *cholera*.
- **Choose** *(चूज)*–चुनना You can *choose* whatever dress you like.
- **Circumstances** *(सरकम्स्टान्सेज)*–परिस्थितियाँ He passed through some very odd *circumstances*.
- **Circus** *(सरकस)*–करतब My son went to see the *circus*.
- **Cite** *(साइट)*–प्रमाण देना Please *cite* a valid example in support of your arguments.

- **Civil** *(सिविल)*–असैनिक Twelve *civilians* were killed in a series of bomb blasts in Delhi.
- **Civilization** *(सिविलाइजेशन)*–सभ्यता The people slowly progressed from barbarism to *civilization*.
- **Clad** *(क्लैड)*–कपड़े पहने हुए She was *clad* in white dress.
- **Clang** *(क्लैंग)*–आवाज We could hear the *clang* of distant bells.
- **Clasp** *(क्लैस्प)*–पकड़ना The child *clasped* my hands.
- **Clatter** *(क्लैटर)*–खड़खड़ करना The windows were *clattering* in the night creating a strange and fearful noise.
- **Claws** *(क्लॉज)*–पंजे The cat tried to cling to the edge by its *claws*.
- **Client** *(क्लाइंट)*–मुवक्किल The advocate supported his *client* with all his might.
- **Climate** *(क्लाइमेट)*–जलवायु The *climate* of the Antarctica is very cold.
- **Climb** *(क्लाइम्ब)*–चढ़ना She tried to *climb* up the tree but failed.
- **Cling** *(क्लिंग)*–चिपकना, पकड़ना The cat tried to *cling* to the edge by its claws.
- **Close friend** *(क्लोज फ्रेण्ड)*–पक्का मित्र Ram and Shyam are *close friends*.
- **Close** *(क्लोज)*–पास, नजदीक He was standing *close* to her mother.
- **Clue** *(क्लू)*–सूत्र, सुराग, संकेत, इशारा The vital *clue* to the identity of the thief was his footprints.
- **Clutch** *(क्लच)*–शिकंजा He smoothly released the *clutch* with one foot and stepped on the gas with the other.
- **Coincidence** *(को-इन्सीड़ेन्स)*–संयोग Success does not depend on *coincidence*.
- **Collapsed** *(कॉलैप्स्ड)*–टूटना The wall *collapsed* due to sudden earthquake.
- **Collection** *(कलेक्शन)*–संग्रह I have sent the cheque for *collection*.
- **Columnist** *(कॉलमिस्ट)*–कॉलम लिखने वाला Khushwant Singh is a *columnist* in various newspapers.
- **Combined** *(कम्बाइन्ड)*–मिलाना, एक करना The success is the *combined* result of hard work and determination.
- **Comfort** *(कम्फर्ट)*–आराम Do whatever you can with *comfort*.
- **Comical** *(कॉमिकल)*–हास्यपूर्ण There was a *comical* look of surprise on her face.
- **Command** *(कमाण्ड)*–आदेश The general *commanded* the troops to march ahead.
- **Commence** *(कॅमेन्स)*–आरम्भ करना The business was *commenced* last year.
- **Commit** *(कमिट)*–करना, किसी बुरे काम का The terrorist *committed* suicide.
- **Commotion** *(कॉमोशन)*–शोरगुल I heard a *commotion* outside.
- **Community** *(कम्यूनिटि)*–समुदाय The team is drawn from all parts of the *community*.
- **Companion** *(कम्पैनियन)*–दोस्त, साथी Be a real *companion* of somebody.
- **Company** *(कम्पनी)*–संगत I like the *company* of religious fellows.

- **Compassion** *(कम्पैशन)*—करुणा, दया He was God-like in his wisdom and *compassion.*
- **Compelling** *(कम्पेलिंग)*—बाध्य कर रही There were *compelling* circumstances that forced her to resign.
- **Complain** *(कम्प्लेन)*—शिकायत He *complained* against the misbehaviour done by the professor.
- **Completely** *(कम्प्लीट्ली)*—पूरी तरह से He failed *completely.*
- **Completion** *(कम्प्लीशन)*—समाप्ति I will leave for my house after *completion* of the assigned duties.
- **Complexion** *(कम्प्लेक्शन)*—चेहरे या मुखड़े का रंगरूप Her *complexion* is fair and height not less than six feet.
- **Compound** *(कम्पाउण्ड)*—सम्मिश्रण *Compound* the ingredients in proper ratio to get the desired mixture.
- **Comprehensive** *(कम्प्रिहेन्सिव)*—समग्र He got his car insured for *comprehensive* risk cover.
- **Comprise** *(कम्प्राइज)*—समाविष्ट करना Women *comprise* 48% of the hospital staff.
- **Conceal** *(कन्सील)*—छिपाना It is the glory of a God to *conceal* a thing.
- **Conceive** *(कन्सीव)*—कल्पना करना She can't *conceive* a baby.
- **Concept** *(कॉनसेप्ट)*—धारणा The *concept* of relativity is still under study.
- **Concerned** *(कन्सर्न्ड)*—सम्बन्धित I am not at all *concerned* with the murder.
- **Condition** *(कन्डीशन)*—शर्त He accepted the job on his own *conditions.*
- **Conduct** *(कन्डक्ट)*—आचरण, व्यवहार Improve your *conduct* towards your colleagues.
- **Confident** *(कॉनफिडेन्ट)*—आश्वस्त I am *confident* of winning the game.
- **Confined** *(कन्फाइन्ड)*—सीमित He *confined* himself to his study room.
- **Confusion** *(कनफ्यूजन)*—घबराहट I have a little *confusion* on this problem.
- **Congealed** *(कानगील्ड)*—जम गया In Georgia, they serve *congealed* salad.
- **Connection** *(कनेक्शन)*—सम्बन्धित The *connection* between church and state is inescapable.
- **Conquer** *(कंकर)*—जीतना *Conquer* your own heart and your own vagaries.
- **Conquest** *(कनक्वेस्ट)*—जीत Despite his *conquest* he remained lonely and isolated.
- **Conscience** *(कॉन्सिएन्स)*—आत्मा He has no *conscience* about his cruelty.
- **Consciousness** *(कॉन्सियसनेस)*—चेतना He lost his *consciousness.*
- **Consent** *(कन्सेन्ट)*—सहमति, स्वीकृति He gave his *consent* to the new venture.
- **Consequence** *(कॉनसिक्वेन्स)*—परिणाम Either ammend your ways or get ready to face the *consequences.*
- **Conservation** *(कन्जर्वेशन)*—संरक्षण Our government is spending a huge amount on energy *conservation.*

- **Conservative** *(कन्जर्वेटिव)*–रूढ़िवादी He is a *conservative*, does't like the rapid changes taking place in fashion.
- **Consider** *(कन्सीडर)*–विचार करना You are requested to *consider* my case sympathetically.
- **Considerable** *(कन्सीडरेबल)*–विचारणीय रूप से Government spent a *considerable* amount on the problems of minorities.
- **Considered** *(कन्सीडर्ड)*–समझा He *considered* me his younger brother.
- **Consist** *(कन्सिस्ट)*–शामिल होना Breakfast *consisted* of porridge served with butter.
- **Consoled** *(कन्सोल्ड)*–सान्त्वना दी He *consoled* her whole heartedly on her mother's death.
- **Constantly** *(कॉन्सटैन्टली)*–निरन्तर रूप से He is watching his progress *constantly*.
- **Constitution** *(कॉन्सटिट्यूशन)*–संविधान Our *Constitution* came into force on 26th January, 1950.
- **Constructive** *(कन्स्ट्रक्टिव)*–रचनात्मक He made progress with his *constructive* ideas.
- **Contact** *(कॉन्टैक्ट)*–सम्बन्ध I will try to make *contact* with him telephonically.
- **Contained** *(कन्टेन्ड)*–रखा गया The mixture *contained* lot of water and milk.
- **Contaminated** *(कन्टैमिनेटिड)*–प्रदूषित The environment is *contaminated* with poisonous gases.
- **Content** *(कन्टेन्ट)*–सन्तुष्ट Don't be *content* with your failures try again and again.
- **Continue** *(कॉन्टीन्यु)*–जारी रहना Keep your efforts *continue*, you will win.
- **Contract** *(कॉन्ट्रैक्ट)*–अनुबन्ध He signed a *contract* with the company for the supply of papers.
- **Contribution** *(कॉन्ट्रीब्यूशन)*–अंशदान, योगदान We must not forget the *contribution* made by our predecessors.
- **Control** *(कन्ट्रोल)*–नियन्त्रण Have a *control* on your anger.
- **Convenience** *(कन्वीनियेन्स)*–सहूलियत, सुविधा Call me at your *convenience*.
- **Conversation** *(कन्वरसेशन)*–बातचीत Doing effective *conversation* is an art.
- **Conviction** *(कनविक्शन)*–दोष सिद्ध The *conviction* came as no surprise.
- **Convinced** *(कनविन्स्ड)*–कायल होना, विश्वास करना They were *convinced* that it would be to their advantage to join our group.
- **Convincing** *(कन्विन्सिंग)*–सन्तुष्ट करने वाला Sachin Pilot won the election with a *convincing* victory.
- **Co-operative** *(को-ऑपरेटिव)*–सहयोग, संगठन Be *co-operative* to your colleagues.
- **Corner** *(कॉर्नर)*–कोना He placed a wooden table in the right *corner*.
- **Correspondence** *(कॉरेसपोन्डेन्स)*–पत्राचार He is doing MA through *correspondence*.
- **Cot** *(कॉट)*–चारपाई I have only one iron *cot*.

- **Cottage** *(कॉटेज)*–मकान, कुटिया He is living in a luxurious *cottage.*
- **Count** *(काउन्ट)*–गिनना *Count* your total books.
- **Countless** *(काउन्टलेस)*–अनगिनत, असंख्य He has *countless* books.
- **Couple** *(कपल)*–दो, जोड़ा The *couple* was caught making love in a public park.
- **Courage** *(करेज)*–साहस You must have *courage* to face the truth.
- **Courteous** *(कर्टियस)*–दयालु He was *courteous* to the poor and the downtrodden.
- **Courtyard** *(कोर्टयार्ड)*–चौक The house has a beautifully decorated *courtyard.*
- **Covered** *(कवर्ड)*–आच्छादित, ढ़की हुई The food was *covered* with dryfruits.
- **Cowardice** *(कोवार्डिस)*–कायरता It was an act of *cowardice.*
- **Cradle** *(क्रैडल)*– झूला, पालना Ram Singh bought a *cradle* for his newly born child.
- **Craft** *(क्राफ्ट)*– शिल्प, दस्तकारी The *craft*-shows represent the ability of an artisan.
- **Crawl** *(क्राउल)*–रेंगना The crocodile was *crawling* along the riverbank.
- **Creation** *(क्रियेशन)*–संरचना From its *creation* the plan was doomed to failure.
- **Creativity** *(क्रियेटिविटि)*–रचना American art reached at the peak of *creativity* in the 50s and 60s.
- **Creep** *(क्रीप)*–रेंगना He *crept* over the walls of the university buildings very slowly.
- **Crescendo** *(क्रिसेन्डो)*–धीरे-धीरे बढ़ाकर चरम पर ले जाना The music *crescendoes.*
- **Crime** *(क्राइम)*–अपराध Theft is a *crime.*
- **Crisis** *(क्राइसिस)*–संकट, संकटावस्था Lehman group is in a financial *crisis.*
- **Crisp** *(क्रिस्प)*–कड़क I like crispy potato *chips.*
- **Critical** *(क्रिटिकल)*–सोचनीय The patient is in a *critical* state.
- **Crowd** *(क्राउड)*–भीड़ The *crowd* moved towards the Parliament.
- **Crown** *(क्राउन)*–मुकुट He donated a *crown,* made of gold, to the temple.
- **Cruel** *(क्रुअल)*–दुष्ट, निर्दयी He is a *cruel* man.
- **Crumple** *(क्रम्पल)*–सिकुड़ना, मुर्झाना She *crumpled* the paper in her hand.
- **Crunched** *(क्रन्च्ड)*–कटर-कटर की आवाज करना His shoes were *crunching* on the gravel.
- **Crystal** *(क्रिस्टल)*–पारदर्शी काँच These are sugar *crystals.*
- **Culprit** *(कलप्रिट्)*–अपराधी The *culprit* was sentenced to jail.
- **Cultivate** *(कल्टीवेट)*–विकसित करना *Cultivate* your musical taste.
- **Cultural** *(कल्चरल)*–सांस्कृतिक He is a man of broad *cultural* interests.
- **Cunning** *(कनिंग)*–चालाक Charles Shobhraj is a *cunning* fellow.
- **Cure** *(क्योर)*–इलाज There is no *cure* of AIDS.
- **Curious** *(क्यूरिअस)*–जिज्ञासु He is *curious* to the new inventions.
- **Curled** *(कर्लड्)*–लपेटना She *curled* farther down under the covers.

- **Curly** *(कर्ली)*–घुँघराले Priyanka Chopra has beautiful *curly* hair.
- **Curse** *(कर्स)--अभिशाप* The bad witch *cursed* the child.
- **Custom** *(कस्टम)*–रिवाज, प्रथाएँ You have the right to withhold your *custom* if you wish so.

D

- **Danced** *(डांस्ड)*–नाचा The crowd *danced* to the tune of music.
- **Dangerous** *(डेन्जरस)*–खतरनाक Tiger is a *dangerous* animal.
- **Dare** *(डेयर)*–साहस They *dared* me to dive off the high board.
- **Dark** *(डार्क)*–अन्धेरा It's very *dark* in that room.
- **Darkness** *(डार्कनेस)*–अन्धकार Darkness cannot drive out darkness; only light can do that.
- **Dashed out** *(डैश्ड आउट)*–टकराया I was in the middle of my cereal when I looked out the window, saw the sky, and *dashed out* to take a couple of shots.
- **Daunted** *(डॉन्टेड)*–चुनौती He got *daunted* by the strange sounds coming from the jungle in the midnight.
- **Dawn** *(डॉन)*–शुरुआत से ही Realization of the danger soon *dawned* on us.
- **Dazed** *(डेज्ड)*–हक्का-बक्का हो गया She wandered in a *daze* through the hundreds of brilliant butterflies.
- **Dead** *(डैड)*–मरा हुआ After examining the patient, the doctor declared him dead.
- **Deal with** *(डील विद)*–के बारे में होना, पर विचार करना Employee should know how to *deal with* arrogant bosses.
- **Dealer** *(डीलर)*–खरीदने-बेचने वाला He is a drug *dealer*.
- **Dear** *(डियर)*–प्यारा In the robbery, I lost everything that was *dear* to me.
- **Dearly** *(डियरली)*–अतिप्रियता He buys his mistress *dearly* with his throne.
- **Debt** *(डेब्ट)*–ऋण, उधार Buying a house put the couple in more *debt* than they imagined.
- **Decade** *(डिकेड)*–दशक The last *decade* was characterized by the rise of the internet.
- **Decay** *(डिके)*–सड़ जाना, क्षय होना, क्षीण होना Nations and empires flourish and *decay*, By turns command, and in their turns obey.
- **Deception** (डिसेप्शन*)*–शंकित An honourable man or woman is one who is truthful and free from every form of *deception*.
- **Decide** *(डिसाइड)*–निर्णय करना A few votes *decided* the election.
- **Decision** *(डिसीजन)*–निर्णय Once you make a *decision*, the universe conspires to make it happen.
- **Deck** *(डेक)*–जहाज He *decked* his sparring partner.

- **Declined** *(डिक्लाइन्ड)*–इनकार किया I *declined* his offer to start a business in partnership.
- **Decreased** *(डिक्रीज्ड)*–घट गई The population growth-rate has *decreased* by a marginal 1%.
- **Dedicate** *(डेडिकेट)*–समर्पित करना We *dedicated* ourselves to starting our own business.
- **Deduce** *(डिड्यूस)*–परिणाम निकालना Based on evidence presented at the trial, the jury was able to *deduce* the accused was innocent.
- **Deed** *(डीड)*–कार्य The smallest good *deed* is better than the grandest malacious intention.
- **Defence** *(डिफेन्स)*–आक्रमण से रक्षा Sanitation is the best *defence* against disease.
- **Defiance** *(डेफियन्स)*–अवज्ञा Workers went on strike in *defiance* of union policy.
- **Definition** *(डेफिनिशन)*–परिभाषा With the drizzle, the trees in the little clearing had lost *definition*.
- **Definite** *(डेफिनिट)*–निश्चित There are no *definite* restrictions on the sale of alcohol.
- **Deforestation** *(डिफॉरेस्टेशन)*–जंगलों को काट डालना This article is about the process of *deforestation* in the environment.
- **Deity** *(डीटी)*–देवता 1. A *deity* is a God or Goddess.
  2. Calves are worshipped as *deities* in Egypt.
- **Delegate** *(डेलीगेट)*–प्रतिनिधि The Manager used to *delegate* all his work to his subordinates.
- **Delicious** *(डिलिशस)*–स्वादिष्ट Yesterday we had a real *delicious* dinner.
- **Diligent** *(डिलिजेन्ट)*–लगनशील, मेहनती His *diligence* is his strength.
- **Delight** *(डिलाइट)*–प्रसन्नता His *delight* to see her was obvious to all.
- **Deliver** *(डिलिवर)*–बाँटना The postman will not be able to *deliver* your letter today.
- **Democracy** *(डेमोक्रैसी)*–लोकतन्त्र There is *democracy* in India.
- **Demoralized** *(डिमॉरैलाइज्ड)*–हौसला गिरा, मनोबल गिरा The behaviour of the boss *demoralized* everyone in the office.
- **Denomination** *(डिनॉमिनेशन)*–मूल्य-वर्ग He flashed a fistful of bills of large *denominations*.
- **Dentist** *(डेन्टिस्ट)*–दन्त चिकित्सक I am going to a *dentist*.
- **Departing** *(डिपार्टिंग)*–विछोह We paid our respect to the *departing* soul.
- **Departure** *(डिपार्चर)*–गमन *Departure* time of the train is 10 am.
- **Depend** *(डिपेन्ड)*–निर्भर You can *depend* on me in case of emergency only.
- **Deplorable** *(डिप्लोरेबिल)*–निन्दनीय, बुरा Up to last year my finances were in a *deplorable* state.
- **Deposit** *(डिपॉजिट)*–जमा करना *Deposit* your fees by tenth of every month.

- **Descended** *(डिसेन्डिड)*–वंशज होना, से उत्पन्न होना She was *descended* from an old Italian noble family.
- **Describe** *(डेस्क्राइब)*–वर्णन करना *Describe* the flood situation in two hundred words only.
- **Description** *(डेस्क्रिप्शन)*–वर्णन The *description* given by the journalist was indeed very pathetic.
- **Desire** *(डिजायर)*–इच्छा, आकांक्षा He is trying his best to fulfil his long cherished *desires.*
- **Despair** *(डेस्पेयर)*–निराशा Don't *despair*–help is on the way.
- **Detached** *(डिटैच्ड)*–अलग या पृथक् She felt *detached* from the group.
- **Determine** *(डिटरमाइन)*–निश्चय करना Experience often *determines* ability.
- **Develop** *(डेवेलप)*–विकसित करना *Develop* your sense of humour.
- **Devotion** *(डिवोशन)*–धर्मनिष्ठ, भक्ति Their *devotion* to each other was admirable.
- **Dialect** *(डायलेक्ट)*–स्थानीय बोली/भाषा The immigrants spoke an odd *dialect* of English.
- **Diamond** *(डायमण्ड)*–हीरा Please show me a *diamond* ring.
- **Dictate** *(डिक्टेट)*–लिखना, आज्ञा देना He *dictated* a report to his secretary.
- **Dig** *(डिग)*–खोदना He is *digging* a pit.
- **Digestion** *(डाइजेशन)*–हाजमा, पाचन My *digestion* is out of order.
- **Dignity** *(डिग्निटि)*–शान He behaved with great *dignity.*
- **Dip** *(डिप)*–डुबोना She *dipped* the clothes in hot water.
- **Disabled** *(डिसएबल्ड)*–अक्षम Three per cent posts are reserved for the *disabled.*
- **Disappear** *(डिस्अपीयर)*–विलुप्त होना The moon *disappeared* in the clouds.
- **Disappointed** *(डिसएपॉइन्टेड)*–निराश Dr Manmohan Singh was *disappointed* with behaviour of opposition.
- **Disaster** *(डिजास्टर)*–अकस्मात् होने वाला विनाश There must be provisions for the *disaster* management.
- **Disciple** *(डिसिपल)*–अनुयायी, शिष्य Many *disciples* of the Mahant were injured in the police lathi charge.
- **Discipline** *(डिसिप्लिन)*–अनुशासन Students must maintain *discipline* in the prayer.
- **Discover** *(डिस्कवर)*–खोजना Amercia was *discovered* by Vasco de Gama.
- **Discussion** *(डिस्कशन)*–वाद-विवाद, वार्तालाप There was a hot *discussion* in the Parliament.
- **Disease** *(डिजीज)*–रोग Malaria is a contagious *disease.*
- **Disgrace** *(डिसग्रेस)*–अनादर He has *disgraced* his family's name.
- **Disgusting** *(डिसगस्टिंग)*–घृणास्पद A *disgusting* smell was emitting from the dead body.

- **Discharge** *(डिस्चार्ज)*–छोड़ना The doctor *discharged* the patient on his earnest request.
- **Dismiss** *(डिसमिस)*–बर्खास्त कर देना He was *dismissed* from his service.
- **Disobey** *(डिसओबे)*–आज्ञा का पालन न करना, मना करना He *disobeyed* his boss, so he was suspended.
- **Dispel** *(डिस्पेल)*–छिन्न-भिन्न करना, भगा देना The report *dispels* the myth that Northerners have a fattier diet than people in the south.
- **Dispensing with** *(डिस्पेन्सिंग विद)*–किसी चीज के अभाव में काम चला लेना Many households have *dispensed with* their old-fashioned wooden tables.
- **Disperse** *(डिसपर्स)*–तितर-बितर होना The police *dispersed* the crowd.
- **Displeasure** *(डिसप्लीजर)*–नाखुशी, अप्रसन्नता He showed his *displeasure* by not attending his marriage ceremony.
- **Disregard** *(डिसरिगार्ड)*–अपमान He *disregarded* the advice of his superiors.
- **Distinguish** *(डिस्टिंग्विश)*–भेद करना, अन्तर बताना Can you *distinguish* between different flavours of tea?
- **Destiny** *(डेस्टिनी)*–भाग्य Success depends a lot on your *destiny*.
- **Distress** *(डिस्ट्रेस)*–निराश The death of his wife caused him great *distress*.
- **Disturbed** *(डिस्टर्ब्ड)*–विचलित He became *disturbed* when he got the news of his demotion.
- **Diversity** *(डाइवर्सिटी)*–भिन्नता The cultural *diversity* of India is well-known.
- **Domestic** *(डोमेस्टिक)*–घरेलू He is a *domestic* servant.
- **Dominion** *(डोमिनियन)*–अधिकार/क्षेत्र France held undisputed *dominion* over vast areas of Africa.
- **Doubt** *(डाउट)*–सन्देह I have no *doubt* about his sincerity.
- **Downstair** *(डाउन स्टेयर)*–सीढ़ियों के नीचे She went *downstairs* to make coffee.
- **Downtrodden** *(डाउनट्रॉडेन)*–गरीब (दबे हुए) The Government must help the *downtrodden*.
- **Dowry** *(डॉवरी)*–दहेज I am against the custom of *dowry*.
- **Drainage** *(ड्रेनेज)*–जल निकास Line the pots with pebbles to ensure good *drainage*.
- **Dreadful** *(ड्रेडफुल)*–भयानक He was looking *dreadfully* ill.
- **Dragged** *(ड्रैग्ड)*–घसीटा He *dragged* me away from the television set.
- **Drowsiness** *(ड्रॉव्जिनेस)*–झपकी Big meals during the day cause *drowsiness*.
- **Dull** *(डल)*–मन्द बुद्धि He is *dull* and foolish.
- **Dump** *(डम्प)*–डालना, पटकना, ढ़ेर लगाना She *dumped* all her books in a corner.
- **Dung** *(डंग)*–गोबर Cow *dung* is used for growing fodder in countryside.
- **Dusted** *(डस्टेड)*–धूल साफ की He *dusted* the car before we started.
- **Duty** *(ड्यूटी)*–कर्त्तव्य I am *duty* bound to take action.

E

- **Eager** *(ईगर)*–उत्सुक I am *eager* to meet my wife.
- **Earn** *(अर्न)*–प्राप्त करना He *earns* a wage of 500 rupess per day.
- **Ease** *(ईज)*–आराम से I can wake up early with a great *ease*.
- **Echo** *(इको)*–अनुगूँज The followers *echoed* the cries of their leaders.
- **Eclipse** *(एक्लिप्स)*–ग्रहण The Sun *eclipses* the moon today.
- **Economise** *(इकोनोमाइज)*–मितव्ययिता Hollywood has been talking about *economising* on movie budgets.
- **Ecstasy** *(एक्स्टैसी)*–अतिआनन्द Her mother was in *ecstasy* when she gave birth to a male child.
- **Edge** *(ऐज)*–किनारा He rounded the *edges* of the box.
- **Educated** *(एजुकेटेड)*–शिक्षित It's very important to be sufficiently *educated* in this age of competition.
- **Effectiveness** *(इफेक्टिवनेस)*–प्रभावकारिता A meeting was called to discuss the *effectiveness* of computers as an educational tool.
- **Effort** *(एफर्ट)*–प्रयास He put all his *efforts* to get success.
- **Elated** *(इलेटेड)*–उत्साहित हुआ He *elated* with joy when he came first in CBSE Exam.
- **Elder** *(एल्डर)*–बड़ा He is my *elder* brother.
- **Elected** *(इलेक्टेड)*–चुने हुए Smt Pratibha Patil is *elected* first lady President of the country.
- **Elevated** *(ऐलिवेटेड)*–ऊँचा उठाया हुआ A meeting was held at the *elevated* platform.
- **Elusive** *(इल्यूसिव)*–छली In London late-night taxis are *elusive* and far from cheap.
- **Embarrassment** *(एम्बैरैसमेन्ट)*–घबराहट, गड़बड़ It was a real *embarrassment* for me to find my pant's zip open in the party.
- **Embraced** *(एम्ब्रेस्ड)*–आलिंगन कर लिया She *embraced* her husband firmly.
- **Empire** *(एम्पायर)*–साम्राज्य The British created a great *empire*.
- **Employment** *(एम्लायमेन्ट)*–रोजगार, काम-धन्धा The youth should be given proper *employment*.
- **Enable** *(इनेबल)*–योग्य बनाना This skill will *enable* you to find a job.
- **Encouragement** *(एनकरेजमेन्ट)*–साहस I also had friends who gave me a great deal of *encouragement*.
- **Endeavour** *(एन्डीवर)*–प्रयास His *endeavour* to start a business on his own deserves praise.
- **Enemies** *(एनिमीज)*–शत्रु Your best friend can turn out to be your worst *enemy*.
- **Energetic** *(एनर्जेटिक)*–ऊर्जावान Rahul Gandhi is an *energetic* young man.

- **Engulf** *(एन्गाल्फ)*–घेर लेना, निगल लेना The sea *engulfed* the entire ship.
- **Enormous** *(इनॉरमस)*–बहुत बड़ा There we saw an *enormous* tortoise.
- **Enough** *(एनफ)*–पर्याप्त 1. India has *enough* of skilled man power.
  2. The space is not *enough* for the hotel.
- **Enterprising** *(एन्टरप्राइजिंग)*–उद्यमी, साहसी He is an *enterprising* young man likely to go far.
- **Entertain** *(एन्टरटेन)*–सत्कार करना, मनोरंजन करना They *entertained* the guests with drinks and nice dinner.
- **Enthusiasm** *(एन्थ्यूजिएज्म)*–उत्साह *Enthusiasm* for the cultural programme is growing.
- **Entirely** *(ऐन्टायरलि)*–पूर्णतया He is *entirely* responsible for the loss.
- **Epidemic** *(एपिडेमिक)*–महामारी A flu like *epidemic* is sweeping through the capital.
- **Epoch** *(इपोक्)*–काल The birth of Christ was the beginning of a major *epoch* of world history.
- **Equator** *(इक्युएटर)*–भूमध्य रेखा The *equator* is the boundary between the northern and southern hemispheres.
- **Essential** *(असेन्शियल)*–आवश्यक At least a fund of rupees one lac is *essential* to the completion of the project.
- **Etiquette** *(एटीक्वेट)*–शिष्टाचार One must learn the *etiquettes* in one's childhood.
- **Evade** *(इवेड)*–कतराकर निकलना, दूर भागना This man always hesitates and *evades*.
- **Evidence** *(एवीडेन्स)*–प्रमाण Indian Legal System blindly relies on the physical *evidence* to give the final verdict.
- **Exactly** *(एक्जैक्टली)*–बिल्कुल, सही रूप से He was doing *exactly* what she had told him to do.
- **Examined** *(एग्जामिन्ड)*–जाँच की The doctor *examined* her thoroughly.
- **Excellent** *(एक्सीलेन्ट)*–शानदार, श्रेष्ठ He made an *excellent* speech.
- **Exceptionally** *(एक्सेप्शनली)*–असाधारण रूप से He is *exceptionally* intelligent.
- **Exchange** *(एक्सचेन्ज)*–विनिमय व आदान-प्रदान *Exchange* rate of dollar attracts every investor.
- **Exciting** *(एक्साइटिंग)*–मजेदार The movie has many *exciting* songs.
- **Exclaimed** *(एक्सक्लेम्ड)*–आश्चर्य से He *exclaimed* with surprise.
- **Excommunication** *(एक्सकम्यूनिकेशन)*–धर्म आदि से बहिष्कृत करना He was *excommunicated* from the village for his involvement in a rape case.
- **Exhausted** *(एक्जॉस्टेड)*–थका-माँदा He was appearing *exhausted*.
- **Exile** *(एक्साइल)*–निष्कासित करना The poet was *exiled* because he signed a letter protesting the government's actions.
- **Existence** *(एक्जिस्टेन्स)*–अस्तित्व There are many unwritten customs and laws, in *existence* for centuries.

- **Expect** *(एक्सपेक्ट)*–आशा करना We should not *expect* a lot from others.
- **Expensive** *(एक्सपेन्सिव)*–महँगा The gift seems very *expensive*.
- **Experienced** *(एक्सपिरियेन्स्ड)*–अनुभवी Mr Sharma is an *experienced* teacher.
- **Exploitation** *(एक्सप्लॉयटेशन)*–शोषण Government has issued many guidelines to prevent the *exploitation* of women in work places.
- **Exploration** *(एक्सप्लोरेशन)*–अनुसन्धान, खोज यात्रा He called for a careful *exploration* of the consequences.
- **Expose** (एक्सपोज)–उघाड़ना, अनावृत करना Inspector Mohan Chand Sharma with his colleagues *exposed* Delhi bomb blasts of 2008.
- **Expressed** *(एक्सप्रेस्ड)*–व्यक्त किया He *expressed* his anger in hot words.
- **Extremely** *(एक्सट्रीमली)*–सर्वोच्च, अत्यधिक रूप से I am *extremely* sorry for my inability to attend the function.
- **Eye-witness** *(आई-विटनेस)*–चश्मदीद गवाह He is the *eye-witness* to the murder.

F

- **Faced** *(फेस्ड)*–सामना किया He *faced* many difficulties in his childhood.
- **Facilities** *(फैसिलिटीज)*–सुविधाएँ, साधन *Facilities* of water and electricity are provided to all the people of the nation.
- **Fact** *(फैक्ट)*–तथ्य We must know the *facts* before we take any action.
- **Fair play** *(फेयर प्ले)*–न्याय व्यवहार, ईमानदारी I believe in hard labour and *fair play*.
- **Faith** *(फेथ)*–विश्वास Have *faith* in God and you will win.
- **Fame** *(फेम)*–यश, प्रसिद्धि The book earned him international *fame*.
- **Familiar** *(फैमिलियर)*–परिचित He seems very *familiar* to her habits.
- **Famous** *(फेमस)*–प्रसिद्ध India is *famous* for its diverse culture.
- **Far** *(फार)*–दूर His house is quite *far* from here.
- **Fare** *(फेयर)*–किराया The Government has increased the roadways *fare* due to price hike of diesel.
- **Fascinate** *(फैसीनेट)*–मोह लेना The snake charmer *fascinates* the cobra.
- **Fashionable** *(फैशनेबल)*–रीति, लोकाचार के अनुरूप Priyanka Chopra is a *fashionable* lady.
- **Faster** *(फास्टर)*–ज्यादा तेज He walks *faster* than his wife.
- **Fault** *(फाल्ट)*–दोष, दुर्गुण Don't find *fault* in others.
- **Favourable** *(फेवरेबल)*–पक्ष में It was a *favourable* decision from the employees' point of view.
- **Favourite** *(फेवरिट)*–पसन्दीदा Kheer is my *favourite* dish.
- **Fear** *(फियर)*–भय *Fear* not from the people but from your misdeeds.
- **Fearless** *(फियरलेस)*–निडर He is a *fearless* boy.

- **Feast** *(फीस्ट)*–भोज, उत्सव A 'thanksgiving *feast*' was arranged after the election.
- **Feebly** *(फीबली)*–धीमी आवाज़ में I said 'Sorry', very *feebly*, feeling rather embarrassed.
- **Feel** *(फील)*–महसूस किया I *feel* that she doesn't like me.
- **Ferocious** *(फेरोसियस)*–खूँखार A *ferocious* battle to select a new parliamentary candidate is in progress.
- **Fertile** *(फर्टाइल)*–उपजाऊ This land is not *fertile* but it is barren.
- **Fervour** *(फरवर)*–तीव्रता They were concerned only with their own religious *fervour.*
- **Festival** *(फेस्टिवल)*–पर्व, उत्सव, त्योहार Deepawali is a *festival* of Hindus.
- **Fetch** *(फेच)*–लाना Please *fetch* a glass of water.
- **Fiercely** *(फियर्सली)*–जोर से They fought *fiercely* to win.
- **Firmly** *(फर्मली)*–मजबूती से He caught my hand *firmly*.
- **Flag** *(फ्लैग)*–झण्डा India's *flag* is also known as 'Tri coloured'.
- **Fly** *(फ्लाई)*–उड़ाना They are *flying* kites.
- **Flock** *(फ्लॉक)*–झुण्ड Tourists *flocked* to the shrine where the statue was said to have shed tears.
- **Flow** *(फ्लो)*–प्रवाह, बहना The champagne *flowed* like water at the wedding.
- **Flushed** *(फ्लशड)*–चमकना, लाल होना The sky *flushed* with rosy splendour.
- **Foe** *(फो)*–शत्रु They had been political *foes* for years.
- **Foiled** *(फॉयल्ड)*–परास्त किया Their secret attempt to capture the thief was *foiled* by some staff members.
- **Follow** *(फॉलो)*–अनुसरण करना *Follow* my instructions.
- **Folly** *(फॉली)*–मूर्खता, अज्ञानता Trying to drive through a blizzard is the height of *folly*.
- **Fond of** *(फॉण्ड ऑफ)*–शौकीन He is *fond of* ice tea.
- **Foothills** *(फूटहिल्स)*–तल, तलहटी Pasadena lies in the *foothills* of the San Gabriel mountains.
- **Footsteps** *(फूटस्टेप्स)*–दहलीज, पद-चिह्न We heard *footsteps* on the porch last night.
- **Forcibly** *(फोर्सिबली)*–जबर्दस्ती He snatched my bike *forcibly*.
- **Forehead** *(फोरहैड)*–माथा There is a sign of injury on the right side of his *forehead.*
- **Foretelling** *(फॉरटेलिंग)*–भविष्य बताना I do not believe in *foretelling* about future events.
- **Forget** *(फॉरगेट)*–भूल जाना She *forgot* my name.
- **Forgive** *(फॉरगिव)*–क्षमा करना Please *forgive* me for not attending your birthday party.

- **Formulate** *(फॉर्मुलेट)*–योजना बनाना *Formulate* some good plans to tackle the slump in sales.
- **Frail** *(फ्रेल)*–दुर्बल She lay in bed looking quite *frail*.
- **Frankly** *(फ्रैंकली)*–खुले रूप से *Frankly* speaking I can't trust her.
- **Fraud** *(फ्रॉड)*–धोखाधड़ी Charles Shobhraj is involved in many *frauds*.
- **Freedom** *(फ्रीडम)*–आजादी We attained *freedom* in 1947.
- **Frequently** *(फ्रीक्वेण्टली)*–बार-बार, अक्सर He comes here *frequently* to visit his mother.
- **Friendship** *(फ्रेण्डशिप)*–मित्रता *Friendship* is very valuable, we must respect it.
- **Fright** *(फ्राइट)*–डर The birds smashed into the top of their cages in *fright*.
- **Furnish** *(फर्निश)*–सुसज्जित करना, सजाना He *furnished* his house in classical style.
- **Fuss** *(फस)*–खलबली What is all this *fuss* about?

G

- **Gain** *(गेन)*–प्राप्त करना, लाभ The stock market *gained* 240 points today.
- **Gathered** *(गैदर्ड)*–इकट्ठा हुए Let's *gather* in the dining hall.
- **Gaze** *(गेज)*–नजर Don't *gaze* at the girls.
- **Geared** *(गीयर्ड)*–तैयार, अनुकूल Management *geared* well to take stern action against the irregulars.
- **Generation** *(जेनरेशन)*–पीढ़ी We had to wait a *generation* for that prejudice to fade.
- **Generosity** *(जेनेरोसिटी)*–उदारशीलता, दानशीलता He can show great amount of *generosity* to impress upon her girl friend.
- **Generous** *(जेनेरस)*–उदार, दानी He is *generous* and liberal.
- **Gently** *(जेन्टली)*–नम्रतापूर्वक He *gently* asked the reason for not attending the meeting.
- **Genuine** *(जेन्युइन)*–वास्तविक The hologram shows its *genuineness*.
- **Giant** *(जायण्ट)*–विशालकाय Reliance built a retail *giant*.
- **Giggling** *(गिगलिंग)*–मूर्ख की तरह हँसना The girls *giggled* when the rock star came into the classroom.
- **Give up** *(गिव अप)*–त्याग देना John has *given up* smoking.
- **Gleam** *(ग्लीम)*–चमकना Her face was *gleaming* like a full moon.
- **Good bye** *(गुड बाय)*–अलविदा She bade *good bye* to her husband.
- **Good luck** *(गुड लक)*–सौभाग्य By saying '*Good Luck*' she wished me.
- **Goodwill** *(गुडविल)*–प्रतिष्ठा We do not want to lose the *goodwill* built up over 77 years.

- **Gossip** *(गॉसिप)*–गपशप We spoke, discussed *gossips* during the night.
- **Grace** *(ग्रेस)*–शालीनता This is a place where the company of others are accepted with good *grace*.
- **Gradual** *(ग्रेजुअल)*–धीरे-धीरे We are witnessing a *gradual* increase in prices.
- **Grand** *(ग्रान्ड)*–भव्य, शानदार The party was *grand* success.
- **Grapple** *(ग्रेपल)*–झगड़ना The two men *grappled* with each other for several minutes.
- **Grateful** *(ग्रेटफुल)*–कृतज्ञ I am *grateful* to you for your timely help.
- **Grave** *(ग्रेव)*–गम्भीर होना, घबरा देना He faced a *grave* decision in a time of crisis.
- **Greatness** *(ग्रेटनेस)*–महानता It was his *greatness* that he forgave you.
- **Grief** *(ग्रीफ)*–दु:ख Her death was a great *grief* to me.
- **Grieved** *(ग्रीव्ड)*–शोकाकुल His behaviour *grieved* his mother.
- **Grinning** *(ग्रिनिंग)*–दाँत पीसते हुए They cannot stand the sight of each other, but they will just have to *grin* and bear it.
- **Group** *(ग्रुप)*–समूह A *group* of ministers will take a decision in this matter.
- **Grudge** *(ग्रज)*–दुर्भावना He appears to have a *grudge* against certain players.
- **Guess** *(गैस)*–अनुमान, अन्दाजा लगाना Can you *guess* who stole the statue?
- **Guile** *(गाइल)*–धूर्तता I love children's innocence and their lack of *guile*.
- **Gushes** *(गशेज)*–फूट निकलना, बह निकलना There was a little *gush* of blood from the head injury.

H

- **Habits** *(हैबिट्स)*–आदतें He has some very good *habits*.
- **Half hearted** *(हाफ हार्टेड)*–अधूरे मन से, अनमना I can't do anything *half heartedly*.
- **Hullabaloo** *(हलाबलू)*–कोलाहल, शोरगुल She was scared by the *hullabaloo* over her arrival.
- **Halt** *(हाल्ट)*–ठहराव The train will *halt* here for one minute only.
- **Hand in hand** *(हैण्ड इन हैण्ड)*–हाथ में हाथ डाले Doctors and nurses worked *hand in hand* to save the lives of the accident victims.
- **Hand over** *(हैण्ड ओवर)*–देना She *handed* over her original certificates to the Chairman.
- **Handsome** *(हैण्डसम)*–सुन्दर Abhishek Bachchan is a *handsome* young man.
- **Hanging around** *(हैंगिंग अराउण्ड)*–आवारा फिरना Who is this man that is *hanging around* the girls' hostel?
- **Happen** *(हैपन)*–घटित होना, घटना What *happened* so that you are so much disturbed?
- **Happiness** *(हैपीनेस)*–खुशी Don't hide your *happiness*.

- **Hard of hearing** *(हार्ड ऑफ हियरिंग)*–सुनने में कठिनाई, बधिर He is a deaf fellow, so we can say that he is *hard of hearing.*
- **Hard working** *(हार्ड वर्किंग)*–मेहनती He is a *hard working* guy.
- **Hardly** *(हार्डली)*–मुश्किल से *Hardly* had he reached there than the train arrived.
- **Hardship** *(हार्डशिप)*–मुश्किल, कठिनाई Hritik has faced many *hardships* in his life.
- **Harm** *(हार्म)*–नुकसान These pills won't *harm* your body.
- **Harmony** *(हार्मनी)*–सामंजस्य, समरसता, मैत्री We must try to live in peace and *harmony* with ourselves and those around us.
- **Harsh** *(हार्श)*–कठोर Do not use *harsh* words in your friend circle.
- **Hawkers** *(हॉकर्स)*–फेरी वाले *Hawkers* were busy in selling newspapers and magazines.
- **Headache** *(हैडेक)*–सिरदर्द I have had a terrible *headache* for the last two days.
- **Heard** *(हर्ड)*–सुना I *heard* a strange sound last night.
- **Heaven** *(हैवन)*–स्वर्ग God lives in *heaven.*
- **Heavily** *(हैविली)*–जोरदार It rained *heavily* yesterday.
- **Heedless** *(हीडलेस)*–असावधान, लापरवाह He drove the car *heedlessly.*
- **Heir apparent** *(हेअर अपैरेन्ट)*–युवराज या उत्तराधिकारी He is only *heir apparent* to the thrown.
- **Hell** *(हेल)*–नरक "Go to *hell*", she said.
- **Helpless** *(हैल्पलेस)*–निःसहाय Help the *helpless.*
- **Heritage** *(हेरिटेज)*–विरासत, पैतृक सम्पत्ति, परम्परा That historic building is as much part of our *heritage* as the paintings.
- **Hermit** *(हरमिट)*–साधु The *hermits* were arrested by the police for their involvement in a theft case.
- **Hesitate** *(हेजीटेट)*–झिझकना, हिचकिचाना Don't *hesitate,* tell me the truth.
- **Hiding** *(हाइडिंग)*–छिप रहा What are you *hiding* here, it is being recorded in a camera?
- **Hold** *(होल्ड)*–पकड़ना Please *hold* my hand tightly.
- **Hole** *(होल)*–छेद, खोखला There are several *holes* in the cloth.
- **Holy** *(होली)*–पवित्र The Quran is a *holy* book.
- **Honest** *(ऑनेस्ट)*–ईमानदार She is an *honest* lady.
- **Honour** *(ऑनर)*–सम्मान He was received with deserving *honour* by the Chairman himself.
- **Hope** *(होप)*–आशा I have no *hope* of his recovery.
- **Horror** *(हॉरर)*–डर, भय Today children prefer to watch *horror* movies.
- **Hospitality** *(हॉसपिटैलिटि)*–आतिथ्य India is known for its respectful *hospitality.*
- **Huge** *(ह्यूज)*–बड़ा There is a *huge* popular demand for higher education to the girls.

- **Humming** *(हमिंग)*–गुनगुनाता हुआ I can hear the sweet *humming* of bees.
- **Hungry** *(हंग्री)*–भूखा I gave five rupees to the *hungry* man.
- **Hurriedly** *(हरीड़ली)*–जल्दी से, फुर्ती से He came *hurriedly* and went to bed.
- **Husky** *(हस्की)*–भर्राई आवाज़ His voice was *husky* with grief.

I

- **Ideal** *(आइडियल)*–आदर्श My father is my *ideal.*
- **Idle** *(आइडल)*–आलसी An *idle* man is a curse himself.
- **Ignorance** *(इग्नोरैन्स)*–अज्ञानता *Ignorance* of laws is no excuse.
- **Illegal** *(इल्लीगल)*–अवैधानिक It is *illegal* to keep a lady here by force.
- **Imagine** *(इमेजिन)*–कल्पना करना, अनुमान करना *Imagine* that you win the match.
- **Immediately** *(इमीडिएटली)*–तुरन्त Go there *immediately.*
- **Immunity** *(इम्युनिटी)*–प्रतिरक्षा, प्रतिरोधकता The President was granted *immunity* from prosecution.
- **Impartiality** *(इम्पार्शियेलिटी)*–निष्पक्षता *Impartiality* was as characteristic of Indians.
- **Impelled** *(इम्पेल्ड)*–धकेलना Courage and competitiveness *impelled* him to take risks.
- **Important** *(इम्पोर्टैन्ट)*–महत्त्वपूर्ण It is an *important* document.
- **Impossible** *(इम्पॉसिबिल)*–असम्भव Nothing is *impossible* in this world.
- **Impressed** *(इम्प्रेस्ड)*–प्रभावित किया The young tennis player Sania Mirza *impressed* the spectators a lot.
- **Improve** *(इम्प्रूव)*–सुधारना *Improve* your English grammar.
- **In spite of** *(इन स्पाइट ऑफ)*–के बावजूद *In spite of* hard work he failed.
- **In touch with** *(इन टच विद)*–के सम्पर्क में Keep *in touch with* me.
- **Incident** *(इन्सीडेंट)*–घटना The police investigated an *incident* at the railway station.
- **Incessant** *(इनसेसेंट)*–सतत्, बिना रुके Night and day we live with the *incessant* noise of the city.
- **Incompetent** *(इनकॉम्पीटेन्ट)*–अयोग्य, अक्षम He is an *incompetent* officer.
- **Increase** *(इनक्रीज)*–बढ़ना The price of the petrol has *increased* recently.
- **Indeed** *(इनडीड)*–वास्तव में He is *indeed* responsible for the loss.
- **Indelibly** *(इन्डेलिबलि)*–अमिट रूप से This tradition has left its mark *indelibly* upon the society.
- **Independence** *(इन्डिपेन्डेन्स)*–आजादी We maintained close relations with England even after *independence.*
- **Indestructible** *(इनडेस्ट्रक्टिबल)*–अविनाशी This type of plastic is *indestructible.*

- **Indicate** *(इन्डिकेट)*–बताना, दिखाना *Indicate* your choice at the earliest.
- **Indiscretion** *(इनडिस्क्रीशन)*–बिना विचार Occasionally they paid for their *indiscretion* with their lives.
- **Indiscriminate** *(इनडिस्क्रिमिनेट)*–बिना सोचे समझे, अन्धाधुन्ध The *indiscriminate* use of chemical fertilizers is injurious to the environment.
- **Indivisible** *(इनडिविजिबल)*–अविभाज्य Some numbers like 2, 3, 5 are *indivisible.*
- **Infinity** *(इनफिनिटी)*–अनन्तता, असीमता These permutations multiply towards *infinity.*
- **Influence** *(इनफ्लुऐन्स)*–प्रभावित करना The artist's work *influenced* the young painter.
- **Inhabitants** *(इनहैबिटैन्टस)*–निवासी Kangaroos are *inhabitants* of Australia.
- **Inhale** *(इनहेल)*–श्वास लेना, साँस खींचना He smoked marijuana but never *inhaled.*
- **Injured** *(इन्जर्ड)*–घायल He got severely *injured* in the accident.
- **Injustice** *(इनजस्टिस)*–अन्याय One should not tolerate the *injustice.*
- **Innocent** *(इन्नोसेन्ट)*–मासूम She is an *innocent* girl.
- **Inquire** *(इनक्वायर)*–जाँच, पूछताछ करना The police is *inquiring* the matter.
- **Insist** *(इनसिस्ट)*–जोर देना He *insisted* upon me to attend the function.
- **Insistence** *(इनसिस्टेन्स)*–हठ *Insistence* on grammatical correctness is a conservative position.
- **Inspite of** *(इन्स्पाइट ऑफ)*–के बावजूद *Inspite of* hard work he failed.
- **Instance** *(इन्स्टान्स)*–उदाहरण Can you quote an *instance* in support of your claim?
- **Instant** *(इन्सटैन्ट)*–पल, क्षण I do not believe in *instant* gratification.
- **Instil** *(इन्स्टिल)*–भरना, मन में बैठना He tried to *instil* confidence to his son's mind.
- **Instinct** *(इनसटिंक्ट)*–सहज वृत्ति He always knew what time it was, as if by *instinct.*
- **Instructed** *(इन्स्ट्रक्टेड)*–निर्देशित किया He *instructed* the students to wear uniform on every Monday.
- **Insult** *(इनसल्ट)*–अपमान He tried to *insult* me.
- **Intention** *(इन्टेन्शन)*–नीयत, भावना His *intentions* are not fair.
- **Intervene** *(इन्टरवीन)*–बीच में आना My father never *intervened* in a dispute between the brothers.
- **Intimate** *(इन्टीमेट)*–अभिन्न He is my *intimate* friend.
- **Introduced** *(इन्ट्रोड्यूस्ड)*–परिचय कराया, ज्ञान कराया, प्रारम्भ किया She *introduced* me with her boss.
- **Invasion** *(इनवेजन)*–आक्रमण Is reading a child's diary always a gross *invasion* of privacy?
- **Invested** *(इनवेस्टेड)*–धन लगाया I *invested* one lac rupees in shares.
- **Invincible** *(इनविन्सिबल)*–अजेय He tried again with *invincible* spirit.

- **Invisible** *(इनविजिबल)*–अदृश्य A thin coil of smoke rose almost *invisibly* into the sharp, bright sky.
- **Involved** *(इनवॉल्वड)*–सम्मिलित था She was found *involved* in the murder of her husband.
- **Irresolute** *(इर्‌रिजोल्यूट)*–डाँवाडोल, अनिश्चित् The committee was timid and *irresolute* in its decision.

J

- **Jealous** *(जीलस)*–ईर्ष्या I am *jealous* of his success.
- **Jibe** *(जिब्)*–मजाक उड़ाना He made a cheap *jibe* about my hair loss.
- **Jolly** *(जॉली)*–खुशी से She was in a *jolly* mood yesterday.
- **Justice** *(जस्टिस)*–न्याय Delayed *justice* is no justice.

K

- **Kindle** *(किन्डल)*–प्रज्वलित करना, जलाना The setting sun *kindled* the sky with orange and red colours.
- **Knew** *(न्यू)*–जानता था He *knew* me well.
- **Knowledge** *(नॉलेज)*–ज्ञान A little *knowledge* is a dangerous thing.

L

- **Lack** *(लैक)*–कमी होना This soup *lacks* salt.
- **Lad** *(लैड)*–बालक, कुमार When I was a *lad* of his age I would laugh at the strangest things.
- **Language** *(लैंग्वेज)*–भाषा Use pure *language* when you write in examination.
- **Later** *(लेटर)*–बाद में She came *later* than her husband.
- **Lauded** *(लॉडेड)*–प्रशंसा करना Dickens was *lauded* for his social and moral sensitivity.
- **Laughed** *(लॉफ्ड)*–हँसा They *laughed* loudly at the joke.
- **Laughter** *(लॉफ्टर)*–हँसी She enjoyed the *laughter* of the crowd.
- **Launched** *(लॉन्चड)*–आरम्भ करना She *launched* her new project on this day last year.
- **Lavishly** *(लैविशली)*–अति उदारता से The house was *lavishly* decorated.
- **Leaning** *(लीनिंग)*–झुकते हुए She felt *leanings* toward frivolity.
- **Learned** *(लरनेड)*–विद्वान् He is a *learned* scholar.
- **Legend** *(लीजेन्ड)*–पौराणिक कथा The play was based on mythological *legend.*

- **Legitimate** *(लेजिटिमेट)*–न्यायसंगत Only *legitimate* demads can be considered.
- **Leisure** *(लीजर)*–फुरसत, छुट्टी How do you pass your *leisure*?
- **Lifeless** *(लाइफलेस)*–जीवन रहित Her face looks *lifeless*.
- **Lift** *(लिफ्ट्)*–उठाना Can you *lift* this bag for me?
- **Lighter** *(लाइटर)*–अपेक्षाकृत हल्की Cotton is *lighter* than wool.
- **Lightning** *(लाइटनिंग)*–तड़ित विद्युत There was *lightning* in the sky.
- **Linger** *(लिंगर)*–ठहरना The shy student *lingered* in the corner.
- **Literally** *(लिटरलि)*–शाब्दिक The book was *literally* translated into English.
- **Livelihood** *(लिवलिहुड)*–जीविका He could no longer earn his own *livelihood* by fair means.
- **Lodging** *(लॉजिंग)*–अस्थायी निवास The regular opening of technical institutions eneouraged *lodging*.
- **Lonely** *(लोनली)*–अकेलापन I feel *loneliness* sometimes.
- **Loyalty** *(लॉयल्टी)*–वफादारी Your *loyalty* will pay you one day.
- **Lump** *(लम्प)*–ढ़ेर They *lumped* together all the applications.
- **Lurking** *(लर्किंग)*–छुपते हुए I saw someone *lurking* near the chamber during my address.
- **Luscious** *(लुसियस)*–स्वादिष्ट What I like most about my friend, is her *luscious* lips.
- **Lust** *(लस्ट)*–तीव्र लालसा His *lust* for power made him commit this crime.

M

- **Madness** *(मैडनेस)*–पागलपन Poetry is a sort of divine *madness*.
- **Maid** *(मेड)*–नौकरानी, कुमारी The *maid* brought me breakfast at 10 am.
- **Majestic** *(मैजेस्टिक)*–शाही, शानदार There is something *majestic* about his stature.
- **Manliness** *(मैनलिनेस)*–पौरुष, मर्दानगी I have no doubt about his *manliness*.
- **Manners** *(मैनर्स)*–तौर-तरीके He dressed well and had impeccable *manners*.
- **Markings** *(मार्किंग्स)*–निशान A plane with Indian *markings* was over-flying his vessel.
- **Matter** *(मैटर)*–मामला Serial bomb blasts is a serious *matter*.
- **Meadow** *(मीडो)*–घास का मैदान You can see cattle grazing in the nearby *meadow*.
- **Meagre** *(मीगर)*–थोड़ी When resources are *meagre*, you should not spend lavishly.
- **Mean** *(मीन)*–अर्थ होता है, तात्पर्य What is the *meaning* of 'lust'?
- **Means** *(मीन्स)*–साधन With small *means* one should not spend lavishly.
- **Meditated** *(मेडिटेटिड)*–ध्यान लगाया On the day her son began school, she *meditated* on the uncertainties of his future.

- **Memory** *(मेमोरी)*–याद्दाश्त His *memory* is fading gradually.
- **Mental** *(मेन्टल)*–मानसिक His *mental* power has weakened a lot.
- **Mention** *(मेन्शन)*–बताना, जिक्र करना *Mention* your father's name here.
- **Mere** *(मीयर)*–केवल He is *merely* a child.
- **Merit** *(मेरिट)*–गुण The *merits* will prevail over the demerits.
- **Merry** *(मेरी)*–खुशी Be *merry* and enjoy!
- **Message** *(मैसेज)*–सन्देश The *messages* of the terrorists disturb the routine work of police.
- **Messenger** *(मेसेन्जर)*–सन्देशवाहक A *messenger* delivered a gift to her.
- **Migrated** *(माइग्रेटिड)*–विस्थापित, देशागमन The workers *migrate* to the place where the crops need harvesting.
- **Mingle** *(मिंगल)*–मिलना He was about to *mingle* in an unpleasant affair.
- **Miracle** *(मिरैकल)*–चमत्कार India is a land of strange *miracles.*
- **Mirth** *(मिर्थ)*–उत्साह The win of the team caused considerable *mirth* amongst the players.
- **Mischief** *(मिस्चीफ)*–अनिष्ट Sunita's mother scold her for making *mischief* on arrival of guests.
- **Miserable** *(मिजरेबिल)*–दयनीय, दुःखी When I met her, she was in a *miserable* condition.
- **Misery** *(मिजरी)*–परेशानी She was exhausted by her *misery* and grief.
- **Misfortune** *(मिसफॉरच्यून)*–दुर्भाग्य She seems to enjoy the *misfortune* of others.
- **Mistake** *(मिस्टेक)*–गलती Don't commit any *mistake*, work slowly.
- **Modesty** *(मॉडेस्टि)*–विनम्रता Don't be shy and succumb to false *modesty.*
- **Moment** *(मोमेन्ट)*–क्षण, पल, समय I will reach you within a *moment.*
- **Monstrous** *(मॉन्स्ट्रस)*–भयानक She endured his *monstrous* behaviour for years.
- **Mortal** *(मॉर्टल)*–विनाशी Man is *mortal.*
- **Mourn** *(मॉर्न)*–दुःखी होना Pakistanis *mourned* on the sudden death of Benazir Bhutto.
- **Mysterious** *(मिस्टीरियस)*–रहस्यपूर्ण He died in *mysterious* circumstances.

N

- **Native** *(नेटिव)*–मूल He is a *native* of Brazil.
- **Natural** *(नैचुरल)*–प्राकृतिक It was a *natural* thing to happen.
- **Nature** *(नेचर)*–प्रकृति His *nature* is very nice and cordial.
- **Naught** *(नॉट)*–तुच्छ, शून्य All this fuss was for *naught.*
- **Naughty** *(नॉटी)*–शरारती He is a *naughty boy.*

- **Nay** *(ने)*–नहीं, न केवल The House of Commons can merely say yea or *nay* to the executive judgement.
- **Nearly** *(नीयरलि)*–लगभग,. प्रायः There were *nearly* hundred persons in the marriage.
- **Necessary** *(नेसेसरी)*–आवश्यक What is *necessary* should be purchased immediately.
- **Necessity** *(नेसेसिटी)*–आवश्यकता *Necessity* is the mother of invention.
- **Nibbled at** *(निबल्ड एट)*–कुतरा The woman tenderly *nibbled at her* baby's ear.
- **Nine-pin** *(नाइन पिन)*–मामूली चीज़ There was a time when Liverpool players never seemed to get injured, but now they are going down like *nine-pins*.
- **Noble** *(नोबल)*–कुलीन She is from a *noble* family.
- **Nocturnal** *(नॉक्टर्नल)*–रात्रिकालीन *Nocturnal* animals are active at night.
- **Nod** *(नॉड)*–सिर हिलाना He *nodded* his approval.
- **Nonchalantly** *(नॉन शैलेन्ट्ली)*–उदासीनतापूर्वक "Will she accompany us?" he asked *nonchalantly*.
- **Nonsense** *(नॉनसेन्स)*–बकवास, मूर्खतापूर्ण Most orthodox doctors rejected it as *nonsense*.
- **Nothing** *(नथिंग)*–कुछ नहीं *Nothing* can be done in this case.
- **Novice** *(नोविस)*–नौसिखिया As a *novice* writer there are so many expected errors in the composition.
- **Nuisance** *(न्यूसैन्स)*–कण्टक, उपभोग, बाधा He could be a bit of a *nuisance* when he was drunk.
- **Numerous** *(न्यूमरस)*–अनेक, असंख्य Sex crimes were just as *numerous* as they are today.

O

- **Obligation** *(ऑब्लीगेशन)*–कर्त्तव्य He is under an *obligation* to finish the job.
- **Observance** *(ऑब्जर्वैन्स)*–प्रेक्षण के आधार पर, प्रथाओं के अनुसार किया जाने वाला कार्य Local councils should use their powers to ensure strict *observance* of laws.
- **Obstacle** *(ऑब्स्टेकल)*–विघ्न, बाधा He faced the *obstacles* boldly and at last got a splendid win.
- **Obstinacy** *(ऑब्सटीनेसी)*–हठधर्मिता I might have become a dangerous man with all that stubbornness and *obstinacy* built into me.
- **Obvious** *(ऑब्वियस)*–स्पष्टतः There is an urgent need to rectify the *obvious* injustice.
- **Occasion** *(ओकेजन)*–अवसर There was never an *occasion* for her to demonstrate her skill.

- **Occult** *(ऑकल्ट)*–तान्त्रिक, गुप्त Planets and stars often are *occulted* by other celestial bodies.
- **Occupation** *(ऑक्युपेशन)*–व्यवसाय, धन्धा Please specify your *occupation* in the form.
- **Offender** *(ऑफेन्डर)*–आक्रमण करने वाला The authorities often know that sex *offenders* will attack again with their release.
- **Offered** *(ऑफर्ड)*–प्रस्तुत की She *offered* us all a cold drink.
- **Omen** *(ओमेन)*–शकुन He looked for an *omen* before going into battle.
- **Omitted** *(ओमिटेड)*–छिपा दिया, मिटा दिया His new girlfriend had *omitted* to tell him she was married.
- **Opportunities** *(ऑपोर्च्युनिटीज)*–अवसर, मौके You will get many *opportunities* in your life to succeed.
- **Origin** *(ओरिजिन)*–उत्पत्ति Several words have their *origin* from the Sanskrit.
- **Original** *(ओरिजिनल)*–मौलिक This is an *original* letter written by Nehruji.
- **Orphan** *(ऑरफन)*–अनाथ A ten years' old boy was left *orphaned* by the recent disaster.
- **Occurrence** *(ऑकरेन्स)*–घटना Complaints seemed to be an everyday *occurrence.*
- **Otherwise** *(अदरवाइज)*–अन्यथा Either say sorry *otherwise* you will be expelled.
- **Outskirts** *(आउटस्कर्ट्स)*–किनारा, बाहरी सीमा He has built his house at the *outskirts.*
- **Outstanding** *(आउस्टैण्डिंग)*–उत्कृष्ट, श्रेष्ठ He is an *outstanding* sportsman.
- **Owed** *(ओव्ड)*–उधार लिया, अनुगृहीत He *owed* me rupees five thousand.
- **Own** *(ओन)*–अपना I have my *own* business.

P

- **Packed** *(पैक्ड)*–खचाखच भरा होना The crowd *packed* the auditorium.
- **Pail** *(पेल)*–बाल्टी I need a *pail* of water.
- **Pain killer** *(पेन किलर)*–दर्द निवारक Vinayak used *pain killer* to release his pain.
- **Palace** *(पैलेस)*–महल Jaipur *palace* is excellent.
- **Pang** *(पैंग)*–दर्द She is having delivery *pangs.*
- **Parched** *(पार्च्ड)*–गर्मी से सूखा हुआ The sun *parched* the earth.
- **Pardon** *(पार्डन)*–क्षमा I beg your *pardon* sir.
- **Particle** *(पार्टिकल)*–कण There is no *particle* of truth in his statement.
- **Parting** *(पार्टिंग)*–अलगाव It was an emotional *parting.*
- **Partition** *(पार्टिशन)*–विभाजन Now offices are divided by glass *partitions.*
- **Partly** *(पार्टली)*–कुल अंश में, अंशतः These are *partly* paid shares.
- **Pass** *(पास)*–गुजारना He is *passing* through very crucial period.

- **Passed** *(पास्ड)*–उत्तीर्ण की He has *passed* his graduation this year itself.
- **Pastime** *(पास्टाइम)*–मनोविनोद Book reading is a good *pastime.*
- **Pasture** *(पाश्चर)*–चारागाह Some cattle are grazing in the *pasture.*
- **Pathetic** *(पैथेटिक)*–करुणाजनक The site of the accident was *pathetic.*
- **Patted** *(पैटेड)*–थपथपाया I *patted* him on the shoulder.
- **Peaceful** *(पीसफुल)*–शान्तिपूर्ण We should opt *peaceful* means to solve any problem.
- **Peasantry** *(पीजेन्ट्री)*–किसान वर्ग The Indian *peasantry* are very simple living fellows.
- **Pebble** *(पेबल)*–कंकड़ The crow put some *pebbles* into the pot and the water level became high.
- **Pell-mell** *(पेल-मेल)*–हड़बड़ी में All of us rushed *pell-mell* into the kitchen.
- **Perfect** *(परफेक्ट)*–पूर्ण He is a *perfect* match for her.
- **Perform** *(परफॉर्म)*–पूरा करना The pandit will *perform* the wedding.
- **Perhaps** *(परहैप्स)*–शायद *Perhaps* you are right.
- **Period** *(पीरियड)*–अवधि One month *period* is not enough for the preparations.
- **Perish** *(पेरिश)*–बर्बाद होना All the property *perished* in the fire.
- **Permanent** *(परमानेन्ट)*–स्थायी He is a *permanent* employee.
- **Permission** *(परमिशन)*–अनुमति, इजाजत You can't enter the hall without *permission.*
- **Persist** *(परसिस्ट)*–कायम रहना The child *persisted* and kept on asking questions.
- **Personal** *(पर्सनल)*–व्यक्तिगत It is my *personal* matter.
- **Personality** *(पर्सनैलिटि)*–व्यक्तित्व He enjoys a very robust *personality.*
- **Persuade** *(परसुएड)*–मनाना He tried to *persuade* me to accept the terms.
- **Pertinent** *(परटिनेन्ट)*–प्रासंगिक She asked some *pertinent* questions.
- **Petition** *(पेटिशन)*–प्रार्थना-पत्र He filed a review *petition* in the court.
- **Physical** *(फिजिकल)*–शारीरिक Take some *physical* exercises daily.
- **Physique** *(फिजिक)*–शारीरिक गठन He has a sound *physique.*
- **Picked** *(पिक्ड)*–उठा लिया He *picked* a stone and threw it at the monkey.
- **Pile** *(पाइल)*–ढ़ेर She *piled* clothes in a suit case.
- **Pilgrim** *(पिलग्रिम)*–तीर्थयात्री *Pilgrims* flocked to the tiny country to mark the Millennium.
- **Plan** *(प्लान)*–योजना, युक्ति Chalk out a *plan* to increase the sale.
- **Play** *(प्ले)*–नाटक He is participating the *play* named 'Akbar the Great'.
- **Pleaded** *(प्लीडेड)*–प्रार्थना की
  1. He *pleaded* ernestly in favour of his client but of no avail.
  2. The thief *pleaded* not guilty.
- **Pleased** *(प्लीज्ड)*–प्रसन्न हुआ I am *pleased* to meet you.

- **Pleasure** *(प्लेजर)*–खुशी It's my *pleasure*, sir.
- **Plenty** *(प्लेन्टि)*–प्रचुरता There was *plenty* of food for everyone.
- **Plough** *(प्लो)*–खेत जोतना He is *ploughing* his field.
- **Plunge into** *(प्लन्ज इनटू)*–कूद पड़ना He *plunged into* the battle without much thinking.
- **Ponder** *(पॉन्डर)*–सोचना I am *pondering* about the future plannings of my son.
- **Possessed** *(पजेस्ड)*–अधिकार में Leer My father *possessed* a unique Vintage car.
- **Poverty** *(पॉवर्टी)*–गरीबी He is living below the *poverty* line.
- **Praised** *(प्रेज्ड)*–प्रशंसा की Everybody *praised* his wisdom and planning skills.
- **Precious** *(प्रेशस)*–कीमती Gold is a *precious* metal.
- **Prefer** *(प्रिफर)*–प्राथमिकता देना I *prefer* coffee to tea.
- **Prejudice** *(प्रिज्युडिस)*–दुराग्रह I have spent a lot of time fighting against racism and *prejudice*.
- **Prescribe** *(प्रेस्क्राइब)*–दवा के सेवन की सलाह देना The doctor *prescribed* three capsules a day.
- **Preserve** *(प्रिजर्व)*–सुरक्षित रखना We must preserve our archaeological monuments.
- **Presume** *(प्रिज्यूम)*–मानना I *presume* you are here on business tour.
- **Pretend** *(प्रिटेण्ड)*–बहाना करना Sometimes boys *pretended* to be asleep.
- **Pretentious** *(प्रिटेन्शस)*–बनावटी, ढोंगी, पाखण्डी His response was full of *pretentious* nonsense.
- **Pretty** *(प्रेटी)*–सुन्दर She is a *pretty* lady with a generous attitude.
- **Prevalent** *(प्रेवैलेण्ट)*–प्रचलित The *prevalent* view is that the interest rates will fall.
- **Prevent** *(प्रिवेन्ट)*–रोकना I tried to *prevent* him from entering the room.
- **Prey** *(प्रे)*–शिकार Police officers lie in wait for the gangs who stalk their *prey* at night.
- **Pride** *(प्राइड)*–गर्व He takes *pride* in his son's success.
- **Primitive** *(प्रिमिटिव)*–आदिकालीन They are using rather some *primitive* technologies.
- **Process** *(प्रोसेस)*–प्रक्रिया The institute of Birlas insists on transparency in admission *process*.
- **Prodding** *(प्रोडिंग)*–उलटना, पलटना She was *prodding* at a boiled egg.
- **Prodigal** *(प्रोडिगल)*–फिजूलखर्च He is *prodigal* in his expenditure on wines.
- **Production** *(प्रोडक्शन)*–उत्पादन Increase the *production* of tea leaves.
- **Profession** *(प्रोफेशन)*–धन्धा, व्यवसाय Your *profession* is absolutely neat and clean.
- **Professional** *(प्रोफेशनल)*–व्यावसायिक Indira Noe is a *professional* lady.
- **Profitable** *(प्रोफिटेबिल)*–लाभप्रद It is not a *profitable* business now.

- **Progress** *(प्रोग्रेस)*–प्रगति, उन्नति India has made rapid *progress* in the field of Information Technology.
- **Prohibited** *(प्रोहिबिटिड)*–निषिद्ध Smoking is *prohibited* in public places.
- **Promulgate** *(प्रोमलगेट)*–कानून लागू करना The President has *promulgated* an ordinance recently.
- **Proportion** *(प्रोपोरशन)*–अनुपात, परिमाण A dry martini has a large *proportion* of gin.
- **Propound** *(प्रोपाउण्ड)*–प्रस्तुत करना Zoologist Eugene Morton has *propounded* a general theory of the vocal sounds that animals make.
- **Prosperity** *(प्रोसपेरिटी)*–खुशहाली, समृद्धि May God grant you peace and *prosperity*.
- **Protested** *(प्रोटेस्टेड)*–विरोध किया He *protested* against the price rise.
- **Proud** *(प्राउड)*–गर्व का अनुभव करना, गर्वित I am *proud* of my country.
- **Prove** *(प्रूव)*–सिद्ध करना You *prove* your innocence.
- **Provided** *(प्रोवाइडेड)*–उपलब्ध कराया We *provided* the room with an electric heater.
- **Provoked** *(प्रोवोक्ड)*–उकसाना, छेड़ना Her behaviour *provoked* a quarrel between the couple.
- **Prowess** *(प्राउऐस)*–वीरता He is always bragging about his *prowess* as a batsman.
- **Put on** *(पुट ऑन)*–पहनना She *put on* jeans and top on her wedding day.

Q

- **Quality** *(क्वालिटि)*–गुण Tell me about your *qualities*.
- **Quarrel** *(क्वैरल)*–लड़ाई-झगड़ा 1. He was *quarrelling* with his neighbour.
  2. Have no *quarrel* with neighbour.
- **Quench** *(कवेन्च)*–बुझाना The cold water *quenched* his thirst.
- **Quick** *(क्विक)*–तेजी से 1. He is *quick* in his work allotted to him.
  2. He finished his work *quickly*.
- **Quietly** *(क्वाइटली)*–चुपचाप He completed his project peacefully and *quietly*.
- **Quote** *(कोट)*–उद्धरण This is a *quote* from Geeta.

R

- **Radiant** *(रेडयेन्ट)*–तेजस्वी On the wedding day the bride looked truly *radiant*.
- **Rage** *(रेज)*–क्रोधित होना She was red cheeked with *rage*.
- **Ragged** *(रैग्ड)*–रूक्ष, जीर्ण She was wearing a *ragged* furcoat.
- **Rammed** *(रैम्ड)*–ठूँसा She *rammed* her mind into focus.
- **Rapidly** *(रैपिडली)*–तेजी से India is progressing *rapidly*.

- **Rarely** *(रेअरली)*–कभी-कभार She comes here *rarely*.
- **Rash** *(रैश)*–उतावला It was a *rash* attempt to mount the everest.
- **Realized** *(रियलाइज्ड)*–महसूस किया He *realized* his mistake.
- **Rear** *(रियर)*–पिछला भाग Before turning your car watch in the *rear* mirror.
- **Reason** *(रीजन)*–कारण I have no *reason* to believe your story.
- **Rebel** *(रेबेल)*–विद्रोही She had been a *rebel* at school.
- **Recapture** *(रीकैप्चर)*–पुनः कब्जा कर लेना She could not *recapture* that feeling of happiness.
- **Reckless** *(रेक्लेस)*–असावधान He is charged with causing death by *reckless* driving.
- **Recognize** *(रेक्गनाइज)*–पहचानना The forces could not *recognize* the extremist.
- **Recount** *(रिकाउन्ट)*–पुनर्गणना The candidate demanded for the *recounting* of votes.
- **Rectitude** *(रेक्टिट्यूड)*–ईमानदारी से He is a man of utmost moral *rectitude*.
- **Redress** *(रिड्रेस)*–दुरुस्त करना More and more victims turn to litigation to *redress* wrongs done to them.
- **Reduce** *(रिड्यूस)*–कम करना If you want to stay fit *reduce* your daily fat intake.
- **Refill** *(रिफिल)*–दुबारा भरना *Refill* this can with milk.
- **Refined** *(रिफाइन्ड)*–शोधित This is *refined* vegetable oil.
- **Reform** *(रिफॉर्म)*–सुधार More economic *reforms* are necessary in India.
- **Refuge** *(रिफ्यूज)*–शरण She took *refuge* in a lonely house.
- **Refuse** *(रिफ्यूज)*–इनकार करना He *refused* to grant me leave.
- **Regain** *(रिगेन)*–पुनः प्राप्त करना · You can't *regain* your youth.
- **Regime** *(रेजिम)*–शासन पद्धति She is fully devoted to the Soviet *regime*.
- **Regulation** *(रेगुलेशन)*–रीति-रिवाज, नियम Implementation of fiscal *regulations* is in the hands of tax officials.
- **Reign** *(रेन्)*–शासन There was a *reign* of terror in the valley.
- **Rejoicing** *(रिजोइसिंग)*–आनन्द People were dancing and *rejoicing*.
- **Relation** *(रिलेशन)*–सम्बन्ध He is in my wife's *relation*.
- **Released** *(रिलीज्ड)*–छोड़ा गया The Court *released* him on five lac rupees' personal bond.
- **Relegated** *(रेलिगेटिड)*–बहिष्कृत, देश निकाला If we lose we shall be *relegated* out of country.
- **Relevance** *(रेलेवैन्स)*–प्रासंगिकता What is the *relevance* of this argument?
- **Relic** *(रेलिक)*–अवशेष This is a museum of war *relics*.
- **Relieve** *(रिलीव)*–राहत This is a pain *relieving* tablet.
- **Religious** *(रिलिजिअस)*–धार्मिक Geeta is a *religious* epic.

- **Reluctantly** *(रिलक्टैण्टली)*–अनिच्छा से She agreed to the proposal *reluctantly*.
- **Remarkable** *(रिमार्केबल)*–असाधारण, विशिष्ट His achievements are *remarkable*.
- **Remedy** *(रेमेडी)*–इलाज, उपाय The *remedy* lies in the hands of the government.
- **Remorse** *(रेमोर्स)*–पश्चात्ताप, दु:ख, विपत्ति She was full of *remorse*.
- **Remote** *(रिमोट)*–दूरस्थ That is a *remote* controlled television.
- **Remove** *(रिमूव)*–हटाना, दूर करना *Remove* this bandage immediately.
- **Reported** *(रिर्पोटेड)*–सूचना दी The matter has been *reported* to the police.
- **Represent** *(रिप्रेजेन्ट)*–प्रतिनिधित्व करना I *represent* my country.
- **Repute** *(रेंप्यूट)*–ख्याति He is a man of great *repute*.
- **Requisite** *(रिक्विसिट)*–आवश्यक She filled in the *requisite* application form.
- **Rescued** *(रेस्क्यूड)*–बचाया, रक्षा की Helicopters *rescued* nearly 20 people from the roof of the burning building.
- **Research** *(रिसर्च)*–शोध, अनुसन्धान The student *researched* the history of that word.
- **Resemble** *(रिजेम्बल)*–मिलता-जुलता Soha Ali Khan *resembles* her mother very much.
- **Resident** *(रेजिडेन्ट)*–निवासी We are the *residents* of Indian countryside.
- **Resign** *(रिजाइन)*–त्यागना He *resigned* from the job.
- **Resolute** *(रेजोल्यूट)*–दृढ़ He *resolutely* refused to speak on this topic.
- **Resolved** *(रिजोल्व्ड)*–ठाना, निश्चय किया He *resolved* never to drink again.
- **Resource** *(रिसोर्स)*–संसाधन Mulayam Singh Yadav is a man of *resource*.
- **Respect** *(रेसपेक्ट)*–आदर Pay due *respect* to the elders.
- **Restrain** *(रेस्ट्रेन)*–रोकना She was unable to *restrain* her desperate anger.
- **Resume** *(रिज्यूम)*–दोबारा शुरू करना He *resumed* his job after one year.
- **Retaliated** *(रिटेलियेटेड)*–चुकाया, प्रतिकार किया The Israeli army *retaliated* for the Hamas bombing.
- **Return** *(रिटर्न)*–लौटना I will *return* to Delhi tomorrow.
- **Revenge** *(रिवेन्ज)*–बदला She tried to *revenge* herself on her former lover.
- **Reverie** *(रेवरि)*–दिवा स्वप्न, दिन का सपना The announcer's voice brought her out of *reverie*.
- **Revive** *(रिवाइव)*–पुनर्जीवित करना She *revived* after the doctor gave her an injection.
- **Revolt** *(रिवॉल्ट)*–क्रान्ति, आन्दोलन People *revolted* when petrol prices increased again.
- **Reward** *(रिवार्ड)*–ईनाम She was *rewarded* for her good performance.
- **Rewarding** *(रिवार्डिंग)*–लाभप्रद, करने योग्य Engineering is a *rewarding* career now-a-days.

- **Ridiculous** *(रिडिकुलस)*–हास्यास्पद It is *ridiculous* to presume that we are having a romance.
- **Rigorous** *(रिगरस)*–कठिन He was sentenced to three years' *rigorous* imprisonment.
- **Risk** *(रिस्क)*–खतरा There is a *risk* of immediate loss in share's trading business.
- **Rites** *(राइट्स)*–रिवाज Most traditional societies have transition *rites* at puberty.
- **Rituals** *(रिच्युअल्स)*–धार्मिक अनुष्ठान या कृत्य The statue was *ritually* bathed and anointed.
- **Roar** *(रोअर)*–दहाड़ना I hear the *roar* of tiger.
- **Roast** *(रोस्ट)*–भूनना She *roasted* a turkey for dinner.
- **Robbed** *(रोब्ड)*–लूटा गया The burglars *robbed* him of all his money.
- **Roof** *(रूफ)*–छत The *roof* of the cave was very high.
- **Rotate** *(रोटेट)*–धुरी पर घूमना Ballet dancers can *rotate* their legs out by 90 degrees.
- **Rubbed** *(रब्ड)*–रगड़ा He *rubbed* scented oil onto her skin.
- **Rude** *(रूड)*–असभ्य, गंवार Amit is a *rude* fellow.
- **Ruffians** *(रफियन्स)*–उपद्रवी A gang of *ruffians* tried to loot some shops in the market.
- **Ruin** *(र्यून)*–बर्बाद करना He has *ruined* his career.
- **Rush** *(रश)*–दौड़कर जाना I *rushed* to the site where accident took place.
- **Rustle** *(रसल)*–सरसराहट I hear *rustle* of clothes behind the almirah.

S

- **Sack** *(सैक)*–बोरा, झोला The grocer *sacked* the onions.
- **Sacred** *(सैकरेड)*–पवित्र Ramayan is a *sacred* book of Hindus.
- **Saddle** *(सैडल)*–घोड़े की काठी He *saddled* me with that heavy responsibility.
- **Safety** *(सेफ्टी)*–सुरक्षा One should take *safety* measures while working on electricity poles.
- **Salutation** *(सेल्यूटेशन)*–अभिवादन The old man moved away, raising his hand in *salutation*.
- **Salvation** *(साल्वेशन)*–मुक्ति The *salvation* of his party was the president's major concern.
- **Sanctuary** *(सैंक्चुरी)*–पक्षी विहार There is a bird *sanctuary* in Bharatpur of Rajasthan.
- **Sanitation** *(सैनिटेशन)*–सफाई का प्रबन्ध The *sanitation* system of the city is very poor.
- **Satisfied** *(सेटिसफाइड)*–सन्तुष्ट I am quite *satisfied* with his performance.

- **Savage** *(सेवेज)*–जंगली, असभ्य लोग This was a *savage* attack on the young girl.
- **Scarcely** *(स्केअर्सली)*–मुश्किल से We *scarcely* ever used the emergency generator.
- **Scarcity** *(स्केअर्सिटि)*–कमी There is a *scarcity* of water these days.
- **Scented** *(सेन्टिड)*–सुगन्धित Please give me a *scented* powder.
- **Scepticism** *(सेप्टिसिस्म)*–सन्देह करने की आदत Never show *scepticism* on your near and dear.
- **Schedule** *(शेड्यूल)*–कार्यक्रम I've *scheduled* a concert next week.
- **Scoff** *(स्कॉफ)*–मजाक उड़ाना At first I *scoffed* at the notion.
- **Scorn** *(स्कॉर्न)*–तिरस्कार The professor *scorns* the students who don't catch on immediately.
- **Scold** *(स्कॉल्ड)*–झिड़कना, डाँटना The mother *scolded* the child for entering a stranger's car.
- **Scratch** *(स्क्रैच)*–खरोंचना *Scratch* the card to win a prize.
- **Scream** *(स्क्रीम)*–चिल्लाना Don't *scream* please.
- **Scruple** *(स्क्रूपल)*–नैतिक विचार, सिद्धान्त He is a man with no moral *scruple.*
- **Scrupulous** *(स्क्रुपुलस)*–सचेत, सावधान I have been *scrupulous* about telling them the truth of dangers.
- **Secret** *(सीक्रेट)*–रहस्य Tell me *secret* of the statue.
- **Seek** *(सीक)*–खोजना She always *seeks* to do good in the world.
- **Seep** *(सीप)*–धीमा रिसाव Gas is *seeping* out of the rocks.
- **Seized** *(सीज्ड)*–जब्त करना Police *seized* drugs from a youth.
- **Selfless** *(सेल्फलेस)*–निःस्वार्थ Perhaps the only all-enduring and *selfless* love was that of a mother for her child.
- **Sensational** *(सेन्सेशनल)*–सनसनीखेज The world champions suffered a *sensational* defeat.
- **Sensitive** *(सेन्सिटिव)*–संवेदनशील, भावुक Her skin is very *sensitive.*
- **Serious** *(सीरियस)*–गम्भीर He was *serious* with his preparations for the ensuing examination.
- **Serve** *(सर्व)*–पूर्ति करना, परोसना She *served* tea with samosas.
- **Service** *(सर्विस)*–सेवा She is in bank *service.*
- **Several** *(सेवेरल)*–कई There were *several* ministers in the meeting.
- **Severe** *(सीवर)*–गम्भीर The house suffered a *severe* damage.
- **Sewage** *(सिवेज)*–गन्दा Thousands of tons of filth and *sewage* pour into the Ganges every day.
- **Sewing** *(स्वीइंग)*–सिलने का कार्य She is learning *sewing* and embroidery work now-a-days.
- **Shade** *(शेड)*–परिछाया It is much cooler in the *shade.*
- **Shake** *(शेक)*–हिलाया My hands were *shaking.*

- **Sharp** *(शार्प)*–नुकीले I need a *sharp* knife.
- **Shatter** *(शैटर)*–बिखरना The wine glass *shattered* with a bang sound.
- **Sheer** *(शीयर)*–निरा, सामान्य, शुद्ध She got the job through *sheer* persistence.
- **Shelter** *(शेल्टर)*–शरण We took *shelter* in an old house.
- **Shield** *(शील्ड)*–ढ़ाल He used his left hand as a *shield* against the reflecting sunlight.
- **Shine** *(शाइन)*–चमकना The sun is *shining* brightly.
- **Shivering** *(शिवरिंग)*–काँपते हुए The children are *shivering*, turn on the heat!
- **Shock** *(शॉक)*–सदमा He was numb with *shock*.
- **Shook** *(शूक)*–हिलाया The chemist *shook* the flask vigorously.
- **Shortcoming** *(शॉर्टकमिंग)*–कमियाँ Marriages usually break down as a result of the shortcomings of both partners.
- **Shot** *(शॉट)*–मारा He was *shot* dead by an unknown person.
- **Showered** *(शॉवर्ड)*–बरसाया गया, बौछार कर दी Her parents *showered* her with kisses.
- **Shrugging** *(श्रगिंग)*–कन्धे उचकाते हुए That man is *shrugging* his shoulders.
- **Shunned** *(शन्ड)*–त्याग दिया, किसी चीज़ से दूर रहना He has always *shunned* publicity.
- **Shut** *(शट्)*–बन्द करना *Shut* the window please.
- **Shyness** *(शाइनेस)*–शर्म Eventually he overcame his *shyness*.
- **Sick** *(सिक्)*–बीमार They devote their lives to caring for the *sick*.
- **Sigh** *(साई)*–आँह भरना She sighed sadly.
- **Sight** *(साइट)*–दृष्टि He caught *sight* of the king's men coming over the ridge.
- **Significant** *(सिग्निफिकैन्ट)*–महत्त्वपूर्ण The Finance Minister Pranab Mukherjee is trying to make a *significant* change in tax structure.
- **Silence** *(साइलेन्स)*–चुप्पी Keep *silence* please.
- **Simple** *(सिम्पल)*–साधारण Live *simple* and think high.
- **Sin** *(सिन)*–पाप Theft is a *sin*.
- **Sincerity** *(सिनसियरिटी)*–ईमानदारी, निष्ठा She got the promotion because of her *sincerity* and honesty.
- **Situated** *(सिचुएटेड)*–स्थित His house is *situated* near the Vishnu temple.
- **Situation** *(सिचुएशन)*–परिस्थिति The *situation* in the city is under control now.
- **Skilful** *(स्किलफुल)*–कुशल Proper effects were achieved by *skilful* retouching.
- **Slack** *(स्लैक)*–धीमा, मन्द As he *slacked* his attention, he lost a point.
- **Slay** *(स्ले)*–मारना This is the hill where St George *slew* the dragon.
- **Sleep** *(स्लीप)*–सोना He is *sleeping*.
- **Slid** *(स्लिड)*–खिसकाना, फिसलना They *slid* through the wicket in the big gate.

- **Slip** *(स्लिप)*–फिसलना The ship *slipped* away in the darkness.
- **Slippery** *(स्लिपरी)*–फिसलन भरा The road was very *slippery*.
- **Slope** *(स्लोप)*–ढ़लान We climbed the steep *slope*.
- **Slums** *(स्लम्ज)*–झुग्गी-झोंपड़ी वाला क्षेत्र Dharavi in Mumbai is the area notorious for *slums* and crimes in Mumbai.
- **Smothered** *(स्मूदर्ड)*–घुटा हुआ, दबा हुआ The butter cream *smothered* the cake.
- **Sneered** *(स्नीयर्ड)*–उपहास किया She *sneered* at her little sister's efforts to play (operate) the piano.
- **Sneezing** *(स्नीजिंग)*–छींकना Pepper makes me *sneeze*.
- **Sob** *(सोब)*–सिसकी He was *sobbing* inconsolably.
- **Softly** *(सॉफ्टली)*–मधुरता से She speaks *softly*.
- **Soil** *(सॉयल)*–मिट्टी American troops were stationed on Japanese *soil*.
- **Solitary** *(सॉलिटरी)*–अकेला He was held in a *solitary* cell.
- **Solve** *(सॉल्व)*–हल करना You can *solve* this sum.
- **Soothe** *(सूथ)*–पीड़ा को कम करना The medicine *soothes* the pain of the inflammation.
- **Span** *(स्पैन)*–फैलाव, अव The job was finished in the *span* of an hour.
- **Speak** *(स्पीक)*–बोलना *Speak* the truth, don't hesitate.
- **Spell bound** *(स्पैल बाउन्ड)*–मन्त्र-मुग्ध Her beauty and looks made me *spell bound*.
- **Spend** *(स्पेन्ड)*–बिताना I *spend* two hours with my friend.
- **Spot** *(स्पॉट)*–चिह्नित जगह या स्थान There was a bright *spot* on the planet.
- **Sprawl** *(स्प्रॉल)*–पसरना, धराशायी होना They both *sprawled* on the bed tired and exhausted.
- **Spread** *(स्प्रेड)*–फैला A big oil spot *spread* across the water.
- **Squeamishness** *(स्क्वीमिशनेस)*–नकचढ़ापन, तुनक मिजाजी The programme was withdrawn because of the *squeamishness* of some viewers.
- **Stack** *(स्टैक)*–ढ़ेर *Stack* your books up on the shelves.
- **Starve** *(स्टार्व)*–भूखों मरना The political prisoners *starved* to death.
- **Stature** *(स्टेचर)*–कद He is a man of great *stature*.
- **Steadily** *(स्टीडिली)*–लगातार रूप से He could not walk *steadily*.
- **Steady** *(स्टीडि)*–दृढ़, लगातार Slow and *steady* wins the race.
- **Steal** *(स्टील)*–चुराना He was caught *stealing* a bread.
- **Storey** *(स्टोरी)*–मंजिल, तल He is living at third *storey*.
- **Strange** *(स्ट्रेन्ज)*–अजीब I heard some *strange* sounds last night.
- **Stranger** *(स्ट्रेन्जर)*–अजनबी Don't trust the *strangers*.
- **Strategy** *(स्ट्रेटेजी)*–विधा, रणनीति Chalk out your *strategy* before taking any action.

- **Stress** *(स्ट्रेस)*–दबाव He was under mental *stress.*
- **Strength** *(स्ट्रेन्थ)*–शक्ति We faced an army of great *strength.*
- **Strict** *(स्ट्रिक्ट)*–कठोर, सख्त Rules must be followed *strictly.*
- **Strike** *(स्ट्राइक)*–टकराना, ठोंकना *Strike* the iron when it is hot.
- **Strive** *(स्ट्राइव)*–संघर्ष She *strived* hard to achieve success.
- **Strut** *(स्ट्रट)*–इठलाना He *struts* around like a rooster in a hen house.
- **Stumbled** *(स्ट्म्बल्ड)*–गिर पड़ना The drunk man *stumbled* about.
- **Submit** *(सबमिट्)*–जमा करना *Submit* your forms at counter number three.
- **Substance** *(सबस्टांस)*–तत्त्व DNA is the *substance* of our genes.
- **Sudden** *(सडन)*–अचानक He stood up *suddenly* and started shouting.
- **Sufficient** *(सफीसियेन्ट)*–पर्याप्त I don't have *sufficient* money to buy a car.
- **Suitable** *(सूटेबल)*–उपयुक्त, लायक The cloth is not *suitable* for the groom.
- **Summon** *(सम्मन)*–बुलावा He was *summoned* through a Court notice.
- **Superb** *(सुपर्ब)*–उत्कृष्ट This is a *superb* book.
- **Superficial** *(सुपरफीशियल)*–ऊपरी, सतही The *superficial* report didn't give the true picture.
- **Superstition** *(सुपरस्टीशन)*–अन्धविश्वास Fortune-telling is a very much debased art surrounded by *superstition.*
- **Supply** *(सप्लाई)*–आपूर्ति, संभरण He is *supplying* goods from door-to-door.
- **Support** *(सपोर्ट)*–सहारा, सहयोग He *supported* the genuine cause.
- **Suppose** *(सपोज)*–मानना, कल्पना करना *Suppose* a tiger comes to your room, what would you do?
- **Supreme being** *(सुप्रीम बीइंग)*–भगवान, परमात्मा God is a *supreme being.*
- **Surplus** *(सरप्लस)*–अतिरिक्त, अधिशेष I have no *surplus* money to invest in shares.
- **Surprise** *(सरप्राइज)*–आश्चर्य I was *surprised* to see her here.
- **Surrounded** *(सराउन्डेड)*–चारों ओर से घिरी The castle was *surrounded* by a ditch.
- **Survival** *(सर्वाइवल)*–उत्तरजीविता, जीवित बने रहना An animal's sense of smell is still crucial to its *survival.*
- **Suspected** *(ससपेक्टेड)*–सन्देह किया Telagi is a *suspected* criminal.
- **Sustaining** *(ससटेनिंग)*–सम्भालना We *sustained* ourselves on bread and water.
- **Swaggering** *(स्वैगरिंग)*–इठलाकर चलना Ajay Jadeja was an arrogant, *swaggering* young man.
- **Swear** *(स्वीयर)*–कसम खाना Before God I *swear* I am innocent.
- **Sweep** *(स्वीप)*–सफाई Sweep your house and kitchen daily.
- **Swelled** *(स्वेल्ड)*–फूल गया *Swelling* in body is a harmful disease which must be cured immediately.
- **Swelling** *(स्वैलिंग)*–सूजना, फूलना The bellies of the starving children are *swelling.*

- **Swiftly** *(स्विफ्टली)*–तीव्रता से He picked the coin *swiftly*.
- **Sworn** *(स्वोर्न)*–कसम लेना He was *sworn* in as cabinet minister.
- **Symbol** *(सिम्बल)*–प्रतीक 1. Lotus is our national *symbol*.
  2. The election *symbol* of BSP is elephant.
- **Symptom** *(सिम्पटम)*–लक्षण She is having flu *symptoms*.

T

- **Tackle** *(टैकल)*–समाधान करना, सम्भालना Try to *tackle* the staff yourself.
- **Take up** *(टेकअप)*–हाथ में लेना Can you *take up* this task individually.
- **Taken aback** *(टेकन एबैक)*–चकित हो गई I was *taken aback* to see my husband in the New Year party.
- **Tale** *(टेल)*–कहानी My grandmother told me many *tales* about the freedom struggle of India.
- **Tame** *(टेम)*–पालना He has *tamed* a cat to work for him.
- **Tangible** *(टैन्जिबल)*–वास्तविक, ठोस What is his *tangible* networth, is important to know.
- **Tan** *(टैन)*–धूप से चमड़ी का ताँबे जैसा रंग हो जाना She is lying in sunlight to *tan* her skin.
- **Task** *(टास्क)*–कार्य You can surely complete this *task* within a week.
- **Tear** *(टीयर)*–आँसू She was in *tears*.
- **Tease** *(टीज)*–छेड़ना, सताना Don't try to *tease* her.
- **Technique** *(टेक्निक)*–प्रणाली, क्रियाविधि This is a new *technique* to draw water from the earth.
- **Temper** *(टेम्पर)*–सन्तुलन Keep your *temper* cool and calm.
- **Temperature** *(टेम्परेचर)*–तापमान Today the *temperature* is very high.
- **Temple** *(टेम्पल)*–मन्दिर I am going to *temple*.
- **Tempted** *(टेम्पटेड)*–लालच दिया We were *tempted* by the delicious looking food.
- **Tend** *(टेंड)*–किसी दिशा में चलना, झुकना She *tends* to be nervous before her lectures.
- **Terms** *(टर्म्स)*–शर्तें, हिदायतें I agree to your *terms* and conditions.
- **Terrible** *(टेरिबिल)*–भयानक There happened a *terrible* accident between a truck and a car yesterday.
- **Therefore** *(देयरफोर)*–इसलिए I love her *therefore* I can do anything for her.
- **Thoroughly** *(थोरोली)*–भली प्रकार से Check everything *thoroughly* before you buy that house.
- **Threatened** *(थ्रेटेन्ड)*–धमकी दी He *threatened* me with dire consequences.
- **Thrift** *(थ्रिफ्ट)*–किफायत They were rightly praised for their *thrift* and enterprise.

- **Throne** *(थ्रोन)*–सिंहासन, गद्दी The king sat on his *throne.*
- **Thunder** *(थण्डर)*–गरजना Clouds were *thundering* and it was raining heavily last night.
- **Thus** *(दस)*–इस प्रकार *Thus* you can solve this question.
- **Tight** *(टाइट)*–सख्त The nut was very *tight.*
- **Time** *(टाइम)*–समय The present *time* is favourable to you.
- **Tiny** *(टाइनी)*–छोटा Though he is *tiny* he has a fertile mind.
- **Tired** *(टायर्ड)*–थका हुआ You look very much *tired.*
- **Tiring** *(टायरिंग)*–थकाने वाला The Amarnath journey was *tiring.*
- **Toil** *(टॉयल)*–मेहनत करना *Toil* hard to get success.
- **Tomorrow** *(टुमॉरो)*–कल I shall meet you *tomorrow* in the morning.
- **Tonight** *(टुनाइट)*–आज रात We shall enjoy a beer party *tonight.*
- **Tools** *(टूल्स)*–उपकरण, औजार Science has given us new *tools* to fight disease.
- **Tormented** *(टॉरमेन्टेड)*–तड़पाना/प्रताड़ित करना The children *tormented* the stuttering teacher.
- **Tortured** *(टॉर्चर्ड)*–पीड़ित किया The police was convinced that she was *tortured* and killed.
- **Traced** *(ट्रेस्ड)*–पीछा किया, खोजा She *traced* the circumstances of her birth.
- **Tradition** *(ट्रैडिशन)*–परम्परा We should respect our *traditions.*
- **Traffic** *(ट्रैफिक)*–यातायात *Traffic* has increased tremendously within a few years.
- **Trained** *(ट्रेन्ड)*–प्रशिक्षित She is a *trained* teacher.
- **Tramp** *(ट्रैम्प)*–कदमों की आवाज We heard the slow and heavy *tramp* of feet on the stairs.
- **Trample** *(ट्रैम्पल)*–कुचलना The passerby was *trampled* by an elephant.
- **Transfer** *(ट्रान्सफर)*–स्थानांतरित करना He was *transfered* to Jodhpur.
- **Translate** *(ट्रान्सलेट)*–अनुवादित *Translate* this paragraph in English.
- **Transparent** *(ट्रान्सपेरेन्ट)*–पारदर्शक The transfer policy must be *transparent* and justified.
- **Travel** *(ट्रैवल)*–यात्रा He *travelled* by bus.
- **Treacherous** *(ट्रेचरस)*–धोखेबाज One should be careful of the *treacherous* friends.
- **Tread** *(ट्रीड)*–चलना, पैर रखना Fools rush in where angels fear to *tread.*
- **Treasure** *(ट्रैजर)*–खजाना It was here, the buried *treasure,* she knew it was.
- **Treat** *(ट्रीट)*–व्यवहार करना She *treated* us very nicely.
- **Treatise** *(ट्रीटीस)*–शोध प्रबन्ध A *treatise* on adulterations of food, exposed the widespread use of potentially lethal additives in edibles.

- **Treaty** *(ट्रीटि)*–सन्धि A peace *treaty* was signed between the two countries.
- **Tremble** *(ट्रेम्बिल)*–काँपना She was *trembling* with fear.
- **Tremendous** *(ट्रिमेन्डस)*–विशाल, जबर्दस्त There was a *tremendous* demand of sugar and wheat.
- **Trial** *(ट्रायल)*–जाँच *Trials* for the semifinals began yesterday.
- **Tribal** *(ट्राइबल)*–जनजाति He is from a *tribal* family.
- **Tribulation** *(ट्रिब्यूलेशन)*–दु:ख Our life is full of *tribulations.*
- **Trick** *(ट्रिक)*–चालाकी She warned me not to play *tricks.*
- **Trifle** *(ट्राइफल)*–मामूली बात One should avoid conflict on *trifles.*
- **Trip** *(ट्रिप)*–यात्रा He took a *trip* to the shopping centre.
- **Triumph** *(ट्रांयम्फ)*–विजेता Her sense of *triumph* was short lived.
- **Trivial** *(ट्रीवियल)*–तुच्छ One should not fight on *trivial* matters.
- **Trouble** *(ट्रबल)*–परेशानी He is *troubling* me.
- **Trousers** *(ट्राउजर्स)*–पायजामा I want to purchase a pair of *trousers.*
- **Trumpet** *(ट्रमपेट)*–चिंघाड़ Elephants are *trumpeting.*
- **Trusted** *(ट्रस्टेड)*–विश्वासपात्र He is my *trusted* employee.
- **Tumble** *(टम्बल)*–लड़खड़ा कर गिरना The tower of the World Trade Centre *tumbled* after the plane hit it.
- **Turban** *(टरबन)*–साफा, पगड़ी He was wearing a red *turban.*
- **Turbulent** *(टर्बुलेंट)*–आन्दोलित, उग्र, अशान्त The sea looks *turbulent.*
- **Twice** *(ट्वाइस)*–दुगुना/दो बार I warned her *twice.*
- **Twinkle** *(ट्विंकल)*–पलक झपकाना There was a perpetual *twinkle* in his eyes.
- **Tying** *(टाइंग)*–बाँधना She was *tying* a rope in the hall.

U

- **Ugly** *(अगली)*–भद्दा, कुरूप She makes me feel rowdy and *ugly.*
- **Unashamed** *(अनअशेम्ड)*–बेशर्मी She grinned at him in an *unashamed* delight.
- **Uncanny** *(अनकैनी)*–अद्भुत, विलक्षण For this *uncanny* ability, she won four gold medals.
- **Unconsciously** *(अनकॉन्शयसली)*–अचेतनता She jumped up *unconsciously* when he entered the room.
- **Under-rate** *(अण्डर-रेट)*–कम आँकना Don't under-rate him , he is a great scholar.
- **Undergone** *(अण्डरगोन)*–सामना किया He has *undergone* a serious heart operation.
- **Understand** *(अण्डरस्टैण्ड)*–समझना Try to *understand* what I mean to say.
- **Undivided** *(अनडिवाइडेड)*–अविभाजित The cabinet was *undivided* on the issue.

- **Undoubtedly** *(अनडाउटेडली)*–निःसन्देह *Undoubtedly* we shall support the bill.
- **Uneducated** *(अनएजूकेटेड)*–निरक्षर, अनपढ़ He is an *uneducated* fellow.
- **Unfortunate** *(अनफॉरच्यूनेट)*–दुर्भाग्यशाली He was *unfortunate* otherwise he could win the game.
- **Uniform** *(यूनिफॉर्म)*–वर्दी, वेशभूषा Wear your *uniform* daily.
- **Union** *(यूनियन)*–संघ *Union* is strength.
- **Universe** *(यूनिवर्स)*–विश्व, सृष्टि In the *universe* there are several astrological events.
- **Unusual** *(अनयूज्वल)*–असामान्य He is a man of *unusual* abilities.
- **Upstairs** *(अपस्टेयर्स)*–सीढ़ियों से ऊपर जाना There is a restaurant *upstairs.*
- **Urge** *(अर्ज)*–विनती I *urged* him to finish his project at the earliest.
- **Used to** *(यूज्ड टू)*–अभ्यस्त होना I *used to* smoke ten cigarettes daily.
- **Usually** *(यूजुअली)*–सामान्यतः साधारणतया *Usually* he comes in the evening after seven.

V

- **Vacancy** *(वेकेन्सी)*–रिक्त पद Fifty *vacancies* of software engineers are to be filled up soon.
- **Vacation** *(वेकेशन)*–छुट्टी We shall go to Agra in summer *vacation.*
- **Vain** *(वेन)*–व्यर्थ He tried his best to win the game but all in *vain.*
- **Vain** *(वेन)*–दम्भी, गर्वीला I think he is shallow, *vain* and untrustworthy.
- **Valuable** *(वेल्यूबल)*–कीमती Gold is a *valuable* metal.
- **Vanish** *(वेनिश)*–खत्म हो गई, लुप्त होना The gas effect *vanished* as the sun rose.
- **Vapour** *(वेपर)*–भाप Water *vapour* condenses to form clouds.
- **Variety** *(वैरायटी)*–किस्म The range and *variety* of his work is amazing.
- **Various** *(वेरियस)*–विभिन्न He cited *various* reasons for his behaviour.
- **Vase** *(वास)*–फूलदान She has a beautiful brass *vase* full of roses.
- **Vexed** *(वैक्स्ड)*–हैरान हुआ We are living in a *vexed* and troubled time.
- **Veil** *(वेल)*–पर्दा, बुर्का Women in Afghanistan are forced to *veil* their faces.
- **Velvet** *(वेल्वेट)*–मखमल This is a *velvet* dress for kids.
- **Venture** *(वेन्चर)*–साहस We *ventured* into the world of high-tech and bought a super computer.
- **Vermin** *(वरमिन)*–फसलों को नष्ट करने वाला प्राणी Cereals must be protected from mice and other *vermin.*
- **Vice** *(वाइस)*–व्यसन, अवगुण, दोष Gambling is a *vice.*
- **Victim** *(विक्टिम)*–शिकार She is a *victim* of domestic violence.

- **Vigour** *(विगर)*–जोश He had a rugged appearance and a raw *vigour* that made him seem indestructible.
- **Virtue** *(वरच्यू)*–सद्गुण Honesty is a *virtue*.
- **Visitor** *(विजिटर)*–आगन्तुक The other day we had many foreign *visitors*.
- **Visualize** *(विजुअलाइज)*–कल्पना करना The radiologist can *visualize* the affected part of cancerous liver.
- **Voice** *(वॉयस)*–आवाज A shrill *voice* sounded behind us.
- **Volume** *(वॉल्यूम)*–आकार या मात्रा Mix one *volume* of the solution with ten volumes of water.
- **Voluntarily** *(वोलन्टेरिली)*–स्वेच्छापूर्वक He retired *voluntarily*.
- **Vouch** *(वाउच)*–प्रमाणित करना I *vouch* for the quality of my products.
- **Voyage** *(वॉयेज)*–यात्रा (*समुद्री यात्रा*) Good Bye, Bon *voyage*!

W

- **Wages** *(वेजेज)*–मजदूरी 1. The workers are offered very low *wages*.
  2. He earns a *wage* of ₹ 100 per day.
- **Wailed** *(वेल्ड)*–विलाप करना The wind *wailed* through the trees.
- **Wailing** *(वेलिंग)*–विलाप करते हुए 1. *Wailing* mourners gathered around the gate.
  2. Stop *wailing* at the spilt milk.
- **Wait** *(वेट)*–इन्तजार (*प्रतीक्षा*) करना 1. Please *wait* for just ten minutes.
  2. We will *wait* for you in the car.
- **Waiting on table** *(वेटिंग ऑन टेबल)*–बैरे का कार्य करना He was *waiting on the table* while the rich guests lavished him a large tip.
- **Waiting room** *(वेटिंग रूम)*–प्रतीक्षालय The guests were asked to wait in the *waiting room*.
- **Wake** *(वेक)*–जगाना I *wake* up at 5 o'clock in the morning.
- **Wallet** *(वैलेट)*–थैली He doesn't carry a *wallet*.
- **Wall** *(वाल)*–दीवार The *walls* of the house are very high.
- **Wander** *(वाण्डर)*–भटकना, घूमना The river *wanders* among the rocks.
- **Warmly** *(वार्मली)*–गर्मजोशी से We greeted them *warmly* on their marriage anniversary.
- **Warned** *(वार्न्ड)*–चेताया I *warned* him about the bad weather.
- **Warning** *(वार्निंग)*–चेतावनी We fired a *warning* at the intruders.
- **Warrior** *(वारियर)*–योद्धा Rana Pratap was a great Rajput *warrior*.
- **Wastage** *(वेस्टेज)*–क्षय, छीजन, क्षति, अपव्यय Annual *wastage* of time due to illness is appalling.
- **Waste** *(वेस्ट)*–कूड़ा-करकट, अपशिष्ट, बर्बाद करना We shouldn't *waste* water.

- **Watch** *(वाच)*–निगरानी Keep a *watch* on him.
- **Waving** *(वेविंग)*–हिलाते हुए I was *waving* hand to him while his train was leaving.
- **Way** *(वे)*–रास्ता Find out some *way* to tackle this problem.
- **Wealth** *(वैल्थ)*–सम्पत्ति, दौलत She has a *wealth* of talent.
- **Weapon** *(वेपन)*–हथियार Gandhiji used the *weapon* of non-violence to free India.
- **Wear** *(वियर)*–पहनना Jitendra always prefers to *wear* white clothes.
- **Weary** *(वियरी)*–थका हुआ He was feeling *weary* after the whole day's work.
- **Weaver** *(वीवर)*–बुनकर He is an excellent *weaver*.
- **Wedding** *(वेडिंग)*–शादी
  1. They invited guests to their silver *wedding*.
  2. It was a perfect *wedding* of conservatism and liberalism.
- **Wee** *(वी)*–छोटा I go to gym in the *wee* hours of the morning.
- **Weeding** *(वीडिंग)*–घास-पात हटाना, निराई करना The gardener is *weeding* the garden.
- **Weeds** *(वीड्स)*–खरपतवार, घास-फूस The vacant lot was covered with *weeds*.
- **Weekend** *(वीकेण्ड)*–सप्ताहान्त What are you doing this *weekend* ?
- **Weird** *(वियर्ड)*–अलौकिक, भयानक Drugs can make you do all kinds of *weird* things and they all said it was a good proposal.
- **Weight** *(वेट)*–भार, वजन His *weight* is 60 kg.
- **Welcome** *(वेलकम)*–स्वागत The whole board *welcomed* his suggestion of flexible timings.
- **Welfare** *(वेलफेयर)*–भलाई We should always keep in mind the *welfare* of the society.
- **Went** *(वेन्ट)*–गया We *went* to Puri on the weekend.
- **Whenever** *(व्हेनएवर)*–जब कभी We can leave *whenever* you're ready.
- **Wherever** *(व्हेयरएवर)*–जहाँ कहीं *Wherever* you go, you'll find Indians.
- **While** *(व्हाइल)*–जबकि Just a *while* ago, I met her.
- **Whimsical** *(व्हिम्सिकल)*–सनकी Everybody knows Sunil because of his *whimsical* behaviour.
- **Whip** *(व्हिप)*–चाबुक Criminals used to be *whipped* for minor offenses.
- **Whirlpool** *(व्हर्लपूल)*–भंवर, जलावर्त The ship enterd a *whirlpool* of water.
- **Whirling** *(व्हर्लिंग)*–गोल-गोल घूमते हुए My head is *whirling* with data.
- **Whiskers** *(व्हिस्कर्स)*–मूँछ के बाल The *whiskers* on his face don't suit his personality.
- **Whispering** *(व्हिस्परिंग)*–कानाफूसी करना I found her *whispering* in his ears in the meeting.

- **White elephant** *(व्हाइट ऐलीफेन्ट)*–सफेद हाथी, खर्चीले साधन Our Victorian bric-a-brac and furniture were *white elephants*.
- **White** *(व्हाइट)*–सफेद *White* is my favourite colour.
- **Whole** *(होल)*–पूरा-का-पूरा His *whole* family had come to attend the marriage.
- **Wholesome** *(होलसम)*–पुष्टिकर Fresh air is *wholesome* for lungs.
- **Whooping** *(हूपिंग)*–हाँकना, भगा देना He was *whooping* the cattle down the road.
- **Wicked** *(विकेड)*–शैतान, दुष्ट These *wicked* kittens upset everything.
- **Wide** *(वाइड)*–चौड़ा Her eyes were *wide* with surprise.
- **Widely** *(वाइडली)*–व्यापक रूप से M F Hussain is a *widely* known artist.
- **Widow** *(विडो)*–विधवा A young *widow* has to face several challenges in the society.
- **Wife** *(वाइफ)*–पत्नी His *wife* is a lawyer.
- **Wild** *(वाइल्ड)*–जंगली He was driving his bike in a *wild* manner.
- **Will** *(विल)*–इच्छा Where there is a *will* there is a way.
- **Willing** *(विलिंग)*–इच्छुक He is *willing* to go to US.
- **Windfall** *(विन्डफाल)*–हवा में उड़कर आने वाला फल, अचानक लाभ होना The winning of the lottery was like a *windfall* for him.
- **Window** *(विन्डो)*–खिड़की Could you please close the *window*?
- **Wine** *(वाइन)*–शराब *Wine* is prepared from grapes.
- **Wired** *(वायर्ड)*–तार द्वारा सूचित किया He *wired* the halves together.
- **Wisdom** *(विज्डम)*–बुद्धि, विवेक It is a characteristic of *wisdom* not to do desperate things.
- **Wise** *(वाइज)*–बुद्धिमान It was a *wise* decision of him to stay silent in the quarrel.
- **Wish** *(विश)*–कामना We *wish* Subhash Chandra Bose alive today.
- **Withdrew** *(विदड्रू)*–वापस ले लेना He *withdrew* his leave request.
- **Without** *(विदाउट)*–बिना We can't imagine life *without* electricity.
- **Witness** *(विटनेस)*–गवाह There was no *witness* to support his claim.
- **Wonder** *(वन्डर)*–आश्चर्य It's no *wonder* travelling to moon today.
- **Wondered** *(वन्डर्ड)*–आश्चर्य किया The health officer *wondered* that most of the eatables are adulterated.
- **Wonderful** *(वन्डरफुल)*–आश्चर्यजनक Taj Mahal is a *wonderful* piece of architecture.
- **Wool** *(वूल)*–ऊन *Wool* is used to make winter wears.
- **Wore** *(वोर)*–पहने हुए He *wore* a pink shawl for the party.
- **Work** *(वर्क)*–कार्य I don't have much *work* to do today.
- **Worker** *(वर्कर)*–श्रमिक He is a hard *worker*.
- **Worm** *(वॅर्म)*–कीड़ा I felt the black *worm* of treachery growing in his heart.

- **Worn out** *(वॉर्न आउट)*–फटना/थक जाना His wife is *worn out* looking after the children.
- **Worried** *(वरीड)*–चिन्तित The mother *worried* about her son.
- **Worry** *(वरी)*–चिन्ता I have no *worries* about the result.
- **Worst** *(वर्स्ट)*–सबसे खराब Your best friend can turn out to be your *worst* enemy.
- **Worth** *(वर्थ)*–योग्यता, अच्छाई He owns stocks having a *worth* of ten million dollars.
- **Worthiness** *(वर्दिनेस)*–योग्यता He was able to keep the *worthiness* of his post.
- **Worthless** *(वर्थलेस)*–निकम्मा Conviction is *worthless* unless it is converted into conduct.
- **Worthwhile** *(वर्थह्वाइल)*–मूल्यवान 'Jodha Akbar' is a *worthwhile* movie to watch.
- **Worthy** *(वर्दी)*–योग्यता The parents found the girl *worthy* for their son.
- **Wrap** *(रैप)*–लपेटना *Wrap* up your work and come.
- **Wrathfully** *(रैथफुली)*–घृणा से He looked at her *wrathfully*.
- **Wrestler** *(रेसलर)*–पहलवान Dara Singh is a well-known *wrestler* of India.
- **Wrinkled** *(रिंकल्ड)*–सिकुड़ा हुआ The skin gets *wrinkled* with age.
- **Wrong** *(रॉंग)*–गलत What's *wrong* with you?

Y

- **Yankee** *(यांकी)*–अमेरिकी Infosys has recruited foreigners; some of them are *yankees* too.
- **Yard** *(यार्ड)*–गज The cricket pitch is 22 *yards* long.
- **Yawning** *(यानिंग)*–उबासी लेते हुए Audience was found *yawning* during the concert.
- **Yell** *(येल)*–चिल्लाना The landlord *yelled* at the children.
- **Yield** *(यील्ड)*–उत्पन्न करना The atomic bomb dropped on Hiroshima had a *yield* of 20 kilotons.
- **Yield** *(यील्ड)*–उत्पन्न होना Look for an investment that *yields* high percentages.
- **Yoke** *(योक)*–जूड़ा (*लकड़ी का*) The pioneers knew there was trouble when the oxen's *yoke* broke and they were no longer able to pull the wagon.

Z

- **Zest** *(जैस्ट)*–उमंग There is no *zest* left in his life.
- **Zeal** *(जील)*–उत्साह She felt a kind of religious *zeal*.

UNIT 2

Synonyms

किसी शब्द-विशेष का समान अर्थ देने वाला शब्द Synonym कहलाता है। Synonym is a word same in meaning to another.

Word	Meaning	Synonyms
Abandon	छोड़ना	Leave, forsake, desert.
Abduct	अपहृत करना	Kidnap, seize.
Abhor	घृणा	Hate, detest, despise,loathe.
Abnormal	असामान्य	Irregular, unusual, uneven.
Abode	रहने का स्थान	Dwelling, home, house.
Abolish	समाप्त करना	Eradicate, remove, destroy.
Abound	भरा होना	Flourish, overflow, teem, luxuriate.
Abortive	व्यर्थ	Fruitless, futile.
Abridge	संक्षिप्त करना	Curtail, shorten.
Absolute	स्वत: पूर्ण	Autocratic, dictatorial, lordly, dogmatic.
Absorb	आत्मसात करना	Consume, exhaust, swallow.
Abundant	प्रचुर	Copious, plentiful, ample.
Academician	पुस्तकीय ज्ञाता	Bookish, learned, lettered, scholarly.
Accede	मान लेना	Consent, agree, acquiesce.
Accept	स्वीकार करना	Agree, concur.
Accident	दुर्घटना	Mishap, calamity, misadventure, disaster.
Accord	सहमति	Agreement, harmony, conformity.
Acquaintance	परिचित	Companionship, familiarity, intimacy.
Accumulate	संचित करना	Collect, amass, gather, store.
Accurate	ठीक, शुद्ध	Correct, exact, precise.
Accuse	दोष लगाना	Blame, fault, charge.
Act	कार्य	Deed, achievement, execution.
Acquire	प्राप्त करना	Obtain, procure, gain.
Actual	वास्तविक	Real, genuine, true.
Active	सक्रिय	Agile, alert, energetic, lively.
Admire	सराहना करना	Appreciate, esteem, praise, reverence.
Addicted	अभ्यस्त हुआ	Habituated, prone, accustomed.

Word	Meaning	Synonyms
Address	सम्बोधित करना	Accost, greet, appeal to, speak to.
Adequate	पर्याप्त	Sufficient, suitable, fit, fitting.
Adore	पूजा करना	Worship, revere, venerate.
Adversity	विपदा	Calamity, distress, anguish.
Adept	कुशल	Expert, apt, skilful, dextrous.
Affable	मिलनसार	Sociable, amiable, genial.
Affliction	दुःख	Distress, grief, misery, agony.
Affront	तिरस्कार	Insult, indignity.
Aggravate	उकसाना	Intensify, heighten, provoke.
Aid	सहायता	Help, assistance.
Aim	उद्देश्य	Goal, purpose, objective, intent.
Allay	शान्त करना	Assuage, calm, soothe, pacify.
Allow	आज्ञा देना	Permit, authorize, consent.
Alien	विदेशी	Foreigner, stranger.
Alliance	मित्रता, समझौता	Coalition, confederation, league, union.
Amass	एकत्र करना	Accumulate, gather, hoard, store, heap up.
Amazement	आश्चर्य	Astonishment, confusion, surprise.
Ameliorate	सुधारना	Improve, better, reform.
Amiable	रमणीक	Lovable, agreeable, pleasing, attractive.
Ample	पर्याप्त	Enough, considerable.
Anger	क्रोध	Rage, resentment, wrath.
Anguish	पीड़ा	Agony, pain, suffering.
Ancient	प्राचीन	Old, primitive, pre-historic.
Annihilate	मिटाना	Destroy, finish.
Announce	घोषणा करना	Proclaim, declare, reveal, notify, advertise.
Annual	वार्षिक	Yearly, regular.
Answer	उत्तर	Reply, rojoinder, riposte.
Antagonist	शत्रुतापूर्ण	Adversary, hostile, unfriendly.
Anxiety	चिन्ता	Anguish, disquiet, worry, care.
Anticipate	पूर्वानुमान लगाना	Forestall, apprehend, expect.
Appeal	अपील करना	Entreat, request, invoke.
Apology	क्षमा माँगना	Excuse, pardon, regret.
Attack	आक्रमण	Aggression, invasion, onslaught, assault.
Attain	प्राप्त करना	Win, gain, achieve, succeed.
Arrogant	घमण्डी	Haughty, insolent, proud.
Assent	सहमति	Consent, agreement.
Ascent	चढ़ाई	Rise, lift, elevation, upswing.
Audacious	साहसी	Bold, daring, adamant.

Word	Meaning	Synonyms
Augment	बढ़ाना	Enlarge, extend, increase.
Austere	उग्र, रूक्ष	Rigorous, severe.
Authentic	प्रामाणिक	Genuine, reliable, accredited, accepted.
Avenge	बदला लेना	Take revenge, vindicate, retaliate.
Averse	परान्मुख	Loth, disinclined.
Awkward	भद्दा	Blundering, clumsy, gauche.
Banish	देश निकाला देना	Exile, evict, oust, expatriate.
Bane	अभिशाप	Curse, mischief, harm, scourge.
Barbarous	जंगली, असभ्य	Animal, brute, creature.
Bard	चारण	Singer, minstrel.
Base	तुच्छ	Mean, low.
Battle	युद्ध	Fight, encounter, conflict.
Beautiful	सुन्दर	Lovely, attractive, charming, pretty.
Beast	पशु	Animal, brute, creature.
Beg	भीख माँगना	Beseech, entreat, start.
Bear	सहन करना	Endure, suffer, tolerate, sustain.
Belief	विश्वास	Faith, trust, confidence, credence.
Benefit	लाभ	Profit, advantage, gain, good.
Beneficent	दानशील	Generous, liberal, bounteous.
Blame	दोष देना	Accuse, censure.
Bleak	धुँधला, कमजोर	Dismal, desolate, blank, exposed.
Bliss	आनन्द	Felicity, joy, pleasure.
Blunder	भारी गलती	Big mistake, error.
Boisterous	ऊधमी	Clamorous, noisy, hilarious.
Bold	साहसी	Fearless, dauntless, courageous.
Boon	वरदान	Benediction, favour, blessing.
Brawl	झगड़ा	Squabble, noisy, quarrel.
Brave	वीर	Courageous, fearless, valiant, bold.
Brevity	सूक्ष्मता	Conciseness, curtness, economy.
Brutal	बर्बर	Savage, cruel, callous.
Build	बनाना	Construct, develop, make.
Busy	व्यस्त	Engaged, occupied, engrossed.
Breach	दरार	Violence, rift.
Boundary	चहारदीवारी, सीमा	Confines, barrier, limit, border, frontier.
Calculation	गणना	Compute, count, enumerate.
Calm	शान्त	Serene, pacific, quiet, placid.
Calumny	दुष्प्रचार, बदनामी	Slander, defamation.
Candid	निष्कपट	Frank, blunt, outspoken.

Word	Meaning	Synonyms
Capture	गिरफ्तार करना	Arrest, nab, apprehend.
Captive	कैदी	Prisoner, convict.
Castle	किला	Fort, citadel.
Change	बदलना	Alter, shift, convert, exchange.
Champion	विजेता	Defender, protector, victor.
Charming	आकर्षक	Attractive, bewitching, enchanting.
Chaste	पवित्र	Pure, clean, virtuous, undefiled.
Cheerful	प्रसन्नचित्त	Happy, joyful.
Chide	फटकारना	Reproach, admonish, scold, rebuke.
Clear	स्वच्छ	Lucid, plain, evident, open, obvious.
Catch	पकड़ना	Grab, grasp.
Clever	चतुर	Skilful, ingenious, dexterous, able.
Collision	टक्कर	Clash, conflict, impact, encounter.
Comfortable	आरामदेह	Agreeable, cheerful, genial.
Compel	मजबूर करना	Coerce, constrain, oblige, force.
Complain	शिकायत करना	Grumble, murmur, grunt, growl, croak.
Complete	पूर्ण	Entire, whole, one.
Compromise	समझौता करना	Conciliation, settlement, agreement.
Commend	प्रशंसा करना	Praise, applaud, approve, compliment.
Conceal	छिपाना	Hide, veil, shroud, disguise.
Concern	चिन्ता	Anxiety, worry, solicitude, import.
Condemn	दोष देना	Blame, censure, denounce, reprove.
Confess	स्वीकार करना	Accept, concede, grant, disclose, admit.
Conflict	संघर्ष	Fight, clash, strife, collision.
Congratulate	बधाई देना	Applaud, felicitate, praise.
Conquer	जीतना	Vanquish, subdue, rout, crush, beat.
Conscious	ज्ञान होना	Aware, assured, certain.
Consolation	सान्त्वना	Solace, comfort, sympathy, hopefulness.
Consider	विचार करना	Think, deem.
Contain	रखना	Receive, include, hold, comprise.
Continual	लगातार	Continuous, incessant, constant, ceaseless.
Contrast	तुलना	Compare, differentiate, oppose.
Contribute	योगदान करना	Give, help, assist, subscribe.
Convert	बदलना	Change, remove.
Convey	देना, भेजना	Transfer, shift, transport.
Convict	अपराधी	Criminal, prisoner, captive.
Copious	विपुल	Plentiful, ample, abundant, adequate.

Word	Meaning	Synonyms
Corrupt	भ्रष्ट	Dishonest, demoralized, debased, pervert.
Costly	मूल्यवान	Precious, valuable.
Couple	जोड़ा, युगल	Pair, two.
Courage	साहस	Boldness, valour, bravery, audacity.
Criminal	अपराधी	Guilty, nefarious, vile, sinful, culpable.
Cultivate	उत्पन्न करना	Grow, farm, develop, foster.
Cunning	चालाक, धूर्त	Clever, wicked.
Curtail	छोटा करना	Shorten, abate, reduce, diminish.
Dacoit	डाकू	Robber, bandit.
Damage	आहत करना	Injure, harm , hurt, wound.
Danger	खतरा	Hazard, peril, risk, insecurity
Daring	साहसी	Bold, fearless, courageous.
Decay	ह्रास	Rot, spoil, decompose.
Defend	रक्षा करना	Guard, protect, save.
Defer	टालना	Postpone, suspend, hang, dwindle.
Deference	प्रणाम	Reverence, respect.
Deficient	कमी होना	Lacking, wanting.
Defect	दोष	Fault, weakness.
Definite	निश्चित	Exact, certain.
Dejected	निराश	Sad, worried.
Deformity	विरूपता	Defect, disfigurement, malformation.
Deleterious	हानिकारक	Harmful, detrimental.
Delicious	स्वादिष्ट	Dainty, luscious, delightful, exquisite.
Demolish	गिराना, नष्ट करना	Destroy, raze, ruin, overthrow.
Delicate	नाजुक	Tender, brittle, soft.
Delight	आनन्द	Pleasure, joy, happiness.
Denounce	दोष ठहराना	Condemn, declaim.
Design	उद्‌देश्य	Aim, intent, purpose, end.
Desire	इच्छा	Wish, longing, inclination, aspiration.
Despair	निराशा	Hopelessness, dejection.
Dead	मृत	Lifeless,comatose, inert.
Deceive	धोखा देना	Cheat, mislead, hoodwink, defraud.
Decline	इनकार करना	Refuse, turndown, rebuff.
Decide	तय करना	Settle, finalize, fix, determine.
Decorate	सजाना	Adorn, embellish, beautify, garnish.
Direction	दिशा, झुकाना	Inclination, fondness, proclivity.
Dispute	झगड़ा	Quarrel, conflict, discord , tension.
Distinct	स्पष्ट	Clear, diverse.

Word	Meaning	Synonyms
Deride	उपहास करना	Mock, jeer, ridicule.
Desecrate	दूषित करना	Pollute, profane.
Desolate	वीरान, सुनसान	Deserted, lonely.
Despicable	घृणास्पद	Hateful, contemptible, detestable.
Destitute	निस्सहाय, अभावग्रस्त	Wanting, insolvent, penniless.
Devotion	श्रद्धा	Loyalty, fidelity.
Dexterity	निपुणता	Skill, adroitness.
Distress	संकट	Calamity, disaster, mishap.
Diverse	विभिन्न	Different, varied.
Dim	धुँधला	Faint, indistinct.
Diligent	परिश्रमी	Industrious, hard working, persevering.
Detain	रोकना	Stop, prevent.
Despotic	अत्याचारी	Tyrant, autocrat.
Dejected	निराश	Disappointed, frustrated, disenchanted.
Disease	रोग	Sickness, ailment.
Disclose	प्रकट करना	Divulge, reveal, uncover.
Discuss	विवाद करना	Argue, debate.
Displease	रुष्ट होना	Anger, offend.
Disseminate	फैलाना	Scatter, spread, sprinkle.
Disgrace	लज्जित करना	Discredit, dishonour.
Divine	दैवी	Godly, heavenly.
Dread	भय	Fear, fright, awe, horror.
Doctrine	सिद्धान्त	Belief, principle, dogma, teaching.
Duplicate	प्रतिकृति	Copy, counterpart, replica, imitation.
Eager	उत्सुक	Anxious, animated, earnest.
Earnest	गम्भीर	Serious, solemn, fervent, determined.
Ecstasy	परम आनन्द	Joy, bliss, rapture, enthusiasm.
Effort	प्रयास	Attempt, endeavour, trial, venture.
Elegant	शानदार	Graceful, refined.
Emancipate	मुक्त करना	Liberate, deliver.
Emerge	प्रकट होना	Issue, appear, arise, come forth.
Eligible	योग्य	Suitable, qualified.
Employ	नौकरी पर लगाना	Engage, hire, engross.
Endeavour	प्रयत्न	Attempt, essay, strive, try, undertake.
Enmity	शत्रुता	Hostility, animosity.
Enrage	क्रोधित करना	Infuriate, anger.
Entertain	मनोरंजन करना	Amuse, cheer, please, gratify, enliven.

Word	Meaning	Synonyms
Enthusiasm	उत्साह	Excitement, frenzy, fervency, fanaticism.
Encourage	प्रोत्साहन	Inspire, animate, strengthen, embolden.
Endure	सहन करना	Continue, last, abide, sustain.
Enormous	बहुत बड़ा	Huge, excessive, tremendous.
Entreat	विनती करना	Request, implore, plead, solicit.
Entrance	प्रवेश द्वार	Gate, doorway, admittance, gateway.
Envious	ईर्ष्यालु	Jealous, suspicious.
Eternal	अमर	Endless, deathless, immortal, unending.
Event	घटना	Chance, fact, outcome.
Evident	स्पष्ट	Apparent, clear, conspicuous, obvious.
Example	उदाहरण	Instance, ideal, sample, type, specimen.
Exceptional	अपवाद	Unusual, rare.
Exquisite	विशिष्ट	Marvellous, grand.
Exult	उल्लासित	Rejoice.
Extraordinary	असाधारण	Exceptional, uncommon, unusual.
Extravagant	फिजूलखर्च	Prodigal, lavish.
Fabricate	बनाना	Construct, concoct, forge, build, make-up.
Fabulous	उत्कृष्ट, उम्दा, काल्पनिक	Awesome, immense, fictitious.
Fade	फीका पड़ना	Pale, dim, vanish, languish.
Faint	मूर्छित होना	Swoon, fade, weaken, dim.
Faith	विश्वास	Belief, conviction, trust, doctrine.
Faithful	स्वामिभक्त	Devoted, loyal, trusty, trustworthy, true.
Fame	प्रसिद्धि	Distinguished, eminent, popular.
Fancy	कल्पना	Imagination, supposition, conceit, liking.
Fanciful	काल्पनिक	Imaginative, capricious, unreal.
Fastidious	दुराराध्य	Squeamish, finical.
Fatal	घातक	Deadly, lethal, mortal, fateful.
Felicity	आनन्द	Bliss, joy.
Flimsy	तथ्यहीन	Trivial, unsubstantial.
Feminine	जनाना	Womanish, womanly.
Fiction	असत्य कथा	Fabrication, myth, falsehood, invention.
Fierce	भयानक	Violent, aggressive, savage, ferocious.
Ferocious	भयंकर	Fierce, barbarous, savage.
Fictitious	नकली	Unreal, false.
Fiendish	पैशाचिक	Devilish, diabolical.
Fine	बढ़िया	Admirable, elegant, polished, excellent.

Word	Meaning	Synonyms
Fit	ठीक	Adequate, fitting, suitable, apt, decent.
Flock	झुण्ड	Drove, litter, pack, swarm.
Flaw	त्रुटि	Defect, fault, mistake, imperfection.
Follow	पीछे चलना	Imitate, pursue, chase, practice.
Forbid	मना करना	Prohibit, inhibit, ban, interdict.
Fortification	किला	Stronghold, entrenchment, fortress.
Fortitude	साहस	Courage, endurance, heroism, resolution.
Frenzy	उन्माद	Fury, rage, excitement, enthusiasm.
Fraud	धोखा-धड़ी	Deceit, treason, cheat, swindler, trickery.
Gaiety	प्रसन्नता	Jollity, hilarity.
Garrulous	बातूनी	Loquacious, talkative.
Ghastly	वीभत्स	Deathlike, pallid, spectral.
Gigantic	विशाल	Colossal, huge.
Gift	उपहार	Present, donation, bounty, contribution.
Gloom	विषाद	Dejection, shadow, obscurity, darkness.
Gorgeous	भड़कीला	Dazzling, splendid.
Grandeur	शान	Majesty, splendour, magnificence.
Graphic	सुचित्रित	Pictorial, vivid.
Gratification	सन्तुष्टि	Happiness, satisfaction.
Grief	शोक	Sorrow, sadness, regret, distress.
Grievous	दुखदायी	Painful, hurtful.
Grotesque	विरूप	Distorted, Bizarre, old.
Hamper	रोकना	Impede, retard, obstruct, hinder.
Happiness	प्रसन्नता	Delight, gladness, pleasure, bliss.
Hard	कठोर	Difficult, stern, firm, cruel.
Hardship	कठिनाई	Difficulty, adversity, calamity, affliction.
Harmony	सामंजस्य	Accord, uniformity, conformity, consent.
Haven	शरण	Refuge, shelter, protection, sanctuary.
Healthy	स्वस्थ	Hale, healthful, wholesome, hearty.
Haughty	मगरूर, घमण्डी	Arrogant, imperious, swollen, headed.
Headstrong	हठीला	Obstinate, stubborn.
High	ऊँचा	Lofty, exalted, elevated, eminent.
Holy	पवित्र	Pious, saintly, blessed, godly.
Humane	दयालु	Benevolent, kind, compassionate.
Humble	विनीत	Modest, meek, submissive, paltry.
Humility	विनम्रता	Modesty, humbleness.
Heaven	स्वर्ग	Elysium, paradise.

Word	Meaning	Synonyms
Ideal	आदर्श	Standard, model, pattern.
Idle	सुस्त	Lazy, inert, inactive, sluggish.
Industrious	परिश्रमी	Diligent, engaged, busy, sedulous.
Incite	उत्तेजित करना	Stir, urge, provoke, instigate.
Indifference	उदासीनता	Apathy, unconcern, coldness, neutrality.
Infinite	अनन्त	Endless, timeless, limitless, boundless.
Illegal	गैर-कानूनी	Actionable, unlawful, wrong.
Inherit	उत्तराधिकार में प्राप्त	Inborn, natural, essential.
Inner	अन्दरूनी	Internal, interior.
Imperial	शाही	Kingly, royal.
Insanity	पागलपन	Madness, delirium, lunacy, mania.
Imagine	कल्पना करना	Conceive, fancy, think.
Imminent	होने वाला, आसन्न	Impending, looming, near.
Impostor	ठग	Charlatan, cheat.
Inanimate	निर्जीव	Lifeless, motionless, unconscious.
Incessant	निरन्तर, लगातार	Continuous, unceasing.
Indignant	क्रोधित	Angry, wrathful.
Intend	इरादा करना	Propose, mean.
Isolation	एकान्त	Solitude, loneliness, dreariness.
Insane	पागल	Crazy, lunatic, mad.
Injure	आहत करना	Harm, wound.
Jovial	हँसमुख	Merry, jolly, cheerful.
Journey	यात्रा	Travel, tour, trip.
Jubilant	प्रफुल्लित	Exultant, joyful.
Judicious	विवेकशील	Prudent, discreet.
Junk	कबाड़	Rubbish, waste, refuse, trash.
Just	न्यायोचित	Right, proper.
Justice	न्याय	Justness, fairness, integrity, impartiality.
Juvenile	तरुण	Youthful, young.
Knave	दुष्ट	Cirminal, villain.
Knowledge	ज्ञान	Information, scholarship, recognition.
Laborious	परिश्रमी	Industrious, diligent, assiduous.
Lament	विलाप करना	Bewail, mourn.
Large	विशाल	Gigantic, massive, huge, spacious, grand.
Lack	अभाव	Want, need, shortage, deficiency.
Laxity	शिथिलता	Looseness, slackness.
Lank	दुबला-पतला	Lean, straight, thin.
Lecherous	कामुक	Lustful, lascivious, passionate, libidinous.

Word	Meaning	Synonyms
Legend	पौराणिक कथा	Myth, saga, story.
Lenient	मृदु	Mild, liberal.
Lethargy	आलस्य	Sluggishness, laziness.
Lethal	घातक	Deadly, fatal.
Liberate	मुक्त करना	Free, emancipate.
Liberty	स्वतन्त्रता	Freedom, independence.
Labour	श्रम	Drudgery, effort.
Lad	लड़का	Boy, kid.
Lass	लड़की	Girl, virgin.
Leap	छलाँग लगाना	Jump, leapfrog, skip.
Light	जलाना	Ignite, inflame, kindle.
Likeness	समानता	Resemblance, similarity.
Likelihood	सम्भाव्यता	Possibility, probability.
Lively	सजीव	Sprightly, vivacious, active.
Loathe	घृणा करना	Despise, abhor, detest.
Loth	अनिच्छुक	Reluctant, unwilling.
Loyal	वफादार	Devoted, faithful.
Lucky	भाग्यशाली	Appropriate, fortunate.
Lucrative	लाभप्रद	Profitable, remunerative.
Lure	लुभावना	Seduce, tempt.
Magnificent	शानदार	Grand, splendid, noble, superb.
Malice	द्वेष	Ill-will, spite.
Malign	बदनाम करना	Defame, vilify.
Manifest	स्पष्ट	Devious, evident.
Masculine	मर्दाना	Male, manful, manlike, manly, mannish.
Massacre	कत्लेआम	Killing, butchery, slaughter, carnage.
Marvel	अचम्भा	Praise, wonder.
Massive	विशाल	Huge, large, big.
Meagre	कमी होना	Abject, low.
Melancholy	उदासी	Gloomy, morose.
Mercenary	भाड़े का	Money-mad, venal.
Mercy	दया	Pity, compassion.
Might	शक्ति	Strength, power.
Mind	मस्तिष्क	Brain, reason, intellect, thought.
Misery	दुःख	Distress, gloom.
Mock	उपहास करना	Deride, ridicule, satirize.
Morbid	विकृत	Ailing, sickly.
Mournful	मातमी	Sorrowful, tearful.

Word	Meaning	Synonyms
Mourn	विलाप करना	Lament, grieve, bewail, bemoan.
Mutiny	विद्रोह करना	Rebellion, revolt, uprising, insurgence.
Myth	पौराणिक कथा	Fable, legend.
Mix	मिलाना	Amalgamate, join, mingle, combine.
Modesty	विनम्रता	Coyness, timidity, constraint.
Mysterious	रहस्यमय	Baffling, obscure, enigmatic.
Native	स्वाभाविक	Innate, natural, original.
Naughty	शरारती	Mischievous, wayward, disobedient.
Neglect	अवहेलना करना	Ignore, overlook.
Negligent	लापरवाह	Heedless, careless.
Nefarious	बुरा	Evil, wicked, shameful, unlawful.
Niggardly	कृपण	Miserly, parsimonious.
Nonplus	व्याकुल होना	Puzzle, confound, perplex.
Notable	उल्लेखनीय	Remarkable, renowned.
Nuptial	वैवाहिक	Bridal, of wedding.
Obligatory	अनिवार्य	Compulsory, imperative, necessary.
Obsolete	अप्रचलित	Antiquated, extinct, discarded, outworn.
Obscene	अश्लील	Filthy, indecent, lewd.
Obscure	पुरातन	Antiquated, outdated.
Obstinate	जिद्दी	Mulish, resolute, heady, obdurate.
Obtain	प्राप्त करना	Get, attain, acquire, procure.
Obvious	स्पष्ट	Manifest, clear, evident, plain.
Offence	अपमान	Insult, affront, attack, wrong.
Oppressive	निर्दयी	Cruel, tyrannical, grinding.
Outlaw	अपराधी	Criminal, bandit, fugitive, desperado.
Onerous	भारी, वजनी	Burdensome, heavy, ponderous, weighty.
Opulent	धनी	Rich, wealthy.
Ostentation	दिखावा	Display, show, pompousness.
Pact	सन्धि	Treaty, accord, agreement, bargain.
Pain	दर्द	Ache, agony, anguish, distress.
Palatable	स्वादिष्ट	Delicious, eatable, edible.
Pathetic	दर्दनाक	Moving, touching.
Pardon	क्षमा करना	Forgive, excuse, tolerate, overlook.
Paucity	कमी	Dearth, shortage, scarcity.
Peak	चोटी	Top, apex, summit, pinnacle.
Pensive	विचारशील	Contemplative, thoughtful.
Perceive	देखना, समझना	Apprehend, conceive, understand.

Word	Meaning	Synonyms
Perennial	हमेशा रहने वाला	Perpetual, continual.
Permanent	स्थायी	Abiding, constant, invariable.
Persuade	फुसलाना	Induce, incite, urge.
Petty	तुच्छ	Puny, insignificant, trifling.
Pious	शुद्ध, पवित्र	Holy, devout, sacred.
Pierce	चुभोना	Bore, wound, puncture, penetrate.
Plentiful	प्रचुर	Ample, abundant.
Plead	तर्क करना	Argue, advocate, solicit, entreat.
Pledge	प्रतिज्ञा करना	Promise, vow, oath, security.
Precarious	जोखिमपूर्ण	Hazardous, perilous, risky.
Prejudice	पूर्वाग्रह	Bias, partiality, presumption, unfairness.
Principal	मुख्य	Capital, predominant, supreme, prime.
Promote	आगे बढ़ाना	Advance, encourage, forward, prefer.
Portray	चित्रित करना	Delineate, sketch.
Pretence	बहाना	Excuse, facade, feint.
Proscribe	मना करना	Prohibit, restrict, stop.
Quarrel	झगड़ा	Dispute, controversy, wrangle.
Queer	विचित्र	Odd, strange, unique.
Quiet	शान्त	Peaceful, silent, serene, tranquil.
Quit	छोड़ना	Leave, abandon, resign, stop.
Quell	दमन करना	Crush, subdue, suppress.
Quote	उद्धृत करना	Cite, recite, extract.
Quest	खोज	Search, pursuit.
Radiant	चमकीला	Bright, dazzling.
Rare	दुर्लभ	Unique, curious, peculiar, odd.
Rebellion	विद्रोह	Mutiny, revolt.
Rebuff	फटकारना	Reprimand, rebuke.
Refinement	सुधार	Cultivation, civilization, culture, elegance.
Relevant	युक्तिसंगत	Pertinent, proper, relative.
Reluctant	अनिच्छुक	Averse, disinclined, unwilling, indisposed.
Rely	भरोसा करना	Depend, trust.
Remorse	पश्चात्ताप	Repentance, regret, penitence.
Remote	दूरवर्ती	Distant, far off.
Renounce	बहिष्कार करना	Abandon, discard, disclaim, disown.
Renowned	विख्यात	Reputed, popular.
Reprove	फटकारना	Admonish, condemn, reproach.
Reside	निवास करना	Dwell, live.

Word	Meaning	Synonyms
Restrain	बाधा देना, रोकना	Hinder, circumscribe, suppress, restrict.
Reticent	सदाचारी	Just, virtuous.
Revelation	प्रकटीकरण	Disclosure, manifestation, apocalypse.
Revolution	क्रान्ति	Revolt, discord, insurrection, anarchy.
Righteous	सदाचारी	Just, virtuous.
Rigid	कठोर	Unyielding, rigorous, stern, stiff.
Royal	शाही	Kingly, magnificent, regal, kinglike.
Ruinous	विनाशक	Destructive, devastating, dire.
Satiate	सन्तुष्ट	Satisfied.
Scandal	बदनामी	Infamy, slander.
Scholar	विद्यार्थी	Student, pupil, disciple, learner.
Sensual	वासनायुक्त	Fleshy, carnal.
Serious	गम्भीर	Grave, earnest, solemn.
Servile	दासोचित	Slavish, submissive.
Shapely	सुडौल, सुशील	Elegant, graceful.
Shore	समुद्र तट	Beach, coast.
Shudder	काँपना	Shade, shiver, tremble.
Sin	पाप	Vice, fault, guilt, crime.
Sketch	रेखाचित्र	Outline, drawing, plan, skeleton.
Skilful	चतुर	Accomplished, dexterous, proficient.
Sloth	आलस्य	Indolence, lethargy.
Solace	राहत, सुकून	Comfort, relief.
Solitary	अकेली	Lonely, lonesome.
Sombre	उद्विग्न	Gloomy, serious.
Sordid	अधम	Squalid, ugly.
Specimen	नमूना	Sample, model.
Spurious	नकली	False, imaginary, ingenuine.
Squalor	गन्दगी	Dirt, meanness.
Stagnant	गतिहीन, रुका हुआ	Motionless, still and stale.
Sterile	बाँझ	Barren, unproductive.
Stupidity	मूर्खता	Foolishness, insensibility.
Supernatural	प्रतिप्राकृतिक	Miraculous, preternatural, superhuman.
Superficial	अनावश्यक, फालतू	Unwanted, shallow.
Sublime	उत्कृष्ट	Elevated, exalted.
Surmise	अनुमान	Guess, conjecture, inference.
Surplus	आवश्यकता से अधिक	Excess, extra.
Tame	पालतू	Domesticated, gentle.
Tedious	उबाने वाला	Monotonous, wearisome.

Word	Meaning	Synonyms
Teeming	भरा हुआ	Abounding, thriving.
Temperate	संयमी	Moderate, reasonable.
Temporal	सांसारिक	Worldly, earthly, mundane, terrestrial.
Thankful	कृतज्ञ	Grateful, obliged.
Theatrical	नाटकीय	Dramatic, farcical.
Thrifty	मितव्ययी	Economical, provident.
Thrive	वृद्धि होना	Flourish, progress.
Tired	थका हुआ	Exhausted, weary.
Transient	क्षणिक	Fleeting, temporary.
Tyranny	तानाशाही	Autocracy, despotism.
Ugly	कुरूप	Repulsive, nasty.
Union	संघ	Coalition, combination, concert.
Unique	अद्वितीय	Matchless, peerless, unparalleled.
Urbane	शीलवान	Courteous, polite.
Vacant	रिक्त	Empty, blank, void, unemployed.
Various	विभिन्न	Several, diverse.
Venerable	सम्माननीय	Esteemed, honourable, adorable.
Veracity	विश्वसनीयता	Truthfulness, frankness, honesty.
Vex	चिढ़ाना	Annoy, irritate.
Victory	विजय	Conquest, triumph, mastery, achievement.
Vigilant	जागरूक	Watchful, wary, cautious.
Vindictive	प्रतिशोध	Revengeful.
Virtue	गुण	Integrity, honesty, excellence.
Vital	मुख्य	Crucial, critical, pivotal.
Voracious	लालची	Greedy, miserly.
Vulgar	भद्दा	Coarse, rough.
Waver	डगमगाना	Falter, oscillate.
Waive	कम करना	Lessen, decrease, diminish, fade.
Wealth	सम्पत्ति	Abundance, fortune, plenty, luxury.
Wicked	पापी	Evil, bad, cruel, hearties.
Wisdom	बुद्धिमता	Enlightenment, perspicacity.
Wretched	दयनीय	Miserable, pitiable.
Yearn	चाहना	Pine, long, hanker, grieve.
Yield	आत्मसमर्पण	Submit, surrender.
Zeal	उत्साह, जोश	Fervour, earnestness, passion.
Zenith	चोटी	Summit, top.
Zeal	जोश	Enthusiasm, eagerness, earnestness.
Zest	जायका	Gusto, relish.

UNIT 3

Antonyms

किसी शब्द-विशेष का विपरीत अर्थ देने वाला शब्द Antonym कहलाता है।
Antonym is a word opposite in meaning to another.

Word	Meaning	Antonym	Meaning
Abandon	छोड़ना	Retain	बनाए/सम्भाले रखना
Abbreviate	छोटा करना	Elongate	लम्बा करना
Able	योग्य	Unable	अयोग्य
Ability	योग्यता	Inability	अयोग्यता
Abnormal	असामान्य	Normal	सामान्य
Abolish	समाप्त करना	Establish	स्थापित करना
Above	ऊपर	Below	नीचे
Absent	अनुपस्थित	Present	उपस्थित
Abundance	अधिकता	Scarcity	न्यूनता
Accept	स्वीकार करना	Reject	अस्वीकार करना
Accord	सहमति	Discord	असहमति
Accurate	यथार्थ	Inaccurate	गलत
Acknowledge	स्वीकार करना	Deny	अस्वीकार करना
Acquit	दोषमुक्त करना	Convict	दोषी ठहराना
Active	चुस्त	Passive/Idle	सुस्त
Acquire	पाना	Lose	खोना
Add	जोड़ना	Subtract	घटाना
Adequate	पर्याप्त	Inadequate	अपर्याप्त
Advance	आगे बढ़ना	Retreat	पीछे हटना
Advantage	लाभ	Disadvantage	हानि
Adversity	आपत्ति	Prosperity	उन्नति, समृद्धि
Admire	प्रशंसा करना	Despise	निन्दा करना
Alive	जीवित	Dead	मृत
Allow	स्वीकार करना	Disallow	अस्वीकार करना
Always	सदैव	Never	कभी नहीं
All	सब	None	कोई नहीं
Analysis	विश्लेषण	Synthesis	संश्लेषण
Angel	देवदूत	Devil	शैतान
Ancient/Antique	प्राचीन	Modern	नवीन
Animate	जीवित	Inanimate	अजीवित, मृत

Word	Meaning	Antonym	Meaning
Appear	प्रकट होना	Disappear	अन्तर्धान होना
Appreciate	प्रशंसा करना	Depreciate	अवमूल्यन करना
Approve	पुष्टि करना	Disapprove	रद्द करना
Armament	शस्त्रीकरण	Disarmament	निःशस्त्रीकरण
Arrival	आगमन	Departure	बहिर्गमन, प्रस्थान
Arrogance	अड़ियलपन	Humility	विनम्रता
Ascend	चढ़ना	Descend	उतरना
Atheist	नास्तिक	Theist	आस्तिक
Attach	संलग्न करना	Detach	पृथक् करना
Attract	आकर्षित करना	Repel	विकर्षित करना
Auspicious	शुभ	Inauspicious	अशुभ
Awake	जाग्रत	Asleep	निद्रित
Awareness	चेतनता	Ignorance	अचेतनता
Barren	बंजर	Fertile	उपजाऊ
Beginning	आदि	End	अन्त
Beautiful	सुन्दर	Ugly	कुरूप, असुन्दर
Behave	व्यवहार करना	Misbehave	दुर्व्यवहार करना
Belief	विश्वास	Doubt	संशय
Backward	पिछड़ा	Forward	उन्नत
Beneficial	लाभप्रद	Harmful	हानिप्रद
Benefactor	लाभकारक	Malefactor	हानिप्रद
Benevolent	परोपकारी	Malevolent	दुष्टकारी
Bitter	कड़वा	Sweet	मीठा
Big	बड़ा	Small	छोटा
Blame	दोष लगाना	Applaud	प्रशंसा करना
Blessing	वरदान	Curse	अभिशाप
Blunt	मौरा, खोटा	Sharp	तेज धार वाला
Bold	साहसी	Timid	डरपोक
Broad	चौड़ा	Narrow	संकुचित
Borrow	उधार लेना	Lend	उधार देना
Boastful	शेखीबाज, घमण्डी	Modest	विनम्र
Bottom	तल	Top	चोटी
Bravery	वीरता	Cowardice	कायरता
Bright	चमकीला	Dim/Dark	धुँधला, अन्धकारपूर्ण
Before	पहले	After	बाद में
Cheap	सस्ता	Costly	महँगा
Comfortable	आरामदायक	Uncomfortable	कष्टदायक
Common	साधारण	Uncommon	असाधारण
Calm	शान्त	Turbulent	उद्विग्न, तूफान
Care	चिन्ता	Neglect	अवहेलना

Word	Meaning	Antonym	Meaning
Carnivorous	मांसाहारी	Herbivorous	शाकाहारी
Cause	कारण	Effect	प्रभाव
Cautious	सावधान	Careless	असावधान, लापरवाह
Celestial	दैविक	Earthly	पार्थिव
Censure	निन्दा	Applause	सराहना
Certain	निश्चित	Uncertain	अनिश्चित
Chaste	पवित्र	Unchaste	अपवित्र
Cheerful	प्रसन्नचित्त	Cheerless	दुःखी
Childish	अपरिपक्व, बच्चों जैसा	Mature	परिपक्व, वयस्कों जैसा
Circular	वृत्ताकार	Linear	रैखिक
Civilized	सभ्य	Savage/Barbarous	असभ्य, बर्बर
Coarse	भद्दा	Fine	बढ़िया
Coherent	अनुरूप, स्पष्ट	Incoherent	अस्पष्ट
Comedy	सुखान्त	Tragedy	दुखान्त
Competent	योग्य	Incompetent	अयोग्य
Compare	तुलना करना	Contrast	अन्तर करना
Complex	जटिल	Simple	सरल
Component	अवयव	Whole	पूर्ण
Compress	दबाना	Expand	बढ़ाना
Conceal	छिपाना	Reveal	उजागर करना
Confess	स्वीकार करना	Deny	इनकार करना
Confident	विश्वासपूर्ण	Diffident	शंकालु, संकोची
Connect	जोड़ना, मिलाना	Disconnect	तोड़ना, अलग करना
Consent	सहमति	Dissent	असहमति, विमति
Conscious	सचेत	Unconscious	अचेत
Considerate	लिहाज करने वाला	Inconsiderate	लिहाज न करने वाला
Consistency	अनुकूलता	Inconsistency	प्रतिकूलता
Continue	जारी रखना	Discontinue	अधूरा छोड़ना
Contract	सिकुड़ना	Expand	फैलना
Correct	सही, उचित	Incorrect	गलत, अनुचित
Create	रचना करना	Destroy	नष्ट करना
Credit	उधार	Cash	नकद
Crude	अंपक्व, कच्चा	Refined	शोधित
Cool	ठण्डा	Warm	गर्म
Clean	साफ	Dirty	गन्दा
Clear	स्पष्ट	Vague	अस्पष्ट
Cruel	क्रूर	Kind	दयालु
Danger	खतरा	Safety	सुरक्षा
Death	मृत्यु	Life	जीवन
Debtor	देनदार	Creditor	लेनदार

Word	Meaning	Antonym	Meaning
Decent	शोभनीय	Indecent	अशोभनीय
Decision	निर्णय	Indecision	अनिर्णय
Decrease	घटना	Increase	बढ़ना
Deep	गहरा	Shallow	उथला
Defeat	हार	Victory/Conquest	जीत
Defence	सुरक्षा	Offence	आक्रमण
Deficient	अकुशल	Efficient	कुशल
Definite	निश्चित	Indefinite	अनिश्चित
Delightful	आनन्ददायक	Boring	नीरस
Dense	घना	Sparse	छीदा
Dependent	आश्रित, परतन्त्र	Independent	स्वाधीन, स्वतन्त्र
Deposit	जमा करना	Withdraw	निकालना
Despair	निराशा	Hope	आशा
Destructive	विघटनात्मक	Constructive	रचनात्मक
Difficult	कठिन	Easy	सुगम
Diminish	घटना	Increase	बढ़ना
Direct	प्रत्यक्ष	Indirect	अप्रत्यक्ष
Discourage	निरुत्साहित करना	Encourage	उत्साहित करना
Dethrone	राजगद्दी से उतारना	Enthrone	राजगद्दी पर बैठाना
Discord	झगड़ा	Concord	सुलह
Disparity	असमानता	Parity	समानता
Distant	दूरस्थ	Near	निकटस्थ
Distinct	स्पष्ट	Indistinct	अस्पष्ट
Do	करना	Undo	किये को मिटाना
Domestic	पालतू	Wild	जंगली
Dream	स्वप्न	Reality	वास्तविकता
Dwarf	बौना	Giant	विशालकाय
Different	भिन्न	Same	समान
Down	नीचे	Up	ऊपर
Early	जल्दी	Late	देर से
Earn	अर्जित करना	Spend	व्यय करना
Ease	आराम	Difficulty	कठिनाई
Economy	मितव्ययिता	Extravagance	फिजूलखर्ची
Elevation	उठाना	Depression	ढ़लान
Eligible	योग्य	Ineligible	अयोग्य
Emancipate	मुक्त करना	Enslave	दास बनाना
Empty	खाली	Full	भरा हुआ
Enmity	शत्रुता	Friendship	मित्रता
Enjoy	मौज करना	Suffer	तकलीफ सहना

Word	Meaning	Antonym	Meaning
Enrich	धनी बनाना	Impoverish	निर्धन बनाना
Entrance	प्रवेश द्वार	Exit	निकास द्वार
Equality	समानता	Inequality	असमानता
Eternal	अनन्त	Transitory	क्षणिक
Examiner	परीक्षक	Examinee	परीक्षार्थी
Exceptional	अपवादमूलक	Ordinary	सामान्य
Exclude	अलग करना	Include	सम्मिलित करना
Experience	अनुभव	Inexperience	अनुभवहीनता
Explicit	स्पष्ट, व्यक्त	Implicit	अस्पष्ट, अव्यक्त
Expose	उजागर करना	Conceal	छिपाना
External	बाह्य	Internal	आन्तरिक
Extensive	विस्तृत	Intensive	गहन
Exterior	बाहरी	Interior	अन्दरूनी
Extreme	चरम सीमा तक	Moderate	सामान्य
Extrinsic	अनावश्यक	Intrinsic	आवश्यक
Export	निर्यात	Import	आयात
Fabulous	काल्पनिक	Actual/ Real	वास्तविक
Fact	तथ्य	Fiction	काल्पनिक
Failure	असफलता, विफलता	Success	सफलता
Fair	उचित	Foul	अनुचित
Faithful	वफादार	Unfaithful	बेवफा
Fall	पतन	Rise	उत्थान
False	झूठा	True	सच्चा
Familiar	परिचित	Strange	अपरिचित
Famous	प्रसिद्ध	Notorious	बदनाम
Farewell	अलविदा	Welcome	स्वागत
Fat	मोटा	Thin	पतला
Favour	पक्ष लेना	Disfavour	पक्ष से गिराना
Fierce	निर्दयी	Gentle	विनम्र
Fickle	चंचल	Steadfast	स्थिर
Fictitious	नकली	Genuine	असली
Fidelity	स्वामीभक्ति	Infidelity	बेवफाई
Folly	मूर्खता	Wisdom	बुद्धिमत्ता
Foreign	विदेशी	Native	देशीय
Fortune	भाग्य	Misfortune	दुर्भाग्य
Freedom	स्वतन्त्रता	Slavery	दासता
Fresh	ताजा	Stale	बासी
Friend	मित्र	Foe	शत्रु
Futile	व्यर्थ	Utility	उपयोगिता
Frown	भृकुटि पर बल	Smile	मुस्कान

Word	Meaning	Antonym	Meaning
Few	कुछ	Many	अनेक
Found	पाना	Lose	खोना
Gain	लाभ	Loss	हानि
Gay	प्रसन्नचित्त	Gloomy	उदास
General	सामान्य	Particular	विशेष
Generous	उदार	Miserly	कंजूस
Generosity	उदारता	Stinginess	कृपणता
Genial	विनीत	Impolite	अविनीत
Genuine	असली	Spurious	नकली
Give	देना	Take	लेना
Go	जाना	Come	आना
Good	अच्छा	Bad	बुरा
Govern	शासन करना	Obey	आज्ञा मानना
Grant	मंजूर करना	Refuse	नामंजूर करना
Great	महान्	Small	तुच्छ
Guilty	अपराधी	Innocent	निरपराधी, निर्दोष
Guide	पथ-प्रदर्शन करना	Misguide	भटकाना
Growth	विकास	Decline	ह्रास
Guest	अतिथि	Host	मेजबान
Handsome	सुन्दर	Ugly	भद्दा
Happy	प्रसन्न	Unhappy	अप्रसन्न
Hard	कठोर	Soft	कोमल
Haste	जल्दी	Delay	देरी
Haughty/Proud	दम्भी/घमण्डी	Humble	विनम्र
Healthy	स्वस्थ	Unhealthy	अस्वस्थ
Heaven	स्वर्ग	Hell	नर्क
Heedful	सचेत	Heedless	लापरवाह
Height	ऊँचाई	Low	नीचा
Holy	पवित्र	Unholy	अपवित्र
Hollow	खोखला	Solid	ठोस
Honest	ईमानदार	Dishonest	बेईमान
Honour	सम्मान	Dishonour	तिरस्कार
Hopeful	आशावान्	Despondent	निराशा
Huge	विशाल	Tiny	छोटा
Hypocrite	पाखण्डी	Sincere	ईमानदार
Illusive	भ्रामक	Real	वास्तविक
Immaterial	अभौतिक, तत्त्वहीन	Material	भौतिक, तत्त्वशाली
Individual	व्यक्तिगत	Joint	सामूहिक
Industrious	कर्मठ	Lazy	सुस्त

Word	Meaning	Antonym	Meaning
Inferior	घटिया	Superior	बढ़िया
Inhale	साँस अन्दर खींचना	Exhale	साँस बाहर छोड़ना
Initial	आरम्भिक	Final	अन्तिम
Insolent	ढ़ीठ	Meek	विनीत
Intrepid	निर्भय	Timid	भीरू, डरपोक
Irksome	दुखदायी	Pleasant	सुहावना
Imprudent	अविवेकी	Prudent	विवेकी
Ignorance	अज्ञानता	Knowledge	ज्ञान
Insult	निरादर	Respect	आदर
Immortal	अमर	Mortal	मरणशील, नश्वर
Join	जोड़ना, सन्धि करना	Disjoin	अलग रखना
Joy	प्रसन्नता	Sorrow	दुःख
Junior	कनिष्ठ	Senior	वरिष्ठ
Justice	न्याय	Injustice	अन्याय
Keen	तीक्ष्ण	Dull	भोथरा
King	राजा	Queen	रानी
Last	अन्तिम	First	प्रथम
Lasting	टिकाऊ	Temporary	अस्थायी
Latent	गुप्त	Apparent	प्रकट
Lawful	कानूनी	Illegal	गैरकानूनी
Leader	नेता	Follower	अनुयायी
Lean	दुबला-पतला	Fleshy	मोटा-ताजा
Legible	पठनीय	Illegible	अपठनीय
Legitimate	तथ्य परक	Illegitimate	तथ्य परक न होना
Lie	झूठ	Truth	सच
Liberty	स्वाधीनता	Slavery	दासता
Like	पसन्द करना	Dislike	नापसन्द करना
Likely	सम्भावना	Unlikely	असम्भावना
Limited	सीमित	Unlimited	असीमित
Liquid	तरल	Solid	ठोस
Literate	साक्षर	Illiterate	निरक्षर
Little	थोड़ा	Much	ज्यादा
Living	जीवित	Dead	मृत
Lofty	ऊँचा	Low	नीचा
Logical	तर्कसंगत, न्यायसंगत	Illogical	अतार्किक, न्यायविरुद्ध
Loose	ढ़ीला	Tight	तंग, कसा हुआ
Love	प्यार करना	Hate	घृणा करना
Lovely	मनोहारी	Ugly	कुरूप
Loyal	वफादार	Disloyal	बेवफा
Lower	निचला	Upper	ऊपर का

Word	Meaning	Antonym	Meaning
Light	प्रकाश	Darkness	अन्धकार
Light	हल्का	Heavy	भारी
Major	वयस्क, प्रमुख	Minor	अवयस्क, क्षुद्र
Make	बनाना	Mar	बिगाड़ना
Meagre	थोड़ा	Profuse	अधिक
Malice	द्वेष	Goodwill	सद्‌भावना
Married	विवाहित	Bachelor	अविवाहित
Masculine	पुल्लिंग	Feminine	स्त्रीलिंग
Material	भौतिक	Spiritual	आध्यात्मिक
Maximum	अधिकतम	Minimum	न्यूनतम
Memory	स्मरण शक्ति	Forgetfulness	भुलक्कड़पन
Merit	गुण	Demerit	दोष
Mild	मृदु	Stern	कर्कश
Modest	विनीत	Immodest/Vain	अविनीत
Mount	चढ़ना	Dismount	उतरना
Movable	चल	Immovable	अचल
Moral	नैतिक	Immoral	अनैतिक
Master	स्वामी	Servant	नौकर
Natural	कुदरती, प्राकृतिक	Artificial	बनावटी, अप्राकृतिक या कृत्रिम
Neat	साफ-सुथरा	Untidy	मैला-कुचैला
New	नया	Old	पुराना
Negative	नकारात्मक	Positive	सकारात्मक
Noble	नेक	Vicious	नीच
Noise	शोर	Silence	शान्ति
Obligatory	बाध्यकारी	Voluntary	ऐच्छिक
Obedient	आज्ञाकारी	Disobedient	अवज्ञाकारी
Obstruct	बाधा डालना	Assist	सहायता करना
Opaque	अपारदर्शी	Transparent	पारदर्शी
Optimism	आशावाद	Pessimism	निराशावाद
Optional	ऐच्छिक	Compulsory	अनिवार्य
Oral	मौखिक	Written	लिखित
Organic	चेतनायुक्त	Inorganic	चेतनाहीन
Outward	बाहरी	Inward	अन्दरूनी
Own	स्वीकार करना	Disown	अस्वीकार करना
Open	खोलना	Shut	बन्द करना
Opponent	विरोधी	Support	सहायक
Part	भाग	Whole	सम्पूर्ण
Partial	आंशिक, पक्षपातपूर्ण	Impartial	पक्षपातरहित
Pathetic	करुणामय	Joyous	आनन्दपूर्ण
Peace	शान्ति	War	युद्ध

Word	Meaning	Antonym	Meaning
Penalty	दण्ड	Reward	पुरस्कार
Penury	निर्धनता	Affluence	समृद्धि
Perfect	पूर्ण	Imperfect	अपूर्ण
Permanent	स्थायी	Temporary	अस्थायी
Permission	अनुमति	Prohibition	मनाही
Persuade	उकसाना	Dissuade	हतोत्साहित करना
Petty	तुच्छ	Significant	महत्त्वपूर्ण
Please	प्रसन्न करना	Displease	अप्रसन्न करना
Pleasure	सुख	Pain	दुःख
Plenty	प्रचुरता	Scarcity	न्यूनता
Polite	शिष्ट, विनम्र	Impolite	अशिष्ट, कर्कश
Poor	निर्धन	Rich	धनी
Pollute	प्रदूषित करना	Purify	शुद्ध करना
Popular	लोकप्रिय	Unpopular	अप्रिय
Posterior	बाद वाला	Anterior	पहले वाला
Practical	प्रयोगात्मक	Theoretical	सैद्धांतिक
Precious	कीमती	Cheap	सस्ता
Presence	उपस्थिति	Absence	अनुपस्थिति
Premium	लाभ	Discount	बट्टा, कटौती
Preserve	सुरक्षित रखना	Destroy	नष्ट करना
Pride	घमण्ड	Humility	विनम्रता
Profound	गहरा	Simple	सादा
Prolong	बढ़ाना, लम्बा करना	Shorten	कम या छोटा करना
Prosaic	गद्य जैसा	Poetical	पद्य जैसा
Public	सार्वजनिक	Private	निजी
Purchase	खरीदना	Sell	बेचना
Patriot	देशभक्त	Traitor	देशद्रोही
Question	प्रश्न	Answer	उत्तर
Quick	तेज	Slow	धीमा
Quiet	शान्त	Noisy	शोर करने वाला
Raise	ऊपर उठाना	Lower	नीचे गिराना
Rational	युक्तिसंगत	Irrational	युक्तिविहीन
Raw	कच्चा	Ripe	पका हुआ
Rear	पिछला	Front	सामने का
Recollect	याद करना	Forget	भूल जाना
Regular	नियमित	Irregular	अनियमित
Religious	धार्मिक	Irreligious	अधार्मिक
Remote	दूर का	Near	नजदीक का
Repulsive	निषेधक	Attractive	आकर्षक
Revolution	क्रान्ति	Evolution	विकास

Word	Meaning	Antonym	Meaning
Remember	याद करना	Forget	भूलना
Rough	खुरदरा	Smooth	चिकना
Ruthless	निर्दयी	Merciful	रहम दिल
Sacred	पवित्र	Profane	कलुषित
Sane	बुद्धिमान	Insane/Mad	पागल
Sensible	बुद्धियुक्त	Senseless	बुद्धिहीन
Satisfaction	सन्तोष	Dissatisfaction	असन्तोष
Shy	शर्मीला	Imprudent	ढ़ीठ
Similar	समान	Dissimilar	असमान
Stable	स्थिर	Unstable	अस्थिर
Straight	सीधा	Crooked/ Curved	टेढ़ा-मेढ़ा/तिर्यक
Surplus	फालतू	Deficit	घाटा
Swift	तेज	Slow	धीमा
Synonym	समानार्थी	Antonym	विपरीतार्थी
Thankful	कृतज्ञ	Thankless	अकृतज्ञ
Thrift	मितव्ययी	Extravagant	फिजूलखर्च
Thick	मोटा	Thin	पतला
Tie	बाँधना	Untie	खोलना
Tolerant	सहनशील	Intolerant	असहनशील
Transparent	पारदर्शी	Opaque	अपारदर्शी
Unanimous	सम्मत, एकमत	Divided	विभाजित
Unity	एकात्मता	Diversity	विविधता
Universal	सार्वजनिक	Particular	व्यक्तिगत
Uphold	समर्थन करना	Oppose	विरोध करना
Urban	शहरी, नगरीय	Rural	देहाती, ग्रामीण
Useful	उपयोगी	Useless	बेकार
Usual	सामान्य	Unusual	असामान्य
Valid	वैध	Invalid	अवैध
Victor	विजेता	Vanquished	पराजित
Victory	जीत, विजय	Defeat	हार, पराजय
Virile	पौरुषेय	Sterile	नपुंसक
Virtue	गुण, अच्छाई	Vice	दोष, बुराई
Visible	सदृश्य	Invisible	अदृश्य
Vulgar	अश्लील	Refined	शोधित, श्लील
Weal	सुख	Woe	दु:ख
Wise	बुद्धिमान	Foolish	मूर्ख
Wrong	गलत	Right	सही
Yield	समर्पित करना	Resist	विरोध करना
Youth	युवा	Aged	वृद्ध
Young	नवयुवक	Old	वृद्ध

UNIT 4

Contranyms

Contranyms ऐसे words, जिनके synonyms, एक-दूसरे के antonyms होते हैं अर्थात् ऐसे शब्द जिनके दो meanings एक-दूसरे के विपरीत अर्थ देते हैं। नीचे कुछ ऐसे ही contranyms की list दी जा रही है जिसमें दो meanings (A) एवं (B) एक-दूसरे के antonym हैं। Contranyms भी एक प्रकार के Homographs (ऐसे शब्द जिनके दो अलग-अलग अर्थ होते हैं।) ही हैं।

The word contranym (also the synonym autoantonym) is used to refer to words that, by some freak of language evolution, are their own antonyms. Both contranym and autoantonym are relatively recent neologisms. Contranyms are the special cases of homographs (two words with the same spelling).

ऐसे कुछ उदाहरण निम्नलिखित हैं–

Word	Contranyms	
Anabasis	(A) Military advance,	(B) Military retreat
Aught	(A) All,	(B) Nothing
Bolt	(A) Secure,	(B) Run away
Buckle	(A) Fasten,	(B) Fall apart
By	(A) Multiplication *(eg, A three by five matrix),* (B) Division *(eg, Dividing eight by four)*	
Chuffed	(A) Pleased,	(B) Annoyed
Cleave	(A) Separate,	(B) Adhere
Clip	(A) Fasten,	(B) Detach
Consult	(A) Ask for advice,	(B) Give advice
Copemate	(A) Partner,	(B) Antagonist
Custom	(A) Usual,	(B) Special
Deceptively	(A) Smarter than one appears, smart (B) Dumber than one appears	
Dike	(A) Wall,	(B) Ditch
Discursive	(A) Proceeding coherently from topic-to-topic, (B) Moving aimlessly from topic-to-topic	
Dollop	(A) A large amount,	(B) A small amount
Dust	(A) Add fine particles,	(B) Remove fine particles
Enjoin	(A) Prescribe,	(B) Prohibit
Fast	(A) Quick,	(B) Unmoving

Word	Contranyms	
First degree	(A) Most severe *(eg, Murder)*	(B) Least severe *(eg, Burn)*
Fix	(A) Restore,	(B) Castrate
Flog	(A) Criticize harshly,	(B) Promote aggressively
Garnish	(A) Enhance *(eg, Food),*	(B) Curtail (eg, Wages)
Give out	(A) Produce,	(B) Stop production
Grade	(A) Incline,	(B) Level
Handicap	(A) Advantage,	(B) Disadvantage
Help	(A) Assist,	(B) Prevent *(eg, I Can't help it if...)*
Left	(A) Remaining,	(B) Departed from
Liege	(A) Sovereign lord,	(B) Loyal subject
Mean	(A) Average,	(B) Excellent *(eg, 'Plays a mean game')*
Off	(A) Off,	(B) On *(eg, 'The alarm went off')*
Out	(A) Visible *(eg, Stars),*	(B) Invisible *(eg, Lights)*
Out of	(A) Outside,	(B) Inside *(eg, Work out of one's home)*
Oversight	(A) Error,	(B) Care
Put out	(A) Extinguish,	(B) Generate *(eg, Something putting out light)*
Quiddity	(A) Essence,	(B) Trifling point
Quite	(A) Rather,	(B) Completely
Rent	(A) Buy use of,	(B) Sell use of
Rinky	(A) Insignificant,	(B) One who frequents rinkworks
Sanction	(A) Approve,	(B) Boycott
Sanguine	(A) Hopeful,	(B) Murderous *(Obsolete synonym for Sanguinary)*
Screen	(A) Show,	(B) Hide
Seed	(A) Add seeds *(eg, 'To seed a field'),*	(B) Remove seeds *(eg, 'To seed a tomato')*
Strike	(A) Hit,	(B) Miss *(In Baseball)*
Table	(A) Propose *(In the United Kingdom),*	(B) Set aside *(In the United States)*
Transparent	(A) Invisible,	(B) Obvious
Unbending	(A) Rigid,	(B) Relaxing
Variety	(A) One type *(eg, 'This variety'),*	(B) Many types *(eg, 'A variety')*
Wear	(A) Endure through use,	(B) Decay through use
Weather	(A) Withstand,	(B) Wear away
Wind Up	(A) End,	(B) Start up *(eg, A watch)*
With	(A) Alongside,	(B) Against

UNIT 5

Homonyms

Words similar in sound or pronunciation, but different in meaning are called Homonyms.

English में ऐसे बहुत से शब्द हैं जिनका उच्चारण लगभग एक जैसा होने के बावजूद उनके अर्थ में अन्तर होता है। ऐसे शब्दों को Homonyms या Homophones कहा जाता है; pewmes—Affect, effect, Access; excess आदि। इन शब्दों का उचित ज्ञान न होने पर, एक ही जगह पर दूसरे शब्द को लिख देने से वाक्य का भाव गलत हो जाता है। अतः छात्रों को ऐसे शब्दों का बहुत ध्यानपूर्वक अध्ययन व प्रयोग करना चाहिए।

- **Affect** *(to act upon, to pretend–प्रभाव डालना)*
  (a) She *affects* too much innocence.
  (b) The drought *affected* a large part of the district.

  Effect *(result–प्रभाव)* Internet produces a bad *effect* on the young generation.
- **Adapt** *(accomodate–व्यवहार)* One should *adapt* oneself to the new circumstances.

  Adept *(expert–निपुण)* He is an *adept* in folk dance.

  Adopt *(take up–ग्रहण करना)* One should not *adopt* unfair means to secure good marks.
- **Addition** *(putting more–जोड़न)* I am to buy two more copies in *addition* to this one.

  Edition *(printing books–प्रकाशन)* The first *edition* of this book has sold like hot cakes.
- **Accede** *(agree–स्वीकार करना)* He will not *accede* to your request.

  Exceed *(to be greater–बढ़ना, बढ़ाना)* Write an essay not *exceeding* three hundred words.
- **Access** *(approach, reach–पहुँच)* Now-a-days every person has an easy *access* to the temples irrespective of his caste.

  Excess *(more than enough–अधिकता)* *Excess* of everything is bad.
- **Accept** *(to take–स्वीकार करना)* He cannot *accept* this gift.

  Except *(leaving out–बजाय)* *Except* Nisha everyone was present in the party.
- **Alter** *(change–बदलना)* You cannot *alter* my opinion about her.

  Altar *(place of offering–वेदी)*
  (a) In India incense is burnt at the *altar* in temples.
  (b) Subhash Chandra Bose sacrificed everything at the *altar* of freedom.

- **Antic** *(odd, strange–विलक्षण, अद्‌भुत)* His behaviour on yesterday was *antic.*

  Antique *(Ancient–प्राचीन)* I am fond of collecting *antique* items.
- **Assay** *(attempt–प्रयास; testing the purity of metals धातुओं की शुद्धता की जाँच)*
  (a) He *assayed* hard to secure top position.
  (b) He *assayed* the gold ornaments.

  Essay *(a piece of composition–निबन्ध)* Write a brief essay on 'Indian Films'.
- **All ready** *(all are ready–सभी तैयार)* They were *all ready* to welcome the groom.

  Already *(earlier–पूर्व में)* I have *already* informed him.
- **Allusions** *(indirect reference–अप्रत्यक्ष संकेत)* The poem is full of *allusions.*

  Illusion *(a deceptive show–मृगतृष्णा)* Indian mythology regards the material world as an *illusion.*
- **Apposite** *(proper–योग्य)* His arguments were not *apposite* to the subject.

  Opposite *(contrary, in front of–विपरीत, सामने)* His house is *opposite* to the college.
- **Assent** *(agreement–स्वीकारोक्ति)* He gave his *assent* to the new proposal.

  Ascent *(going up–ऊपर चढ़ना)* He pushed the button and the elevator began its slow *ascent.*
- **Arc** *(part of circle–त्रिज्या)* If a straight line is drawn in a circle it will divide it into two **arcs.**

  Ark *(covered floating vessel–ढ़की हुई नाव)* He crossed the Black Sea with his family in an *ark.*
- **Aloud** *(high volume–ऊँचा स्वर)* I can't hear you well, please speak *aloud.*

  Allowed *(permitted–इजाजत दी)* He was *allowed* to enter.
- **Angle** *(an angle of degree–कोण)* This is a ninety degree *angle.*

  Angel *(a divine being–फरिश्ता)* *Angels* reside in heaven while men reside on earth.
- **Advice** *(guidance–परामर्श)* I need your expert *advice* in this matter.

  Advise *(to councel–सलाह देना)* Please *advise* me in this matter.
- **Amiable** *(lovable–प्यार योग्य)* She is not only beautiful but an *amiable* girl also.

  Amicable *(friendly–मित्रवत्)* Finally they came to an *amicable* settlement.
- **Ail** *(to be ill–बीमार होना)* What *ails* the Industry is to be sorted out ?

  Ale *(a type of liquor–शराब)* He has gone to the *ale*-house.
- **All together** *(in a body–साथ-साथ)* Let us move there *all together.*

  Altogether *(completely–पूर्णतया)* It seems *altogether* impossible to cross the river in the night.
- **Ad** *(short for advertisement–विज्ञापन)* He has given an *ad* in the newspaper.

  Add *(short for addition–जोड़ना)* *Add* two to three.

  Aid *(to assist–सहायता करना)* He has given *aid* of Rs 50,000/- to the poor family.

  Aide *(an assistant–सहयोगी)* He is a close *aide* to the Prime Minister.

- **Aerie** *(eagle's nest–घोंसला)* There is an *aerie* on this tree.

  Airy *(breezy–हवादार)* The house is quite *airy*.

- **Aisle** *(walkway–रास्ता)* (a) I am in no hurry to walk down the *aisle*.

  (b) An *aisle* is a long narrow gap that people can walk along between rows of seats in a public building such as a church or between rows of shelves in a super market.

  (c) The *aisle* is also used in expressions such as walking down the aisle to refer to the activity of getting married.

  Isle *(island–द्वीप)* I have seen many isles but this is the best *isle*.

- **All** *(everything–सब)* He has donated *all* his property.

  Awl *(a small pointed tool for pricking or piercing holes, esp. such a tool used by shoemakers–मोची का एक औजार)* Awl is an essential tool for shoe repair.

- **Ate** *(past tense of eat–खाया)* He *ate* two apples.

  Eight *(the number base of octal, seven, eight, nine–आठ)* I have *eight* pens.

- **Auger** *(a drill tool–औजार)* I need an *auger* to make a hole.

  Augur *(foretell–भविष्य)* The recent communal riots do not *augur* well for the smooth running of government.

- **Aural** *(of hearing–सुनने से सम्बन्धित)* He became famous as an inventor of astonishing visual and *aural* effects.

  Oral *(of the mouth–मौखिक)* He presented his ideas in a nice way *orally*.

- **Auricle** *(external part of the ear–कान का बाहरी हिस्सा)* *Auricle* protects all the sensitive parts of the ear.

  Oracle *(seer–श्रेष्ठ)* He regards himself as an *oracle* on architecture.

- **Away** *(distant–दूर)* Do not go far *away* from the house.

  Aweigh *(just clear of the bottom)* Ship anchors *aweigh*!

- **Awed** *(in a state of wonder–चकित)* *Awedly* she was unable to recall his name.

  Odd *(not even–अयुग्म)* Always mention *odd* numbers on the right side.

- **Aye** *(Aye means yes–हाँ)* Used generally in some dialects of British English : 'Do you remember your first day at school?' 'Oh *aye*. Yeah.'

  Eye *(ocular organ–आँख)* Her *eyes* are very beautiful.

- **Bale** *(package–गाँठ)* I received thirty *bales* of cotton last month.

  Bail *(security–जमानत)* The magistrate didn't grant him *bail* in theft case.

- **Berth** *(sleeping place in train–ट्रेन में सोने का स्थान)* I have booked two *berths* in Shatabdi Express.

  Birth *(coming to life–जन्म)* This is not the *birth* place of Buddha.

- **Bare** *(uncovered–नंगा, बिना ढ़का)* He came here *bare* footed.

  Bear *(to tolerate–सहन करना)* *(a)* I cannot *bear* your insulting remarks.

  (an animal–रीछ) *(b)* There are three *bears* in that circus.

  Beer *(a kind of wine–बीयर)* I prefer to take *beer*.

- **Blow** *(to whistle–बजाना)* Cool wind is *blowing*. Don't blow the whistle.

  Below *(underneath–नीचे)* Hitting *below* the belt is not allowed.
- **Born** *(to take birth–जन्म)* My wife was *born* in 1960.

  Borne *(supported–आश्रय दिया हुआ)* He is suffering from water *borne* disease.
- **Bad** *(not good–बुरा)* He is a *bad* man.

  Bed *(sleeping place–बिस्तर)* I go to *bed* at 11 pm.
- **By** *(assistance–द्वारा)* A snake was killed *by* Ram with a stick.

  Buy *(purchase–खरीदना)* I want to *buy* a car.
- **Beet** *(a vegetable–चुकन्दर)* I prefer mango to *beet*.

  Beat *(to thrash–पीटना)* It is wrong to *beat* the students with a stick.
- **Borrow** *(to take loan–उधार लेना)* I have *borrowed* some money from Bank.

  Burrow *(a hole in earth–छेद)* A mouse lives in this *burrow*.
- **Cell** *(a small cottage–छोटी कोठरी)* There are more than twenty *cells* in that prison.

  Sell *(to dispose off–बेचना)* He *sells* fruits and vegetables.

  Sale *(act of selling–बिक्री)* I have purchased this dress from the *sale*.
- **Beach** (shore–किनारा) Many people like to walk along the sea *beach*.

  Beech *(a kind of tree–पेड़)* There are many *beech* trees near the railway station.
- **Brake** *(lever–ब्रेंक)* I am going to get the *brake* wire changed .

  Break *(to make a part–तोड़ना)* You can easily *break* this stick with your hands.
- **Bow** *(bend–झुकना)* Let us *bow* to our motherland India.

  Bough *(a branch of tree–टहनी)* Many birds are sitting on the *bough* of the tree.
- **Bridal** *(pertaining to marriage–शादी से सम्बन्धित)* She is looking beautiful in her *bridal* dress.

  Bridle *(reins–लगाम)* It is not easy to *bridle* a vicious horse.
- **Baron** *(a landlord–जमींदार)* There was a time when all powers rested in the hands of rich *barons*.

  Barren *(not fertile–अनुपजाऊ)* In *barren* land you can't cultivate any thing.
- **Blue** *(a colour–नीला)* I like *blue* colour.

  Blew *(whistled–सीटी बजाई)* The referee *blew* the whistle again and again.
- **Bait** *(food placed on a hook or in a trap to entice fish–ललचाना)* Let your *bait* falls gently upon the water.

  Bate *(to lessen–कम करना)* We listened with *bated* breath the stories of grand mother's travel.
- **Bald** *(hairless–गंजा)* She is *bald* headed.

  Balled *(carnal knowledge)* He picked up the sheets of paper and *balled* them tightly in his fists.

  Bawled *(cried aloud–जोर से चीखना)* Someone in the audience *bawled* out 'Once More'.

- **Band** *(a group–समूह)* A *band* is a group of trained musicians.

  Banned *(forbidden–प्रतिबन्धित)* Drinking is *banned* in Gujarat.

- **Bard** *(a poet–कवि)* People sometimes refer to William Shakespeare as the *Bard.*

  Barred *(enclosed by poles–घेरना)* The windows were closed and shuttered and the door was *barred.*

- **Basal** *(forming the base–आधार बनाना)* The *basal* layer of the skin was also torn.

  Basil *(an herb–तुलसी)* *Basil* is used in cooking also.

- **Base** *(the bottom support for anything–आधार)* The *base* of the bottle is very narrow.

  Bass *(the lowest musical pitch or range–धीमी आवाज)* A *bass* is also a man with deep singing voice.

- **Bask** *(to warm oneself pleasantly–गर्म करना)* Crocodiles *bask* on the small sandy beaches.

  Basque *(tight fitting bodice or tunic–कसे हुए कपड़े)* She was advised to wear *basque.*

- **Baud** *(bits per second–बिट्स प्रति सेकेण्ड)* *Baud* is a unit of data transmission speed equals to one information unit per second·

  Bawd *(brothel manager–करनी)* She is the *bawd* of that brothel.

- **Beau** *(male friend–नर मित्र)* A woman's *beau* is her boy friend or lover.

  Bow *(a curve or bend–मुड़ा हुआ)* He *bowed* slightly for taking her bag.

- **Bell** *(ding ding–घण्टी)* Don't try to *bell* the cat.

  Belle *(charming woman–सुन्दर स्त्री)* She was the *belle* in last night party.

- **Besot** *(to get drunk–नशे में होना)* He became so *besotted* with her that even he forgot his children.

  Besought *(past tense of beseech–आग्रह करना)* She *besought* him to cut his drinking and reduce his smoking.

- **Better** *(superior–अच्छा)* It is always *better* to drive carefully.

  Bettor *(one who bets–शर्त लगाने वाले)* The person who bets is called a *bettor.*

- **Bight** *(a loop–घुमाव)* The loop of a rope is called *bight.*

  Bite *(a mouthful–दाँतों से काटा हुआ)* You can have a *bite* of chocolate.

  Byte *(eight bits–बाइट)* *Byte* is a unit of data storage in computers.

- **Bloc** *(an alliance–मित्रों का संगठन)* .A *bloc* is a group of countries which have similar aims and interests and generally work together over some issues.

  Block *(a block in a town is an area of land with streets on all its sides–पंक्तिबद्ध)* She walked four *blocks* down high street.

- **Boar** *(wild pig–जंगली सूअर)* We can find wild *boars* in the valleys.

  Boer *(a South African of Dutch descent)* He is a *boer,* his father was a Dutch from South Africa.

Boor *(tasteless buffoon–स्वादरहित)* If we refer someone as a *boor*, we think his behaviour and attitude rough and rude.

Bore *(not interesting–अरुचिकर)* He *bored* me all through the meal with stories of the army life.

- **Bode** *(an omen–शकुन)* She says the way bill was passed bodes ill for the democracy.

  Bowed *(curved–मुड़ा हुआ)* He has *bowed* legs.

- **Bole** *(trunk–पेड़ का धड़ या तना)* He was standing behind the *bole* of a tree.

  Bowl *(dish–बर्तन)* Put all the soup in a large *bowl.*

- **Boos** *(disparaging sounds from audience–आवाज)* Demonstrators *boosed* and jeered him.

  Booze *(whiskey–व्हिस्की)* I have five empty bottles of *booze.*

- **Bough** *(tree branch–पेड़ की टहनी)* I rested my fishing rod against a pine *bough.*

  Bow *(front of a ship, respectful bend–जहाज का उगता भाग)* I gave a theatrical *bow* and waved.

- **Bra** *(brassiere–महिलाओं का अंगवस्त्र)* She wears beautiful coloured *bra.*

  Braw *(well-groomed–तैयार रहना)* He always keeps himself in *braw* shape.

- **Braid** *(a narrow piece of twisted thread or cloth used to decorate clothes–गोटा)* He was wearing a coloured uniform with lots of gold *braid.*

  Brayed *(a donkey cried–गधे की आवाज)* The donkey *brayed* and tried to bolt.

- **Braise** *(cook with oil and water–पकाना)* I like *braised* cabbage.

  Brays *(loud, harsh cry of donkey–गधे की आवाज)* A donkey is *braying.*

- **Bread** *(a loaf– रोटी)* *Bread* is necessary for the living.

  Bred *(past tense of breed–नस्ल का भूतकाल)* He is an ill *bred* fellow.

- **Brewed** *(fermented–शराब बनाना)* I like nicely *brewed* beer.

  Brood *(family–परिवार, सोचना)*

  (a) *Brood* is a group of baby birds that were born at the same time to the same mother.

  (b) If someone *broods* over something they think about it a lot, seriously.

- **Bruise** *(an injury–चोट)* I think that the *bruise* on your cheek is a serious one.

  Brews *(making beer–बीयर बनाना)* I *brew* my own beer.

- **Broach** *(to raise a subject–मुद्दा उठाना)* At last I *broached* the subject of her early life.

  Brooch *(an ornament fastened to clothes which has a pin at the back–वस्त्रों मे लगाई जाने वाली सुरक्षित पिन)* I have five *brooches.*

- **Brows** *(multiple foreheads–भौहें)* Your *brows* are on your forehead.

  Browse *(grazing–चरना)* Three red deer were *browsing* near my lodge.

- **Burger** *(meat sandwich–बर्गर)* I do not like eating *burger.*

  Burgher *(merchant–व्यवसायी)* The *burghers* of a town are the people who live there, especially the richer or more respectable people.

- **But** *(except–लेकिन)* He is *but* a good man.

  Butt *(the thick end–सिरा)* A number of cigarette *butts* are lying there.

- **Buyer** *(one who purchases–खरीदार)* Only a prospective *buyer* can purchase this house.

  Byre *(a cow barn–गौशाला)* A *byre* is a cowshed.

- **Check** *(to verify, to stop–जाँचना)*

  (a) He *checked* my passport.

  (b) He *checked* me from leaving the function.

  Cheque *(bank document–चेक)* I issued a *cheque* favouring PNB.

- **Calendar** *(chart showing dates etc.–कैलेण्डर)* I have only one *calendar* in my office.

  Calender *(to press paper, cloth etc.–प्रेस करना)* Please *calender* my dress.

- **Cannon** *(big gun–तोप)* A *cannon* of ancient time is placed near the Railway Station.

  Canon *(rule–सिद्धान्त)* He believes in *canons* of justice.

- **Canvas** *(a kind of rough cloth–तिरपाल)* My shoes are made of *canvas.*

  Canvass *(to solicit votes– वोट माँगना)* Now-a-days students are busy in *canvassing* for their friends.

- **Casual** *(accidental, occasional–आकस्मिक)* I was granted only one day *casual* leave.

  Causal *(showing cause–कारण बताने वाला)* There is a *causal* link between balanced diet and sound mind.

- **Corpse** *(dead body–लाश)* The *corpse* was covered with a white bedsheet.

  Corps *(a body of troops–सेना की टुकड़ी)* I want to join National Cadet *Corps.*

- **Coma** *(state of senselessness–बेहोशी)* The patient has been in *coma* since Monday.

  Comma *(mark of punctuation–कॉमा)* One should be careful about proper use of *comma.*

- **Cession** *(to yield–छोड़ना)* India should not have made a *cession* of an inch of its land for the establishment of Pakistan.

  Session *(sitting of an assembly or court–सत्र)* The winter *session* of parliament will be over tomorrow.

- **Censer** *(a pot in which incense is burnt–यज्ञ की वेदी)* Place some incense into the *censer.*

  Censor *(an official to examine–निरीक्षक)* The *censor* board has awarded 'U' certificate to this film.

  Censure *(criticize adversely–निन्दा)* His conduct was *censured* by Parliament.

- **Chord** *(a string of musical instrument– वाद्य-यन्त्र का तार)* He is playing with the *chords* of the violin.

  Cord *(a thin rope– रस्सी)* I need a fifteen fit *cord* for packing the luggage.

- **Cease** *(discontinue–छोड़ना)* He resigned and thus *ceased* to be the Chairman of our society.

  Seize *(to catch–पकड़ना)* Heroin worth two lac rupees *seized* from his office.

  Seize *(surrounded–घेरना)* Akbar's army *seized* the castle of Chittorgarh.

- **Career** *(profession–व्यवसाय)* For better *career* opportunities these days, you need to join computer courses.

  Carrier *(one who carries–ले जाने वाला)* Mosquitoes are *carrier* of virus.

- **Coarse** *(rough–खुरदरा)* Do not use a *coarse* cloth to clean the glasses.

  Course *(line of action–कार्य की दिशा)* A disciplined *course* of action is required to achieve success.

- **Collision** *(clashing–टकराना)* In a *collision* between train and bus, three persons died on the spot.

  Collusion *(secret agreement for an evil plan–षड़यन्त्र)* He planned to execute a robbery in *collusion* with the clerk.

- **Cloth** *(unstitched cloth–बिना सिले कपड़े)* I want to purchase *cloth* for a shirt and a pair of trousers.

  Clothe *(stitched clothes–सिले हुए कपड़े)* I have given my *clothes* to washerman for drycleaning.

- **Capital** *(centre of administration–राजधानी)* Delhi is the *capital* of India.

  Capitol *(Roman temple of Jupiter, US Congress House–एक बिल्डिंग का नाम)* A meeting of US Congress will be held in capitol tomorrow.

- **Defy** *(challenge–चुनौती)* One should not *defy* the orders of one's superiors.

  Deify *(worship a God–ईश्वर की तरह पूजना)* Gandhiji is *deified* by all Indians.

- **Complacent** *(self-satisfied–सन्तुष्ट)* He seems *complacent* with his job and earning.

  Complaisant *(polite–नम्र)* He is a man of very *complaisant* nature.

- **Complement** *(which completes–पूरक)* Husband and wife are **complementary** to each other.

  Compliment *(regards–अभिनन्दन)* Please convey my best *compliments* to your parents.

- **Cautious** *(aware–जागरूक)* I am quite *cautious* of his activities.

  Conscientious *(careful, scrupulous–धार्मिक आस्था)* My mother is very hard working, sincere and *conscientious* lady.

- **Council** *(assembly–सदन)* He was nominated to the *Council* of State.

  Counsel *(advice–सलाह)* He *counsels* in a right way.

- **Credible** *(believable–विश्वास योग्य)* He is not a *credible* person.

  Creditable *(worthy of praise–प्रशंसनीय)* His achievements are indeed *creditable.*

- **Cymbal** *(a musical instrument–मंजीरा)* I like the melodious sound of the *cymbal.*

  Symbol *(sign–चिह्न)* The elephant is the *symbol* of Bahujan Samaj Party.

- **Current** *(present–वर्तमान, ताजा)* AIR airs *current* news.

  Currant *(dried grapes–किशमिश)* I am fond of *currants.*

- **Cite** *(speak–कहना)* He *cited* the example of bravery of Maharana Pratap.

  Site *(location–स्थान)* In my opinion this *site* for the departmental store is commercially viable.

  Sight *(view–दृश्य; vision–दृष्टि)*

  (a) It was a pitiable *sight.*

  (b) Get your eye *sight* checked at the earliest.

- **Caste** *(community–जाति)* He belongs to the scheduled *caste.*

  Cast *(to give–देना)* Please *cast* your votes in favour of me.

- **Cattle** *(animal–पशु)* *Cattle* were grazing in the field.

  Kettle *(vessel–पतीली)* Put the *kettle* on the stove.

- **Corporal** *(pertaining to body–शारीरिक)* *Corporal* punishment are banned now-a-days in all schools and colleges.

  Corporeal *(bodily–शरीर सम्बन्धित)* God has no *corporeal* existence.

- **Cache** *(hidden storage–कोई वस्तु या चीज छिपाना)* A huge arms *cache* was discovered by police.

  Cash *(legal tender– नकद)* I do not accept *cash,* but cheque.

- **Canter** *(a moderate gallop–कदम चाल)* When a horse *canters,* it moves at a speed that is slower than a gallop but faster than a trot.

  Cantor *(singer–गायक)* An official *cantor* who sings liturgical music and leads prayer in a synagogue.

- **Carat** *(unit of weight for precious stones, equal to 200 milligrams–मात्रक)* Diamond is measured in *carat* for purity.

  Caret *(proofreader's insertion mark–छूटा हुआ शब्द दिखाने का चिह्न)* Here the *caret* shows the blank space.

  Carrot *(edible orange root–गाजर)* The *carrot* is a delicious vegetable.

  Karat *(a measure of purity of–सोने की गुणवत्ता की माप)* The ornaments of 24 *karat* are called as purest.

- **Carol** *(Christmas song–गाना)* *Carols* are the religious songs that are sung at Christmas.

  Carrel *(study enclosure–अध्ययन कक्ष)* His seat in the *carrel* was close to book-shelf.

- **Cause** *(generative force–कारण)* Smoking is the biggest *cause* of death.

  Caws *(sounds of crows–कौओं की आवाज)* When a crow *caws* it makes a loud sound.

- **Cent** *(one hundredth part of a dollar–डॉलर का सौवाँ हिस्सा)* I have five *cents* in my pocket.

  Scent *(an aroma–सुगन्ध)* I like the *scent* of freshly baked bread .

  Sent *(dispatched–भेजा)* I have *sent* you a bag of wool.

- **Sciens** *(knowingly–जानते हुए भी)* There is no chance of your getting bail as you were driving *sciens* the people were sleeping on the pavement.

  Sense *(physical abilities of sight, smell, hearing, touch and taste–चेतना)* She has a good *sense* of humour.

- **Cere** *(waxy fleshy covering at the base of the upper beak in some birds–पक्षियों में चोंच का ऊपरी हिस्सा)*–A bird looks lovely with its cere.

  Sear *(to burn its surface with a sudden intense heat–झुलसाना)* Grass fires have *seared* the land near the farming village.

  Seer *(a prophet–महान्)* A *seer* is a person who foretells about the future.

- **Chalk** *(calcareous earthy substance–चाक)* He writes on the board with a *chalk*.

  Chock *(wedge to keep wheels from rolling–रोक)* The small roads are *chock* a block with traffic.

- **Chard** *(spinach-like vegetable–सब्जी)* She is fond of *chard* and relishes it.

  Charred *(burnt–जला हुआ)* In the fire, broke out yesterday, seven persons were *charred* to ash.

- **Chased** *(quickly followed–पीछा करना)* I *chased* the thief for 100 yards.

  Chaste *(virginal–पवित्र)* If you describe a person or their behaviour as *chaste*, you mean that they do not have sex with anyone or they only have sex with their legal partner.

- **Chews** *(masticating–चबाना)* His *chews* made the other people uncomfortable at the dining table.

  Choose *(to select–चुनना)* They will be able to *choose* their own leader through election.

- **Chile** *(a South American country–एक दक्षिण अमेरिकी देश)* *Chile* is a small country.

  Chili *(dried pod of red pepper–मिर्ची)* *Chilies* are used in cooking for taste.

  Chilly *(uncomfortably cool–अत्यधिक ठण्डा)* It was a *chilly* night.

- **Choir** *(church singers–गायक)* A *choir* is a group of people who sing together, for example, in a church or school.

  Quire *(the twentieth part of a ream of paper–कागज के रिम का बीसवाँ हिस्सा)* They require a *quire* essentially.

- **Collar** *(around your neck–कॉलर)* The *collar* of this shirt has worn out.

  Choral *(music sung by a choir–गीत)* His collection of *choral* music is very large and wonderful.

  Coral *(a hard substance formed from the bones of very small sea animals–मूँगा)* *Coral* is available for wearing in the ring.

  Corral *(a space surrounded by a fence where cattle or horses are kept–तबेला)* The *corral* was full of horses.

- **Clack** *(a chattering sound–आवाज)* The windshield wipers *clacked* back and forth.

  Claque *(a group hired to applaud, sycophants–प्रशंसक)* Whenever our team scored a goal the *claque* made a superb clappings which further boosted the spirit of the team.

- **Claus** *(fat, jolly guy with presents–सान्ता क्लॉज)* Santa *Claus* comes to town on every Christmas.

  Clause *(a syntactic construction containing a subject and predicate; a distinct article or provision in a contract, treaty, will, or other formal or legal document–Meyo-mecetn)* According to *Clause* 8 of the contract you have to donate one-fourth of your income to the uplipment of poor children.

  Claws *(big fingernails–पंजा)* The cat tried to cling to the edge by its *claws*.

- **Click** *(ticking noise–क्लिक करना)* You can check your e-mail with a *click* of your mouse.

  Clique *(exclusive group–अलग समूह)* *Clique* is a group of people that spend a lot of time together and seem unfriendly towards people who are not in the group.

- **Climb** *(ascending–चढ़ना)* He *climbed* the stairs.

  Clime *(climate–वातावरण)* She left Britain for the sunnier *climes* of Southern France.

- **Coal** *(black mineral–कोयला)* A number of families even today use *coal* for cooking.

  Cold *(opposite to warm–ठण्डा)* I like tea neither too hot nor too *cold*.

- **Coax** *(persuade–बहलाना)* The government *coaxed* them to giveup their strike by promising them some temporary benefits.

  Cokes *(more than one soft drink–विभिन्न पेय पदार्थ)* Several kinds of *cokes* were available in the party.

  Cocks *(more than one male bird–मुर्गे)* I have two beautiful *cocks*.

  Cox *(a coxwain–नाव में अधिकारी)* In a rowing boat, the *cox* is the person who gives instructions to the rowers.

- **Coddling** *(tenderly treating–स्नेहपूर्ण व्यवहार)* She *codled* her youger daughter madly.

  Codling *(small, unripe apples–छोटे सेब)* I am eating *codling*.

- **Conch** *(spiral shell–शंख)* A *conch* is a shellfish with a large shell.

  Conk *(blow to the head–जोर की ध्वनि)* The dynamo *conked* out so we have no electricity.

- **Coo** *(a soft murmuring sound–धीमी आवाज)* 'Isn't she beautiful?' he *cooed*.

  Coup *(a successful stroke–सच्चा आघात)* He was sentenced to death for his part in the *coup*.

Copes *(gets along with adversity–मुकाबला करना)* It was amazing how my mother *coped* with bringing up three children on less than rupees one thousand a month.

Copse *(a stand of trees–पेड़ों की पंक्ति)* A *copse* is a small group of trees growing very close to each other.

Cops *(police officer–पुलिस अधिकारी)* I do not like the *cops* standing near my house.

- **Creak** *(a short high pitched sound–तीव्र ध्वनि)* The door *creaked* open by the storm.

Creek *(small stream–जल की धारा)* If someone is up the *creek*, he is in a difficult situation.

- **Desert** [a waste track of land रेगिस्तान *(noun)*; to forsake–त्यागना *(verb)*]

(a) Churu is a *desert* area in Rajasthan.

(b) He has *deserted* his wife.

Dessert *(fruit served after dinner–भोजन के बाद फल आहार)* The *dessert* course after dinner was liked by all.

- **Decry** *(to cry down–निन्दा करना)* The Pak Policy of US government is *decried* by Indian Govt.

Descry *(to see dimly–दूर से देखना)* Across the river you can *descry* a hut near the palm tree.

- **Dye** [*to colour–रँगना (verb)*] *Dye* my shirt in sky blue.

Die *(expire–मरना)* He *died* from cholera.

- **Dose** *(quantity of medicine–दवा की खुराक)* I have already taken four *doses* of this medicine by now.

Doze *(sleep–ऊँघना)* You were *dozing* in the class yesterday.

- **Draught** *(a quantity of liquid–तरल की मात्रा)* The patient was given a *draught* of medicine.

Drought *(want of rain–सूखा)* Due to scanty rain whole of the district is in the grip of *drought*.

- **Dam** *(surrounding area to stop flow of water–बाँध)* A *dam* is being build up here for the storage of the rainy water.

Damn *(condemn–निन्दा)* His behaviour is *damned* by all the members of the society.

- **Dear** *(loving–प्रिय)* He is my very *dear* friend.

Deer *(an animal–हिरण)* I saw many *deer* in that forest.

- **Deduce** *(draw conclusion–नतीजा निकालना)* You can't *deduce* such a conclusion of the discussion.

Deduct *(to take something–कम करना)* *Deduct* cash discount 3% and make the payment by tomorrow.

- **Deference** *(respect–आदर)* I treat my elders with due *deference*.

Difference *(dissimilarity–अन्तर)* There was a *difference* of opinion on this point.

- **Decent** *(good–बढ़िया)* Because of his *decent* behaviour he was promoted to the post of General Manager.

  Descent *(coming down–नीचे उतरना)* That hill has a steep *descent* to the south.

  Dissent *(to differ–मतभेद)* He recorded his *dissent* on this proposal.

- **Device** [*plan–योजना (noun)*] He used all *devices* to popularize the game.

  Devise [*to plan– योजना बनाना (verb)*] You are to *devise* a plan to increase the turn over.

- **Duel** *(a fight between two–दो के बीच युद्ध)* There was a *duel* between Dara Singh and Kingkong.

  Dual *(double–दोहरा)* *Dual* system of governance is a bad governance.

- **Disease** *(illness–रोग)* Malaria is a curable *disease.*

  Decease *(death–मृत्यु)* The sudden *decease* of his father forced him to abandon his studies.

- **Dam** *(holds back water–बाँध)* Government is building a *dam* on Yamuna river.

  Damn *(a curse–शाप देना)* Don't be flippant, *damn* it! This is serious.

- **Darn** *(to mend–रफ़ू करना)* She is *darning* the old socks to wear in winter.

  Darne *(a fish steak–मछली पकड़ने का मांस)* He had a *darne* with his lunch.

- **Dine** *(to eat–खाना)* He *dines* alone most nights.

  Dyne *(unit of energy–ऊर्जा को मापने की इकाई)* Three *dyne* energy is needed to pull this pump.

- **Dire** *(desperate–भयानक)* He was in *dire* need of hospital treatment.

  Dyer *(one who dyes–रँगने वाला)* Raju is working as a *dyer.*

- **Do** *(an auxiliary in grammar–करना)*

  (a) They *do* not know me.

  (b) *Do* come tomorrow again.

  Doe *(a female deer–मादा हिरण)* There are several *does* in the forest.

  Dough *(uncooked bread–सना हुआ गीला आटा)* Roll out the *dough* into one large circle.

  DOS *(a computer operating system–कम्प्यूटर संचालन का कार्यक्रम)* He is learning *DOS* now-a-days.

- **Done** *(completed–पूर्ण करना)* I have *done* my job.

  Dun *(a dark colour–गहरा रंग)* Something that is *dun* is a dull grey-brown colour.

- **Eruption** *(bursting out–फटना)* There was an *eruption* of volcano near Gujarat border.

  Irruption *(invasion–आक्रमण)* The *irruption* of Mughals destroyed the glory of Rajput empire.

- **Emerge** *(to come out– बाहर आना)* He *emerged* successfully out of the miserable circumstances.

  Immerge *(to plunge into–डूबना)* He is *immerged* in mythological thoughts.

- **Eminent** *(distinguish–विशिष्ट)* Indira Gandhi was an *eminent* politician.

  Imminent *(impending–तुरन्त)* Indian forces are always ready to face any *imminent* attack of Pakistan.

- **Eligible** *(fit to be chosen–योग्य)* He is *eligible* for the post.

  Illegible *(that which cannot be read–अपठनीय)* His writing is *illegible.*

- **Earn** *(to come to deserve–कमाना)* *Companies must earn a reputation for honesty.*

  Urn *(a jar–बर्तन)*

  (a) An *urn* is a container in which a dead person's ashes are kept.

  (b) An *urn* is a metal container used for making a large quantity of tea or coffee and keeping it hot.

- **Elude** *(to escape from–बचाना)* He *eluded* the police for ten years.

  Allude *(refer–संकेत करना)* She also *alluded* to her rival's post marital troubles.

- **Epic** *(a narrative poem or story–काव्य)* Like 'Gone with the Wind' it's an unashamed *epic* romance.

  Epoch *(a noteworthy period in history–ऐतिहासिक काल)* The birth of Christ was the beginning of a major *epoch* of world history.

- **Eunuchs** *(a castrated male–हिजड़ा)* In India *eunuchs* are turning to politics.

  Unix *(operating system–ऑपरेटिंग सिस्टम)* *Unix* is an operating system for computers.

- **Ewe** *(female sheep–मादा भेड़)* A *ewe* is an adult female sheep.

  Yew *(a type of tree–पेड़)* *Yew* is an evergreen tree which has sharp leaves.

  You *(the second person–तुम)* *You* are a good fellow.

- **Eyelet** *(small hole for laces–छोटे छिद्र)* My shoes have eight *eyelets.*

  Islet *(small island–छोटा द्वीप)* An *islet* is a small *island.*

- **Ere** *(before–पूर्व)* Take the water *ere* the clock strikes four.

  Err *(to make a mistake–गलती या भूल करना)* If you make a mistake be sure to carry it out if he *errs* again.

  Heir *(one who will inherit–वारिस)* The younger prince was declared *heir* to the throne.

- **Facility** *(ease, opportunity–सुविधा)* *Facility* of STD is also available in this hotel.

  Felicity *(happiness–प्रसन्नता)* True *felicity* can't be enjoyed by a dishonest man.

- **Foul** *(unfair–अनुचित)* One can't achieve true success through *foul* means.

  Fowl *(a bird–पक्षी)* He is fond of *fowl's* meat.

- **Find** *(to get–पाना)* Go there you will *find* a tree near the river.

  Fined *(to charge–जुर्माना)* The court *fined* him Rs 20,000 for the offence.

- **Floor** *(surface–फर्श)* Clean the *floor* with dettol and water.

  Flour *(wheat meal–आटा)* He has a *flour* mill.

- **Forth** *(onward–आगे आना)* He alone came *forth* to assist that poor lady.

  Fourth *(ordinal of four–चौथा)* April is the *fourth* month of the year.

- **Farther** *(more distant–दूर)* Delhi is *farther* from Alwar in comparison to Jaipur.

  Further *(next–आगे)* Please settle the case without any *further* delay.

- **Faint** *(to swoon–बेहोश होना)* She *fainted* after taking wine yesterday .

  Feint *(pretention–दिखावा)* She made a *feint* of reading the books.

- **Fain** *(gladly–खुशी से)* She would *fain* on seeing me.

  Feign *(pretend–दिखावा)* When his boss scolded him, he *feigned* as a deaf.

- **Fair** *(a show, pure–मेला, पवित्र)* (a) Let us go to the *fair.*

  (b) I believe in using *fair* means to achieve the target.

  Fare *(cost of conveying passengers–किराया)* A strike was called by the truckers demanding hike in minimum *fare.*

- **Feat** *(courageous work–साहसिक कार्य)* A racing car is an extraordinary *feat* of engineering.

  Feet *(plural of foot–पाँव)* Do not put your *feet* on the table.

- **Forego** *(go before–पहले जाना)* We have already discussed this point in *foregoing* lessons.

  Forgo *(to let go–त्याग देना)* I cannot *forgo* my rights.

- **Fairy** *(imaginary magic person–जादूगर)* *Fairies* are often represented as small people with wings.

  Ferry *(river-crossing boat–छोटी नाव)* They crossed the river by *ferry.*

- **Fey** *(whimsical–सनकी)*

  (a) Her *fey* charm and eccentric ways were legendary.

  (b) If you describe someone as *fey*, you mean that they behave in a shy, childish, or unpredictable way, and you are often suggesting that this is unnatural or insincere.

  Fays *(more than one fairy–एक से अधिक छोटे जीव)* The *fays* were out dancing.

- **Faze** *(to stun–आश्चर्य)* He was *fazed* to see such a big hall.

  Phase *(state of change–परिवर्तन की स्थिति)* The crisis is entering a crucial *phase.*

- **Ferrate** *(a salt containing iron and oxygen)* He was making *ferrate* in the lab.

  Ferret *(a domesticated pole cat–छोटी बिल्ली)* A *ferret* is a small fierce animal which is used for hunting rabbits and rats.

- **Feted** *(celebrated–कार्य करने वाला)* If someone is *feted*, they are celebrated, welcomed or admired by the public.

  Fetid *(stinking–बदबूदार)* *Fetid* water or air contains a very unpleasant and harmful smell.

- **Few** *(not many–थोड़ा)* I gave a dinner party for a *few* close friends.

  Phew *(expression of relief–राहत का भाव)* *Phew*! What a relief I am getting now!

- **File** *(a folder for holding papers–फाइल)* Please put this paper in a *file*.

  Phial *(a small glass bottle–छोटी बोतल)* A *phial* is a small tube shaped glass bottle used to hold medicine.

- **Finish** *(to complete–समाप्त)* I will *finish* my work by tomorrow.

  Finnish *(from Finland–फिनलैण्ड के निवासी)* *Finnish* is the language spoken in Finland.

- **Flair** *(verve, talent–प्रवृत्ति)* If you have a *flair* for a particular thing, you have a natural ability to do it well.

  Flare *(to spread–बढ़ाना)* Camp fire *flares* like beacons in the dark.

- **Flea** *(parasitic insect–मक्खी)* A *flea* feeds on the blood of humans or animals.

  Flee *(to run away–भाग जाना)* He tried to *flee* from the sight, but he was caught.

- **Flecks** *(many tiny specks–छोटा धब्बा जैसा)* His hair is dark grey with *flecks* of ginger.

  Flex *(to bend–मोड़)* He slowly *flexed* his muscles and tried to stand.

- **Flew** *(past tense of fly–उड़ाना)* He *flew* many kites yesterday.

  Flu *(short for influenza–बुखार)* I got *flu* day before yesterday.

  Flue *(chimney pipe–चिमनी पाइप)* The *flue* of the chimney required to be changed.

- **Floe** *(sheet of floating ice–तैरती बर्फ की परत)* Ice *floe* is a large area of ice floating in the sea.

  Flow *(to glide along–बहना)* A stream *flowed* gently down into the valley.

- **For** *(in place of–के लिए)* It is enough *for* me.

  Fore *(in front–सामने)* There is no direct damage in the *fore* part of the ship.

  Four *(number after three–चार)* I have *four* pens.

- **Frees** *(releasing–छोड़ना)* He *frees* the bird from the cage.

  Freeze *(very cold–ठण्डा)*

  (a) The trees are damaged by a *freeze* in December.

  (b) We want the government to *freeze* the prices.

  Frieze *(a wall decoration–दीवार सजाने की वस्तु)* A *frieze* is a decoration high up on the walls of a room or just under the roof of a building. It consists of a long panel of carving or a long strip of paper with a picture or pattern on it.

- **Friar** *(a monk–तपस्वी)* He is a *friar*.

  Fryer *(a utensil–बर्तन)* A *fryer* is a type of deep pan which is used to fry food in hot oil.

- **Gild** *(thin coating of metal–धातु का पत्तर चढ़ाना)* *Gilded* ornaments look more beautiful than the original.

  Guild *(group of same profession–संघ)* Now-a-days all the workers have organized themselves into *guilds*.

- **Gage** *(security–जमानत)* I do not lend without sufficient *gage*.

  Gaze *(to look attentively–एकटक देखना)* She stood *gazing* at herself in the mirror.

- **Gait** *(manner of walk–चाल)* That model girl has a graceful and sexy *gait.*

  Gate *(large door–दरवाजा)* You should not enter through the main *gate.*

- **Goal** *(aim–उद्‌देश्य)* To achieve this *goal* you are to work hard.

  Gaol *(jail–जेल में)* He has been to *gaol* earlier also for some crime.

- **Gaff** *(a barbed spear–भाला)* A *gaff* is a pole with a point or hook at one end, which is used for catching large fish.

  Gaffe *(a stupid mistake–मूर्खतापूर्ण गलती)* He made an embarrassing *gaffe* at the convention last weekend.

- **Galley** *(ship's kitchen–जहाज की रसोई)* The *galley* of this ship is well maintained and full of eatables.

  Gally *(to frighten or terrify–डराना)* He tried to *gally* the child with a mask of demon.

- **Gilt** *(gold plated–सोने की परत चढ़ाना)* This is a *gilt* ornament .

  Guilt *(culpable–दोषी)* You aren't convinced of Mr Charles' *guilt.*

- **Gnawed** *(chewed–चबाना)* He *gnawed* his long fingernail.

  Nod *(head tilting–सर हिलाना)* 'Are you fine?' I asked. She *nodded* and smiled.

- **Gnu** *(African deer–अफ्रीकन हिरन)* I saw *gnu* in the zoo.

  Knew *(past tense of know–जानना)* He *knew* me well.

  New *(not old–नया)* Nano is *newer* in the market.

- **Gored** *(pierced by an animal's horns–जानवर द्वारा सींग घोंप देना)* He was *gored* to death in front of his family.

  Gourd *(fleshy fruit with hard skin–फल)* I like *gourd* very much.

- **Gorilla** *(large ape–गोरिल्ला)* *Gorilla* has long arm, black fur and a black face.

  Guerrilla *(irregular soldier–अनियमित सिपाही)* The *guerrillas* threatened to kill their hostages.

- **Grade** *(rank–श्रेणी)* He belongs to *grade* one service.

  Grayed *(turned gray–ग्रे रंग)* I like *grayed* walls.

- **Graft** *(to attach–जोड़ना)* The top layer of skin has to be *grafted* on to the burns.

  Graphed *(plotted–ग्राफ बनाना)* You can see a *graphed* diagram of the progress made by the country in population control.

- **Grate** *(a lattice–जाली)* (a) A wood fire burned in the *grate.*

  (b) A *grate* is a frame-work of metal bars in a fireplace, which holds the coal or wood.

  Great *(extremely good–बड़ा, महान्)* Gandhiji was a *great* man.

- **Grill** *(to sear cook–पकाना)*

  (a) Place the omelette under a gentle *grill.*

  (b) A *grill* is a flat frame of metal bars on which food can be cooked over fire.

  Grille *(an iron gate–लोहे की जाली)* *Grille* is used to protect anything from the public.

- **Groan** *(a long low sound uttered in pain–कराहना)* He opened his eyes and he began to *groan* with pain.

  Grown *(has gotten larger–बड़ा होना, बढ़ना)* Dad, I am *grown*, I know what I am doing.
- **Guise** *(appearance–दिखना)* She presented the dance in the *guise* of a rabbit.

  Guys *(man–व्यक्ति)* Hi, *guys*. You are doing well.
- **Hail** *(frozen rain–ओले)* (a) It is *hailing*.

  (b) It *hailed* yesterday.

  Hale *(healthy–स्वस्थ)* May God keep you *hale* and healthy.
- **Horde** *(a gang–समूह)* A *horde* of mischievous students attacked the shop-keepers.

  Hoard *(to store–एकत्र करना)* *Hoarding* of sugar beyond the prescribed limit is an offence.
- **Hair** *(dry elastic filaments growing from the skin–बाल)* She has black *hair*.

  Heir *(successor–उत्तराधिकारी)* He is an *heir* apparent to the throne.
- **Hurt** *(injury–चोट)* Your comments can *hurt* her feelings.

  Hart *(a male deer–हिरण)* I have a beautiful pair of *harts*.

  Heart *(an organ in the body–दिल)* He is suffering from *heart* disease.
- **Humane** *(kind–दयालु)* UNO has advised its member countries to mete out *humane* treatment to prisoners of war.

  Human *(pertaining to mankind–मनुष्यता से सम्बद्ध)* You will find almost the same *human* nature everywhere.
- **Heel** *(part of shoe–जूते की एड़ी)* The *heels* of my shoes are pinching.

  Heal *(to cure–अच्छा होना)* This medicine will help you in quick *healing*.
- **Hole** *(a burrow–छेद)* A serpent lives in this *hole*.

  Whole *(complete–सम्पूर्ण)* He ate *whole* of the breakfast.
- **Hall** *(a large room–बड़ा कमरा)* He has hired a *hall* for the concert.

  Haul *(a pull with force–उठाना)*

  (a) If you *haul* something which is heavy or difficult to move, you move it using a lot of effort.

  (b) A crane had to be used to *haul* the car out of the stream.

  (c) If someone is *hauled* before a court or someone in authority, they are made to appear before them because they are accused of having done something wrong.

  (d) He was *hauled* before the managing director and fired.
- **Hammock** *(rope bed–रस्सी वाली खाट)* A *hammock* is a piece of strong cloth or netting which is hung between two supports and used as a bed.

  Hummock *(low, rounded hill–छोटी पहाड़ी)* A *hummock* is a small raised area of ground, like a very small hill.

- **Hangar** *(garage for airplanes—हवाई जहाज खड़ा करने का स्थान)* Some repairing is going on in the *hangar* of the airport.

  Hanger *(from which things hang—लटकाने वाला)* I want to purchase a coat *hanger.*
- **Ho** *(an expression of admiration or surprise—हो हो)* *Ho* ! you are here.

  Hoe *(a garden tool—औजार)* Today he is *hoeing* in the vineyard.
- **He'll** *(contraction of 'he will')* *He'll* come tomorrow.

  Heal *(to make well—घाव करना)* Therapies like acupuncture do work and many people have been *healed* by them.

  Hill *(smaller than a mountain—छोटी पहाड़ी)* There is a temple on that *hill.*

  Heel *(hind part of foot—एड़ी)* I need a pair of shoes with high *heel.*
- **Hear** *(to listen—सुनना)* I *hear* his voice.

  Here *(at this location—यहाँ)* Come here.
- **Heard** *(listened to—सुनना)* I *heard* a strange sound yesterday in the night.

  Herd *(a group of animals—भीड़)* They are individuals. They will not follow the **herd**.
- **Hi** *(greetings—हाय)* '*Hi* Luis', she said.

  High *(way up—ऊँचा)* I looked down from the *high* window.
- **Heroin** *(narcotic—अफीम)* *Heroin* is a powdery illegal drug.

  Heroine *(female actor—अभिनेत्री)* My favourite *heroine* is Deepika Padukone.
- **Hew** *(to chop—काटना)* He fell, peeled and *hewed* his own timber.

  Hue *(a color—रंग)* The same *hue* will look different in different light.
- **Higher** *(farther up—ऊँचा)* He has gone to USA for *higher* studies.

  Hire *(to employ—किराए पर लेना)* Cars are available for *hire.*
- **Him** *(pronoun—उसका)* I know *him.*

  Hymn *(religious song—धार्मिक गीत)* I like singing *hymns.*
- **Hoarse** *(rough voice—कर्कश ध्वनि)* His voice is *hoarse.*

  Horse *(equine—घोड़ा)* He has a black *horse.*
- **Hold** *(to grip—पकड़ना)* *Hold* the bucket please.

  Holed *(full of holes—छिद्रिल)* The wall seems to be *holed* by a drill.
- **Holy** *(with religious significance—पवित्र)* Ayodhya is a *holy* place for the Hindus.

  Wholly *(completely—पूर्णतया)* This approach for the urban area is *wholly* inadequate.
- **Hostel** *(residence of students—छात्रावास)* He is living in the college *hostel.*

  Hostile *(unfriendly—अमित्र)* Pakistan has not yet changed its *hostile* attitude towards India.
- **Idle** *(indolent—निकम्मा)* An *idle* man can't make any progress.

  Ideal *(visionary—आदर्श)* My teacher Mr Shrivastava is an *ideal* for me.

  Idol *(an image of a deity—मूर्ति)* A section of the Hindus believe in *idol* worship.

- **Ingenious** *(clever–चतुर)* He is an *ingenious* engineer.

  Ingenuous *(simple–सीधा)* His *ingenuous* attitude is liked by all.
- **Incite** *(to provoke–उत्तेजित करना)* His arrogant behaviour *incited* me a lot.

  Insight *(a clear vision–स्पष्ट देखना)* Everyone knows the *insight* story of this murder.
- **Indite** *(to compose–रचना)* Though he *indited* the letter carefully, yet it was not liked by the Chairman.

  Indict *(to accuse–दोषारोपण करना)* He was *indicted* for theft and murder.
- **In** *(expressing inclusion–में)* He is *in* the room.

  Inn *(hotel–होटल)* This is a well maintained *inn*.
- **Inc.** *(short for incorporated–समायोजित)* *Inc.* is an abbreviation for 'Incorporated' when it is used after a company's name.

  Ink *(writing fluid–स्याही)* I have an *ink* pen.
- **It's** *(contraction of 'it is')* *It's* a large hotel.

  Its *(possessive pronoun)* I know *its* true position.
- **Jealous** *(envious–ईर्ष्यालु)* He is not liked by anybody because of his *jealous* nature.

  Zealous *(enthusiastic–उत्साही)* She is very *zealous* about her new book.
- **Jewel** *(precious stone–बहुमूल्य रत्न)* This watch contains many *jewels*.

  Joule *(unit of energy measure–ऊर्जा की इकाई)* In Physics *joule* is a unit of energy or work.
- **Juggler** *(one who juggles–जादूगर)* He is a good *juggler*.

  Jugular *(artery to head–सर की नस)*

  (a) A *jugular* or *jugular* vein is one of the three important veins in your neck that carry blood from your head back to your heart.

  (b) If you say that someone went for the *jugular*, you mean that they strongly attacked another person's weakest points in order to harm them.
- **Naughty** *(mischievous–शैतान)* She is a *naughty* girl.

  Knotty *(difficult–कठिन)* This was indeed a *knotty* problem.
- **Knap** *(crest of a hill; break with a hammer–ऊँची चोटी, हथौड़े से तोड़ना)* We unfurled the flag at the *knap* of the hill at 6.30 p.m. He *knapped* the glass box to uncountable pieces.

  Nap *(a short sleep–झपकी)* You should use your lunch hour to have a *nap* in your chair.
- **Knead** *(working bread dough–गूँथना)*

  (a) He *kneaded* the mixture on a floured surface.

  (b) She felt him *knead* the aching muscles.

  Need *(must have–आवश्यकता)* He *needs* your help.

- **Knight** *(chivalrous man–बहादुर)* He was *knighted* on the queens birthday.

  Night *(darkness–रात)* *Night* comes after day.

- **Knit** *(interlocking loops of yarn–बुनना)* She has already started *knitting* baby sweators.

  Nit *(louse egg–जूँ के अण्डे)*

  (a) *Nits* are the eggs of insects called lice which live in people's hair.

  (b) If you refer to someone as a *nit*, you think they are stupid or silly.

  (c) I'd rather leave the business than working with such a *nit*.

- **Knob** *(handle–हैण्डिल का सिरा)* He turned the *knob* and pushed against the door.

  Nob *(rich person–धनी व्यक्ति)* The *nobs*, who live in that big house, are very generous.

- **Knock** *(to rap–ठोकना)* (a) Someone had *knocked* him unconscious.
  (b) She heard a *knock* at the front door.

  Nock *(a notch in an arrow–तीर का सिरा जैसा)* *Noch* is a 'V' shape cut or indentation in an edge or across a surface.

- **Knot** *(fastening in cord–गाँठ)* He tied a *knot* at the end of the lace.

  Naught *(or nought is zero–शून्य)* Sales rose by *nought* point four per cent last month.

  Not *(negation–नहीं)* He was *not* present in the party.

- **Know** *(to possess knowledge–जानना)* I *know* him.

  No *(negation–नहीं)* I have *no* pen.

- **Knows** *(to recognize–जानना)* He *knows* my father.

  Nose *(a body part on face–नाक)* My *nose* is hurting.

- **Lightening** *(make lighter–हल्का करना)* We had appealed to the Court for *lightening* the punishment, but of no avail.

  Lightning *(electric discharge in clouds–बिजली चमकना)* There was occasional *lightning* in the sky last night.

- **Loath** *(unwilling–इच्छा विरुद्ध)* Nothing *loath* he did, as he was saying.

  Loathe *(to dislike greatly–घृणा करना)* I *loathe* her dressing pattern and arrogant way of talking.

- **Latter** *(antonym of former–बाद में आने वाला)* Between Ram and Shyam, the *latter* (Shyam) is a diligent student.

  Later *(comparative of late–देरी से आने वाला)* He came *later* than his friend.

- **Lose** *(to part with–खोना)* Where did you *lose* your briefcase?

  Loose *(to slack–ढ़ीला करना)* He was wearing a *loose* cotton shirt.

- **Lesson** *(chapter–पाठ)* Learn your *lesson* well.

  Lessen *(to make less–कम करना)* Even this medicine has not *lessen* my pain.

- **Last** *(antonym to first–अन्तिम)* Bahadur Shah was the *last* Emperor of India.

  Latest *(superlative of late–ताजा)* She always prefers *latest* design clothes.

- **Lacks** *(does not have–नहीं होना)* He *lacks* the judgement and political acumen for the post of General Manager.

  Lax *(loose discipline–अनुशासन में कमी)* One of the point of contention is the *lax* security for the airport personnel.

- **Lain** *(past tense of lay or lie–लेटना)* He has *lain* there for sometime.

  Lane *(narrow road–तंग गली)* Shyam lives at the end of the *lane*.

- **Lam** *(head long flight–भागना)*

  (a) He was on the *lam* for seven years.

  (b) If someone is on the *lam* or if they go on the *lam*, they are trying to escape or hide from someone such as the police or an enemy.

  Lamb *(baby sheep–भेड़ का बच्चा)* A *lamb* is a young sheep.

- **Lay** *(to recline–समर्पण)* *Lay* a sheet of paper on the floor.

  Lei *(a flower necklace–फूलों का हार)* A garland made of flowers, feathers, shells, etc, often given as a symbol of affection is a *lei*.

- **Lea** *(a meadow–घास का मैदान)* They live in a hut constructed in the *lea*.

  Lee *(downwind–नीची हवा)* The *lee* of a place is the shelter that it gives from the wind or bad weather.

  Lease *(rented–किराए पर)* She *leased* out her bungalow at a good rent.

- **Leach** *(a dish consisting of sliced meat, eggs, fruits, and spices in jelly etc–खाने की डिश)* She made a delicious *leach*.

  Leech *(sucking parasite–छोटा जन्तु)*

  (a) A *leech* is a small animal which looks like a worm and lives in water.

  (b) *Leeches* feed by attaching themselves to other animals and sucking their blood.

  (c) If you describe someone as a *leech*, you disapprove of them because they deliberately depend on other people, often making money out of them.

  (d) They're just a bunch of *leeches* cadging off others.

- **Leak** *(accidental escape of liquid–रिसना)* The roof is *leaking*.

  Leek *(variety of onion–प्याज)* I like *leek* vegetables.

- **Lean** *(angle of repose–झुकना)* They stopped to *lean* over the gate.

  Lien *(a claim on property–अधिकार)* Please mark my *lien* over the property.

- **Liar** *(tells falsehoods–झूठा)* He is a *liar* and a cheat.

  Lyre *(stringed instrument–यन्त्र)* A *lyre* is a stringed instrument that looks like a harp.

- **Lichen** *(a fungus–एक प्रकार का पौधा)* *Lichen* is a group of tiny plants like moss and grows on the surface of things such as rocks, trees and walls.

  Liken *(to compare–तुलना करना)*

  (a) If you *liken* one thing or person to another thing or person, you say that they are similar.

  (b) The pain is often *likened* to being drilled through the side of the head.

- **Lie** *(an untruth–झूठ)* He is telling a *lie*.

  Lieu *(instead–बजाय)* He gave his TV to the landlord in *lieu* of rent.
- **Loo** *(British toilet–ब्रिटिश टॉयलेट)* I asked if I could go to the *loo*.

  Lou *(short for Louis)* Where has *lou* gone so early?

  Low *(not high–नीचा)* He put it down on the *low* table.
- **Limb** *(tree branch–पेड़ की शाखा)*

  (a) The entire structure was hanging from the *limb* of an enormous leafy tree.

  (b) She would be able to stretch out her cramped *limbs* for some time.

  Limn *(illuminate–चमकना)* His face was *limned* in the dim glow from the match.
- **Links** *(pieces of chain–चेन के टुकड़े)* I have no *links* with that man.

  Lynx *(a wild animal similar to a large cat–बड़ी बिल्ली जैसा)* *Lynx* is a wild animal.
- **Literal** *(taking words in their primary sense–वास्तविक)* He was saying no more than the *literal* truth.

  Littoral *(having to do with the shore–किनारा)* In Geography, the *littoral* means the coast.
- **Load** *(cargo–सामान)* I have just *loaded* my truck up.

  Lowed *(a cow mooed–रम्भाना)* The cow *lowed* in agony.
- **Loan** *(allow to borrow–ऋण)* She has taken *loan* from a bank.

  Lone *(by itself–अकेला)* He was shot by a *lone* gunmen.
- **Loch** *(a lake–नहर)* A *loch* is a large area of water that is almost surrounded by land.

  Lock *(a security device–ताला)* I need a good *lock*.
- **Loot** *(ill-gotten gains–लूटना)* The trouble began when the students began the *looting* of shops.

  Lute *(stringed instrument–यन्त्र)* A *lute* is a stringed instrument with a rounded body that is quite like a guitar and is played with the fingers.
- **Lumbar** *(lower part of back–पीठ का नीचे का हिस्सा)* *Lumbar* support is very important if you are driving a long way.

  Lumber *(dimensional wood–लकड़ी)*

  (a) *noun* : It was made of soft *lumber*.

  (b) *verb* : He turned and *lumbered* back to his chair.
- **Meat** *(flesh–मांस)* I don't like eating *meat*.

  Meet *(to assemble–मिलना)* She came here only to *meet* me.
- **Mead** *(a meadow–चारागाह)* I met a beautiful girl in the *mead* yesterday.

  Meed *(reward–प्रतिफल)* Kalidas has got a universal *meed* of praise.
- **Metal** *(iron, brass etc–धातु)* Silver is a white *metal*.

  Mettle *(spirit, courage–साहस)* Our leaders have no *mettle* to fight against corruption.

- **Metre** *(poetic rhythm–छन्द)* Can you tell me, in what *metre* Shelley's 'Skylark' is written.

  Meter *(a measuring instrument =100 cm, मीटर)* One *meter* is equal to hundred centimetres.

- **Minor** *(under age–छोटा, नाबालिग)* *Minors* are not allowed to open current accounts in banks.

  Miner *(one who works in mine–खान में काम करने वाला)* He is a *miner*, works in a coal mine.

- **Moat** *(a ditch surrounding a castle–खाई)* There is a bridge over the *moat* near main gate.

  Mote *(a particle of dust–धूल का कण)* You cannot see small *mote* by naked eyes.

- **Monetary** *(pertaining to money–मुद्रा सम्बन्धित)* Have you any book on *monetary* theory ?

  Monitory *(giving advice– सलाह देना)* He acted against the *monitory* advise of his friends and so failed.

- **Male** *(opposite to female–पुरुष)* A *male* candidate can't be posted against the post reserved for a woman.

  Mail *(post–डाक)* Have you received my *mail* ?

- **Mite** *(small thing–अल्प मात्रा)* He contributed his *mite* for the service of mankind.

  Might *(strength–शक्ति)* Your *might* will be tested in battle against the foreign power.

  Might *(past of may–सकना)* He told me that he *might* come to attend the function.

- **Marry** *(to get married–विवाह करना)* I want to *marry* your sister.

  Merry *(joyous–आनन्द करना)* Don't lose heart and be *merry*.

- **Main** *(chief–मुख्य)* Ramesh is the *main* culprit in the bank robbery.

  Mane *(long hair of an animal's neck–गर्दन के बाल)* His horse had a fine *mane*.

- **Marshal** *(a military officer–मार्शल)* He is a *marshal* of the Court.

  Martial *(war like–युद्ध जैसा)* He has *martial* spirit and courage to fight in odd circumstances.

- **Maize** *(corn–मक्का)* I like to eat *maize* cake.

  Maze *(labyrinth–घुमाव)* This castle has many hidden *mazes*.

- **Mach** *(speed of sound–ध्वनि की गति)* *Mach* is used as a unit of measurement in stating the speed of a moving object in relation to the speed of sound. For example, if an aircraft is travelling at *Mach* 1, it is travelling at exactly the speed of sound.

  Mock *(parody–व्यंग्य)* I thought you were *mocking* me.

- **Made** *(accomplished–बनाया)* Our table is *made* of wood.

  Maid *(woman servant–नौकरानी)* Kanta is our *maid*.

- **Mall** *(a large shopping area–सम्पूर्ण शॉपिंग की जगह)* Presently *malls* are convenient medium of shopping.

  Maul *(savage–क्रूर)* He had been *mauled* by a tiger.

  Moll *(gangster's girlfriend–महिला मित्र)* She is the *moll* of the don.

- **Manner** *(method–तरीका)* (a) She smiled in a friendly *manner*.

  (b) I am a professional and I have to conduct myself in a professional *manner*.

  Manor *(lord's house or a large private house–बड़ा निजी घराना)* Thieves broke into the *manor* at night.

- **Marc** *(coarse brandy–ब्राण्डी)* I don't like the taste of *marc*.

  Mark *(a sign–निशान)* He made some peculiar *marks* with a pen.

- **Marquee** *(a rooflike projection over a theatre entrance–बड़ा टैण्ट)*

  (a) A *marquee* is a large tent which is used at a fair, garden party, or other outdoor event, usually for eating and drinking in.

  (b) A *marquee* is a cover over the entrance of a building, for example a hotel or a theatre.

  Marquis *(title of nobility–समानता का द्योतक)* *Marquis* Harry came to the king's Court.

- **Marshal** *(to organise–संयोजक)* He was *marshalling* the teachers and other officials showing them where to go.

  Martial *(warlike–युद्ध समान स्थिति)* The newspapers were banned during **martial** regime.

- **Massed** *(grouped together–समूह)* He could not escape the *massed* ranks of newsmen.

  Mast *(sail pole–जहाज का मस्तूल)* The *mast* of a boat are the tall upright poles that support its sails.

- **Mews** *(stables–घुड़शाला)* The house is in a secluded *mews*.

  Muse *(creative inspiration–प्रेरणा)* (a) *noun* : Once she was a nude model and *muse* to French artist Henri.

  (b) (think) *verb* : Many scholars *muse* on the role of President in Indian polity.

- **Mince** *(chop finely–टुकड़े करना)* I'll buy lean meat and *mince* it myself.

  Mints *(aromatic candies–सुगन्धित खाद्य)* *Mint* is a herb with fresh tasting leaves.

- **Mind** *(thinking unit–मस्तिष्क)* *Mind* your business please.

  Mined *(looked for ore–खनिज कार्य)* The pit was shut down because it hadn't enough that can be *mined* economically.

- **Missal** *(hymn book–किताब)* *Missal* is a book containing the service of the mass for the whole year; *loosely* a Roman Catholic book of prayers.

  Missile *(projectile–मिसाइल)* The football supporters began throwing *missiles* one of which is the captain of the rival team.

- **Mist** *(fog–कोहरा)* The *mist* made the flying impossible.

  Missed *(not hit–चुकना)* He scored four of the goals but *missed* a penalty.

- **Moan** *(to groan–कराहना)* She gave a low choking *moan* and began to tremble.

  Mown *(the lawn is freshly cut–घास काटना)* He has *mown* the lawn today itself.

- **Mood** *(emotional state–मानसिक स्थिति)* She is in a jolly *mood* today.

  Mooed *(what the loquacious cow did–गाय की ध्वनि)* When cattle especially cows *moo*, they make a long low sound that cattle typically make.

- **Moor** *(swampy coastland; to anchor–रुकना, बाँधना)* I decided to *moor* near some tourist boats.

  More *(additional–अपेक्षाकृत अधिक)* I need some *more* rice.

- **Moose** *(a large elk–बड़ा हिरण)* *Moose* are large type of deer having big flat horns.

  Mousse *(dessert of whipped cream and eggs भोजनोपरान्त मिष्ठान)* *Mousse* is a sweet light after food made from nutritious eggs and cream.

- **Morning** *(first part of the day–प्रात:काल)* I get up early in the *morning*.

  Mourning *(remembering the dead–मृतक हेतु प्रार्थना)* On the death of Benazir Bhutto the whole of Pakistan was in the *mourning*.

- **Muscle** *(fibrous, contracting tissue–मांसपेशी)* He is doing a lot of exercises to keep his *muscles* strong.

  Mussel *(a kind of mollusc that is edible–घोंघा जो खाया जा सकता है)* Fresh water *mussels* are really tasty after being cooked.

- **Mussed** *(made messy–गड़बड़ी)* His clothes are all *mussed* up.

  Must *(required–आवश्यक)* You *must* go there to get his support.

- **Mustard** *(plant with oily ungent seeds–सरसों)* The fish is fried in *mustard* oil.

  Mustered *(assembled for roll call–एकत्र होना)* He travelled throughout India to *muster* support for his movement.

- **Nice** *(good–अच्छा)* She is a *nice* and beautiful girl.

  Niece *(daughter of brother–भतीजी)* I am to attend the marriage of my *niece* positively.

- **Naval** *(pertaining to ships and the sea–जहाज से सम्बन्धित)* He is a captain in *naval* forces.

  Navel *(pertaining to the belly button–नाभिक)* There is a black mole near her *navel*.

- **Nay** *(no–नहीं)* The Rajya Sabha can merely say yea or *nay* to such a bill.

  Neigh *(a horse's cry–हिनहिनाना)* The horse gave a loud *neigh*.

- **Our** *(plural of 'my'–हमारा)* This is *our* house.

  Hour *(a period of time–घण्टा)* I have been waiting for you for half an *hour*.

- **Oar** *(used for rowing a boat–नाव का डण्डा)* Life without aim is like a boat without an *oar*.

  Ore *(mineral from which metal can be extracted–खनिज)* Iron is extracted from its *ore* by melting.

- **Ordinance** *(a rule–अध्यादेश)* The President has promulgated an *ordinance* for administering the minority community.

  Ordnance *(gun–युद्ध सामग्री)* There is an *ordnance* factory in Jamshedpur of Jharkhand.

- **Oohs** *(People say 'ooh' when they are surprized, looking forward to something, or find something pleasant or unpleasant. (INFORMAL–ऊह)*

  '*Ooh* dear me, that's a bit of a racist comment isn't it.'... 'Red? Ooh how nice.'

  Ooze *(बाहर निकलना)*

  (a) The lava will just ooze gently out of the crater...

  (b) The wounds may heal cleanly or they may ooze a clear liquid.

  (c) When a thick or sticky liquid *oozes* from something or when something *oozes* it, the liquid flows slowly and in small quantities.

- **Overdo** *(carried to excess–अधिक)* It is important never to *overdo* new exercises.

  Overdue *(past time for payment or some action–देर)* The meeting is long *overdue*.

- **Pray** *(entreat–प्रार्थना)* I *pray* to God every day.

  Prey *(hunt–शिकार)* Do not *prey* upon the innocent animals.

- **Principal** *(head of school or college–प्राचार्य)* Sh RC Jha is the new *principal* of our college.

  Principle *(rule–सिद्धान्त)* Do you understand anything about the *principles* of justice.

- **Prophecy** *(noun-foretold–भविष्यवाणी)* It is his *prophecy* that America will not attack Iraq.

  Prophesy *(verb-to foretell–भविष्यवाणी)* He *prophesied* that Iraq would attack Kuwait.

- **Proffer** *(offer–प्रस्ताव)* Many lucrative proposals were *proffered* to him for acceptance.

  Prefer *(like–पसन्द)* I *prefer* coffee to tea.

- **Practice** *(noun-constant use in an art–अभ्यास)* *Practice* makes a man perfect.

  Practise *(verb-to perform habitually–अभ्यास करना)* Don't preach but *practise*.

- **Plain** *(easy, simple–साधारण)* One should try to write his thoughts in *plain* language.

  Plane *(to level–समकक्ष करना)* I use cream to *plane* my hair.

- **Peel** *(to remove the skin–छीलना)* You cannot eat a banana without *peeling* it.

  Peal *(sound of thunder or bells–घण्टियों की ध्वनि)* I am hearing *peals* of trumpets.

- **Pare** *(to trim–टुकड़े करना)* *Pare* your nails and then polish them.

  Pair *(set of two–जोड़ी)* I have only three *pairs* of shoes.

- **Peace** *(tranquillity–शान्ति)* *Peace* of mind is more precious than the materialistic richness.

  Piece *(fragment–टुकड़ा)* The dog found a *piece* of meat suddenly.

- **Price** *(value–कीमत)* The price of this *coat* is on its tag.

  Prize *(reward–ईनाम)* She could not win any *prize* this time.
- **Persecute** *(to harass–परेशान करना)* Talibans *persecute* the innocents in a very cruel manner.

  Prosecute *(to bring before a Court–अभियोग चलाना)* He was *prosecuted* for murdering his wife.
- **Physic** *(medicine–दवा)* No *physic* could cure him of this disease.

  Physique *(bodily fitness–शारीरिक बनावट)* He possesses an attractive *physique.*
- **Prescribe** *(to direct–निर्देश देना)* The doctor has *prescribed* three doses of medicine after four hours daily.

  Proscribe *(to banish–देश निकाला देना)* The minister was *proscribed* by the king.
- **Patrol** *(going round–गश्त लगाना)* A chowkidar was *patrolling* at the main gate.

  Petrol *(oil–पेट्रोल)* *Petrol* is required to run vehicles.
- **Popular** *(familiar–लोकप्रिय)* Rajeev Gandhi was a very *popular* leader.

  Populous *(thickly inhabited–आबादी वाला)* Delhi is a highly *populous* city.

  Pail *(bucket–बाल्टी)* I have two *pails* full of water.

  Pale *(yellowish appearance–पीला)* On seeing a lion, his face turned *pale.*
- **Paced** *(measured by footsteps–कदम)* This excellent thriller is fast *paced* and believable.

  Paste *(thick glue–चिपकाना)* I *pasted* some graphics in my note book.
- **Pain** *(it hurts–दर्द)* I felt a sharp *pain* in my lower back.

  Pane *(a single panel of glass–पैनल)* The left *pane* of this window required change.
- **Pair** *(a set of two–जोड़ा)* I need a new *pair* of socks.

  Pare *(cutting down–काटना)* Local authorities were instructed to *pare* their budget.

  Pear *(bottom-heavy fruit–नाशपाती)* I am fond of eating *pears.*
- **Palate** *(the roof of the mouth–मुँह के ऊपर का भाग)* The top part of the inside of your mouth is called *palate.*

  Pallet *(a bed of strane–फूस का बिस्तर)*

  (a) A *pallet* is a narrow mattress filled with straw which is put on the floor for someone to sleep on.

  (b) A *pallet* is a hard, narrow bed. He was given only a wooden pallet with a blanket.

  (c) A *pallet* is a flat wooden or metal platform on which goods are stored so that they can be lifted and moved using a forklift truck.

  (d) The warehouse will hold more than 90000 *pallets* storing 30 million Easter eggs.

- **Pall** *(to become wearisome–अरुचिकर)* Already the allure of meals in hotels and restaurants begun to *pall.*

  Pawl *(locks a ratchet–रोक)* A pivoted, usually curved, bar or lever whose free end engages with the teeth of a cog-wheel or ratchet so that it can only turn or move in one way.

- **Pause** *(to hesitate–रुकना)* He talked for three hours regularly without *pausing* for a minute.

  Paws *(the foot of a beast–पंजा)* The cat has white front *paws.*

- **Pea** *(round, green legume–मटर)* I like *peas* vegetable.

  Pee *(piss–पेशाब करना)* The baby *peed* on the bed and wet the matress.

- **Peak** *(mountain top–पहाड़ की चोटी)* He climbed up to the *peak* of the mountain.

  Peek *(secret look–चोरी से देखना)* On one occasion she had *peeked* at him through a crack in the door.

  Pique *(to stimulate–नाराज होना)*

  (a) *Pique* is the feeling of annoyance you have when you think someone has not treated you properly.

  (b) Simi had gotten over her *pique* at Rue's refusal to accept the job.

  (c) If something *piques* your interest or curiosity, it makes you interested or curious. This phenomenon *piquoed* Dr Mohit's interest.

  (d) If someone does something in a fit of *pique*, they do it suddenly because they are annoyed at not being treated properly. Lally, in a fit of *pique*, left the Army and took up a career in the town.

- **Pearl** *(round, luminescent gem from an oyster–मोती)* She wore a string of **pearls** at her throat.

  Purl *(a cord of metal for embroidery–धातु का तार)* *Purl* is a thread or cord of twisted gold or silver wire, used especially for edging etc made from this.

- **Pedal** *(foot control–पैडल)* I am too tired to *pedal* again.

  Peddle *(to sell–बेचना)* He attempted to *peddle* his paintings around the city.

- **Peer** *(a nobleman–कुलीन व्यक्ति)*

  (a) If you *peer* at something, you look at it very hard, usually because it is difficult to see clearly. I had been peering at a computer print-out that made no sense at all.

  (b) In Britain, a *peer* is a member of the nobility who has or had the right to vote in the House of Lords. Lord Swan was made a life peer in 1981.

  (c) Your *peers* are the people who are the same age as you or who have the same status as you. His engaging personality made him popular with his *peers.*

  Pier (a structure in a water used as a landing stage–सेतुबन्ध, धार*)* A *pier* is a platform sticking out into water, usually the sea, which people walk along or use when getting onto or off boats.

- **Pi** (3.1416—पाई) *Pi* is a number, approximately 3.1416, which is equal to the distance round a circle divided by its width. It is usually represented by the Greek letter p.

  Pie *(baked tasty dish—खाने की स्वादिष्ट वस्तु)* A *pie* consists of meat, vegetables or fruit baked in pastry.

- **Pieced** *(assembled from pieces—टुकड़े)* Do you want another *piece*?

  Piste *(a ski run of compacted snow—बर्फ)* Piste is a track of firm snow for skiing on.

- **Pincer** *(claw-like gripping action—पंजे से पकड़ना)* The *pincers* of an animal such as a crab or a loberster are its front claws.

  Pincher *(one who pinches—परेशान करने वाला)* None likes a *pincher.*

  Pinscher *(terrier—छोटा कुत्ता)* I have *pinscher* as a pet.

- **Pistil** *(female organ of a flower—गर्भ केसर)* *Pistil* is a seed-bearing organ of a flower.

  Pistol *(hand gun—पिस्तौल)* He was caught with a *pistol* in hand.

- **Place** *(a location—स्थान)* This is a good *place* to live in.

  Plaice *(an edible brown flat fish—एक प्रकार की मछली)* *Plaice* is a type of flat sea fish.

- **Plait** *(braid—तह बनाना)* She parted her hair and then began to *plait* it into two thick braids.

  Plate *(a dish—थाली)* She pushed her *plate* away. She had eaten nothing.

- **Plum** *(purple fruit—बेर)* A *plum* is a small, sweet fruit with a smooth red or yellow skin and a stone in the middle.

  Plumb *(straight up and down—पाइप कार्य)* He knows how to *plumb* the pipe well.

- **Pole** *(a person from Poland—पोलैण्ड का निवासी)* He is a *pole.*

  Pole *(big stick—बड़ी लकड़ी)* I need a *pole* to climb up that house.

  Poll *(a voting—चुनाव कार्य)* More than 60 per cent of those *polled* said that they approved of his record as Chairman.

- **Poor** *(no money—निर्धन)* A *poor* man can't afford a car.

  Pore *(careful study; microscopic hole—गहन अध्ययन, छोटा छिद्र)* We spent hours *poring* over the visa rules.

  Pour *(to flow freely—बहना)* He *poured* himself another drink.

- **Precedence** *(priority—प्राथमिकता)* Enjoy fully but don't let it take *precedence* over work.

  Precedent *(established course of action—पूर्व कार्य)* This case can set an important *precedent* for dealing with such cases in future.

  President *(the chief—प्रधान)* The *president* is all in all of this society.

- **Presence** *(the state of being present—उपस्थिति)* The meeting took place in the *presence* of the Judge.

  Present *(gift—उपहार)* He gave a nice *present* to his friend on his wedding anniversary.

- **Pride** *(ego–गर्व)* We take *pride* in offering you the best services.

  Pried *(opened–खोलना)* I *pried* the top off a can of chilli.
- **Profit** *(money earned–लाभ)* The company has earned good *profit* in this quarter.

  Prophet *(seer–सिद्ध व्यक्ति)* He did it as per the instructions of the *prophet.*
- **Pros** *(multiple experts–फायदा)* Motherhood has both its *pros* and cons.

  Prose *(ordinary language–गद्य)* Shute's *prose* is stark and chillingly unsentimental.
- **Quite** *(altogether–पूरी तरह से)* I am *quite* well now.

  Quiet *(silent–शान्त)* Please keep *quiet.*
- **Rein** *(bridle–लगाम)* Keep the *rein* tight, otherwise you may be thrown out by the horse.

  Reign *(rule–शासन)* The *reign* of Akbar is known for communal harmony.
- **Rite** *(ceremony–रस्म)* Only a few *rites* were performed in his wedding.

  Write *(compose–लिखना)* I am about to *write* a letter to her.

  Right *(antonym of left–दायाँ)* This is my *right* leg.

  Right *(antonym to wrong–सही)* You have taken a *right* decision.

  Wright *(a worker–बनाने वाला)* He is a wonderful play *wright.*
- **Route** *(course–रास्ता)* By which *route* you came here?

  Rout *(flight–भगाना)* The Pakistan armies were put to *rout.*
- **Rap** *(a sharp blow–थप्पड़)* He *rapped* her on the cheek.

  Rape *(to ravish–बलात्कार)* He *raped* a college girl.

  Wrap *(to enclose–बन्द करना)* The book was *wrapped* in a piece of white paper.
- **Reclaim** *(to win back–सुधारना)* He was *reclaimed* from his bad habits by his devoted wife.

  Re-claim *(to claim again–पुनः दावा करना)* He is thinking to *re-claim* the property on some other ground.
- **Recover** *(regain–ठीक होना)* He has now *recovered* a lot from the weakness.

  Re-cover *(to cover again–पुनः ढ़कना)* *Re-cover* the sweets with some clean cloth.
- **Road** *(way–रास्ता)* The *road* has recently been repaired.

  Rode *(past of ride–सवारी की)* He *rode* on the horse yesterday.
- **Ring** *(an ornament for fingers–अंगूठी)* This *ring* is made of gold.

  Wring *(to twist, to squeeze–ऐंठना, निचोड़ना)* *Wring* the clothes well and put them on the ground.
- **Rest** *(respite–आराम)* I want some *rest* before starting the next assignment.

  Wrest *(snatch by force–छीनना)* Ram *wrested* a bag from Shyam.

- **Roll** *(to run over–लोटपोट होना)* (a) Your *roll* number is easy to remember.
(b) He *rolled* over the log to the right side of river.

Role *(part–भाग लेना)* I am playing the *role* of Ravana in this serial.

- **Raise** *(elevate–उठाना)* He *raised* his hand in support of the resolution.

Rays *(thin beams of light–किरण)* The sun *rays* can penetrate water up to ten feet.

Raze *(to tear down completely–नष्ट करना)* Many of villages have been *razed*.

- **Read** *(having knowledge from reading–पढ़ना)* I have *read* this novel.

Red *(a primary colour–लाल रंग)* I like *red* colour.

- **Rede** *(advice–सलाह)* It is always fruitful to listen to the *rede* of your elders.

Reed *(tall, thin water plant–जलीय पौधा)* He has a beautiful *reed* plant.

- **Real** *(authentic–वास्तविक)* Yes, it is a *real* story.

Reel *(wavering move–चक्कर)* He lost his balance and *reeled* back.

- **Recede** *(to move backward–पीछे जाना)* As he *receded* she waved goodbye.

Reseed *(to plant again–पुन: बीजारोपण)* He is trying to *reseed* the rose plant.

- **Reek** *(smells bad–दुर्गन्ध)* Your breath *reeks* of stale cigar smoke.

Wreak *(to inflict–बदला लेना)* She threatened to *wreak* vengeance on the man who toppled him some years ago.

- **Rest** *(stop working–आराम)* He is much tired. He is taking some *rest*.

Wrest *(take away–ले लेना)* The thief *wrested* the suitcase from him.

- **Retch** *(heave–वमन करना)* (a) The smell made me *retch*.
(b) If you *retch*, your stomach moves as if you are vomiting.

Wretch *(wicked–नीच व्यक्ति)* Oh, what have you done, you *wretch*!

- **Review** *(a general survey or assessment–विचार करना)* The PM *reviewed* the situation with his cabinet.

Revue *(a light theatrical show with sketches or songs–एक हल्का-फुल्का नाट्य शो)* A *revue* is a theatrical performance consisting of songs, dances and jokes about recent events.

- **Rheum** *(watery discharge of mucous–नाक बहना)* A *rheum* is caused by infection with a cold.

Room *(partitioned space–कमरा)* I need a three *room* set.

- **Rho** *(seventeenth letter of Greek alphabet–ग्रीक भाषा का सत्रहवाँ शब्द)* :

Roe *(fish eggs–मछली के अण्डे)* He is fond of cod's *roe*.

Row *(aisle; pull an oar–पंक्ति)* They were standing in *rows*.

- **Rigger** *(one who rigs–छल करने वाला)* A person who works with lifting-tackle; a person who erects and maintains scaffolding.

Rigour *(discipline–अनुशासित)* He found the *rigours* of the tour too demanding.

- **Rise** *(to stand up–उगना)* The sun *rises* in the east.

Rye *(variety of grain–अन्न की किस्म)* I am fond of cheese on *rye*.

- **Roam** *(to wander–घूमना)* Barefoot children *roamed* in the streets.

  Rome *(Italian capital–रोम)* *Rome* was not built in a day.

- **Roil** *(to make turbid–अशान्त)*

  (a) If water *roils*, it is rough and disturbed. (mainly am*)*

  (b) The water *roiled* to his left as he climbed carefully at the edge of the waterfall.

  (c) Something that *roils* a state or situation makes it disturbed and confused.

  (d) Times of national turmoil generally *roil* a country's financial markets.

  Royal *(worthy of a king or queen–शाही)* He belongs to a *royal* family.

- **Rood** *(a cross–क्रॉस चिह्न)* A cross as an instrument of execution; The Cross on which Jesus suffered; the cross as the symbol of the Christian faith.

  Rude *(coarse–असभ्य)* He is *rude* to his friends and obsessively jealous.

- **Rot** *(decay–सड़न)* Sugary canned drinks can *rot* your teeth.

  Wrought *(made–बना हुआ)* The recent results of presidential elections in USA *wrought* a change in US policy towards India.

  Rote *(by memory–कण्ठस्थ करना)* I am very sceptical about the value of *rote* learning.

  Wrote *(has written–लिखा)* He *wrote* a letter yesterday.

- **Rough** (coarse–कठोर*)* His hands are *rough*.

  Ruff *(pleated collar–कॉलर)* A *ruff* is a stiff strip of cloth or other material with many small folds in it, which some people wore round their neck in former times.

- **Rude** *(impolite–असभ्य)* I am unable to understand as to why she behaved so *rudely*.

  Rued *(regretted–पश्चात्ताप)*

  (a) If you *rue* something that you have done, you are sorry that you did it, because it has had unpleasant results.

  (b) If you *rue* the day that you did something, you are sorry that you did it, because it has had unpleasant results.You'll live to rue the day you said that to me, my girl.

- **Rye** *(variety of grain–अन्न की किस्म)* *Rye* is a kind of grain.

  Wry *(twisted–विकृत किया हुआ)* (a) There is a *wry* sense of humour in his work.

  (b) A *wry* remark or piece of writing refers to a bad situation or a change in a situation in an amusing way.

  (c) If someone has a *wry* expression, it shows that he finds a bad situation or a change in a situation slightly amusing.

  (d) He allowed himself a *wry* smile.

- **Sooth** *(truth–सच)* *Sooth* to speak, he is not a good boy.

  Soothe *(to calm–शान्त करना)* You can't *soothe* his anger with lame excuses.

- **Spacious** *(enough space–खुला)* His office is quite *spacious* and well decorated.

  Specious *(attractive–आकर्षक)* With your *specious* looks, you can't befool her.

- **Stationary** *(fixed–स्थिर)* Earth is not *stationary*, it moves round the sun.

  Stationery *(writing material–स्टेशनरी)* I am going to market to purchase *stationery* essential for the office.

- **Straight** *(opposed to curved–सीधा)* I believe in *straight* talks.

  Strait *(narrow–संकरा)* The lane is too *strait* to allow an elephant to pass.

- **Sore** *(painful–दर्दकारक)* I can't sing as my throat is *sore*.

  Soar *(to fly high–ऊँचा उड़ना)* Birds *soar* in sky.

  Sour *(not sweet–खट्टा)* The grapes were *sour*.

- **Suit** *(an action in court–दावा)* Bank has filed a civil *suit* against Abdul Karim Telagi for recovery.

  Suite *(a set of rooms–कमरों का सेट)* I have reserved a *suite* for you in Alaska Hotel.

- **Story** *(a tale–कहानी)* My grandmother told me a *story* of an old man.

  Storey *(floor of a building–मंजिल)* I have taken a room at first storey.

- **Serge** *(a kind of cloth–एक प्रकार का कपड़ा)* This suit is made of *serge*.

  Surge *(move like waves–तरंगों की तरह)* The waves of ocean *surge* violently in night.

- **Shear** *(to clip the wool–ऊन कतरना)* Wool is being *sheared* off the sheep.

  Sheer *(downright–एक मात्र)* He achieved success by the *sheer* force of his hard labour.

- **Sun** *(sun–सूर्य)* The *sun* is a planet.

  Son *(male descendent–पुत्र)* He is my *son*.

- **Sole** *(lower surface of shoes–जूते का तला)*

  (a) The *sole* of the right shoes requires repairing.

  (b) The *sole* aim of my life is to earn reputation in the society.

  Soul *(immaterial part–आत्मा)* (a) You can't see the *soul*.

  (b) *Soul* is immortal.

- **Stair** *(step–सीढ़ी)* Let us go up *stairs*.

  Stare *(gaze–घूरना)* It is wrong to *stare* at girls.

- **Sing** *(melodious sound–मधुर आवाज)* She will *sing* a sweet song.

  Swing *(to oscillate–झूलना)* She has gone to enjoy *swing* ride.

- **Sale** *(to exchange for money–बिक्री)* This is not for *sale*.

  Sail *(to travel in water–तैरना)* Ships can *sail* in deep sea only.

- **Sachet** *(a small bag containing small quantity of something–छोटा पैकेट)* I found twenty *sachets* of coffee.

  Sashay *(to strut or flounce–इठलाकर चलना)* The models *sashay* down the catwalk.

- **Sacks** *(bags–थैले)* I found twenty *sacks* for potatoes.

  Sax *(short for saxophone)* The former President of USA Bill Clinton was fond of playing sax.

- **Sail** *(wind powered water travel–तैरना)* The ship had *sailed* from Sri Lanka to India.

  Sale *(the act of selling–बेचना)* We are putting very hard to increase the *sale.*

- **Sane** *(mentally normal–मानसिक रूप से स्वस्थ)* He is perfectly *sane.*

  Seine *(fishing net–मछली पकड़ने का जाल)* A large fishing net having floats at the top and weights at the bottom so as to hang vertically in the water, the ends being drawn together to enclose the fish and the net usually hauled ashore.

- **Saver** *(one who saves–बचाने वाला)* Low interest-rates are bad news for *savers.*

  Savor *(to relish a taste–स्वादिष्ट)* People come here to *savor* the exquisite food provided by the owner.

- **Sawed** *(cut timber–लकड़ी काटना)* He *sawed* the timber very quickly.

  Sod *(to express anger–गुस्सा व्यक्त करना)* If someone uses an expression such as '*sod* it', '*sod* you' or '*sod* that', they are expressing anger or showing that they do not care about something.

- **Scull** *(rowing motion–नाव चलाना)* *Scull* are small oars which are held by one person and used to move a boat through water.

  Skull *(head bone–खोपड़ी)* He was treated for a fractured *skull.*

- **Seal** *(to close–बन्द करना)* He *sealed* the envelope and put on a stamp.

  Seel *(to close someone's eyes–आँखें बन्द करना)* Close the eyes of (a hawk etc) by stitching up the eyelids.

- **Seam** *(row of stitches–सिलाई)*

  (a) A *seam* is a line of stitches which joins two pieces of cloth together.

  (b) If something is coming apart at the *seams* or is falling apart at the *seams,* it is no longer working properly and may soon stop working completely. Britain's university system is in danger of falling apart at the *seams.*

  (c) If a place is very full, you can say that it is bursting at the *seams.*

  (d) The hotels of New Delhi were bursting at the *seams* during Asia 96 Trade Fair.

  Seem *(appears–दिखना)* Everyone *seem* very busy here.

- **Seaman** *(sailor–नाविक)* He emigrated to work as *seaman.*

  Semen *(male discharge–वीर्य)* He is being treated for some *semen* problem.

- **Sear** *(scorched–मुरझाया या सूखा)* To *sear* something means to burn its surface with a sudden intense heat. Grass fires have *seared* the land near the farming villages of Haryana.

  Seer *(a person who sees visions– भविष्यदृष्टा)* A *seer* is a person who tells what will happen in the future.

- **Serf** *(slave–दास)* In former times, *serfs* were a class of people who had to work on a particular person's land and could not leave without that person's permission.

  Surf *(mass of white bubbles–लहर)* *Surf* is the mass of white bubbles that is formed by waves as they fall upon the shore.

(a) If you *surf*, you ride on big waves in the sea on a special board.
I'm going to buy a surfboard and learn to *surf*...
I'm going to be *surfing* bigger waves when I get to Australia!
(b) If you *surf* the Internet, you spend time finding and looking at things on the Internet. (COMPUTING)
No one knows how many people currently *surf* the Net.

- **Sewer** *(channel for carrying off waste and filth–मल मार्ग)* *Sewer* is medium to flow extracts in a safe manner.

Sower *(one who sows–बोने वाला)*

Suer (one who sues–दावा करने वाला)

- **Shell** *(the hard covering of anything–वाह्य आवरण)* They cracked the nuts and removed their *shell*.

She'll *(contraction of she will)* *She'll* cooperate you positively.

Shill *(a decoy–प्रलोभन)* A decoy, an accomplice, esp. one posing as an enthusiastic or successful customer to encourage buyers, gamblers.

- **Shear** *(to cut or wrench–कतरना)* He *shears* his sheep's hair twice in a year.

Sheer *(pure–शुद्ध)*
(a) *Sheer* material is very thin, light, and delicate....*sheer* black tights.
(b) You can use *sheer* to emphasize that a state or situation is complete and does not involve or is not mixed with anything else.
His music is *sheer* delight...
Sheer chance quite often plays an important part in making career.
(c) A *sheer* cliff or drop is extremely steep or completely vertical.
There was a *sheer* drop just outside my window...

- **Sic** *(thus–इस प्रकार से)* You write *sic* in brackets after a word or expression when you want to indicate to the reader that although the word looks odd or wrong, you intended to write it like that or the original writer wrote it like that.
The latest school jobs page advertises a 'wide range *(sic)* of 6th form courses.'

Sick *(ill–बीमार)* He is very *sick*. He needs medication.

Six *(whole number–छः)* I have *six* pencils.

- **Side** *(position–स्थिति)* There is a park on the left *side* of the road.

Sighed *(breathed sorrowfully–आह भरना)* He *sighed* wearily.

- **Sign** *(display board bearing information–निराश)* Equations are generally written with a two bar equals *sign*.

Sine *(reciprocal of the cosecant)* Find the *sine* value of this angle.

- **Sink** *(to submerge–डूबना)* A fresh egg will *sink* and an old egg will float.

Synch *(together in time–साथ-साथ)* If two things are out of *synch*, they do not match or do not happen together as they should. If two things are in *synch*, they match or happen together as they should. Normally, when demand and supply are out of sync, you either increase the supply, or you adjust the price mechanism...

- **Slay** *(kill–मारना)* He *slew* a man with a sword.

  Sleigh *(snow carriage–बर्फ की गाड़ी)* A *sleigh* is a vehicle usually pulled by dogs or reindeers.

- **Slew** *(past tense of slay–हत्या की)* He *slew* his neighbour.

  Slough *(shed–झुकना)*

  (a) All reptiles have to *slough* their skin to grow.

  (b) When a plant *sloughs* its leaves, or an animal such as a snake sloughs its skin, the leaves or skin come off naturally.

  Sloe *(blackthorn berries–जंगली बेर)* A *sloe* is a small, sour fruit that has a dark purple skin. It is often used to flavour gin.

  Slow *(not fast–धीमा)* The traffic is heavy and *slow*.

- **Solace** *(comfort–आराम)* I found *solace* in writing when my friend died three months ago.

  Soulless *(lacking a soul–मृत)*

  (a) If you describe a thing or person as *soulless*, you mean that he lacks human qualities and the ability to feel or produce deep feelings.

  (b) Vivek is a *soulless* person.

- **Some** *(a few–कुछ)* Please give me *some* money.

  Sum *(result of addition–योग)* The *sum* of all the angles of a *triangle* is 180 degree.

- **Soot** *(black residue of burning–काजल)*

  (a) This wall is blackened by *soot*.

  (b) *Soot* is black powder which rises in the smoke from a fire and collects on the inside of chimneys.

  Suit *(set of clothes–पहनने का सूट)* Shreya has a blue *suit*.

  Suite *(a set of rooms–कमरों का समूह)* We expended our time during this week in a *suite* at London.

- **Spade** *(shovel–फावड़ा)* He used a *spade* for digging this pit.

  Spayed *(to sterilize a female animal–मादा को बधिया करना)*

  (a) When a female animal is *spayed*, it has its ovaries removed so that it cannot become pregnant.

  (b) All bitches should be *spayed* unless being used for breeding.

- **Spoor** *(trail of an animal–गन्ध से पशु की खोज करना)* The *spoor* of an animal is the mark or substance that it leaves behind as it moves along, which hunters can follow.

  Spore *(single cell reproductive body–जीवाणु)* *Spores* are cells produced by bacteria and fungi which can develop new bacteria or fungi.

- **Staid** *(reserved–गम्भीर)* If you say that someone or something is *staid*, you mean that they are serious, dull, and rather old fashioned.

  Stayed *(remained–ठहरना)* In the old days the woman *stayed* at home and the man earned the livelihood.

- **Stake** *(a competitive situation–दाँव)*
  - (a) If something is at *stake*, it is being risked and might be lost or damaged if you are not successful.
    The tension was naturally high for that game with so much at *stake*.
  - (b) If you *stake* something such as your money or your reputation *on* the result of something, you risk your money or reputation on it.
    He has *staked* his political future on this election victory.
  - (c) If you have a *stake* in something such as a business, it matters to you, for example because you own part of it or because its success or failure will affect you.
    He was eager to return to a more entrepreneurial role in which he had a big financial *stake* in his own efforts.
  - (d) A *stake* is a pointed wooden post which is pushed into the ground, for example in order to support a young tree.
  - (e) If you *stake* a claim, you say that something is yours or that you have a right to it.
  - (f) Jasmine is determined to *stake* her claim as an actress.

Steak *(slice of meat–मांस का टुकड़ा)* He hates eating *steak*.

- **Step** *(a measure taken–कदम)* The next *step* is to put the theory into practice.

Steppe *(a level, grassy, unforested plain–बिना सोचा हुआ)* *Steppes* are large areas of flat grassy land where there are no trees, especially the area that stretches from Eastern Europe across the south of the former Soviet Union to Siberia.

- **Stile** *(narrow passage–संकरा रास्ता)* A *stile* is an entrance to a field or path consisting of a step on either side of a fence or wall to help people climb over it.

Style *(mode–तरीका)* She had not lost her grace and *style*.

- **Stoop** *(to bent down–झुकना)*
  - (a) If you *stoop*, you stand or walk with your shoulders bent forwards.
    She was taller than he was and *stooped* slightly.
  - (b) If you *stoop*, you bend your body forwards and downwards.
  - (c) He *stooped* to pick up the carrier bag of groceries.
  - (d) If you say that a person *stoops* to do something, you are criticizing him because they do something wrong or immoral that they would not normally do.
  - (e) He had not, until recently, *stooped* to personal abuse.
  - (f) How could anyone *stoop* so low?
  - (h) A *stoop* is a small platform at the door of a building, with steps leading up to it. They *stood* together on the stoop and rang the bell.

Stoup *(a kind of drinking pot–पानी पीने का बर्तन)* She served wine in a beautiful *stoup*.

- **Succour** *(help given at the time of need–समयानुकूल सहायता)* Helicopters fly in appalling weather to *succour* ship wrecked mariners.

Sucker *(one who sucks–चूसने वाला)* If you call someone a *sucker*, you mean that it is easy to cheat him.

- **Suede** *(split leather–एक प्रकार का चमड़ा)* He wore a *suede* jacket and jeans.

  Swayed *(to govern–प्रवृत्त करना)*

  (a) When people or things *sway*, they lean or swing slowly from one side to the other. The people *swayed* back and forth with arms linked.
  (b) The whole boat *swayed* and tipped.
  (c) If you are *swayed* by someone or something, you are influenced by them.
  (d) Don't ever be *swayed* by fashion.
  (e) If someone or something holds *sway*, they have great power or influence over a particular place or activity.
  (f) South of the Usk, a completely different approach seems to hold *sway*.
  (g) If you are under the *sway* of someone or something, they have great influence over you. How mothers keep daughters under their *sway* is the subject of the next five sections ?

- **Sundoe** *(a dish of icecream–आइसक्रीम)* *Sundoe* is a tall glass of icecream with whipped cream and nuts or fruit on top.

  Sunday *(first day of the week–रविवार)* Today is *Sunday*.

- **Team** *(a group of players–टीम)* Our college *team* has won the trophy.

  Teem *(to be full of–बहुतायत)* Rajasthan is a state *teeming* with natural resources.

- **Toe** *(a part of foot–पैर का अँगूठा)* She hurt her left *toe* in an accident.

  Tow *(to draw by a rope–बाँधना)* The boat was *towed* with a tree near the shore.

- **Tail** *(part of body–पूँछ)* Cow has a long *tail*.

  Tale *(story–कहानी)* My grandmother told me an interesting *tale*.

- **Their** *(belong to them–उनका)* They have learnt *their* lesson.

  There *(at that place–वहाँ)* I am to go *there* now.

- **Throne** *(Royal seat–सिंहासन)* All the brothers are fighting for the *throne*.

  Thrown *(III form of throw–फेंक दिया)* She has *thrown* her certificates into the river.

  Thorn *(impediment–काँटा)* You need a needle to get the *thorn* out.

- **Tenor** *(substance–तात्पर्य)* The *tenor* of his speech was important from religious point of view.

  Tenure *(right of holding an estate–भूमि नियमन)* The Zamindari Abolition Act has finished the big problem of land *tenure* system in our country.

  Tenner *(English slang for a ten pound note–दस पाउण्ड का नोट)* I have only a *tenner* in my pocket.

- **Tare** *(the seed of a vetch used in reference to its small size–एक प्रकार की घास)* When the harvest is gleaned the evil *tares* will be separated from the good wheat.

  Tear *(salty drops from eyes–आँसू)* Her eyes filled with *tears*.

  Tier *(a horizontal row–पंक्ति)* I have booked your seats in two *tier* compartment.

- **Taught** *(past tense of teach–पढ़ाया)* Bakshi Ji *taught* English in an interesting way.

  Taut *(stretched tight–तना हुआ)* The clothes line is pulled *taut* and secured.

- **Tea** *(herbal infusion–चाय)* I am fond of *tea.*

  Tee *(golf ball prop–गोल्फ से सम्बन्धित)* The *tee* was broken accidentally.
- **Tern** *(a shore bird–एक चिड़िया)* A *tern* is a small black and white seabird with long wings and a forked tail.

  Terne *(alloy of lead and tin–मिश्रित धातु)* This plate is made of *terne.*

  Turn *(rotate–घुमाव)* He *turned* left and went away.
- **The** *(denoting persons already mentioned–आर्टिकल)* *'The'* is a definite article.

  Thee *(objective case of thou–तुझे)* I missed *thee*, beloved mother.
- **Through** *(from end to end–बीच से)* Go straight *through* that door under the 'exit' word.

  Throe *(a spasm of pain–दर्द)* A violent physical spasm or pang, especially in the pain and struggle of childbirth or death. Also, a spasm of feeling; mental agony; anguish.

  Throw *(to discharge through the air–फेंकना)* The crowd began *throwing* stones.
- **Thyme** *(herb–एक प्रकार का पौधा)* *Thyme* is a type of herb generally used in cooking.

  Time *(nature's way of keeping everything from happening at once–समय)* The *time* is favourable to you none.
- **Tic** *(twitch–ऐंठना)* If someone has a *tic*, a part of their face or body keeps making a small uncontrollable movement, for example because they are tired or have a nervous illness.

  Tick *(small noise, parasitic bug–टिक-टिक)* He sat listening to the *tick* of the clock.
- **Tighten** *(to make tighter–जोर से बाँधना)* I use my nail to *tighten* the screw of my torch.

  Titan *(a giant–बहुत बड़ा)* He is the richest business *titan* of our country.
- **Timber** *(wood for building–लकड़ी)* In Japan *timber* is used in construction of house.

  Timbre *(musical quality–ध्वनि)* The *timbre* of someone's voice or of a musical instrument is the particular quality of sound that it has. (FORMAL)

  (a) His voice had a deep *timbre.*

  (b) The *timbre* of the violin is far richer than that of the mouth organ.
- **Toad** *(frog–मेंढक)* A *toad* is a creature similar to frog.

  Toed (having toes–छूना) He tried to persuade the rivals to *toe* the line.

  Towed *(pulled ahead–ले जाना)* The policeman threatened to *tow* away my car.
- **Told** *(what was spoken–बोला)* He *told* me how to do it.

  Tolled *(a bell was rung–घण्टी बजाना)* The pilgrims *tolled* the bell.
- **Track** *(narrow path or road–संकरा रास्ता)* We set of once more, over a rough mountain *track.*

  Tract *(a plot of land–भू-भाग)* A vast *tract* of land is available for stadium.

- **Tray** *(a platter–ट्रे)* I need a *tray* for six cups of tea.

  Trey *(three–तीन)* The side of a die marked with trey pips or spots; a throw which turns up this side.

- **Troop** *(a company of soldiers–सिपाहियों का समूह)* Twenty thousand *troops* were deployed on the border.

  Troup *(a company of actors–अभिनेताओं का समूह)* She belongs to a *troup*.

- **Trussed** *(tied up–बाँधना)* She *trussed* him quickly with a rope and gagged his mouth.

  Trust *(faith–विश्वास)* I *trust* you blindly.

- **Umpire** *(a referee–अम्पायर)* You must not disobey the *umpire*.

  Empire *(dominion–राज्य)* The king was unable to manage his *empire* properly.

- **Vein** *(a blood vessel–शिरा)* *Veins* take the blood to all parts of body.

  Vane *(weather vane–वायु की दिशा दर्शाने वाली पंखी)* There is a *vane* at the top of the temple.

- **Vale** *(valley–घाटी)* The beautiful *vale* of Manali is worthseeing.

  Veil *(a cover–पर्दा)* Muslim ladies generally put a *veil* on their face.

  Wail *(to lament–विलाप)* Don't *wail*, he is safe and sound.

- **Wave** *(unevenness–असमता)* The *waves* of ocean are rising higher and higher.

  Wave *(movement–हिलाना)* She *waved* her hand as the bus started.

  Waive *(relinquish–छोड़ना)* I request the officer to *waive* the punishment.

- **Waste** *(useless–व्यर्थ)* Don't *waste* your precious time.

  Waist (part of body–कमर) The boy had a chain round his *waist*.

- **Weather** (atmosphere–मौसम) It is cold *weather* today.

  Whether *(which of the two–यदि)* I asked her *whether* she would come.

- **Vain** *(useless–व्यर्थ)* I made several requests to our Principal but all in *vain*.

  Wane *(to decrease–कम होना)* I see the moon *waning* these nights.

- **Vary** *(to diversify–बदलना)* Your actions *vary* from the promise you made.

  Very *(more–बहुत)* She is a *very* beautiful girl.

  Wary *(cautious of danger–सतर्क)* Because of his *wary* nature, he was saved.

- **Vacation** *(holidays–छुट्टियाँ)* We are going to Delhi in summer *vacation*.

  Vocation *(occupation–पेशा)* Your vocation is safe as well as benevolent.

- **Vary** *(to change–परिवर्तन)* This text *varies* from the earlier versions.

  Very *(extremely–बहुत)* You are *very* beautiful.

- **Verse** *(paragraph–गद्य)* This *verse* describes three reasons of his failure.

  Versus *(against–विपरीत)* India *versus* Pakistan is a greatly contesting Cricket match.

- **Vial** *(narrow glass container–शीशे का छोटा पात्र)*
  (a) A *vial* is a very small bottle which is used to hold something such as perfume or medicine.
  (b) Please give me a *vial* of rose perfume.

  Vile *(despicable, unpleasant–अरुचिकर)* She was in too *vile* a mood to work.

  Viol *(stringed instrument–यन्त्र)*
  (a) *Viols* are a family of musical instruments that are made of wood and have six strings.
  (b) You play the *viol* with a bow while sitting down.
- **Vice** *(bad habit–बुरी आदत)* She described that those responsible for offences are connected with *vice*, like drugs or gaming.

  Vise *(bench-mounted clamp–क्लैम्प)* I need a good *vise* while I repair the furniture.
- **Weigh** *(to ascertain the weight–तौलना)* I am to purchase one *weighing* machine.

  Way *(passage–रास्ता)* This *way* leads to hospital.
- **Weight** *(amount–वजन)* He gained ten kg of *weight* within a month.

  Wait *(to remain inactive until something expected happens–इन्तजार)* Don't *wait* for me, I will go myself.
- **Week** *(period of seven days–सप्ताह)* Sunday is the first day of a *week*.

  Weak *(feeble–कमजोर)* Ram is too *weak* to walk.
- **Ware** *(article–सामान)* He has sold all his cooking *wares*.

  Wear *(to put on–पहनना)* I like to *wear* silk sarees.

  Wear *(to diminish–घिसना)* My shirt has *worn* out.
- **Wine** *(drink–शराब)* Drinking *wine* is harmful for lever.

  Vine *(creeper–बेल)* The hut is covered with grape *vines*.
- **Wax** *(candle stuff–मोम)* Candles had spread pools of *wax* on the furniture.

  Whacks *(several blows–धमाका)*
  (a) Someone *whacked* him on the head.
  (b) He gave the donkey a *whack* across the back with a stick.
- **Wade** *(walk in shallow water–पानी में हलचल)* Rescuers had to *wade* across a stream to reach them.

  Weighed *(weight was measured–वजन मापना)* He *weighed* approximately 270 kilos.
- **Wain** *(a wagon–छकड़ा गाड़ी)* He has hired a *wain* for transporting his household goods.

  Wane *(decrease, fade–कम होना)* His interest in sports began to *wane*, a passion for golf developed.
- **Want** *(desire–इच्छा)* I *want* to become a surgeon.

  Wont *(inclined–जरूरत)*
  (a) If someone is *wont* to do something, they often or regularly do it.
  (b) *Both have committed their indiscretions, as human beings are wont to do.*

(accustomed—परिचित)

(a) If someone does a particular thing as is their *wont*, they do that thing often or regularly.

(b) Ram woke early, as was his *wont*.

- **War** *(large scale armed conflict—युद्ध)* A *war* like situation is prevailed between India and Pakistan.

  Wore *(past tense of wear—पहना)* She *wore* a silken saree last night.

  Ware *(merchandise—सामान)* The box seems to contain glass *wares*.

- **Warship** *(naval implement of destruction—युद्धपोत)* *Warships* played a decisive role in the victory of our forces.

  Worship *(revere in a religious manner—पूजा)* I enjoyed *worshipping* God.

- **Wary** *(cautious—सावधान)* People do not teach their wards to be *wary* of strangers.

  Wherry *(a shallow boat—छोटी नाव)* *Wherry* is used chiefly on rivers and in harbours for carrying passengers.

- **We** *(us—हम)* *We* are going to market.

  Wee *(small—छोटा आकार)*

  (a) He just needs to calm down a *wee* bit.

  (b) To *wee* means to urinate. *Wee* is an informal word used especially by children. He said he wanted to *wee*.

  (c) *Wee* is also a noun.The baby has done a *wee* in his potty.

- **We'd** *(contraction of 'we would')* *We'd* meet you there positively.

  Weed *(wild plants—जंगली पौधे)* If you don't care about the garden it will be soon full of *weeds*.

- **We're** *(contraction of 'we are'—हम हैं)* *We're* friends.

  Weir *(a low dam or a fence in a river for catching fish—नदी का छोटा बाँध)*

  (a) A *weir* is a low barrier which is built across a river in order to control or direct the flow of water.

  (b) A *weir* is a wooden fence which is built across a stream in order to create a pool for catching fish.

  Were *(past tense plural of 'to be' थे)* Where *were* you playing?

  Whir or **whirr** *(prolonged swish or buzz)* When something such as a machine or an insect's wing *whirrs*, it makes a series of low sounds so quickly that they seem like one continuous sound. The camera *whirred* and clicked.

- **We've** (contraction of we have) *We've* twenty pencils only.

  Weave *(to make cloth—कपड़ा बुनना)* They were busy in *weaving* cotton fabrics.

- **Wheeled** *(having wheels—पहियों पर)* We *wheeled* her out on the stretcher.

  Wield *(to apply or use—उपयोग करना)*

  (a) If you *wield* a weapon, tool, or piece of equipment, you carry and use it. The assailant was *wielding* a kitchen knife.

(b) If someone *wields* power, they have it and are able to use it.
(c) He remains President, but *wields* little power at the company.

- **Weld** *(to join metal by melting its edges–वेल्डिंग)* Where did you learn to *weld* ?

  Welled *(pouring forth–अधिक होना)* Her love for him *welled* stronger than ever.

- **Wet** *(watery–गीला)* She towelled her *wet* hair.

  Whet *(prime–भूख बढ़ाने या जगाने वाली वस्तु)* If someone or something *whets* your appetite for a particular thing, they increase your desire to have it or know about it, especially by giving you an idea of what it is like.

  A really good catalogue can also *whet* customers' appetites for merchandise.

- **Which** *(selection–किसका)* *Which* dress do you like most ?

  Witch *(a sorceress–जादूगरनी)* In fairy stories, a *witch* is a woman, usually an old woman, who has evil magic powers. *Witches* often wear a pointed black hat, and have a pet black cat.

- **While** *(during–जबकि)* He was reading *while* she was cooking.

  Wile *(a trick, a stratagem–कपट, छल)* She used all her *wiles* to earn his favour.

- **Whine** *(annoying cry–दर्द भरी आवाज)* I can hear my dog *whining* in the court yard.

  Wine *(fermented grape juice–दारू)* This is a nice *wine*.

- **Whit** *(insignificant amount–बहुत थोड़ी राशि)* He cared not a *whit* for the social, political or religious aspects of literature.

  Wit *(cleverness, sense of humour–चतुराई)* He was at his *wit's* end.

- **Whither** *(to which place, point, condition, etc–कौन-सा स्थान)* They knew not *whither* they went.

  Wither *(shrivel up–मुरझाना)* The flowers *withered* away within three hours.

- **Whoa** *(stop–ठहरो)* You can say *whoa* to someone who is talking to you, to indicate that you think they are talking too fast or assuming things that may not be true.

  Woe *(despair–दुःख निराशा)* She listened to my tale of *woe* very patiently.

- **Yearn** *(to long–इच्छा करना)* I am anxiously *yearning* to meet my wife.

  Yarn *(thread–धागा)* I have purchased three bundles of *yarn*.

- **Yoke** (slavery–दास बनाना) He is under the *yoke* of his master.

  Yolk (yellow portion of an egg–अण्डे की पीली जर्दी) Some people eat only the *yolk* of an egg.

- **Yore** *(the past–भूतकाल)* Of *yore* is used to refer to a period of time in the past. The images provoked strong surges of nostalgia for the days of *yore*.

  You're *(contraction of 'you are')* *You're* a great writer.

  Your *(belonging to you–तुम्हारा)* *Your* house is excellent.

- **You'll** *(contraction of 'you will')* *You'll* be asked to explain your conduct.

  Yule *(Christmas–क्रिसमस)* Everyone makes enjoyment in his own way during *yule* tide.

UNIT 6

Heteronyms

Heteronyms are also a type of Homographs. All heteronyms are homographs, but all homographs are not heteronyms. Many heteronyms are similar in meaning (especially a related noun and verb are spelled the same but pronounced differently), while others are wholly unrelated.

Heteronyms (A) एवं (B) के अर्थ तथा उनका उच्चारण (Pronunciation) भी अलग-अलग होते हैं। निम्न List में ऐसे शब्दों के अंग्रेजी अर्थ के साथ, उसका अलग-अलग उच्चारण भी बताया गया है।

- **Affect** (A) (ah-fect) to change;
  (B) (af-fect) feeling or emotion
- **Alternate** (A) (alt-er-nit) another choice;
  (B) (alt-er-nait) switch back and forth
- **Appropriate** (A) (ap-prope-ri-ate) to take possession of;
  (B) (ap-prope-ri-it) suitable
- **Arc** (A) (air) 100 square meters (a hundredth of a hectare);
  (B) (ahr) plural present tense of 'to be'
- **Arithmetic** (A) (a-rith-me-tic) a branch of mathematics;
  (B) (air-ith-met-ic) characteristic of arithmetic
- **Attribute** (A) (at-trib-ute) to ascribe;
  (B) (at-trib-ute) characteristic
- **Axes** (A) (ax-ez) plural of axe;
  (B) (ax-eez) plural of axis
- **Bass** (A) (base) a stringed instrument;
  (B) (bass) a fish
- **Bow** (A) (rhymes with 'how') to incline the head in greeting;
  (B) (rhymes with 'tow') weapon that shooting arrows;
  (C) front of a ship
- **Bowed** (A) (rhymes with 'how'd') inclined the head in greeting;
  (B) (rhymes with 'towed') bent
- **Buffet** (A) (buf-fet) to hit;
  (B) (buf-fay, boof:fay) a meal at which guests serve themselves from dishes on display
- **Close** (A) (cloze) to shut;
  (B) (clohss) nearby

- **Combine** (A) (com-bine) threshing machine;
(B) (com-bine) put together
- **Conduct** (A) (con-duct) behaviour;
(B) (con-duct) to direct or manage
- **Conflict** (A) (con-flict) disagreement or fight;
(B) (con-flict) to be in opposition
- **Console** (A) (con-sole) upright cases also, computer terminal;
(B) (con-sole) to comfort
- **Consort** (A) (con-sort) companion or partner;
(B) (con-sort) to keep company
- **Construct** (A) (con:struct) something constructed;
(B) (con-struct) to assemble
- **Content** (A) (con-tent) substantive part;
(B) (con-tent) satisfied
- **Contest** (A) (con-test) competition;
(B) (con-test) to dispute
- **Contract** (A) (con-tract) agreement;
(B) (con-tract) to shrink or to agree on a project
- **Convert** (A) (con-vert) one whose belief was changed;
(B) (con-vert) to change one's belief
- **Converse** (A) (con:verse) opposite;
(B) (con-verse) to talk
- **Convict** (A) (con-vict) prisoner;
(B) (con-vict) to find guilty
- **Crooked** (A) (crooked) bended;
(B) (crook-ed) bent
- **Deliberate** (A) (de:lib-er:ate) carefully considered;
(B) (de-lib-er-ate) to consider
- **Desert** (A) (des-ert) arid region;
(B) (de-sert) to leave, also, something deserved
- **Digest** (A) (die-jest) collection of published material;
(B) (die-jest) absorb nutrients
- **Do** (A) (doo) to accomplish;
(B).(doe) musical note
- **Does** (A) (duz) performs;
(B) (doze) multiple one female deer
- **Dove** (A) (rhymes with 'love') a bird;
(B) (rhymes with 'hove') jumped off
- **Drawer** (A) (dror) compartment that is opened by pulling out;
(B) (draw-er) one who draws

- **Ellipses** (A) (ee-lip-sez) plural of ellipse;
  (B) (ee-lip-seez) plural of ellipsis
- **Entrance** (A) (en-rance) entry way;
  (B) (en-trance) to captivate
- **Evening** (A) (eve-ning) the time of day between afternoon and night;
  (B) (eve-en-ing) making even
- **Excuse** (A) (ex-cuze) to let someone off;
  (B) (ex-kyewss) justifying explanation
- **House** (A) (howss) building that serves as living quarters;
  (B) (howz) to provide with living quarters
- **Incense** (A) (in-cense) substance that produces a pleasant aroma when burned;
  (B) (in-cense) to anger
- **Intern** (A) (in-tern) a worker in training;
  (B) (in-tern) confine to a prescribed area
- **Invalid** (A) (in-val-id) someone who is sick or disabled;
  (B) (in-val-id) not valid
- **Laminate** (A) (lam-in-it) a layered construct;
  (B) (lam-in-ate) to construct by layering
- **Lather** (A) (hard 'th') foam or suds;
  (B) (soft 'th') one who installs lath (lattice)
- **Lead** (A) (leed) to guide;
  (B) (led) a metallic element
- **Minute** (A) (min-it) sixty seconds;
  (B) (my-noot) tiny
- **Moderate** (A) (mod-er-it) not excessive or extreme;
  (B) (mod-er-ate) to preside over
- **Mow** (A) (rhymes with 'cow') pile of hay stored in a barn;
  (B) (rhymes with 'tow') to cut grass
- **Multiply** (A) (mult-i-ply) to perform the mathematical operation of multiplication;
  (B) (mult-i-plee) in a multiple manner
- **Number** (A) (num-ber) a discrete value or quantity;
  (B) (num-mer) more numb
- **Nun** (A) (nun) women in a religious order;
  (B) (noon) the fourteenth letter of the hebrew alphabet
- **Object** (A) (ob-ject) thing;
  (B) (ob-ject) to protest
- **Overhead** (A) (ove:er:head) operating expenses; also, an overhead projector;
  (B) (ov-er-head) high, above the level of the head

- **Pasty** (A) (pay-stee) like glue;
  (B) (pass-tee) meat pie
- **Pate** (A) (pate) top of the head;
  (B) (pat) porcelain paste, (pa:tay) a minced food
- **Perfect** (A) (per-fect) flawless;
  (B) (per-fect) to make flawless
- **Periodic** (A) (peer-ee-odd-ic) occasional;
  (B) (pure-eye-odd-ic) an iodine compound
- **Permit** (A) (per-mit) document giving permission;
  (B) (per-mit) to allow
- **Present** (A) (prez-ent) gift;
  (B) (pre-zent) to introduce
- **Primer** (A) (prihm-er) elementary book;
  (B) (pry-mer) undercoat of paint
- **Produce** (A) (pro-duce) vegetables;
  (B) (pro-duce) bring forth
- **Project** (A) (pro-ject) task;
  (B) (pro-ject) to forecast; also, to show a movie
- **Protest** (A) (pro-test) an objection;
  (B) (pro-test) to object
- **Pussy** (A) (puhs-ee) having pus;
  (B) (pooh-see) kitten
- **Raven** (A) (ray-ven) a black bird;
  (B) (rav-en) hungry
- **Rebel** (A) (reb-el) one who refuses allegiance or opposes;
  (B) (re-bel) to refuse allegiance or oppose
- **Record** (A) (rec-ord) a documented account;
  (B) (re-cord) to set down to preserve
- **Recreation** (A) (rec-ree-a-shun) entertaining or relaxing pastime;
  (B) (ree-cree-a-shun) something that is remade, recreated
- **Refuse** (A) (ref-yoos) garbage;
  (B) (ref-yooz) to deny
- **Relay** (A) (ree-lay) a race in which members of a team take turns racing;
  (B) (ree-lay) to lay again;
  (C) (rih-lay) to pass along
- **Repeat** (A) (re-peat) repeated television show;
  (B) (re-peat) to perform again
- **Rerun** (A) (re-run) repeated television show;
  (B) (re-run) to run again

- **Resign** (A) (re-zine) to quit;
  (B) (re-sign) to sign again
- **Resume** (A) (ree-zoom) to restart;
  (B) (reh-zoom:ay) document of professional experience
- **Row** (A) (rhymes with 'cow') a fight;
  (B) (rhymes with 'tow') a series of objects; also, to propel a boat with oars
- **Sake** (A) (sake) purpose;
  (B) (sah-kee) alcoholic drink
- **Secreted** (A) (see-cret-ed) placed out of sight;
  (B) (see-creet-ed) emitted
- **Separate** (A) (sep-ar-ate) to set apart;
  (B) (sep-ret) not joined together
- **Sewer** (A) (soe-wer) one who sews;
  (B) (soo-wer) channel for human waste
- **Slough** (A) (rhymes with 'tough') outer layer or covering that is shed;
  (B) (rhymes with 'cow') a hole filled with deep mud or mire;
  (C) (rhymes with 'through') a marsh
- **Sow** (A) (rhymes with 'cow') a pig;
  (B) (rhymes with 'tow') to plant seed
- **Subject** (A) (sub-ject) the theme; also, one ruled by another;
  (B) (sub-ject) to force upon
- **Suspect** (A) (sus-pect) one suspected of a crime;
  (B) (sus-pect) to have suspicion
- **Tear** (A) (tare) to rip;
  (B) (teer) a drop of the clear liquid emitted by the eye
- **Unionized** (A) (yoon-yon-ized) belonging to a union;
  (B) (un-i-on-ized) not converted into ions
- **Wind** (A) (rhymes with 'find') to coil up;
  (B) (winned) moving air
- **Wound** (A) (woond) to injure;
  (B) (wownd) coiled up

Some Examples

(a) When the brush fire was *close*, the authorities had to *close* the road.
(b) I *subject* my friends to pain when I discuss the *subject* of my operation.
(c) The *bass* swam around the *bass* drum on the ocean floor.
(d) She wished she could *desert* him in the *desert*.

UNIT 7

Homographs

A homograph is a word of the same written form as another but of a different origin and meaning. (buck : buck). Following list tells you the use of homographs in sentence (A) and (B), depicting different meanings.

Homograph किसी शब्द का ऐसा प्रतिरूप है, जिसके एक से अधिक अलग-अलग अर्थ होते हैं। Same spelling but different meanings (Homograph) वाले शब्दों का उच्चारण कई बार अलग एवं कई बार समान होता है। Homographs के विभिन्न अर्थों का ज्ञान छात्र के vocabulary सम्बन्धी ज्ञान हेतु आवश्यक है। छात्रों को निम्न Homographs का अध्ययन ध्यानपूर्वक अवश्य करना चाहिए—

- **Act** (A) Jack will *act* in a play.
  (B) He's in the second *act* of the play.
- **Arms** (A) My *arms* and legs hurt.
  (B) The soldiers laid down their *arms*.
- **Block** (A) The puppy ran around the *block*.
  (B) The chairs will *block* the door.
- **Buck** (A) It costs one *buck* to get in.
  (B) The horse will *buck* you off.
- **Blue** (A) I feel very *blue* today.
  (B) She wore a *blue* dress.
- **Box** (A) Put your things in a *box*.
  (B) The fighters will *box* tonight.
- **Brand** (A) They put a *brand* on the horse.
  (B) What *brand* is your computer?
- **Base** (A) The *base* of the statue broke.
  (B) The player ran to third *base*.
- **Back** (A) My *back* hurts.
  (B) The dog came *back* home.
- **Bank** (A) The river overflowed its *bank*.
  (B) I have a $1000 in the *bank*.
- **Bear** (A) The grizzly *bear* is dangerous.
  (B) I cannot *bear* to be alone.
- **Bark** (A) The dog has a loud *bark*.
  (B) The *bark* peeled off the tree.

- **Bit** (A) The tiger *bit* the giraffe.
(B) My finger hurts a little *bit*.
- **Ball** (A) My wife went to a *ball*.
(B) The *ball* bounced off my head.
- **Bright** (A) The light is *bright* in my room.
(B) Some students are very *bright*.
- **Blow** (A) They will *blow* up the bridge.
(B) He received a *blow* to the head.
- **Bangs** (A) The shots were like loud *bangs*.
(B) She wears her hair in *bangs*.
- **Bat** (A) The baseball *bat* was broken.
(B) A *bat* flew out of the cave.
- **Bow** (A) *Bow* to the audience before playing!
(B) The *bow* of the ship was breaking.
- **Bluff** (A) You can *bluff* when playing poker.
(B) The man stood on the *bluff*.
- **Bill** (A) We have received a large *bill*.
(B) The ducks *bill* is orange.
(C) He wants change for a $5 *bill*.
- **Bulb** (A) We planted a daffodil *bulb*.
(B) The light *bulb* is burned out.
- **Bed** (A) My *bed* is warm and soft.
(B) We planted a *bed* of flowers.
- **Coat** (A) She is wearing a new *coat*.
(B) There is a *coat* of dust on the car.
- **Court** (A) The criminal was tried in a *court*.
(B) The man wanted to *court* the lady.
- **Chest** (A) He found a pirate's *chest* of gold.
(B) He pounded his *chest* in rage.
- **Change** (A) I need fifty cents in *change*.
(B) You can *change* my class time.
- **Can** (A) A *can* of food will solve hunger.
(B) You *can* try to come in time.
- **Check** (A) I received a *check* from my bank.
(B) We need to *check* on the date.
- **Charge** (A) You can *charge* your purchase.
(B) Tell me the *charges* for lessons.
(C) Elephants can *charge* at any time.
- **Cast** (A) The *cast* of the play went home.
(B) He had a *cast* on his broken arm.
(C) He *cast* the money into the sea.

- **Calf** (A) A *calf* is a baby cow.
  (B) The *calf* of my leg hurts.
- **Corn** (A) We ate *corn* at dinner.
  (B) I have a *corn* on my foot.
- **Crow** (A) A big black *crow* ate the corn.
  (B) Most roosters *crow* in the morning.
- **Date** (A) I ate a *date* with my lunch.
  (B) I have a *date* with my wife.
- **Dart** (A) She sewed a *dart* in her dress.
  (B) He threw a *dart* at the dartboard.
  (C) Don't *dart* into the street.
- **Dull** (A) The knife is too *dull* to cut.
  (B) The movie was *dull* and stupid.
- **Deck** (A) The captain stood on the *deck*.
  (B) I need a *deck* of cards.
- **Draw** (A) If you *draw* a gun, then shoot.
  (B) I cannot easily *draw* pictures.
  (C) They were down in the *draw*.
- **Down** (A) A duck has *down* on its back.
  (B) Walk *down* the stairs carefully.
- **Duck** (A) *Duck* when walking in a cave.
  (B) A small *duck* swam with its mother.
- **Ear** (A) I cannot hear in one *ear*.
  (B) She ate an *ear* of corn.
- **Fly** (A) A *fly* landed on his nose.
  (B) We shall *fly* to Paris today.
- **Fall** (A) The *fall* weather is cool.
  (B) Be careful that you don't *fall*.
- **Fine** (A) If you speed you will pay a *fine*.
  (B) I feel *fine* today.
- **Float** (A) Astronauts can *float* in space.
  (B) There was a *float* in the parade.
- **Fair** (A) The State *Fair* is in October.
  (B) Today was *fair* and warm.
- **Fast** (A) Some cars can go very *fast*.
  (B) Some people *fast* at Easter.
- **Firm** (A) I work in a law *firm*.
  (B) I sleep on a *firm* mattress.
  (C) They made us a *firm* offer.
- **Foot** (A) The stick is one *foot* long.
  (B) My *foot* won't fit my shoe.

- **Faint** (A) Did you ever *faint* from hunger?
  (B) He heard a *faint* noise.
- **Fool** (A) They tried to *fool* me.
  (B) The *fool* did tricks for the King.
- **Fit** (A) She had a *fit* over the job.
  (B) The pants will not *fit* me.
- **Face** (A) Your *face* is red.
  (B) You must *face* the audience.
  (C) He will lose *face*.
- **Felt** (A) The dress was made from *felt*.
  (B) She *felt* sorry for the victim.
- **Fleet** (A) He owns a *fleet* of taxis.
  (B) She is *fleet* of foot.
- **File** (A) You must *file* the papers.
  (B) You must *file* your fingernails.
  (C) He used a *file* to escape.
- **Ground** (A) The snow covered the *ground*.
  (B) We *ground* up the meat for dinner.
- **Gobble** (A) A pig will *gobble* his food fast.
  (B) A turkey will *gobble* for attention.
- **Game** (A) I enjoy the *game* of football.
  (B) He is playing a *game* of blame with me.
- **Hand** (A) He had a glove in his *hand*.
  (B) We gave the singer a *hand*.
- **Hide** (A) Did you *hide* the money ?
  (B) The *hide* of a cow is very useful.
- **Hit** (A) The movie was a big *hit*.
  (B) I *hit* the ball for a home run.
- **Hang** (A) *Hang* your coat on a hook.
  (B) We will *hang* around for an hour.
- **Head** (A) He is the *head* of our company.
  (B) A book fell on my *head*.
- **Hold** (A) *Hold* onto your money.
  (B) Put the cargo into the ship's *hold*.
  (C) They put us on *hold*.
- **Hard** (A) It was a *hard* test.
  (B) The cement will get *hard* soon.
- **Iron** (A) We seldom *iron* clothes.
  (B) The chair was made of *iron*.
  (C) We must *iron* out our problems.

- **Ice** (A) We will *ice* the cake before eating.
(B) Make sure you don't slip on the *ice*.
- **Jumper** (A) She wore a cotton *jumper*.
(B) She is a good high *jumper*.
- **Jam** (A) I like berry *jam* on toast.
(B) The traffic *jam* made me late.
- **Jar** (A) Put the sugar into the *jar*.
(B) Don't *jar* the doctor's hand.
- **Joker** (A) She is a practical *joker*.
(B) A deck of cards has two *jokers*.
- **Kid** (A) There is a new *kid* in my class.
(B) A *kid* is a baby goat.
(C) He loves to *kid* people.
- **Kind** (A) You should be *kind* to animals.
(B) It is the wrong *kind* of cloth.
- **Lean** (A) I only eat *lean* meat.
(B) You can *lean* on the desk.
- **Letter** (A) I got a *letter* in the mail.
(B) What is the first *letter* in China ?
- **Light** (A) Is that chair *light* or heavy ?
(B) Please turn on the *light*.
- **Like** (A) Do you *like* to watch TV ?
(B) She looks *like* her mother.
- **Log** (A) I keep a *log* of my flying hours.
(B) Put another *log* on the fire.
- **Land** (A) We shall *land* in Paris at noon.
(B) Farmers need *land* to grow crops.
- **Lap** (A) Cats *lap* milk with their tongue.
(B) She sat in my *lap* eating candy.
- **Leaves** (A) In Fall *leaves* drop to the ground.
(B) She *leaves* for London today.
- **Left** (A) I can only write with my *left* hand.
(B) There are two cookies *left*.
(C) She *left* the house an hour ago.
- **Line** (A) She was first in the *line* of workers.
(B) He drew a long *line* on the paper.
- **Loaf** (A) A fresh *loaf* of bread smells good.
(B) Some people *loaf* all day.
- **Lie** (A) A *lie* can get you into trouble.
(B) Cats often *lie* down to sleep.

- **Last** (A) It did not *last* very long.
(B) She came in *last* in the race.
- **Long** (A) I *long* to see my home again.
(B) It is a *long* time until winter.
- **Mine** (A) He worked in an iron *mine*.
(B) That book is *mine*.
- **Match** (A) She is no *match* for him.
(B) Light a *match* for my stove.
- **Miss** (A) Do you *miss* your home?
(B) Your arrow may *miss* the target.
(C) Did *Miss* Brown meet her?
- **Mean** (A) What did she *mean* by that?
(B) He is a *mean* teacher.
(C) The *mean* temperature is low.
- **Mold** (A) The bread has *mold* on it.
(B) Pour wax into the *mold*.
- **Might** (A) We *might* hire her for the job.
(B) *Might* does not make it right.
- **Note** (A) He knows not a *note* of music.
(B) Send her a *note* of apology.
- **Nap** (A) We often take a *nap* at noon.
(B) The blanket has a lot of *nap*.
- **Nail** (A) She painted her *nails*.
(B) He used a *nail* to fasten the shelf.
- **Perch** (A) Birds often *perch* on trees.
(B) Many *perch* live in the ocean.
- **Pen** (A) The pigs are in the *pen*.
(B) My *pen* needs some ink.
- **Pupil** (A) She is the best *pupil* in class.
(B) The *pupil* in her eye is blue.
- **Point** (A) You should not *point* at people.
(B) My knife has a sharp *point*.
(C) You missed the *point* of the story.
- **Pitcher** (A) She is the *pitcher* on our team.
(B) She poured a *pitcher* of juice.
- **Pound** (A) I bought a *Pound* of chocolates.
(B) We bought a dog at the *pound*.
(C) Don't *pound* on the table.
- **Pit** (A) A peach has a large *pit* inside.
(B) We will *pit* her against him.
(C) Some snakes were in the deep *pit*.

- **Plane** (A) A *plane* flew them to Paris.
  (B) We use a *plane* to smooth wood.
- **Play** (A) He is an actor in a *play*.
  (B) We *play* basketball each day.
- **Park** (A) We had a picnic in the *park*.
  (B) I *park* my car near my office.
- **Pop** (A) Do you drink soda *pop*?
  (B) Don't *pop* the balloon.
- **Pipe** (A) My dad smokes a *pipe*.
  (B) The water *pipe* broke.
- **Palm** (A) There is a *palm* tree there.
  (B) He hurt the *palm* of his hand.
- **Part** (A) I *part* my hair on the right.
  (B) I need a *part* to fix my car.
- **Pass** (A) She will *pass* the test easily.
  (B) He threw a *pass* to his friend.
  (C) He went through the narrow *pass*.
- **Pool** (A) She has a *pool* table at her house.
  (B) We swam in the swimming *pool*.
- **Pet** (A) A cat can make a nice *pet*.
  (B) You can *pet* my horse.
- **Peep** (A) A tiny chick can *peep* very loud.
  (B) They can *peep* through the window.
- **Page** (A) It is at the top of the *page*.
  (B) The *page* knelt before the King.
- **Punch** (A) We will drink orange *punch*.
  (B) He *punched* the man on his chin.
- **Pick** (A) *Pick* out the one you like.
  (B) A miner uses a *pick* and shovel.
- **Quack** (A) A duck will *quack* when it sees you.
  (B) The doctor was a *quack*.
- **Rare** (A) I don't like my steak *rare*.
  (B) Diamonds are *rare* jewels.
- **Ruler** (A) The King is the *ruler* of the nation.
  (B) Measure it with the *ruler*.
- **Record** (A) She bought a new *record* album.
  (B) He set the *record* in the high jump.
- **Racket** (A) She bought a new tennis *racket*.
  (B) The kids made a *racket* at dinner.
  (C) His *racket* made him money.

- **Range** (A) The cattle are feeding on the *range*.
  (B) She cooked on her new *range*.
  (C) They *range* in age from 2 to 30.
- **Roll** (A) The ball will *roll* into the road.
  (B) We ate a *roll* for dinner.
- **Rock** (A) She will often *rock* in her chair.
  (B) The *rock* went through my window.
- **Run** (A) She will *run* five miles a day.
  (B) She had a *run* in her stocking.
- **Right** (A) I have a ring on my *right* hand.
  (B) She got all the answers *right*.
- **Race** (A) He ran the school *race*.
  (B) He is a member of the human *race*.
- **Round** (A) Her watch is *round*.
  (B) He was injured in the fifth *round*.
- **Rest** (A) We will *rest* until dinner.
  (B) The *rest* will arrive after dinner.
- **Rose** (A) The *rose* is a pretty flower.
  (B) The crowd *rose* to greet her.
- **Rung** (A) He has *rung* the bell twice.
  (B) A *rung* on the ladder is missing.
- **Rear** (A) The horse will *rear* if frightened.
  (B) We sat at the *rear* of the room.
- **Scales** (A) Fish have many *scales*.
  (B) We weighed on the *scales*.
- **Strike** (A) Did you *strike* her on the arm?
  (B) The workers are on *strike*.
- **Stand** (A) They sold fruit at the *stand*.
  (B) *Stand* up if he comes into the room.
- **Shine** (A) *Shine* your shoes every day.
  (B) *Shine* your flashlight over here.
- **Shock** (A) She got a *shock* from the wire.
  (B) That movie will *shock* my mom.
- **Swallow** (A) The *swallow* flew up into the tree.
  (B) My throat hurts when I *swallow*.
- **Stick** (A) *Stick* the stamp on the letter.
  (B) He broke the *stick* in two pieces.
- **Sink** (A) The kitchen *sink* is full of dishes.
  (B) The boat will *sink* if over loaded.

- **Stump** (A) She sat on the tree *stump*.
  (B) That question will *stump* everyone.
- **Spoke** (A) The bike has a broken *spoke*.
  (B) She often *spoke* to me about that.
- **Sock** (A) He lost his *sock* in the park.
  (B) She got a *sock* on her chin.
- **Skip** (A) Children often *skip* when they are happy.
  (B) *Skip* any question you don't know.
- **Sheet** (A) She put a new *sheet* on the bed.
  (B) I need a *sheet* of paper.
- **Stall** (A) The horse is eating in its *stall*.
  (B) My car will *stall* at times.
- **Spray** (A) We need to *spray* the apple trees.
  (B) The *spray* of flowers is pretty.
- **Spring** (A) *Spring* is a good time of the year.
  (B) The car has a broken *spring*.
- **Speaker** (A) She was a *speaker* in our class.
  (B) My stereo has a new *speaker*.
- **Steer** (A) You must *steer* your car carefully.
  (B) The *steers* were out in the field.
- **Space** (A) The rocket flew into *space*.
  (B) Put your name in that *space*.
- **Set** (A) Our TV *set* is broken.
  (B) Please *set* the table for dinner.
- **Screen** (A) Please set up the movie *screen*.
  (B) The *screen* door slammed.
  (C) *Screen* them for infections.
- **Story** (A) We live on the sixth *story*.
  (B) She told a *story* to the children.
- **Shift** (A) I worked on the night *shift*.
  (B) *Shift* gears when you go uphill.
- **Soil** (A) Plant the flower in good *soil*.
  (B) Do not *soil* your dress.
- **Shed** (A) Cats will *shed* their fur.
  (B) The cow is eating in the *shed*.
- **Seal** (A) The *seal* swam in the ocean.
  (B) *Seal* the envelope before mailing.
  (C) He put a *seal* on the document.
- **Squash** (A) I like to eat *squash*.
  (B) You'll *squash* it if you step on it.

- **Train** (A) We will *train* all students.
  (B) We rode the *train* home.
- **Trip** (A) We will take a long *trip* this year.
  (B) Don't *trip* over the rug.
- **Top** (A) The *top* was spinning fast.
  (B) It is on the *top* of the desk.
- **Tip** (A) He left a *tip* for the waiter.
  (B) He cut the *tip* of his finger.
- **Tablet** (A) Take a *tablet* after dinner.
  (B) I need a new *tablet* of paper.
- **Tag** (A) We played *tag* with the children.
  (B) Put an ID *tag* on each suitcase.
- **Well** (A) She can play the piano *well*.
  (B) The water comes from a *well*.
- **Wave** (A) A large *wave* knocked her down.
  (B) *Wave* goodbye to your mother.
- **Watch** (A) She had a new gold *watch*.
  (B) *Watch* your children at all times.

Exercise

1. Tracey didn't feel ***well*** after falling into the ***well***. *(in good health)*
2. Jim hunts, but he ***does*** not shoot ***does***. *(female deer)*
3. There was a big ***row*** in the first **row** of the theatre. *(fight)*
4. Let's **wind** up the kite string before the **wind** gets too wild. *(moving air)*
5. If the judges are ***fair,*** our rabbit will win a ribbon at the ***fair***. *(just)*
6. That creaking ***sound*** makes me wonder if this building is ***sound***. *(in good condition)*
7. The oil well is yours and the gold ***mine*** is ***mine.*** *(belonging to me)*
8. The ***dove dove*** to the ground to eat the peanut. *(dived)*
9. I ***found*** it hard to believe that he planned to ***found*** a new church. *(establish, or start)*
10. The ***rose*** bushes ***rose*** out of the fertile ground. *(a kind of flower)*
11. I won't shed a ***tear*** if you ***tear*** my old shirt into shreds. *(rip)*
12. The dog was happy when you dropped the ***ground*** beef onto the ***ground***. *(past of grind)*

The meanings of the underlined words are given in the brackets.

UNIT 8

Palindromes

A palindrome is a word or sentence that reads the same forward as it does backward. The words 'A' and 'I' are perhaps the simplest palindromes. The word 'Refer' and the name 'Malayalam' are more interesting and illustrative palindromes.

Palindromes are a type of palingram called letter palingrams. A palingram is a sentence in which the letters, syllables, or words read the same backward as they do forward. The sentence, "I was, was I ?" is a word palingram, because the words can be placed in reverse order and still read the same. The sentence, "I did, did I?" is not only a word palingram but a letter palingram (or palindrome) as well.

A number of interesting palindromes are given below to improve your *knowledge.* Can you make up your own?

Words

Aibohphobia	Alula	Cammac	Civic Deified
Deleveled	Detartrated	Devoved	Dewed
Evitative	Hannah	Kayak	Kinnikinnik
Lemel	Level	Madam	Malayalam
Minim	Murdrum	Peeweep	Racecar
Radar	Redder	Refer	Reifier
Repaper	Reviver	Rotator	Rotavator
Rotor	Sagas	Solos	Sexes
Stats	Tenet	Terret	Testset

Phrases and Sentences

1. A tin mug for a jar of gum, Nita.
2. A Toyota. Race fast, safe car. A Toyota.
3. Able was I ere I saw Elba.
4. Anne, I vote more cars race Rome to Vienna.
5. As I pee, sir, I see Pisa!
6. Cigar ? Toss it in a can. It is so tragic.
7. Dammit, I'm mad!
8. Ten animals I slam in a net.
9. Too bad I hid a boot.
10. Was it a car or a cat I saw?
11. Won't lovers revolt now?

UNIT 9

Pangram

A pangram is a sentence that contains all letters of the alphabet. Such sentences are also called holalphabetic sentences. Constructing a sentence that includes the fewest repeat letters possible is a challenging task.

By far the most well-known pangram is,

"The quick brown fox jumps over a lazy dog."

This sentence is generally used to test out new typewriters, presumably because it includes every letter of the alphabets.

A number of pangrams are given below :

Some examples

1. No kidding—Lorenzo called off his trip to visit Mexico city just because they told him the conquistadores were extinct. *(99 letters)*
2. Six javelins thrown by the quick savages whizzed forty paces beyond the mark. *(64 letters)*
3. The public was amazed to view the quickness and dexterity of the juggler. *(60 letters)*
4. We quickly seized the black axle and just saved it from going past him. *(57 letters)*
5. Six big juicy steaks sizzled in a pan as five workmen left the quarry. *(56 letters)*
6. A mad boxer shot a quick, gloved jab to the jaw of his dizzy opponent. *(54 letters)*
7. A quart jar of oil mixed with zinc oxide makes a very bright paint. *(53 letters)*
8. Crazy Fredericka bought many very exquisite opal jewels. *(48 letters)*
9. Sixty zippers were quickly picked from the woven jute bag. *(48 letters)*
   Heavy boxes perform quick waltzes and jigs. *(36 letters)*
10. Pack my box with five dozen liquor jugs. *(32 letters)*
11. The five boxing wizards jump quickly. *(31 letters)*
12. How quickly daft jumping zebras vex. *(30 letters)*
13. Jackdaws love my big sphinx of quartz. *(31 letters)*

UNIT 10

Idioms and Phrases

दैनिक व्यवहार में प्रयुक्त होने वाले कुछ महत्त्वपूर्ण idoms एवं phrases का उनके English अर्थ सहित वाक्यों में प्रयोग सरल तरीके से नीचे दिया जा रहा है। विद्यार्थियों को इन idioms एवं phrases को ध्यानपूर्वक कण्ठस्थ कर लेना चाहिए। इनका प्रयोग लेखन शैली को प्रभावी बनाता है।

विद्यार्थियों को Fve idiomatic expressions का प्रयोग करने का पर्याप्त अभ्यास करना चाहिए। विभिन्न Competitive Examinations में विद्यार्थियों द्वारा लिखे जाने वाले Explanations, Essays आदि में इनका प्रयोग निश्चय ही उन्हें अधिक सशक्त, सुन्दर एवं प्रभावशाली बनाएगा।

A

- **A gentleman at large** (*an unreliable person*) He is a *gentleman at large*, you must not trust him.
- **A wolf in sheep's clothing**
- **ABC** (*basic knowledge*) He doesn't know *ABC* of Physics.
- **Above board** (*fair and honest*) He is a straightforward man. His financial dealings are *above board*.
- **Again and again**
- **All and sundry** (*without making any distinction*) He invited *all and sundry* in the marriage party of his younger brother.
- **All in all** (*whole sole, most important*) The Forest Minister is *all in all* of our department.
- **Alpha and omega** (*first and last letters of the Greek alphabet, mean beginning and end*) The *alpha and omega* of British policy was to keep the Indians divided.
- **An eye wash** (*a pretence*) He does nothing without self-interest, all his excuses are but *an eye wash*.
- **An iron hand**
- **At sixes and seven** (*persons who are having different opinions*) Economists are *at sixes and seven* on the policy of rationing.

B

- **Back and call** (*at the service*) Don't worry I am at your *back and call*.
- **Bag and baggage** (*with all goods*) He returned to his village with *bag and baggage.*
- **Between Scylla and Charybdis** (*choice between two unpleasant alternatives*) Going to Jaipur or staying back at Delhi was like a choice *between scylla and charybdis*.
- **Between the cup and the lip** (*on the point of achievement*) Until I got the appointment letter in hand, I was not sure of the posting as there are many a slip *between the cup and the lip*.
- **Black and white** (*in writing*) It is always better to get every thing in *black and white.*
- **Blow hot and cold** (*having no stand, shows favour at one time and unfavour at another*) He can't be relied upon as he *blows hot and cold* on this matter.
- **Body and soul** (*entirely*) She devoted *body and soul* to win the medal.
- **By fits and starts** (*irregularly*) Work done *by fits and starts* never gets completed in time.
- **By hook or by crook** (*by any means*) I want to get this licence *by hook or by crook.*
- **By leaps and bound** (*speedily*) The population is increasing *by leaps and bounds.*

C

- **Call a spade-a-spade** (*straight talks*) He believes in *calling a spade-a-spade*.
- **Cats and dogs** (*heavy rain*) It has been raining *cats and dogs* for the last three hours.
- **Cock and bull story** (*untrue story*) All his excuses seems a *cock and bull story*.
- **Confusion worse confounded** (*be in further worse position*) Such demonstrations and communal speeches in present situation make *confusion worse confounded.*
- **Cut and dried** (*readymade form*) There is no *cut and dried* method of English speaking.

E

- **Ever and anon** (*now and then*) She goes to temple *ever and anon*.

F

- **Fair and square** (*honest*) He is *fair and square* in his dealings.
- **Fair field and no favour** (*equal opportunity to all*) All the staff want *fair field and no favour* in the matter of transfer.
- **Far and wide** (*everywhere*) Many tourists come to see the Taj from *far and wide*.
- **Fire and brimstone** (*fearful penalties*) The USA has threatened Iraq with *fire and brimstone* if she refuses to follow the resolutions of UNO.
- **Fire and fury** (*extreme enthusiasm*) The speech of Nepalese Prachand was full of *fire and fury*.
- **First and foremost** (*highest priority*) To be sincere and devoted is the *first and foremost* requirement of a good employee.
- **Fishy** (*doubtful*) There seems to be something *fishy* going on.
- **Free and easy** (*natural and simple*) The principal found his arguments *free and easy*.

G

- **Gall and wormwood** (*source of irritation*) Her remarks about his father were *gall and wormwood* to him.
- **Gird up the loin** (*to be ready*) We should *gird up the loin* to fight the poverty and menace of dowry.
- **Goods and chattels** (*belongings of home*) On transfer he brought all *goods and chattels* by road.

H

- **Hand and gloves** (*very intimate friends*) Ram and Rahim are *hand and gloves* to each other.
- **Hard and fast** (*certain*) There are no *hard and fast* rules to sanction the loan in the banks.
- **Haughty and naughty** (*arrogant and naughty*) The *haughty and naughty* attitude of the president is not liked by any memeber of the society.
- **Heart and soul** (*with full devotion*) He threw himself *heart and soul* in preparation to pass the examination.
- **Herculean task** (*a tedious job*) Getting selected in IAS is a *herculean task* for everybody.
- **Hit below the belt** (*contrary to principles of fairness*) By making his private secretes public he *hit* him *below the belt*.
- **Hither and thither** (*here and there*) He is in the habit of putting his goods *hither and thither*.

- **Hole and corner policy** (*a secret policy for an evil purpose*) The officer adopted *hole and corner policy* to get his PA transferred.
- **Hue and cry** (*great noise*) A lot of *hue and cry* was raised in Parliament against this bill.

I

- **Ins and outs** (*full details*) Before starting any new business you must know all *ins and outs* of it.
- **Intents and purposes** (*practically*) My wife is the incharge of the house for all *intents and purposes*.

K

- **Kith and kin** (*blood relatives*) All *kith* and *kin* were invited in the marriage of his son.

L

- **Latin and Greek** (*unable to understand*) His speech in English was *Latin and Greek* to the rural folk.
- **Law and equity** (*legal and moral justice*) *Law and equity* demands that the reservation should be based on economic parameters.
- **Leave no stone unturned** (*make all possible efforts*) I shall *leave no stone unturned* to get the promotion.
- **Length and breadth** (*all over*) Anti-English agitation spread through the *length and breadth* of the country.
- **Life and soul** (*main support*) Sonia Gandhi is the *life and soul* of Congress (I).
- **Like a fish out of water** (*in every difficult and unsuitable situation*) Ram was given an unremunerative post. He is feeling *like a fish out of water*.
- **Loaves and fish** (*material interests*) Now-a-days Government servants are concerned with the *loaves and fish* of the office than to solve the problems of common public.
- **Lock and key** (*in safe place*) He keeps jewellery under *lock and key*.

M

- **Might and main** (*with all enthusiasm*) If you study with *might and main* you will positively secure the success.
- **Milk and water** (*weak*) The foreign policy of India is nothing more than a *milk and water* policy.

N

- **Neck and crop** (*completely*) The Pak army ruined the border village *neck and crop*.
- **Need of the hour** (*necessity of time*) Providing full security for the residents of border area is the *need of hour*.
- **Nook and corner** (*everywhere*) I searched her in every *nook and corner*.
- **Not born yesterday** (*worldly wise*) You can't fool me as I was *not born yesterday*.
- **Now and then** (*occasionally*) I visit church *now and then*,
- **Null and void** (of no use, without force of application) The law passed by legislature was declared *null and void* by the Supreme Court.

O

- **Odds and ends** (*remaining goods*) Except *odds and ends*, all the items have since been arranged in order.
- **Often and often** (*frequently*) She visits her parents *often and often*.
- **Once and again** (*repeatedly*) I have told you *once and again* that I have no money to purchase the car at the moment.
- **Open and above board** (*very clear, transparent*) He believes in *open and above board* discussion on every point before arriving at a conclusion.
- **Out of gear** (*in disorder*) The strike of employees always put the government machinery *out of gear*.
- **Over and above** (*besides*) I paid him rupees ten thousand *over and above* what he demanded.
- **Over head and ears** (*excessively*) He is *over head and ears* in debt.

P

- **Part and parcel** (*being an important part of*) Each employee should feel himself *part and parcel* of the business enterprises.
- **Pell mell** (*putting one upon the other, in confusion*) He was in such a hurry that he put all the articles *pell mell* and closed the room.
- **Pick and choose** (*to choose spelectively as per wish*) The management adopted *pick and choose* policy in the promotions from clerical to assistant cadre.
- **Pins and needles** (*small items*) It is unwise to use swords and scissors where *pins and needles* can do.
- **Pros and cons** (*merits and demerits*) Before signing this agreement you must understand all *pros and cons* well.

R

- **Rain or shine** (*favourable or unfavourable circumstances*) *Rain or shine*, I will continue to support her on this topic.
- **Rank and file** (*everyone without discrimination*) For the actual prosperity of the nation, the economic conditions of *rank and file* should be improved.
- **Rank and ruin** (*complete destructions*) The present drought has put the farmers at the verge of *rank and ruin*.
- **Rhyme or reason** (*rational cause*) He resigned from the service without any *rhyme or reason*.
- **Right and left** (*in all ways*) The robbers looted the village *right and left* and fled away.
- **Root and branch** (*complete*) Poverty among the public is the *root and branch* of all the crimes.

S

- **Safe and sound** (*quite well*) She reached there *safe and sound*.
- **Speck and span** (*neat and smart*) Pt JL Nehru was always *speck and span* in his dressing style.
- **Stuff and nonsense** (*worthless*) The judge found all his arguments *stuff and nonsense*.
- **Sum and substance** (*the actual theme*) The *sum and substance* of the paragraph must be reflected in a good precis.

T

- **The die is cast** (*decided finally*) *The die is cast* there is not point of discussing over it now.
- **The last nail in the coffin** (*the last action which resulted in the complete end of something*) Delhi's incident of serial blasts was *the last nail in the coffin* of Indian Mujahideen.
- **Thick and thin** (*in all circumstances*) I shall support you through *thick and thin.*
- **Through fire and water** (*in all sort of difficulties*) He can go *through fire and water* to achieve his goal.
- **Time and tide** (*course of time*) *Time and tide* waits for none.
- **To and fro** (*going and coming*) She went *to and fro* Jaipur to check on the health of her parents.
- **To cheek by jowl** (*very near to each other*) As the space was short, so he kept all the articles *cheek by jowl*.
- **To move heaven and earth** (*to make all possible efforts*) Mahendra Rawat *moved heaven and earth* to get success in MAT Exams.

- **To play ducks and drakes** (*to waste money*) He is playing *ducks and drakes* with the parental money.
- **Toil and moil** (*hard labour*) It requires too much of *toil and moil* to secure first position.
- **Tom, Dick and Harry** (*everyone*) Every *Tom, Dick and Harry* knows that Sachin is the greatest cricketer.
- **Tooth and nail** (*with all force*) He fought *tooth and nail* for abolition of reservation policy.

U

- **Ups and downs** (*prosperity and adversity*) There are *ups and downs* in every business, so one must not lose heart.

W

- **Warp and woof** (*essential parts of a thing*) Blood and bones are *warp and woof* of human body.
- **Watch and ward** (*careful guard*) At least three guards are required to have perfect *watch and ward* of the building.
- **Weal and woe** (*prosperity and adversity*) I will abide by you in all *weal and woe* and never let you down.
- **Whips and spur** (*with greatest hurry*) He completed the project *whips and spur*, and never let you down.
- **Why and wherefore** (*the basic roll season*) Please tell me the *why and wherefore* of your decision to take voluntary retirement.
- **Willy-nilly** (*wish or not wish*) He was *willy-nilly* about appearing in CAT exam.

UNIT 11

Words Used As Different Parts of Speech

The grammatical character of a word can be determined by its use in a sentence. It is difficult to say whether a particular word is a noun or a verb. Only by studying the use and position of the word in a sentence we can say that it is used as noun or pronoun or as verb or as an adjective or an adverb. Below we are giving some of the important words which are used as different parts of speech in the sentences. A careful study of the use of these words will help the students increase their grammatical knowledge of words and their uses.

Words	Used As	Examples
All	*Noun*	All is well that ends well.
	Adjective	All men are mortal.
	Adverb	They are now all right.
	Pronoun	All were in favour of the motion.
Any	*Pronoun*	Do any of you know anything about her temperament?
	Adjective	Take any magazine that you like.
	Adverb	We must take lunch before doing any other work?
As	*Pronoun*	He is not such a good man as he looks.
	Adverb	She wrote as fast as she could.
	Conjunction	As he was poor so I helped him.
About	*Adverb*	She wandered about in inner garments.
	Preposition	There is nothing pleasing about her gait.
Above	*Noun*	The blessings came from above.
	Adverb	The God lives above in heaven.
	Preposition	The sun was above our head at that time.
After	*Adverb*	She arrived soon after.
	Conjunction	She went away after her husband had left.
	Preposition	He looks after his mother.
Age	*Noun*	Age is more important than the physical fitness.
	Verb	He is aging, my dear.
Arm	*Noun*	He received a serious wound in his right arm.
	Verb	Border people were asked to arm themselves with weapons.
Before	*Adverb*	I have not met you before.
	Conjunction	She went away before he came.

Words	Used As	Examples
Better	*Noun*	Give place to your betters.
	Adjective	I think yours is a better pen.
	Verb	Let us first better our financial position.
	Adverb	You are working better today.
Both	*Pronoun*	Both of them have gone.
	Adjective	You cannot make it both ways.
	Conjunction	Both the cashier and the clerk are on leave.
But	*Pronoun*	There is no one but praise her.
	Adverb	It is but a natural consequence.
	Conjunction	He tried hard, but failed.
Back	*Noun*	She carried the load on her back.
	Verb	Do not back false friends.
Book	*Noun*	He is writing a book.
	Verb	Please book a cycle for Kota through this train.
Bare	*Adjective*	He has bare feet.
	Adverb	He walked bare feet.
	Verb	Bare your arm.
By	*Adverb*	Time passes by.
	Preposition	He was much loved by his wife.
Close	*Noun*	The meeting came to close at 5 pm.
	Adjective	They are very close friends.
	Verb	The school will close tomorrow.
	Adverb	Both walked close to each other.
Calm	*Noun*	The calm of mind is, in fact, required.
	Adjective	Today the weather is very calm and quiet.
	Verb	First calm yourself and then write your report.
Cold	*Noun*	Wear the woollen clothes lest you should catch cold.
	Adjective	It is very cold today.
Court	*Noun*	Ramesh was summoned to the court.
	Verb	He courted her all the week.
Cane	*Noun*	This is a beautiful cane.
	Verb	He was caned publicly by the teacher.
Cut	*Noun*	I do not like the cut of your hair.
	Verb	Cut the paper in desired sizes.
Cover	*Noun*	Put a cover on your copy.
	Verb	Cover your head lest you should catch cold.
Down	*Noun*	He has seen the ups and downs of life.
	Adjective	The man was thrown from the down train.
	Verb	Down with dowry.
	Preposition	The engine came rushing down the hill very fast.

Words	Used As	Examples
Deep	*Noun*	She fell down into the deep.
	Adjective	Ganga is a very deep river.
	Adverb	My pen fell deep into the tank.
Drive	*Noun*	My brother has gone out for a drive.
	Verb	You are driving very fast.
Date	*Noun*	His date of birth is 26th April.
	Verb	The Vikram Era dates from 57 BC.
Either	*Pronoun*	Ask either of them to bring a pen.
	Adjective	Either pen is good enough.
	Conjunction	He must either work or take rest.
Enough	*Adjective*	There is enough time to go there.
	Adverb	He knows well enough what she mean to say.
Even	*Adjective*	The chances of winning the game are even.
	Verb	Let them even the field first.
	Adverb	He cannot even see me.
Else	*Adjective*	He brought something else for her.
	Adverb	We should look anywhere else.
	Conjunction	Walk fast, else you should miss the bus.
Eye	*Noun*	He has one eye only.
	Verb	The policeman eyed him with suspicion.
Elder	*Noun*	We must show respect to our elders.
	Adjective	He is my elder brother.
For	*Conjunction*	We should help him for he is very poor.
	Preposition	I was looking for her.
Fast	*Noun*	He keeps fast on Tuesday.
	Adjective	He is a very fast today.
	Verb	He fasted for a week.
	Adverb	He ran so fast to win the race.
Free	*Adjective*	We are citizen of a free country.
	Verb	Let us free ourselves from social bondage.
Fix	*Noun*	He was in a terrible fix.
	Verb	Fix some other date for our marriage.
Face	*Noun*	There are red pimples on her face.
	Verb	He faced the situation with courage.
Fool	*Noun*	He is a fool to behave like that.
	Verb	He cannot fool me now.
Fish	*Noun*	Whale is a kind of large fish.
	Verb	Do not try to fish in troubled water.
Half	*Noun*	One half of this task is completed.
	Adjective	Half hearted man do not succeed.
	Adverb	She was half dead with fear.

Words	Used As	Examples
Help	*Noun*	His timely help saved him.
	Verb	God helps those who help themselves.
Hand	*Noun*	A bird in hand is better than two in the bush.
	Verb	The postman handed him two parcels.
Head	*Noun*	She was wearing a large and beautiful hat on her head.
	Verb	He headed the list of successful students.
Less	*Noun*	She won't be happy with less.
	Adjective	He paid less attention to sports and more to studies.
	Adverb	The soil of her garden is less fertile than that of yours.
Like	*Noun*	You cannot see her like again.
	Adjective	They are man of like physic and stature.
	Verb	I like to take some fruit after dinner.
Light	*Noun*	There is no light in the room.
	Adjective	It is not a light matter.
	Verb	Light the candle, please.
Love	*Noun*	I have great love for her.
	Adjective	She does not like love stories.
	Verb	I love you.
Laugh	*Noun*	She raised many a laugh at his cost.
	Verb	Do not laugh at the poor.
Much	*Adjective*	He has wasted much time.
	Adverb	I am much annoyed with you.
More	*Adjective*	He wants more workers like you.
	Adverb	You must talk less and work more.
Meek	*Noun*	God helps the meek and gentle.
	Adjective	She is quite meek.
Master	*Noun*	She was my master in all matters.
	Adjective	He conceived a master plan.
	Verb	She has mastered this book.
Move	*Noun*	This army is on the move.
	Verb	Let us move to some other hotel.
Make	*Noun*	What is the make of your television.
	Verb	Do not make a noise.
Near	*Adjective*	He is my near relative.
	Verb	We are nearing the end of the project.
	Adverb	Come near and listen to me.
	Preposition	His house is near the temple.
Needs	*Noun*	My needs are few.
	Verb	It needs great care.
Neither	*Pronoun*	Neither of them can be relied.
	Adjective	Neither charge is true.
	Conjunction	Neither he nor his brother was present there.

Words	Used As	Examples
No	*Noun*	His answer was a perfect no.
	Adjective	It is no joke.
	Verb	She is no more with me.
Next	*Adjective*	I shall see you next Monday.
	Adverb	What next ?
	Preposition	He was sitting next to her.
Number	*Noun*	Put it on the tenth number.
	Verb	His days are now numbered.
Once	*Noun*	Let me see her for once.
	Adverb	I was young once.
	Conjunction	Once you hesitate, you are dead.
One	*Noun*	The little one cried for joy.
	Pronoun	One would think he was mad.
	Adjective	One day I met her in a function.
Only	*Adjective*	It was his only chance.
	Adverb	He was only foolish.
Over	*Noun*	In first over Praveen Kumar took three wickets.
	Adverb	Read it over carefully.
	Preposition	Last year, a chance came over to him again.
Off	*Adjective*	Ramesh picked the horse's off nail.
	Adverb	He is falling off.
	Preposition	The rider fell off the bike.
Open	*Adjective*	This is an open letter.
	Verb	Please open the door.
Poor	*Noun*	The rich should help the poor.
	Adjective	He is a poor man.
Pocket	*Noun*	I have two rupees in my pocket.
	Verb	He pocketed the insult patiently.
Right	*Noun*	I asked him favour as a right.
	Adjective	He is the right man for the job.
	Verb	This is a fault that will right itself.
	Adverb	She stood right in front of my gate.
Round	*Noun*	That night was a round of pleasures.
	Adjective	It is a round hole.
	Verb	You cannot round it by pen.
	Adverb	He brought her round to my point of view.
	Preposition	The earth revolves round the sun.
Reach	*Noun*	The bunch of grapes was not within his reach.
	Verb	I shall reach there in time.
Refuse	*Noun*	The refuse of hospital is put into public drains.
	Verb	She refused to help her.

Words	Used As	Examples
Since	*Adverb*	I have not seen him since.
	Conjunction	Since there is no way, let us kiss and part.
	Preposition	Since Monday, I have not seen her.
Some	*Pronoun*	Some say one thing and other say another.
	Adjective	We must find some way out of this problem.
	Adverb	Some thirty people were present in the party.
Still	*Noun*	I could hear her cry in the still of night.
	Adjective	Still waters run deep.
	Verb	With his name the mother still their babies.
	Adverb	They are still sleeping.
Such	*Pronoun*	Such was not his meaning.
	Adjective	Don't move in such a hurry.
So	*Adverb*	I am so tired that I cannot go.
	Conjunction	He was poor, so they helped him.
Slow	*Adjective*	He is a very slow writer.
	Verb	The car slowed down as it reached the hotel.
	Adverb	How slow she works?
Sound	*Noun*	Hearing the sound of the trumpets the people woke up.
	Adjective	His arguments were not sound and acceptable.
	Verb	Sound the horn, please.
Spring	*Noun*	It was a spring of fresh-water.
	Adjective	We use spring water for bathing.
	Verb	See how the dog springs upon the cat.
Stone	*Noun*	The house is made of stone.
	Adjective	That house has stone walls.
	Verb	He was stoned to death.
Stand	*Noun*	Everybody praised him for his stand against the injustice.
	Verb	Stand in a queue.
Stay	*Noun*	He has to cut short the period of my stay at Alwar.
	Verb	She will stay with me for a few days.
Second	*Adjective*	He is second to none.
	Verb	No one seconded her candidature.
School	*Noun*	There is no school in our colony.
	Verb	He was not schooled properly.
Silence	*Noun*	There was perfect silence in the hall.
	Verb	He soon silenced her with his arguments and the evidences.
That	*Pronoun*	That is what I want.
	Adjective	What is that noise?
	Adverb	You have done that much only.
	Conjunction	He says that he wants to leave.

Words	Used As	Examples
Till	*Conjunction*	Do not start till I say.
	Preposition	He put off his work till tomorrow.
Than	*Conjunction*	He likes this more than that.
	Preposition	He was fond of any drink other than milk.
Time	*Noun*	What is the time by your watch?
	Verb	The train is timed to come at 10 pm.
Touch	*Noun*	Midas loved the Golden touch.
	Verb	She will not touch this point.
Turn	*Noun*	There is a turn after 5 km.
	Verb	He turned to be a thief.
Up	*Adjective*	She will come by the next up train.
	Adverb	These days prices are up.
	Preposition	Can you climb up this tree?
Well	*Noun*	There are only two wells in the village.
	Adjective	I hope you are now well.
	Adverb	Well begun is half done.
While	*Noun*	Sit down and rest for a while.
	Verb	They while away their days with books and watching TV.
	Conjunction	He was reading while his friends were playing.
Why	*Noun*	You should not be worried about why and wherefore of it?
	Adverb	I know why she did it?
Wrong	*Noun*	The Minister did no wrong.
	Adjective	It is a wrong policy.
	Verb	He was wronged by the leader of his party.
	Adverb	I think that my son is going wrong.
Watch	*Noun*	I have lost my watch.
	Adjective	I require a watch-man.
	Verb	Let us watch her movements.
Water	*Noun*	Bring me some cold water.
	Adjective	There are water snakes and land snakes.
	Verb	He is watering in the garden.
Walk	*Noun*	They go for a walk in the evening.
	Verb	She was so weak that she could not walk.
Which	*Pronoun*	Which of these two pens you like more?
	Adjective	Which coaching you have joined?
Want	*Noun*	Owing to the want of rains, there occurred a drought.
	Verb	I want to purchase a good new set.
Whose	*Pronoun*	He is the man whose brother met me yesterday.
	Adjective	Whose book is this?
Yet	*Adverb*	There is more evidence yet to be given.
	Conjunction	Though he worked hard, yet he failed.

UNIT 12

One Word Substitutions

A

Abdication	Voluntary renouncing throne.
Aborigines	Original inhabitants of a country.
Ablaut	A vowel change that accompanies a change in grammatical function. Same as 'gradation'. *Sing, sang, Nor, sung.*
Accismus	Pretended refusal of something desired.
Acrolect	A variety of language that is closest to a standard main language, especially in an area where a creole is also spoken. Standard Jamaican English, where Jamaican Creole is also spoken.
Adianoeta	An expression that carries both an obvious meaning and a second, subtler meaning.
Adynaton	A declaration of impossibility, usually expressed as an exaggerated comparison with a more obvious impossibility. *"I will sooner have a beard grow in the palm of my hand than he shall get one of his cheek."* —William Shakespeare
Alexia	Inability to read, usually caused by brain lesions; word blindness.
Alliteration	Repetition of the same sound beginning several words placed close together, usually adjacent.
Alphabetism	The expression of spoken sounds by an alphabet.
Ambigram	A word, phrase, or sentence written in such a way that it reads the same way upside down as right.
Anadiplosis	Rhetorical repetition of one or more words, particularly a word at the end of a clause. *"Men in great place are thrice servants : servants of the sovereign or state; servants of fame; and servants of business."* —Francis Bacon
Anagram	A rearrangement of a group of letters, especially a word that can be formed by rearranging the letters in another word.
Accessible	Which can be approached.
Acclimatize	To accustom oneself in new climate.
Aggressor	One who attacks first.
Alimony	Allowance paid to wife on legal separation.
Altruist	One who loves others.

Amateur	Who does thing for pleasure and not for money.
Ambassador	Person representing a state in a foreign country.
Ambidextrous	One who can use either hand without any problem.
Ambiguous	That can be interpreted in any way.
Amnesia	Loss of memory.
Amphibian	Animals live both on land and sea.
Anarchy	Absence of rule or law and order.
Annual	Which happens once a year.
Anomaly	Deviation from common rule.
Anonymous	Which does not bear the name of writer.
Antiseptic	Medicine used to save plants and animals from being rotten or decaying.
Anaphora	Repetition of a word or phrase at the beginning of successive phrases, clauses, or sentences.
Antonym	Words which is opposite in meaning.
Aphasia	Loss of speech.
Aquarium	Vessel in which fish and water plants are kept.
Aquatic	Animals living in water.
Archaeology	Study of Antiquities.
Aristocracy	Government by the rich/aristocrats.
Ascetic	One who tortures himself for the good of soul.
Atheist	One who does not believe in existence of God.
Audible	Sound which can be heard.
Auditor	One who audits the accounts.
Aurist	A specialist with regard to the ear.
Autobiography	Life history written by self.
Autocracy	Government by one man.
Autograph	Getting signature of some important person in his handwriting.

B

Bachelorhood	State of being unmarried.
Bankrupt	One who can't pay the debts.
Bellicose	One who is fond of fighting.
Belligerents	Nations engaged in war.
Billingsgate	Coarsely abusive language.
Bibliophile	One who loves and collects books.
Biennial	Happening every second year.
Bigamy	Have two husband or two wives at a time.
Biography	Life history of a person.
Biped	Animal having two feet.

Blasphemy	Speaking disrespectfully about sacred or religious things.
Bookworm	One who devotes full time in studying books.
Botany	Study of plants.
Brigand	A bandit or robber, especially one of a band living by pillage and ransom.
Brittle	Which can be easily broken.
Bullion	Gold or Silver before using for manufacturing ornaments.
Bureaucracy	Government run by officials.

C

Caducity	The infirmity of old age, senility.
Calligraphy	The art of beautiful handwriting; elegant penmanship.
Cannibal	One who eats human flesh.
Centrifugal	Anything tending to move away from centre.
Centripetal	Anything tending to move towards centre.
Century	One hundred years.
Chrestomathy	A collection of choice literary passages, especially to help in learning a language.
Coprolalia	Uncontrolled, excessive use of obscene or scatological language, sometimes accompanying certain mental disorders.
Cruciverbalist	A constructor of crossword puzzles; also, an enthusiast of word games, especially crossword puzzles.
Colleagues	Persons working in the same office.
Compatriot	Belonging to same country.
Congenital	Belongs to a person by birth.
Contemporaries	Persons living at the same time.
Convalescence	Period of gradual recovery after illness.
Cosmopolitan	A citizen of the world.
Credulous	Who easily believes others.
Cryptography	Study of secret writing and coded words.
Curable	Which can be cured.
Cytology	Study of cell.

D

Dead letter	An unclaimed letter.
Deaf	One who cannot hear.
Democracy	Government of the people, for the people, by the people.
Dermatology	Study of skin.

Digestible	That which can be digested.
Dilogy	An ambiguous speech.
Dittograph	A letter or word repeated unintentionally in writing or copying.
Dittology	Two distinct interpretations of the same text.
Dipsomania	A strong desire to take liquor.
Divisible	That which can be divided.
Dotage	Extreme old age when one behaves like a child.
Drawn	A game in which no party wins.
Dumb	One who can't speak.
Dysgraphia	Impairment of the ability to write, usually caused by brain dysfunction or disease.
Dyslexia	A learning disorder distinguished by impaired ability to recognize and comprehend written words.

E

Edible	A thing fit to eat.
Effeminate	Womanish in habits.
Eligible	One who is fit for the post.
Elision	The omission of a letter or syllable. *'Don't'* instead of 'do not'.
Emigrant	One who goes to live in a foreign country.
Employee	One who is employed.
Employer	One who employs.
Endemic	A disease prevailing in a locality.
Entomology	Study of insects.
Endophoric	Characteristic of a reference to something outside the speech or text in which the reference occurs. See also: exophoric.
Epic	A long narrative poem.
Epanorthosis	Immediate rephrasing for emphasis, intensification, or justification. *"You, young lad, are most brave! Brave, did I say? No, heroic!"*
Epistrophe	Repetition of the same word or phrase at the end of successive phrases, clauses, or sentences.
Epicure	One who is fond of sensuous enjoyment.
Epilogue	A commentary given after conclusion of drama.
Epitaph	Words inscribed on the tomb of the dead.
Etymology	Science deals with formation of words.
Etymology	Study of a word regarding its origin and development.
Etymon	An earlier form of a word in the same language or an ancestor language.
Examinee	One who is taking examination.

Examiner	One who examines the copies to evaluate the knowledge or ability.
Exonym	A name by which one people or social group refers to another but which is not used by said group to refer to themselves.
Expatriate	To send out of native country.
Expurgate	To remove all objectionable matter.
Extempore	A speech without previous preparations.
Extradite	To send back the criminal to the country of his origin.

F

Fanatic (Bigot)	Unreasonably enthusiastic about religion.
Fastidious	Having very selective taste, hard to please.
Fatalist	One who believes in fate.
Feminist	One devoted to the welfare of women.
Foster child	Child brought by persons, who are not his parents.
Franchise	Constitutional right to cast vote.
Fratricide	Murder of brother.

G

Garage	A shed for motor car.
Geology	Study of Earth.
Germicide	Which destroys harmful micro-organisms.
Glossolalia	Fabricated, non-meaningful speech, especially such speech associated with a trancestate or some schizophrenic syndromes.
Glottochronology	The determination of how long ago different languages evolved from a common source language.
Glutton	Fond of eating too much.
Gratis	Without any payment, free.
Gregarious	Animals living in flocks.

H

Harangue	A noisy and loud speech before a large gathering.
Haplology	The process by which a word is formed by removing one of two identical or similar adjacent syllables in an earlier word.
Hearse	Vehicle to carry dead bodies.
Herbivorous	Animals living on herbs.
Hendiadys	The use of a conjunction rather than the subordination of one word to another.

Heterography	A method of spelling in which the same letters represent different sounds in different words, as in ordinary English orthography.
Heterophemy	The unconscious saying, in speech or in writing, of something that one does not intend to say, especially when what is said is the reverse of what was intended.
Heterogeneous	Things of different nature.
Histology	Biological branch concerned with the microscopic structure of tissues.
Hobson Jobson	An anglicized word or phrase corrupted from one or more words of an Asian language.
Holonym	A concept that has another concept as a part.
Homicide	Murder of a human being.
Homogeneous	Things of same nature.
Honeymoon	The first night of newly married couple.
Honorary	A post provided for honour.
Hydra	A serpent with many heads.
Hydrophobia	A fear from water.
Hygienist	Who cares fully of his health.
Hypothesis	A tentative assumption, made to drive a logical conclusion.
Hypallage	Interchange of two elements in a phrase or clause from the order in which they would normally appear. *"A mind is a terrible thing to waste"*, instead of *"To waste a mind is a terrible thing."*
Hypercorrect	Characteristic of an incorrect linguistic construction in which the error is produced from a mistaken effort to be correct. *"Between you and I"*, which should be *"between you and me"*.
Hyponym	A word that is more specific than a given word.

I

Iconoclast	Breaker of art and literature.
Idiosyncrasy	Peculiar temper of an individual.
Idolatry	Worshipping of idols.
Ignorant	Person who has no knowledge of any happening.
Illegal	Against the law.
Illegible	Which is not readable.
Illiterate	One who can neither read nor write.
Illeism	The practice of referring to oneself in the third person.
Imitable	Which can be imitated.
Immigrant	Arrival of a person from other country to settle.

Immovable	Which can't be moved, fixed.
Impostor	One who assumes name or title of someone else for deceiving others.
Impregnable	A fort which can't be entered into.
Incorrigible	Bad habits that cannot be corrected.
Ingressive	Characteristic of a speech sound produced with an inhalation of breath.
Incredible	Which can't be believed.
Inevitable	That can't be avoided.
Infallible	One who cannot make a mistake.
Infanticide	Murder of an infant.
Infection	A disease spread by contact.
Inimitable	Impossible to imitate.
Insomnia	Lack of sleep.
Interpolate	Inserting new matter in a book.
Intervenes	Anything pushed inside veins.
Invisible	That which cannot be seen.
Invulnerable	Impossible to harm.
Irreparable	That can't be repaired.
Irrevocable	A decision that can't be revoked.
Isocolon	A sequence of parallel structures, having the same number of words and sometimes the same number of syllables. *"What else can one do when he is alone in a jail cell, other than write long letters, think long thoughts, and pray long prayers?"* —Martin Luther King
Itinerant	One who travels from place-to-place.

K

Kindergarten	A nursery school for small children.
Kleptomania	An abnormal desire to steal.

L

Linguist	One who knows many languages.
Ligature	A character that combines two or more letters, such as e.
Lipogram	Writing composed of words lacking a certain specific letter or letters.
Litotes	Understatement by negating the opposite; a type of meiosis. *"I was not disappointed with the news."*
Loquacious	A continuous talker.
Lunar	Eclipse of moon.

M

Maiden speech Speech made for the first time.

Mammals Animals which give milk.

Manuscript Study material prepared to publish.

Masochism The condition or state of deriving (especially sexual) gratification from one's own pain or humiliation.

Materialistic One for whom money is the most important thing.

Matins Morning prayer in church.

Matricide Murder of own mother.

Matrimony State of being married.

Maxim An established principle.

Meadow A low level tract of uncultivated grassland.

Meditation The action or practice of profound spiritual or religious reflection or mental contemplation.

Melodrama A sensational dramatic piece with crude appeals to the emotions and usually a happy ending.

Mercenary One who fights for the sake of money.

Mesomorph A person whose build is powerful, compact and muscular.

Meteorology Study of climate or weather.

Meticulous Very particular even about small details.

Migratory That moves from one place to another.

Misogamist One who hates the custom of marriage.

Misogynist Hater of women.

Misologist One who hates learning.

Mobocracy Rule by mob.

Metonymy Substitution of a word or phrase with another which it suggests. *"The pen is mightier than the sword"*, in which both 'pen' and 'sword' are substituted for 'written prose' and 'military'.

Morphology The study of structure and forms of words in any language including inflection, derivation, and formation of compounds.

Monogamy Marrying one at a time.

N

Narcotic Medicine which induces sleep.

Neologism New word coined by an author.

Neology Study of formation of new words.

Notorious A man with bad reputation.

Nosism The practice of referring to oneself as 'we'; a type of enallage.

Numismatics Study of currency and medals.

O

Obsolete	No longer in practice.
Oceanography	Study of ocean.
Odontology	Study of teeth.
Oligarchy	Government by a few.
Omnipotent	One who is all powerful.
Omniscient	One who knows everything.
Omnivorous	One who eats everything.
Opaque	That which can't be seen through.
Ophthalmology	Study and treatment of eyes.
Optics	Study of vision.
Optimist	One who sees bright side of things.
Orthography	The study of correct spelling according to established usage.
Ornithology	Study of birds.
Orography	Study of mountains.
Orphan	A child whose parents are dead.
Orthodox	One who believes in traditional values.
Orthography	Study of correct spelling of words.
Ostracize	To expel from society.

P

Pacifist	One who believes in total abolition of war.
Palaeontology	Study of fossils.
Panacea	A remedy for all ills.
Pantisocracy	Government by all.
Pantomime	A dumb show.
Palilogy	The repetition of a word or phrase in immediate succession, for emphasis.
Palindrome	A word, phrase, clause, or sentence that reads the same regularly as it does when its letters are reversed; a type of palingram.
Palingram	A word, phrase, clause, or sentence that reads the same backwards after rearranging segments. *"Workmate did team-work."*
Pangram	A sentence that uses all the letters of the alphabet; a holalphabetic sentence.
Paragoge	The process by which a new word is formed by adding a letter or syllable to the end of another word. Same as 'proparalepsis', *'Climature'*, derived from 'climate'.

Paraprosdokian	Unexpected ending of a phrase or series.
Parasite	One who survives on others.
Parasol	A lady's umbrella.
Pathology	Medicinal branch to study the causes and effects of diseases.
Patricide	Murder of one's own father.
Patrimony	Properties inherited from one's father.
Patriot	One who loves own country.
Pedagogy	Study of art of teaching.
Pedantic	A style in which an author displays his knowledge.
Perpilocutionist	One who expounds on a subject of which he has little knowledge.
Polyptoton	Repetition of a word in different forms, cases, or with different inflection, in the sentence.
Purr word	A word with positive connotations and therefore desirable to use in building and sustaining good public relations.
Pedestrian	One who travels on foot.
Pessimist	One who sees dark side of things.
Philanderer	One who enjoys by love making.
Philanthropist	A lover of mankind.
Philately	Study of stamp collection.
Philistine	A person who does not care for art or literature.
Philogynist	Lover of womankind.
Philology	Study of words and their roots.
Phonetics	The study of speech sounds.
Phrenology	Study of skull with regard to human character.
Physiology	Study of structure of human body.
Pioneer	One who leads others.
Plagiarism	Literary theft. Using ideas and words of another person presenting them as own.
Platitudes	Common place remarks.
Plutocracy	Government by rich.
Polyandry	Marrying more than one husband at a time.
Polygamy	Marrying more than one wife at a time.
Post-mortem	An examination of body after death to find out the cause of death.
Primogeniture	Right of succession belonging to the first born.
Pseudonym	An imaginary name of author assumed to disguise himself.
Pugnacity	Tendency to quarrel.
Purist	One who is particular about the purity of one's language.

Q

Quadruped	Animal having four foot.

R

Rebel	One who takes up arms against Government.
Red tapism	Too much official formalities.
Regicide	Murder of a king.
Reticule	A lady's purse.
Retrospective	Which takes effect from some earlier date.

S

Sacrilege	Violating sanctity of some religious place.
Sadist	A person who derives (especially sexual) pleasure from inflicting pain, suffering, humiliation.
Shrew	A woman with peevish nature.
Simultaneous	Happening at the same time.
Smuggle	Importing goods illegally without paying custom duties.
Solar	Related to Sun.
Soliloquy	Speaking himself when alone.
Somnambulism	Walking in sleep.
Somniloquism	Talking in sleep.
Spokesman	One who speaks on behalf of other.
Stoic	One who is indifferent to pleasure and pain.
Suicide	Killing of self.
Snarl word	A word with negative connotations and therefore not desirable to use lest good public relations be undermined.
Superordinate	A word that is more generic than a given word.
Syllogism	Deductive reasoning in which a conclusion is derived from two promises. *"All human beings are mortal. I am a human being. Therefore, I am mortal."*
Synesis	Agreement of words to logic rather than grammatical form. *"The wages of sin is death."* —Romans 6:23
Synchronize	Occurring two or more events at a time.

T

Teetotaller	One who does not take alcoholic drinks.
Telltale	One who enjoys talking about others' private affairs.
Thearchy	Government by the God.
Theist	One who believes in the existence of God.
Theomania	A belief that there is one God.
Transmigration	Passing of soul from one body to another after death.
Transparent	That which can be seen through.
Truant	A student who leaves school or class without permission.
Truism	An often repeated truth.
Twins	Two child born together.

U

Usurer	One who lends money at higher rate of interest.
Utopia	A state of highest perfection.
Uxoricide	Murder of wife.

V

Valetudinarian	One who always thinks that he is ill.
Venial	An excusable fault.
Verbatim	Word for word.
Verbicide	The destruction of the sense or value of a word.
Verbose	Style full of words.
Vesper	Evening prayer in a church.
Veteran	A well and long experienced person in a particular occupation.

W

Wardrobe	An almirah where clothes are kept.
Widow	A woman whose husband has died.
Widower	A man whose wife has died.

X

Xenoepist	One with a foreign accent.

Z

Zoology	Study of animals.

UNIT 13

Words Used in the Constitution

भारतीय गणतन्त्र के संविधान-निर्माण में विशेष अर्थ वाले प्रयुक्त शब्दों की महत्ता को समझते हुए हिन्दी में उनके समानार्थी शब्द व पद विद्यार्थियों की सुविधा की दृष्टि से यहाँ दिये जा रहे हैं—

A

Word	Meaning(s)
Abandonment	परित्यजन, परित्याग
Abridgement	न्यूनन
Abrogation	निराकरण
Access	प्रवेश, पहुँच
Account	लेखा गणना
Accrual	प्रापण, प्रोद्भवन
Accrued	प्राप्त, प्रोद्भूत, उपार्जित
Accusation	अभियोग
Accused	अभियुक्त
Acquisition	अर्जन
Act	अधिनियम
Acting	कार्यकारी
Actionable wrong	अभियोज्य दोष
Adaptation	अनुकूलन
Addressed	सम्बोधित
Adherence	अवलम्बन
Ad Hoc	तदर्थ
Adjournment	स्थगन, अवधिदान, कालदान
Administer	प्रशासन करना
Administered	प्रशासित
Administration	प्रशासन
Administrative	प्रशासकीय
Administrative function	प्रशासकीय कृत्य
Administrator General	महाप्रशासक

Word	Meaning(s)
Admiralty	नौकाधिकरण, नावाधिकरण
Admissible	ग्राह्य
Adoption	दत्तक ग्रहण, दत्तक स्वीकरण
Adulteration	अपमिश्रण
Adult suffrage	वयस्क मताधिकार
Advance	अग्रिम, धन पेशगी
Advice	मन्त्रणा, उपदेश, सलाह
Advise	मन्त्रणा देना
Advisory Council	मन्त्रणा परिषद्
Advocate	अधिवक्ता
Advocate-General	महाधिवक्ता
Affect prejudicially	प्रतिकूल प्रभाव डालना
Affirmation	प्रतिज्ञान
Agency	अभिकरण
Agent	अभिकर्ता
Agreement	करार, समझौता
Air Force	वायुसेना
Air navigation	विमान परिवहन
Air traffic	विमान यातायात
Airways	वायु पथ
Alien	अन्य देशी, परदेशी
Alienate	पराधीन करना
Alienation	अन्य संक्रमण, परकीयकरण
Allegation	अभिकथन, आरोप

Word	Meaning(s)
Allegiance	निष्ठा
Allocation	बँटवारा
Allot	बाँटना
Allotment	बँटवारा
Amnesty	सर्वक्षमा
Amount	राशि
Annual	वार्षिक
Annual Financial Statement	वार्षिक वित्त विवरण
Annuity	वार्षिका
Annulment	अस्वीकृति
Appeal	पुनर्विचार-प्रार्थना
Appear	उपस्थित होना
Appended	संलग्न
Application	आवेदन-पत्र
Appointment	नियुक्ति
Appropriation	विनियोग
Appropriation bill	विनियोग विधेयक
Approval	अनुमोदन
Approve	अनुमोदन करना
Arbitral tribunal	मध्यस्थ न्यायाधिकरण
Arbitration	मध्यस्थ निर्णय
Arbitrator	पंचनिर्णय
Area	क्षेत्र
Armed forces	सशस्त्र सेना
Arrest	बन्दीकरण
Article	अनुच्छेद
Assemble	जमा होना
Assembly	सभा
Assent	अनुमति
Assessment	कर-निर्धारण
Assignment	समर्पण, सुपुर्दगी
Association	संस्था, संघ
Assurance of property	सम्पत्ति हस्तान्तरण
As the case may be	यथास्थिति, यथा प्रसंग
Attachment	कुर्की, टांच
Attorney-General	महान्यायवादी

Word	Meaning(s)
Audit	लेखा परीक्षण, गणना परीक्षण
Auditor-General	महालेखा-परीक्षक
Authentication	प्रमाणीकरण
Authority	प्राधिकारी
Authorize	प्राधिकृत करना
Autonomous	स्वायत्त
Autonomy	स्वायत्तता, स्वायत्त शासन
Auxiliary	सहायक
Award	पंचाज्ञा, निर्णय देना

B

Word	Meaning(s)
Bail	प्रतिभूति, जमानत
Ballot	शलाका, शलाका पद्धति, गूढ़पत्र
Bank	बैंक, अधिकोष
Banking	महाजनी, अधिकोषण
Bankruptcy	दिवाला
Bar	रुकावट
Benefit	हित
Betting	पण लगाना, पण क्रिया
Bicameral	दोघरा, द्विगृही
Bill	विधेयक, बिल
Bill of exchange	विनिमय-पत्र
Bill of indemnity	परिहान विधेयक
Bill of lading	वहन पत्र
Board	मण्डली, बोर्ड, परिषद्
Body	निकाय
Body (Corporate)	निगम निकाय
Body (Governing)	शासी निकाय
Bona Vacancia	स्वामिहीनत्व
Borrowing	उधार ग्रहण
Boundary	सीमा
Broadcasting	प्रसारण
Business	कारोबार
By-election	उपनिर्वाचन
By-law	उपविधि

C

Word	Meaning(s)
Calling	आजीविका
Camp	शिविर
Candidate	अभ्यर्थी, उम्मीदवार
Cantonment	छावनी
Capacity	सामर्थ्य
Capital	मूल धन, पूँजी
Capital value	मूल धन मूल्य
Capitation tax	प्रति व्यक्ति कर
Carriage	परिवहन
Casting vote	निर्णायक मत
Cattle pound	पशु अवरोध
Cause	वाद
Cause of action	वाद मूल
Central Intelligence Bureau	केन्द्रीय गुप्त वार्ता विभाग
Certificate	प्रमाण-पत्र
Certiorari	उत्प्रेरण लेख
Cess	उप-कर
Chairman	सभापति, अध्यक्ष
Charge	दोषारोप, अभियुक्त भार
Charitable and religious endowments	दातव्य तथा धार्मिक धर्मस्व
Charitable institution	दातव्य संस्था
Charity	दयालुता, उदारता, कृपा
Cheque	चैक, धनादेश
Chief	मुख्य प्रधान
Chief Commissioner	मुख्य आयुक्त
Chief Election Commissioner	मुख्य निर्वाचन आयुक्त
Chief Judge	मुख्य न्यायाधीश
Chief Justice	मुख्य न्यायाधिपति
Chief Minister	मुख्यमन्त्री
Citizenship	नागरिकता
Civil	व्यवहारिक, असैनिक
Civil Court	व्यवहार न्यायालय, व्यय न्यायालय, दीवानी न्यायालय

Word	Meaning(s)
Civil power	व्यवहार शक्ति, असैनिक
Civil wrong	व्यवहार विषयक अपकृत्य
Claim	दावा
Clarification	स्पष्टीकरण
Clause	धारा
Code	संहिता
Coinage	टंकण
Colonization	उपनिवेशन
Commerce	वाणिज्य
Commercial	वाणिज्य सम्बन्धी
Commission	आयोग
Commissioner	आयुक्त
Committee	समिति
Committee, select	प्रवर समिति
Common good	सार्वजनिक कल्याण
Common seal	सामान्य मुद्रा, सामान्य मुहर
Communicate	संचार करना
Communication, Means of	संचार साधन
Community	लोकसमाज, समुदाय
Commutation	लघुकरण
Company	समवाय, कम्पनी
Compensation	प्रतिकर, क्षतिपूर्ति
Competent	सक्षम
Complaint	फरियाद
Comptroller and Auditor-General	नियन्त्रक तथा महालेखा-परीक्षक
Computation	संगणना
Concurrence	सहमति
Condition	शर्त
Conditions of service	सेवा की शर्तें
Conference want of	विश्वास का अभाव
Conscience	अन्तःकरण
Consent	सम्मति

Word	Meaning(s)
Consent (Previous)	पूर्व सम्मति
Consequential	आनुषंगिक
Consideration	विचार
Consolidated fund	संचित निधि
Constituency	निर्वाचन क्षेत्र
Constituent Assembly	संविधान सभा
Constitution	संविधान
Construe	अर्थ करना
Consul	वाणिज्य दूत
Consultation	परामर्श
Consumption	उपभोग
Contact	सम्पर्क
Contagious	सांसर्गिक
Contempt	अवमानना
Contempt of Court	न्यायालय की अवमानना
Context	सन्दर्भ, प्रसंग
Contingency fund	आकस्मिक निधि
Contract	संविदा
Contravention	प्रतिकूलता उल्लंघन
Contribution	अंशदान
Control	नियन्त्रण
Controversy	प्रतिवाद
Convention	अभिसमय, प्रथा, रूढ़ि, परम्परा
Conveyance	सम्पत्ति हस्तान्तरण
Convicted	सिद्ध दोष, अभिशस्त, दोष प्रमाणित
Conviction	दोष सिद्ध अभिशस्त
Co-operative society	सहकारी संस्था
Copy	प्रतिलिपि, प्रतिकृति
Copyright	प्रकाशनाधिकार, कृति स्वाम्य
Corporation	निगम
Corresponding	तत्स्थानी
Corrupt	भ्रष्ट
Cost	परिव्यय, खर्च, लागत
Council	परिषद्
Council of States	राज्य परिषद्

Word	Meaning(s)
Council of Tribals	जनजातीय परिषद्
Countervailing duty	प्रतिशुल्क
Court	न्यायालय
Court (District)	जिला न्यायालय
Court (Federal)	संघ न्यायालय
Court (Magisterial)	दण्डाधिकारी न्यायालय
Court Martial	सैन्य न्यायालय
Court of Appeal	पुनर्विचार न्यायालय
Court of Wards	प्रतिपालक अधिकरण
Court of Revenue	राजस्व न्यायालय
Court of Session	सत्र न्यायालय
Court Subordinate	अधीन न्यायालय
Credit	प्रत्यय साख, पत्त, आकलन
Crime	अपराध
Criminal	अपराधी, आपराधिक, दण्ड सम्बन्धी
Criminal law	दण्ड विधि
Currency	चल अर्थ, मुद्रा प्रचलन
Custody	अभिरक्षा, निरोध, कावल
Custom	रूढ़ि, आचार
Custom duty	बहिर्शुल्क, सीमा शुल्क
Custom, Frontier	सीमान्त शुल्क

D

Word	Meaning(s)
Dealings	व्यवहार, लेनदेन
Debate	वाद-विवाद
Debenture	ऋण-पत्र
Debit	विकलन
Debt	ऋण
Decision	विनिश्चय
Decree	घोषणा
Dedication	समर्पण, उत्सर्ग
Deed	विलेख
Defamation	मानहानि
Defence	प्रतिरक्षा

Word	Meaning(s)
Deliberation	पर्यालोचन, विचार-विमर्श
Delimitation	परिसीमन
Demand	माँग, अभियाचना
Demarcation	सीमांकन
Demobilization	सैन्य वियोजन, सैन्य विघटन
Deprive	वंचित करना
Deputy Chairman	उपसभापति
Deputy Commissioner	उपायुक्त, मण्डलायुक्त
Deputy President	उपराष्ट्रपति
Deputy Speaker	उपाध्यक्ष
Derogation	अप्रतिष्ठा, अपमान
Descent	उद्भव
Design	रूपांकन
Detrimental	अहितकारी
Diplomacy	राजनय, कूटनीति
Direction	निर्देश
Disability	निर्योग्यता
Discharge	निर्वाह करना, भार हटाना, मुक्त करना
Disciplinary	अनुशासन सम्बन्धी
Discipline	अनुशासन
Discovery	आविष्कार
Discretion	स्वविवेक
Discrimination	विभेद
Discussion	चर्चा, बहस
Dismiss	पदच्युत करना, (मुकदमा) खारिज करना
Disperse	विसर्जन करना
Dispute	विवाद
Disqualification	अनर्हता
Disqualify	अनर्ह या अयोग्य ठहराना
Dissent	विमति
Dissolution	विघटन
Distribution	वितरण, विभाजन
District	जिला

Word	Meaning(s)
District Board	जिला परिषद्
District Council	जिला सभा
District Fund	जिला निधि
Dividend	लाभांश
Divorce	विवाह-विच्छेदन
Document	लेख-दस्तावेज
Domicile	अधिवास गृह, घर (सर्वदा रहने का स्थान)
Domiciled	अधिवासी
Dullness	मतिमान्य
During good behaviour	सदाचार पर्यन्त
During the pleasure of President	राष्ट्रपति प्रसादपर्यन्त
Duty	शुल्क, कर्त्तव्य
Duty, Custom	सीमा शुल्क
Duty, Death	मरण शुल्क, मृत्युकर
Duty, Estate	सम्पत्ति शुल्क
Duty, Excise	उत्पादन शुल्क
Duty, Export	निर्यात शुल्क
Duty, Import	आयात शुल्क
Duty, Stamp	मुद्रांक शुल्क
Duty, Succession	उत्तराधिकार शुल्क

E

Word	Meaning(s)
Economic	आर्थिक
Education	शिक्षा
Efficiency of Administration	प्रशासन कार्यक्षमता
Elect	निर्वाचित करना
Elected	निर्वाचित, चुने हुए
Election	निर्वाचन
Election Commissioner	निर्वाचन आयुक्त
Election (Direct)	प्रत्यक्ष निर्वाचन
Election (General)	साधारण निर्वाचन

Word	Meaning(s)
Election (Indirect)	परोक्ष निर्वाचन
Election tribunal	निर्वाचन अधिकरण
Electoral-roll	निर्वाचन नामावली
Electorate	निर्वाचक मण्डल, निर्वाचक क्षेत्र
Eligibility	पात्रता, योग्यता
Eligible	पात्र, योग्य
Emergency	आपात
Emergent	आपाती
Emigration	उत्प्रवास
Emoluments	उपलब्धियाँ
Employer's liability	नियोजक दातव्य, नियोजक उत्तरवादिता
Enactment	अधिनियम
Encumbered Estate	भारग्रस्त सम्पदा
Endorse	पृष्ठांकन करना, समर्थन करना
Endorsed	पृष्ठांकित अंकित
Endowment	धर्मस्व
Engagement	वचनबन्ध
Engineering	यन्त्रशास्त्र, अभियान्त्रिकी
Enterprise	उद्यम
Entitled	अधिकारी, हकदार
Entrust	न्यस्त करना, सौंपना
Entry	प्रविष्टि, दाखिला
Equality	समता
Equal protection of laws	विधि का समान संरक्षण
Escheat	राजगामी धन
Establishment	स्थापना, संस्थापन कर्मचारी वर्ग
Estate	सम्पदा
Estimate	आकप्राकूलन, आगणन, अनुमान
Evidence	साक्ष्य
Excess profit	अतिरिक्त लाभ
Exclude	अपवर्जन करना
Exclusion	अपवर्जन
Exclusive jurisdiction	अनन्य क्षेत्राधिकार

Word	Meaning(s)
Executive	कार्यपालिका
Executive power	कार्य पालिका शक्ति या अधिकार
Exempt	मुक्त
Exercise	प्रयोग, अनुष्ठान
Ex-officio	पदेन
Expenditure	व्यय
Explanation	व्याख्या, स्पष्टीकरण
Explosives	विस्फोटक
Extend	विस्तार करना, फैलाना
External affairs	वैदेशिक कार्य, बहिःस्थित कार्य
Extradition	प्रत्यर्पण
Extra-territorial operation	राज्य क्षेत्रातीत प्रवर्तन
Export	निर्यात

F

Word	Meaning(s)
Factory	कारखाना
Faith	धर्म भावना, श्रद्धा
Fare	भाड़ा, किराया, खाद्य, भोजन
Federal Court	संघ न्यायालय
Fee	देय शुल्क
Finance	वित्त
Finance Bill	वित्त विधेयक
Finance Commission	वित्त आयोग
Financial	वित्तीय
Financial obligation	वित्तीय भार
Financial Statement	वित्तीय विवरण
Fine	अर्थदण्ड
Fishery	मीन क्षेत्र, मीन पण्य
Forbid	निषेध करना
Forbidden	निषिद्ध
Forces	बल, सेना

Word	Meaning(s)
Foreign affairs	विदेशी कार्य
Foreign exchanges	विदेशी विनियम
Form	रूप, प्रपत्र
Formula	सूत्र
Formulated	सूत्रीय
For the time being	तत्सम, उपस्थित समय के लिए
Freedom	स्वतन्त्रता, स्वातन्त्र्य, आजादी
Freight	वस्तु-भाड़ा
Frontiers	सीमान्त प्रदेश
Function	कृत्य
Function Administrative	प्रशासकीय कृत्य
Fund	निधि
Fund, sinking	निक्षेप निधि
Future market	वायदा बाजार

G

Word	Meaning(s)
Gambling	द्यूत, जुआ
Gazette	सूचना पत्र, राज-पत्र
General Election	साधारण निर्वाचन
Govern	शासन करना
Governance	शासन
Government	सरकार, शासन
Government of State	राज्य की सरकार
Government of India	भारत सरकार
Governor	राज्यपाल
Grant	अनुदान
Grant-in-aid	सहायक अनुदान
Gratuity	उपदान
Guarantee	प्रत्याभूति
Guardian	संरक्षक
Guidance	मार्गदर्शन

H

Word	Meaning(s)
Habeas Corpus	बन्दी प्रत्यक्षीकरण
Handicrafts	हस्तशिल्प, दस्तकारी
Hazardous	संकटमय
Headman	मुखिया
High Court	उच्च न्यायालय
Honorarium	मानदेय
House	सदन
House of People	लोकसभा

I

Word	Meaning(s)
Illegal	अवैध
Illegal practice	अवैध आचरण
Immuned	उन्मुक्त
Immunity	उन्मुक्ति
Impeachment	महाभियोग
Implementing	परिपालन
Impose	दोषारोपण या करारोपण
Imprisonment	कारावास, कैद
Improvement Trust	सुधार प्रन्यास
Incapacity	असमर्थता
Incidental	प्रासंगिक
Incompetency	अक्षमता
Imcompetent	अक्षम
Incorporation	निगमन
Incumbent of an office	पदधारी
Indebtedness	ऋणग्रस्तता
Industry	उद्योग
Ineligible	अपात्र
Infants	शिशु
Infectious	संक्रामक
Influence	प्रभाव
Influence undue	प्रभाव अनुचित

Word	Meaning(s)
Inheritance	दाय, उत्तराधिकार
Initiate	उपक्रमण करना, दीक्षा देना
Injury	क्षति
Inland waterways	अन्तर्देशीय जलपथ
Inoperative Inquiry	अप्रवृत परिपत्र जाँच
Insolvency	दिवाला
Inspection	पर्यवेक्षण, निरीक्षण
Institution	संस्थान
Instruction	शिक्षा, अनुदेश, हिदायत
Instrument	लिखित, संविदा, विलेख दलील, उपकरण, साधन
Insurance	बीमा
Intercourse	समागम
Interest	ब्याज
International	अन्तर्राष्ट्रीय
Interpretation	निर्वचन व्याख्या
Intestacy	इच्छापत्र, हीनत्व, निर्वासीयतता
Intestate	इच्छा-पत्र-हीन, निर्वसीयत
Introduction	पुरःस्थापना
Invalid	अमान्य, असमर्थ
Invalidity pensions	असमर्थता निवृत्तिवेतन
Investigation	अनुसन्धान
Involve	अन्तर्ग्रस्त करना
Involved	अन्तर्ग्रस्त
Irregularity	अनियमितता
Issue	विवाद पद
Introduce	पुरःस्थापन करना

J

Word	Meaning(s)
Joining time	कार्यग्रहण काल
Joint family	अविभक्त या संयुक्त कुटुम्ब या परिवार
Judge	न्यायाधीश
Judge, Additional	अपर न्यायाधीश
Judge, Extra	अतिरिक्त न्यायाधीश
Judgement	निर्णय
Judicial power	न्यायिक शक्ति या अधिकार
Judicial proceeding	न्यायिक कार्यवाही, न्यायिक कार्य-रीति
Judicial stamp	न्यायिक मुद्रांक
Judiciary	न्यायपालिका
Jurisdiction	क्षेत्राधिकार
Justice-Chief	मुख्य न्यायाधीश

K

Word	Meaning(s)
Keep	रखना
Kept in abayance	अस्थगित
Key-words	बीज-शब्द
Key-sentence	मुख्य-वाक्य
Khewat	लेखापाल की पंजी
Knowledge	बोध, ज्ञान

L

Word	Meaning(s)
Labour	श्रम
Labour Union	श्रमिक संघ
Land Records	भू-अभिलेख
Land Revenue	भू-राजस्व
Land-tenure	भू-धृति
Law	विधि
Law of Nations	राष्ट्रों की विधि
Legal	विधि सम्बन्धी
Legislation	विधान
Legislative power	विधायिनी शक्ति

Word	Meaning(s)
Legislative Assembly	विधानसभा
Legislative Council	विधानपरिषद्
Legislature	विधानमण्डल
Levy	आरोपण, उद्ग्रहण, उगाहना
Liability	दायित्व
Libel	अपमान लेख
Liberty	स्वाधीनता
Licence	अनुज्ञप्ति, लाइसेन्स
Lieutenant Governor	उपराज्यपाल
Limitation	परिसीमा
List	सूची
List Concurrent	समवर्ती सूची
List State	राज्य सूची
List Union	संघ सूची
Livelihood	जीविका
Loan	उधार, ऋण
Local area	स्थानीय क्षेत्र
Local authorities	स्थानीय प्राधिकारी
Local board	स्थानीय मण्डली
Local body	स्थानीय निकाय
Local Government	स्थानीय शासन
Local Self Government	स्थानीय स्वशासन
Lockup	बन्दीखाना
Lower House	प्रथम सदन
Lunacy	उन्माद, पागलपन
Lunatic	उन्मत्त, पागल
Letters of Credit	प्रत्यय पत्र

M

Word	Meaning(s)
Maintain	पोषण करना, बनाए रखना
Maintenance	पोषण
Major	वयस्क
Majority	बहुमत
Mandamus	परमादेश
Manufacture	निर्माण
Maritime shipping	समुद्र नौवहन
Maternity relief	प्रसूति सहायता, प्रसूति साहाम्य
Member	सदस्य
Memo	ज्ञाप, स्मृतिपत्र
Memorandum	ज्ञापन
Memorial	स्मारक
Mental deficiency	मनोवैकल्य
Mental weakness	मनोदौर्बल्य
Merchandise Marks	पण्य चिह्न
Merchandise Marine	वणिक पोता
Migration	प्रव्रजन
Mind Unsound	विकृत चित्त
Mineral	खनिज
Mineral resources	खनिज सम्पत्ति
Mining settlement	खनिज वसति
Minor	अवयस्क, अल्पवयस्क, नाबालिग
Minority	अल्पसंख्यक
Misbehaviour	दुराचार, दुष्ट वृत्ति
Modification	रूपभेद सुधार
Money bill	धन विधेयक
Morality	सदाचार
Motion of Confidence	विश्वास प्रस्ताव
Motion of No Confidence	अविश्वास प्रस्ताव
Municipal Area	नगर क्षेत्र
Municipal Committee	नगर समिति
Municipal Corporation	नगर निगम
Municipal Tramways	नगर में ट्राम गाड़ी का पथ, नगर ट्राम-वे

N

Word	Meaning(s)
National Highway	राष्ट्रीय राजपथ
Naturalization	देशीयकरण, अभ्यस्तीकरण
Naval	नौ-सेना
Navigation	नौ-परिवहन
Newspaper	समाचार-पत्र
Nomination	नाम निर्देशन, मनोनयन
Notice in writing	लिखित सूचना
Notification	अधिसूचना

O

Word	Meaning(s)
Obligation	वैधानिक या नैतिक बन्धन, अनुग्रह
Occupation	उपजीविका, धन्धा
Officer	अधिकारी
Official residence	पदावास, अधिकारी का आवास
Opinion	अभिप्राय, राय
Order in council	परिषद्, आदेश
Order standing	स्थायी आदेश
Ordinance	अध्यादेश
Organization	संघटन
Owner	स्वामी

P

Word	Meaning(s)
Parliament	संसद
Partnership	भागिता
Pass	पारण आदेश या परिचय-पत्र
Passed	पारित
Passport	पारपत्र
Patent	एकस्व
Pecuniary Jurisdiction	आर्थिक क्षेत्राधिकार
Penalty	दण्ड, सजा, जुर्माना
Pending	लम्बित, लम्बमान
Pension	निवृत्ति वेतन
Permission	अनुज्ञा
Perpetual succession	शाश्वत उत्तराधिकारी
Perquisite	परिलब्धि
Personal law	निजी कानून, व्यक्तिगत कानून
Piracy	जल दस्युता, ग्रन्थकर्ता की आज्ञा के बिना उसके ग्रन्थ को छापकर लाभ उठाना
Plead	अदालत में बहस करना
Police	आरक्षक, नगरपाल, नगर रक्षक
Police Force	आरक्षक दल
Policy of Insurance	बीमा पत्र
Port-quarantine	पत्तन निरोधा
Possession	स्ववश अधिकार, कब्जा
Preamble	प्रस्तावना
Preference	अधिमान
Prejudice	प्रतिकूल प्रभाव, पक्षपात की भावना
Preside	पीठासीन होना, सभापतित्त्व करना
President	राष्ट्रपति
Presiding officer	अधिष्ठाता
Preventive detention	निवारक
Prisoner	काराबन्दी
Privileges	विशेषाधिकार
Process	आदेशिका विधि
Proclamation	उद्घोषणा
Proclamation of Emergency	आपात की उद्घोषणा

Word	Meaning(s)
Prohibited	प्रतिषेध, निषिद्ध
Prohibition	मद्य-निषेध
Proportional representation	अनुपाती प्रतिनिधित्व
Proposal	प्रस्थापना
Prorogue	सत्रावसान, सभा को बिना व्यवधान के कुछ काल के लिए स्थगित करना
Provided	परन्तु, बशर्ते कि
Proxy	प्रतिपत्री
Publication	प्रकाशन
Public debt	राष्ट्र ऋण
Public demand	सार्वजनिक अभियाचना
Public health	लोक स्वास्थ्य
Public notification	सार्वजनिक अधिसूचना, लोक अधिसूचना
Public order	सार्वजनिक व्यवस्था
Public Service Commission	लोक सेवा आयोग
Public service	लोक सेवा

Q

Word	Meaning(s)
Qualification	अर्हता
Quarantine	निरोधा
Question of law	विधि प्रश्न
Quorum	गणपूर्ति
Quo warranto	अधिकार-पृच्छा

R

Word	Meaning(s)
Ratification	अनुसमर्थन
Reading First	प्रथम पठन
Receipt paper	पावती रसीद
Recommend	सिफारिश या संस्तुति करना
Recommendation	संस्तुति या सिफारिश
Record of Court	अभिलेख न्यायालय
Record of right	अधिकाराभिलेख
Recruitment	भर्ती
Recurring	आवर्तक
Redemption charges	विमोचन भार
Reference	निदेश
Reformatory	सुधारालय
Refundable to	लौटाए जाने योग्य
Regional Commissioner	प्रादेशिक आयुक्त
Regional Council	प्रादेशिक परिषद्
Regional Fund	प्रादेशिक निधि
Registered	पंजीबद्ध, निबद्ध
Registration	पंजीयन, पंजी-बन्धन, निबन्धन
Regulation	विनियम
Relevancy	सुसंगति
Relevant	सुसंगत
Remission	परिहार
Remuneration	पारिश्रमिक
Repeal	निरसन
Representation	प्रतिनिधित्व
Representative	प्रतिनिधि
Reprieve	प्रविलम्बन करना
Repugnancy	विरोध
Repugnant	विरुद्ध
Requisition	अधिग्रहण
Reserved forest	रक्षित वन
Respite	विराम
Restriction	निर्बन्धन
Retire	निवृत्त होना
Retirement	निवृत्ति
Review	पुनरावलोकन
Revoke	प्रतिसंहार करना
Reward	पारितोषिक
Rule of the road	पथ नियम
Ruler	शासक

S

Word	Meaning(s)
Sefeguard	रक्षा, संरक्षण
Sale	विक्रय
Sanction, previous	पूर्व स्वीकृति
Savings	बचत
Security	प्रतिभूति, जमानत
Sentence	दण्डादेश
Service charges	सेवाभार
Session	सत्र
Single transferable vote	एकल संक्रमणीय मत
Sinking fund	निक्षेप निधि
Social custom	सामाजिक रूढ़ि
Social insurance	सामाजिक बीमा
Social service	सामाजिक सेवा
Sovereign	प्रभु, प्रधान, मुख्य, श्रेष्ठ
Sovereign Democratic Republic	सम्पूर्ण प्रभुत्व सम्पन्न लोकतन्त्रात्मक गणतन्त्र
Speaker	अध्यक्ष
Speech, Freedom of	वाक्स्वातन्त्र्य
Staff	कर्मचारी वृन्द
Stamp duties	मुद्रांक शुल्क
Standing orders	स्थायी आदेश
State funds	राज्य निधि
Stock exchange	श्रेष्ठि चत्वर
Subject matter	वाद विषय
Subordinate officer	अधीनस्थ अधिकारी
Succession	उत्तराधिकार
Successor	उत्तराधिकारी
Sue	वाद लाना
Suffrage	मताधिकार
Suit, Civil	व्यवहार वाद
Summon	आह्वान
Superintendence	अधीक्षण
Supplementary Grant	अनुपूरक अनुदान
Supreme command	सर्वोच्च समादेश
Suspend	निलम्बित करना
Slander	अपमान वचन

T

Word	Meaning(s)
Tax (Calling)	आजीविका कर
Tax (Capitation)	प्रति-व्यक्ति कर
Tax (Corporation)	निगम कर
Tax (Employment)	सेवा कर
Tax (Entertainment)	प्रमोद कर
Tax (Export)	निर्यात कर
Tax (Profession)	वृत्ति कर
Tax (Income)	आयकर
Tax (Sales)	विक्रय कर
Tax (Terminal)	सीमा कर
Tax (Trades)	व्यापार कर
Technical Training	शिल्पी प्रशिक्षण
Tenant	असामी, किराएदार
Tender, legal	विधि मान्य
Tenure	पदावधि
Term	निबन्ध अवधि
Territorial charges	प्रादेशिक भार
Territorial Jurisdiction	प्रादेशिक क्षेत्राधिकार
Territorial waters	जल प्रांगण
Territory	राज्य क्षेत्र
Tidal water	वेला जल, ज्वार जल
Tolls	पथ कर
Trade mark	व्यापार चिह्न
Trade Union	कार्मिक या व्यापार संघ
Traffic Human	मानव पणन
Training	प्रशिक्षण
Tramcar	रथयान
Transfer	स्थानान्तरण हस्तान्तरण
Transition	संक्रमण

Word	Meaning(s)
Transport	परिवहन
Transportation	निर्वासन
Treasure troves	निखात निधि
Treaty	सन्धि
Tribal Area	जनजाति क्षेत्र
Tribe	जनजाति
Tribunal	न्यायाधिकरण
Triennial	त्रैवार्षिक, तिसाला
Trust	न्यास

U

Word	Meaning(s)
Undischarged	अनुन्मुक्त
Undue influence	अनुचित प्रभाव
Unemployment	बेकारी
Union	संघ
Unity	एकता
Unsoundness of mind	चित्त विकृति

V

Word	Meaning(s)
Vacancy	रिक्ति, रिक्तता
Vagrancy	आहिंडन, आवारागर्दी
Validity	मान्यता
Vice-President	उपराष्ट्रपति
Village Council	ग्राम परिषद्
Violation	अतिक्रमण
Visas	द्रष्टांक, वीसा
Vocation	व्यवसाय

Word	Meaning(s)
Vote Casting	निर्णायक मत
Voter	मतदाता
Votes on account	लेखानुदान, गणअनुदान
Votes of credit	प्रत्यायानुदान

W

Word	Meaning(s)
Wage	मजदूरी
Wage, Living	निर्वाह मजदूरी
Warrant	अधिपत्र
Will	इच्छा-पत्र, बिल, वसीयत
Winding up	समापन
Writ	लेख, कानूनी आज्ञापत्र

Y

Word	Meaning(s)
Yearly	वार्षिक
Yield	उपज, देना

Z

Word	Meaning(s)
Zaid	अतिरिक्त फसल
Zamindari wahid	एकल जमींदारी
Zeal	उत्साह
Zerab	जलाच्छादित
Zone	क्षेत्र

UNIT 14

The Speaking Tree : Words by Category

Parts of the Body

Word	Pronunciation	Hindi Meaning
Abdomen	एब्डोम्न	पेट
Ankle	एंकल	टखना
Anus	ऐनस	गुदा
Arm	आर्म	भुजा, बाँह
Arm-pit	आर्म-पिट	बगल
Artery	आर्टरी	धमनी
Back	बैक	पीठ
Backbone	बैक-बोन	रीढ़ की हड्डी
Beard	बियर्ड	दाढ़ी
Beak	बीक	चोंच
Belly	बेली	उदर
Bile	बाइल	पित्त
Bladder	ब्लैडर	मूत्राशय
Blood	ब्लड	खून
Bone	बोन	हड्डी
Brain	ब्रेन	मस्तिष्क
Breast	ब्रेस्ट	छाती
Buttock	बुटॉक	नितम्ब
Breath	ब्रेथ	साँस
Calf	काफ	पिण्डली
Cartilage	कार्टिलेज	उपास्थि
Cheeks	चीक्स	गाल
Claw	क्लॉ	पंजा
Chest	चेस्ट	पुरुष की छाती
Chin	चिन	ठोड़ी
Collar bone	कॉलर बोन	हँसली की हड्डी
Ear	इयर	कान, कर्ण
Ear-drum	इयर-ड्रम	कर्ण पटल
Elbow	एल्बो	कोहनी

Word	Pronunciation	Hindi Meaning
Embyro	एम्ब्रओ	भ्रूण
Eye	आई	आँख
Eye-ball	आई-बॉल	आँख की पुतली
Eye-brow	आई-ब्रो	भौंह
Eye-lid	आई-लिड	पलक
Eye-lash	आई-लैश	बरौनी
Face	फेस	चेहरा
Feather	फीदर	पर, पंख
Finger	फिंगर	अँगुली
Fist	फिस्ट	मुट्ठी
Fin	फिन	मछली का पर
Foot	फुट	पैर, पाँव
Forehead	फोरहैड	माथा, ललाट
Fang	फैंग	सर्प का विषाक्त दन्त
Flesh	फ्लेश	मांस
Gum	गम	मसूढ़ा
Groin	ग्रोइन	पेट और जाँघ के बीच का अंग
Hair	हेयर	बाल
Hand	हैण्ड	हाथ
Head	हैड	सिर
Hood	हूड	फन
Heart	हार्ट	दिल, हृदय
Hoof	हूफ	खुर
Heel	हील	एड़ी
Horn	हॉर्न	सींग
Index finger	इंडेक्स फिंगर	तर्जनी
Intestine	इन्टेस्टाइन	आँत
Jaw	जॉ	जबड़ा
Joint	ज्वाइंट	जोड़
Kidney	किडनी	गुर्दा
Knee	नी	घुटना
Lap	लैप	गोद
Leg	लेग	टाँग
Loin	लॉयन	कमर
Lip	लिप	होंठ, अधर
Little finger	लिटिल फिंगर	छोटी अँगुली
Liver	लिवर	जिगर
Lung	लंग	फेफड़ा
Marrow	मैरो	मज्जा
Middle finger	मिडल फिंगर	मध्यमा

Word	Pronunciation	Hindi Meaning
Mole	मोल	मस्सा
Molar teeth	मोलर टीथ	दाढ़
Moustache	मुश्टाश	मूँछ
Mouth	माउथ	मुँह
Muscle	मसल	मांसपेशी
Nail	नेल	नाखून
Navel	नेवल	नाभि
Neck	नेक	गर्दन
Nerve	नर्व	रग, नस
Nipple	निप्पल	चुचुक
Nose	नोज	नाक
Nostril	नॉस्ट्रिल	नासिका छिद्र
Orbit	ऑरबिट	आँख का गड्ढा
Palate	पैलेट	तालू
Palm	पाम	हथेली
Plume	प्लूम	पंख
Penis	पेनिस	शिश्न
Phalange	फ्लैंज	अंगुली का पोर
Pores	पोर्स	रोमकूप
Phlegm	फ्लेम	कफ
Pulse	पल्स	नाड़ी
Pupil	प्युपिल	आँख की पुतली
Pus	पस	पीप
Rib	रिब	पसली
Ring finger	रिंग फिंगर	अनामिका
Rump	रम्प	नितम्ब
Saliva	सैलाइवा	लार
Wrist	रिस्ट	कलाई
Shoulder	शोल्डर	कंधा
Skin	स्किन	त्वचा
Skull	स्कल	खोपड़ी
Snout	स्नाउट	थूथनी
Sole	सोल	पैर का तलवा
Soul	सोल	आत्मा
Spleen	स्पलीन	तिल्ली
Sting	स्टिंग	डंक
Stomach	स्टॉमक	पेट
Spittle	स्पिटल	थूक
Stool	स्टूल	मल
Sweat	स्वैट	पसीना

Word	Pronunciation	Hindi Meaning
Teat	टीट	स्तन, चुचुक
Temple	टैम्पल	कनपटी
Tail	टेल	पूँछ
Thigh	थाइ	जाँघ
Throat	थ्रोट	गला, कण्ठ
Thumb	थम्ब	अँगूठा
Toe	टो	पाँव का पंजा
Tongue	टंग	जीभ
Tooth	टूथ	दाँत
Trachea	ट्रैकिया	श्वास नली
Trunk	ट्रंक	धड़
Tears	टीयर्स	आँसू, अश्रु
Tonsil	टॉन्सिल	गले की गिल्टी
Testicles	टेस्टिकल्स	अण्डकोश
Udders	अडर्स	थन
Womb	वॉम्ब	गर्भाशय
Uterus	यूटरस	गर्भाशय
Waist	वेस्ट	कमर
Uvula	यूव्युला	काग
Urine	यूरीन	मूत्र
Vagina	वेजिना	योनि
Vein	वेन	नस

Conditions of the Body and Diseases

Word	Pronunciation	Hindi Meaning
Abortion	अबॉर्शन	गर्भपात
Acne	एक्ने	मुहाँसे
Acidity	एसिडिटी	अम्ल, पित्त
Anaemia	एनीमिया	खून की कमी
Asthma	अस्थमा	दमा
Asphyxy	ऑसफिक्सी	दम घुटना
Amnesia	एम्नेसिया	स्मृति विभ्रम
Antiseptic	एण्टिसेप्टिक	संक्रमण प्रतिरोधी
Anorexia	अनोरिक्सीया	अरुचि
Bald	बाल्ड	गंजापन
Belching	बेल्चिंग	डकार
Blind	ब्लाइण्ड	अन्धता
Boil	बॉयल	फोड़ा
Breath	ब्रेथ	साँस

Word	Pronunciation	Hindi Meaning
Bronchitis	ब्रोन्काइटिस	श्वांस रोग
Bubo	ब्यूबो	गिल्टी
Blood-flux	ब्लड-फ्लक्स	रक्त अतिसार
Conjunctivitis	कॉनजांक्टिवाइटिस	नेत्र पीड़ा
Cataract	कैटैरैक्ट	मोतियाबिन्द
Carries	कैरीज	दाँत में गड्ढा
Catarrah	कैटर	जुकाम
Chill	चिल	शीतल
Cold	कोल्ड	ठण्डक
Cough	कफ	खाँसी
Consumption	कन्सम्प्शन	क्षय रोग
Colic pain	कॉलिक पेन	उदरशूल
Constipation	कॉन्स्टिपेशन	कब्ज
Cholera	कोलरा	हैजा
Corns	कॉर्न्स	बिवाई फटना
Carbuncle	कार्बन्कल	जहरबाद
Canker	कैंकर	कीड़े पड़ना
Coryza	कोरीजा	जुकाम, नजला
Deaf	डीफ	बहरा
Dengue	डेन्गू	लँगड़ा बुखार
Diabetes	डाइबिटिज	मधुमेह
Diarrhoea	डायरिया	अतिसार
Dropsy	ड्रॉप्सी	जलोदर
Dumb	डम्ब	गूँगा
Dysentery	डिसेन्टरी	पेचिस, आँव
Dwarf	ड्वार्फ	बौना
Debility	डेबिलिटी	कमजोरी
Diphtheria	डिफ्थीरिया	कण्ठरोहिणी
Dyspepsia	डिस्पेप्सिया	अजीर्ण
Eczema	एक्जीमा	उकवत, छाजन
Epilepsy	ऐपिलेप्सी	मिरगी
Eunuch	यूनक	नपुंसक
Eye-sore	आइ-सोर	आँखों का दुखना
Epistaxes	एपिस्टेक्सिस	रक्तपित्त
Emissions	एमिशन्स	स्वप्नदोष
Eschal	एस्चाल	फफोले
Elephantiasis	ऐलिफैण्टियासिस	फील पाँव
Fever	फीवर	बुखार, ज्वर
Fistula	फिस्टूला	भगन्दर
Fainting	फेन्टिंग	बेहोशी

Word	Pronunciation	Hindi Meaning
Giddiness	गिडिनेस	चक्कर आना
Gland	ग्लैण्ड	गिल्टी
Gripping	ग्रिपिंग	पेट की ऐंठन
Goitre	गाइटर	गलगण्ड
Gonorrhoea	गानोरिया	सूजाक
Gout	गाउट	गाँठ पड़ना
Hunch-backed	हंच-बैक्ड	कुबड़ा
Head-ache	हेड-एक	सिरदर्द
Hiccup	हिक्कप	हिचकी
Hiccough	हिक्कफ	हिचकी
Hoarseness	होर्सनेस	गला बैठना
Hysteria	हिस्टीरिया	मूर्छा रोग
Hernia	हर्निया	आँत उतरना
Hydrocele	हाइड्रोसील	अण्डकोश वृद्धि
Haemorrhage	हैमरेज	लहू बहना
Hypermetropia	हायपरमेट्रोपिया	दूर दृष्टि दोष
Hurt	हर्ट	चोट
Insomnia	इन्सोमनिया	नींद न आना
Influenza	इन्फ्लूऐंजा	मोतिझरा
Indigestion	इन्डाइजेशन	अपच
Itch	इच	खुजली
Insanity	इनसैनिटी	पागलपन
Iritis	आइरीटिस	बिलनी
Jaundice	जॉन्डिस	पीलिया
Lame	लेम	लँगड़ा
Lock-jaw	लॉक-जॉ	दाँत बैठना
Lumbago	लुम्बैगो	कमर दर्द
Leucorrhoea	ल्यूकोरिया	श्वेत प्रदर
Leprosy	लेप्रोसी	कुष्ठ रोग
Leucoderma	ल्यूकोडरमा	श्वेत कुष्ठ
Lunacy	लूनैसी	पागलपन
Madness	मैडनेस	पागलपन
Measles	मीजल्स	खसरा
Myopia	मायोपिया	निकट दृष्टि दोष
Malaria	मलेरिया	मलेरिया ज्वर
Melena	मेलिना	खूनी दस्त
Mole	मोल	मस्सा
Mumps	मम्प्स	कनफड़ा
Night blindness	नाइट-ब्लाइण्डनेस	रतौंधी
Nausea	नासिया	जी मिचलाना

Word	Pronunciation	Hindi Meaning
Narcolepsy	नार्कोलेप्सी	निद्रा रोग
Obesity	ओबेसिटी	मोटापा
One-eyed	वन आइड	काना
Ortitis	ऑरटिटिस	कर्ण रोग
Pain	पेन	दर्द
Palpitation	पाल्पीटेशन	धड़कन
Piles	पाइल्स	बवासीर
Pimple	पिम्पल	फुंसी
Plague	प्लेग	प्लेग महामारी
Paralysis	पारालिसिस	लकवा
Pus	पस	पीप
Pneumonia	न्यूमोनिया	न्यूमोनिया
Phycosus	फाइकोसस	दुस्साध्य उन्माद
Phthisis	पाइथिसिस	राजयक्ष्मा रोग
Rheumatism	रूमाटिज्म	गठिया
Ring worm	रिंग वॉर्म	दाद
Scabies	स्केबीज	खाज
Short sightedness	शॉर्ट-साइटेडनेस	अल्प/मन्द दृष्टि
Sneezing	स्नीजिंग	छींक
Sore	सोर	व्रण
Sun stroke	सन स्ट्रोक	लू लगना
Small pox	स्मॉल-पॉक्स	शीतला
Sprain	स्प्रेन	मोच
Swelling	स्वेलिंग	सूजन
Syphilis	सिफिलिस	आतशक, गर्मी
Squint-eyed	स्क्विं-आइड	ऐंचा
Scrofula	स्क्रॉफुला	कण्ठमाला
Stone	स्टोन	पथरी
Semen	सिमेन	वीर्य
Stammer	स्टैमर	हकलाना
Sprue	स्प्रू	संग्रहणी
Spesis	स्पेसिस	विषाक्त खून होना
Sinus	साइनस	नासूर
Tonsil	टॉन्सिल	गलसुआ
Tomour	ट्यूमर	गाँठ, गिलटी
Typhoid	टायफॉइड	मियादी बुखार
Typhus	टायफस	काला ज्वर
Tuberculosis	ट्यूबरक्यूलोसिस	क्षय रोग
Urine	यूरीन	मूत्र
Ulcer	अल्सर	नासूर

Word	Pronunciation	Hindi Meaning
Vomit	वोमिट	उल्टी करना
Vertigo	वर्टिगो	आँखें चौंधियाना
Yawn	यॉन	जम्हाई
Worm	वर्म	कृमि
Wound	वाऊण्ड	घाव

Relations

Word	Pronunciation	Hindi Meaning
Adopted daughter	एडॉप्टेड डॉटर	दत्तक पुत्री
Adopted son	एडॉप्टेड सन	दत्तक पुत्र
Ancestors	ऐनसेस्टर्स	पूर्वज
Aunt	ऑन्ट	मौसी, चाची
Bride	ब्राइड	दुल्हन
Bridegroom	ब्राइड-ग्रूम	दूल्हा
Brother	ब्रदर	सगा भाई
Brethren	ब्रदर्न	भाई-बन्धु
Brother-in-law	ब्रदर-इन-लॉ	देवर, जेठ
Concubine	कॉन्क्युबिन	रखैल
Class-fellow	क्लास-फैलो	सहपाठी
Co-wife	को-वाइफ	उप-पत्नी
Cousin	कजिन	चचेरा भाई/चचेरी बहन
Client	क्लाइंट	मुवक्किल
Customer	कस्टमर	ग्राहक
Daughter	डॉटर	पुत्री
Daughter-in-law	डॉटर-इन-लॉ	पुत्रवधु
Disciple	डिसिपल	शिष्य
Father	फादर	पिता
Fellow	फेलो	संगी-साथी
Father-in-law	फादर-इन-लॉ	ससुर
Foe	फो	शत्रु
Friend	फ्रेन्ड	मित्र
Grand-daughter	ग्रैन्ड-डॉटर	पोती
Grand-father	ग्रैन्ड-फादर	दादा
Grand-mother	ग्रैन्ड-मदर	दादी
Grand-son	ग्रैन्ड-सन	पोता
Guest	गेस्ट	अतिथि
Heir	ऍअर	वारिस
Husband	हसबैण्ड	पति

Word	Pronunciation	Hindi Meaning
Lover	लवर	प्रेमी
Maternal aunt	मैटर्नल ऑन्ट	मामी
Maternal uncle	मैटर्नल अंकल	मामा
Teacher	टीचर	अध्यापक
Uncle	अंकल	चाचा, मौसा
Maternal sister	मैटर्नल सिस्टर	ममेरी/मौसेरी बहन
Mamma	मम्मा	अम्मा
Mother	मदर	माँ
Mother-in-law	मदर-इन-लॉ	सास
Master	मास्टर	स्वामी
Maid-servant	मेड-सर्वेन्ट	नौकरानी
Maternal grand-mother	मैटर्नल ग्रैन्ड-मदर	नानी
Maternal grand-father	मैटर्नल ग्रैन्ड-फादर	नाना
Nephew	नेफ्यू	भाँजा, भतीजा
Neighbour	नेबर	पड़ोसी
Niece	नीस	भाँजी, भतीजी
Parents	पेरेन्ट्स	माता-पिता
Posterity	पॉस्टेरिटी	वंशज
Paramour	पैरामर	यार
Relative	रिलेटिव	सम्बन्धी, नातेदार
Step-brother	स्टेप-ब्रदर	सौतेला भाई
Step-daughter	स्टेप-डॉटर	सौतेली पुत्री
Step-father	स्टेप-फॉदर	सौतेला पिता
Step-mother	स्टेप-मदर	सौतेली माँ
Step-son	स्टेप-सन	सौतेला पुत्र
Servant	सर्वेन्ट	नौकर
Sister	सिस्टर	बहन
Sister-in-law	सिस्टर-इन-लॉ	भाभी, ननद
Son	सन	बेटा
Son-in-law	सन-इन-लॉ	दामाद, जमाई
Wife	वाइफ	पत्नी

Human Beings of Different Ages

Word	Pronunciation	Hindi Meaning
Baby	बेबी	शिशु
Child	चाइल्ड	बच्चा
Infant	इन्फैन्ट	नवजात
Boy	बॉय	लड़का
Girl	गर्ल	लड़की

Word	Pronunciation	Hindi Meaning
Adolescent	एडोलेसेन्ट	किशोर
Minor	माइनर	अल्पवयस्क
Young	यंग	युवा
Mature	मैच्योर	वयस्क
Adult	एडल्ट	प्रौढ़
Man	मैन	मनुष्य
Woman	वोमैन	महिला
Young man	यंग मैन	नवयुवक
Young woman	यंग वोमैन	नवयुवती
Bachelor	बैचलर	कुँवारा
Virgin	विर्जिन	कुँवारी
Bridegroom	ब्राइडग्रूम	दूल्हा
Bride	ब्राइड	दुल्हन
Spinster	स्पिन्स्टर	चिरकुमारी
Widow	विडो	विधवा
Widower	विडोवर	विधुर, रंडवा
Old man	ओल्ड मैन	वृद्ध (पुरुष)
Old woman	ओल्ड वोमैन	वृद्धा (महिला)
Orphan	ऑरफन	अनाथ

Ornaments and Jewels

Word	Pronunciation	Hindi Meaning
Anklet	ऐंकलेट	पायजेब
Armlet	आर्मलेट	बाजूबन्द
Bangle	बैंगल	चूड़ी
Belt	बेल्ट	कमरपेटी
Bracelet	ब्रेसलेट	कंगन
Brooch	ब्रूच	साड़ी का काँटा, रत्नजड़ित पिन
Cat's eye	कैट्स आई	लहसुनिया रत्न
Chain	चेन	जंजीर
Clip	क्लिप	चिमटी
Coral	कोरल	मूँगा
Diamond	डायमण्ड	हीरा
Ear stud	इयर स्टड	कान का तल्ला
Emerald	एमरल्ड	पन्ना
Ear-ring	इयर-रिंग	कान की बाली
Garland	गारलैण्ड	हार, माला
Girdle	गर्डल	कमरबन्द
Gem	जेम	रत्न

Word	Pronunciation	Hindi Meaning
Hair pin	हेयर पिन	बालों की चिमटी
Head locket	हैड लॉकेट	टीका
Locket	लॉकेट	लटकन
Medal	मेड्ल	तमगा
Mother of Pearl	मदर ऑफ पर्ल	मोती की सीप
Necklace	नेकलेस	हार
Nose pin	नोज पिन	लौंग
Nose ring	नोज रिंग	नथ, नथुनी
Opal	ओपल	दूधिया पत्थर
Pearl	पर्ल	मोती
Quartz	क्वार्ट्ज	बिल्लौर
Ring	रिंग	छल्ला, अँगूठी
Ruby	रूबी	माणिक
Sapphire	सफायर	नीलम
Tiara	टियारा	ताज, मुकुट
Tops	टॉप्स	टॉप्स
Topaz	टोपाज	पुखराज
Turquoise	टरक्वाइज	फिरोजा
Wreath	रीथ	माला
Wristlet	रिस्टलेट	कंगन
Wrist-watch	रिस्ट वाच	कलाई घड़ी

Animals

Word	Pronunciation	Hindi Meaning
Ant eater	आन्ट ईटर	चींटीखोर
Antelope	ऐन्टीलोप	मृग
Ape	एप	लंगूर बन्दर
Ass	ऐस	गधा, गर्दभ
Bear	बीअर	भालू, रीछ
Bitch	बिच	कुतिया
Boar	बोर	जंगली सूअर
Buffalo	बफैलो	भैंस
Bull	बुल	साँड, बैल
Beast	बीस्ट	जंगली पशु
Calf	काफ	बछड़ा
Camel	कैमल	ऊँट
Cat	कैट	बिल्ली
Charmois	शैमॉय	पहाड़ी हिरण
Colt	कोल्ट	बछेरा
Cow	काऊ	गाय

Word	Pronunciation	Hindi Meaning
Chimpanzee	चिम्पैंजी	वनमानुष
Deer	डियर	हिरण
Dog	डॉग	कुत्ता
Donkey	डंकी	गधा
Elephant	एलीफेंट	हाथी
Ewe	यू	मेढ़ी
Fawn	फॉन	हिरण का बच्चा
Fox	फॉक्स	लोमड़ी
Giraffe	जिराफ	जिराफ
Goat	गोट	बकरी
Hare	हेअर	खरगोश
Hind	हाइंड	हिरनी
Hippopotamus	हिप्पोपोटैमस	दरियाई घोड़ा
Horse	हॉर्स	घोड़ा
Hound	हाउंड	शिकारी कुत्ता
Hyena	हाएना	लक्कड़बग्घा
Hog	हॉग	सूअर
Jackal	जैकाल	सियार
Kangaroo	कंगारू	कंगारू
Kid	किड	बकरी का बच्चा
Kitten	किट्टन	बिल्ली का बच्चा
Lamb	लैम्ब	भेड़ का बच्चा
Leopard	लिओपार्ड	तेंदुआ
Lion	लायन	शेर
Mare	मेयर	घोड़ी
Mole	मोल	छुछुन्दर
Mongoose	मॉन्गूज	नेवला
Monkey	मंकी	बन्दर
Mouse	माउस	चूहा
Mule	म्यूल	खच्चर
Musk-rat	मस्क-रैट	छुछुन्दर
Musk-deer	मस्क-डियर	कस्तूरी मृग
Ox	ऑक्स	बैल
Panther	पैन्थर	चीता
Pig	पिग	सूअर
Pony	पोनी	टट्टू
Porcupine	पॉर्क्यूपाइन	साही
Puppy	पप्पी	पिल्ला
Rabbit	रैबिट	खरगोश
Ram	रैम	मेढ़ा

Word	Pronunciation	Hindi Meaning
Rat	रैट	चूहा
Reindeer	रेण्डीयर	हिरण
Rhinoceros	राइनोसेरस	गैंडा
She-calf	शी-काफ	बछड़ी
Sheep	शीप	भेड़
She-goat	शी-गोट	बकरी
Sire	सायर	प्रजनक साँड
Spaniel	स्पेनियल	झबरा कुत्ता
Squirrel	स्क्वीरल	गिलहरी
Steer	स्टीयर	बधिया पशु
Stag	स्टैग	बारहसिंगा
Sow	साउ	सुअरी
Swine	स्वाइन	शूकरी
Tiger	टाइगर	बाघ
Wolf	वुल्फ	भेड़िया
Yak	यॉक	पर्वतीय बैल
Zebra	जेब्रा	गोर खर
Zebu	जीबू	साँड

Birds

Word	Pronunciation	Hindi Meaning
Adjutant	एड्जुटैन्ट	सारस
Bat	बैट	चमगादड़
Bittern	बिटर्न	तितलौया
Chicken	चिकन	चूजा
Cock	कॉक	मुर्गा
Crane	क्रेन	सारस
Crow	क्रो	कौआ
Cuckoo	कुक्कू	कोयल
Cygnet	सिगनेट	हंस शावक
Cocato	कॉकैटो	काकातुआ
Dove	डॉव	पेंडुकी
Duck	डक	बत्तख (मादा)
Duckling	डकलिंग	बत्तख का बच्चा
Drake	ड्रेक	बत्तख (नर)
Eagle	ईगल	चील
Egg	ऐग	अण्डा
Falcon	फाल्कन	बाज
Fowl	फाउल	चूजा

Word	Pronunciation	Hindi Meaning
Goose	गूज	बत्तख, कलहंस
Hawk	हॉक	बाज
Hen	हैन	मुर्गी
Heron	हेरॅन	बगुला
Jay	जे	नीलकण्ठ
Kite	काइट	चील
Lark	लार्क	लवा
Magpie	मैग्पी	नीलकण्ठ
Macaw	मैका	मकावी तोता
Nightingale	नाइटिंगेल	बुलबुल
Ostrich	ऑस्ट्रिच	शुतुरमुर्ग
Owl	आउल	उल्लू
Parrot	पैरट	तोता
Partridge	पार्टरिज	चकोर, तीतर
Peacock	पीकॉक	मोर
Peahen	पीहैन	मोरनी
Pigeon	पिजन	कबूतर
Pheasant	फीजैन्ट	तीतर
Quail	क्वेल	बटेर
Rook	रूक	डोम कौआ
Raven	रेवॅन	पहाड़ी कौआ
Sparrow	स्पैरो	गौरैया
Stork	स्टॉर्क	सारस
Swallow	स्वैलो	अबाबील चिड़िया
Swan	स्वैन	हंस
Vulture	वल्चर	गिद्ध
Weaver-bird	वीवर-बर्ड	बया
Wood Pecker	वुडपेकर	कठफोड़वा

Reptiles, Water-Living Creatures, Worms and Insects

Word	Pronunciation	Hindi Meaning
Adder	एड्डर	गेहुँआ साँप
Alligator	एलीगेटर	घड़ियाल
Ant	आण्ट	चींटी
Beetle	बीटल	गुबरैला
Bee	बी	मधुमक्खी (मादा)
Boa	बोआ	अजगर
Body-licer	बॉड़ी-लाइसर	चीलर

Word	Pronunciation	Hindi Meaning
Bug	बग	खटमल
Wasp	वास्प	ततैया, भिड़
Butterfly	बटरफ्लाई	तितली
Centipede	सेन्टीपीड	गोजर
Chameleon	शैमीलियन	गिरगिट
Cobra	कोबरा	काला साँप
Cocoon	कोकून	रेशम का कोआ
Cod-fish	कॉड-फिश	कॉड मछली
Conch	कोंच	शंख
Cowire	कौरी	कोड़ी
Crab	क्रैब	केकड़ा
Cricket	क्रिकेट	झींगुर
Crocodile	क्रोकोडाइल	मगरमच्छ
Drone	ड्रोन	मधुमक्खी (नर)
Earthworm	अर्थवॅर्म	केंचुआ
Eel	ईल	सर्प मछली
Fire-fly	फायर-फ्लाई	जुगनू
Fish	फिश	मछली
Flea	फ्ली	पिस्सू
Fly	फ्लाई	मक्खी
Frog	फ्रॉग	मेढ़क
Gad-fly	गैड-फ्लाई	गोमक्खी, डँस
Grass-hopper	ग्रास-हॉपर	टिड्ढ़ा
Honey-bee	हनी-बी	मधुमक्खी
Hornet	हॉर्नेट	भिड़, बर्र
Leech	लीच	जोंक
Lizard	लिजर्ड	छिपकली
Lobster	लॉब्स्टर	झींगा
Locust	लोकस्ट	टिड्ढ़ी
Louse	लाउस	जूँ
Mosquito	मॉसकीटो	मच्छर
Nit	निट	लीख
Oyster	आयस्टर	सीप
Poison	पॉइजन	विष
Rat Flea	रैट फ्ली	पिस्सू, मूषक
Scorpion	स्कॉरपिअन	बिच्छू
Serpent	सर्पेण्ट	सर्प
Shark	शार्क	शार्क मछली
Silk-worm	सिल्क-वॅर्म	रेशम का कीड़ा
Snail	स्नेल	घोंघा

Word	Pronunciation	Hindi Meaning
Snake	स्नेक	साँप
Spider	स्पाइडर	मकड़ी
Tadpole	टैडपोल	मेढ़क का बच्चा
Termite	टरमाइट	दीमक
Toad	टोड	टोड
Tortoise	टॉर्टाइज	कछुआ
Turtle	टर्टल	कछुआ
Walrus	वालरस	दरियाई घोड़ा

Articles of Domestic Use

Word	Pronunciation	Hindi Meaning
Almirah	अलमीरा	अलमारी
Anvil	एनविल	निहाई
Ash	ऐश	राख
Ash-tray	ऐश ट्रे	राख का पात्र
Attache Case	अटैची केस	अटैची
Auger	ऑगर	पेंचदार बरमा
Axe	ऐक्स	कुल्हाड़ी
Balance	बैलैन्स	तराजू
Basket	बास्केट	टोकरी
Bed	बेड	बिस्तर
Bed-stead	बेड-स्टैड	पलंग
Bed-sheet	बेड-शीट	चादर
Bench	बेन्च	बेन्च
Blanket	ब्लैंकेट	कम्बल
Bobbin	बॉबिन	अन्टा
Bolster	बोल्स्टर	गोल तकिया
Bottle	बॉटल	बोतल
Box	बॉक्स	सन्दूक
Bowl	बाउल	कटोरा
Broom	ब्रूम	झाड़ू
Brush	ब्रश	ब्रुश
Bucket	बकेट	बाल्टी
Bulb	बल्ब	बल्ब
Button	बटन	बटन
Candle	कैन्डिल	मोमबत्ती
Candle-stand	कैन्डिल-स्टैण्ड	शमादान
Cabinet	कैबिनेट	अलमारी
Carpet	कारपेट	गलीचा

Word	Pronunciation	Hindi Meaning
Canister	कैनिस्टर	कनस्तर
Cauldron	काल्ड्रन	कड़ाही
Censor	सेन्सर	धूपदानी
Chair	चेयर	कुर्सी
Chest	चेस्ट	पेटी
Chimney	चिमनी	चिमनी
Cotton	कॉटन	रूई
Chandelier	शैन्डीलियर	झाड़-फानूस
Chisel	चिजल	छेनी
Churn	चर्न	मथानी
Comb	कॉम्ब	कंघी
Cooking gas	कुकिंग गैस	भोजन पकाने की गैस
Cup	कप	प्याला
Curtain	कर्टेन	पर्दा
Cushion	कुशन	गद्दा
China-ware	चाइना-वेअर	चीनी-मिट्टी के बर्तन
Couch	काउच	सेज
Clock	क्लॉक	घड़ी
Cream	क्रीम	क्रीम
Cot	कॉट	चारपाई
Cinders	सिन्डर्स	अंगारे
Cup-board	कबर्ड	अलमारी
Desk	डेस्क	डेस्क
Dish	डिश	रकाबी
Door-mat	डोर-मैट	पायदान
Drawers	ड्राअर्स	दराज
Drill	ड्रिल	बरमा
Electricity	इलेक्ट्रिसिटी	बिजली
Fan	फैन	पंखा
File	फाइल	रेती
Fire	फायर	आग
Fire place	फायर प्लेस	अंगीठी
Flower-vase	फ्लॉवर-वास	फूलदान
Fork	फोर्क	काँटा
Frying pan	फ्राइंग पैन	कड़ाही
Fuel	फ्यूल	ईंधन
Funnel	फनल	कीप
Flagon	फ्लैगॉन	सुराही

Word	Pronunciation	Hindi Meaning
Fire Pan	फायर पैन	अंगीठी
Grate	ग्रेट	चूल्हा
Gramophone	ग्रामोफोन	ग्रामोफोन
Hammer	हैमर	हथौड़ा
Hand-pump	हैण्ड-पम्प	बरमा
Hearth	हार्थ	भट्ठी
Hatchet	हैचेट	फावड़ा
Iron	आयरन	इस्तरी
Ice-box	आइस-बॉक्स	बर्फ पेटी
Iron-plate	आयरन-प्लेट	तवा
Iron-chest	आयरन-चेस्ट	लोहे का सन्दूक
Iron-safe	आयरन-सेफ	लोहे की अलमारी
Jar	जार	मर्तबान
Jug	जग	जग
Kerosene	केरोसिन	मिट्टी का तेल
Kettle	कैटल	केतली
Key	की	चाबी
Knife	नाइफ	चाकू
Kiln	किल्न	भट्ठी
Lancet	लान्सेट	छुरी
Lamp	लैम्प	दीया
Lid	लिड	ढक्कन
Lock	लॉक	ताला
Lantern	लैन्टर्न	लालटेन
Loom	लूम	करघा
Ladle	लैडल	कड़छी
Looking glass	लुकिंग ग्लास	दर्पण
Mackintosh	माकिन्टोश	मोमजामा
Mat	मैट	चटाई
Match-box	मैच-बॉक्स	माचिस
Mallet	मैलेट	हथौड़ा
Mattress	मैट्रेस	गद्दा
Mirror	मिरर	दर्पण
Mortar	मोर्टार	ओखली
Needle	नीडल	सुई
Nut-cracker	नट-क्रैकर	सरोता
News-paper	न्यूज-पेपर	समाचार-पत्र
Oil	ऑयल	तेल
Oven	ओवेन	तन्दूर

Word	Pronunciation	Hindi Meaning
Palanquin	पैलैन्क्विन	पालकी
Pastry-board	पेस्ट्री-बोर्ड	चकला
Pastry-roller	पेस्ट्री-रोलर	बेलन
Paper	पेपर	कागज
Picture	पिक्चर	तस्वीर
Pan	पैन	कड़ाही
Pen	पेन	कलम
Pestle	पैसल	मूसली
Phial	फियल	शीशी
Pillow	पिलो	तकिया
Pillow-case	पिलो-केस	गिलाफ
Pincers	पिन्सर्स	संड़सी
Pitcher	पिचर	घड़ा
Pot	पॉट	मटका
Probe	प्रोब	सलाई
Plate	प्लेट	थाली
Plough	प्लो	हल
Plane	प्लेन	रंदा
Pad-lock	पैड-लॉक	बड़ा ताला
Powder	पाउडर	बुकनी
Quilt	क्विल्ट	रजाई
Rope	रोप	रस्सी
Radio	रेडियो	रेडियो
Razor	रेजर	उस्तरा
Sack	सैक	बोरी
Safe	सेफ	तिजोरी
Saucer	सॉसर	छोटी तश्तरी
Sieve	सीव	चलनी
Soap	सोप	साबुन
Soap-case	सोप-केस	साबुनदानी
Spoon	स्पून	चम्मच
Spittoon	स्पिटन	पीकदान
Stick	स्टिक	छड़ी
Stove	स्टोव	दम चूल्हा
Swing	स्विंग	झूला
Screw-driver	स्क्रू-ड्राइवर	पेचकस
Sickle	सिकल	हँसिया
Shovel	शॉवेल	खुरपी
Spade	स्पेड	फावड़ा

Word	Pronunciation	Hindi Meaning
Saw	सॉ	आरा
Spear	स्पीयर	भाला
Sword	स्वॉर्ड	तलवार
Stool	स्टूल	तिपाई
Sofa	सोफा	सोफा
Shelf	शेल्फ	खुली अलमारी
String	स्ट्रिंग	रस्सी
Switch	स्विच	खटका
Scissors	सिजर्स	कैंची
Sewing machine	स्यूइंग मशीन	सिलाई मशीन
Table	टेबल	मेज
Tap	टैप	नलका
Tumbler	टम्बलर	गिलास
Thimble	थिम्बल	अंगुस्ताना
Tongs	टोंग्स	चिमटा
Tooth brush	टूथ ब्रश	ब्रुश
Tooth powder	टूथ पाउडर	दन्त मंजन
Tray	ट्रे	थाली
Twine	ट्वाइन	रस्सी
Table fan	टेबल फैन	मेज का पंखा
Table lamp	टेबल लैम्प	मेज का लैम्प
Telephone	टेलीफोन	दूरभाष
Umbrella	अम्ब्रेला	छाता
Wick	विक	बत्ती
Wire	वायर	तार

Homes and Abodes

Animal	Hindi Meaning	Lives in	Hindi Meaning
Baby	शिशु	Nursery	नर्सरी
Bee	मधु-मक्खी	Beehive	शहद का छत्ता
Bird	पक्षी	Nest	घोंसला
Convict	अपराधी	Prison	कारावास
Cow	गाय	Shed	गौशाला
Dog	कुत्ता	Kennel	कुत्ताघर
Fox	लोमड़ी	Forest	वन
King	राजा	Palace	महल
Horse	घोड़ा	Stable	अस्तबल
Lion	शेर	Den	माँद
Lunatic	पागल	Asylum	पागलखाना

Animal	Hindi Meaning	Lives in	Hindi Meaning
Man	आदमी	House	घर
Mice	चूहा	Hole	बिल
Monk	भिक्षु	Monastery	मठ
Nun	भिक्षुणी	Convent	विहार
Invalid	दुर्बल व्यक्ति	Sanatorium	स्वास्थ्यालय
Pig	सूअर	Sty	सूअर बाड़ा
Officer	अधिकारी	Quarter	क्वार्टर
Priest	पुजारी	Parsonage	पादरीघर
Peasant	किसान	Cottage	झोंपड़ी
Prisoner	कैदी	Cell	कोठरी
Sheep	भेड़	Pen or Fold	बाड़ा
Soldier	सैनिक	Barrack	सैनिक आवास
Spider	मकड़ी	Web	जाला
Owl	उल्लू	Tree	वृक्ष
Tiger	बाघ	Den	गुफा

Minerals

Word	Pronunciation	Hindi Meaning
Antimony	एन्टीमॉनी	सुरमा
Arsenic	आर्सेनिक	संखिया
Alum	ऐलम	फिटकरी
Bitumen	बिटुमेन	शिलाजीत
Bronze	ब्रोन्ज	काँसा
Brass	ब्रास	पीतल
Bell-metal	बेल-मेटल	काँसा
Bluevitrio	ब्लूविट्रियो	तूतिया
Chalk	चाक	खड़िया
Cinnabar	सिनेबार	सिन्दूर
Charcoal	चारकोल	लकड़ी का कोयला
Coal	कोल	कोयला
Copper	कॉपर	ताँबा
Cornelian	कोर्नेलियन	अकीक
Copper sulphate	कॉपर सल्फेट	तूतिया
Diamond	डायमण्ड	हीरा
Emerald	एमरल्ड	पन्ना
Flint	फ्लिन्ट	चकमक पत्थर
Fuller's earth	फुलर्स अर्थ	मुलतानी मिट्टी
Grey copper	ग्रे कॉपर	भूरा ताँबा
Grey tin	ग्रे टिन	धूसर राँगा

Word	Pronunciation	Hindi Meaning
Gold	गोल्ड	सोना
Greenvitriol	ग्रीनविट्रियोल	कसीह
Iron	आयरन	लोहा
Iron ore	आयरन ओर	खनिज लोहा
Lead	लेड	सीसा
Marble	मार्बल	संगमरमर
Mercury	मर्करी	पारा
Metal	मेटल	धातु
Mica	माइका	अभ्रक
Mine	माइन	खान
Natron	नैट्रॉन	सज्जीखार
Orpiment	ऑर्पिमेण्ट	हरताल
Ochre	ओकर	गेरू
Plastic clay	प्लास्टिक क्ले	सुघट्य मिट्टी
Red ochre	रेड ओकर	गेरू
Ruby	रूबी	लाल
Rock oil	रॉक ऑयल	शैल तेल
Saltpetre	साल्टपीटर	शोरा
Shale	शेल	स्लेटी पत्थर
Silver	सिल्वर	चाँदी
Soapstone	सोप-स्टोन	सेलखड़ी
Steatite	स्टीटाइट	सेलखड़ी
Steel	स्टील	फौलाद
Sulphur	सल्फर	गन्धक
Tin	टिन	राँगा
Touch-stone	टच-स्टोन	कसौटी
Vermilion	वर्मिलियन	सिन्दूर
White lead	व्हाइट लेड	सफेदा
Yellow ochre	येलो ओकर	राजरज
Zinc	जिंक	जस्ता

Professions and Occupations

Word	Pronunciation	Hindi Meaning
Actor	एक्टर	अभिनेता
Accountant	अकाउन्टैन्ट	मुनीम
Advocate	एडवोकेट	वकील, अधिवक्ता
Agent	एजेण्ट	प्रतिनिधि
Agriculturist	एग्रीकल्चरिस्ट	कृषक
Architect	आर्किटेक्ट	नक्शानवीस

Word	Pronunciation	Hindi Meaning
Artist	आर्टिस्ट	कलाकार
Artisan	आर्टिसन	कारीगर
Astrologer	एस्ट्रोलॉजर	ज्योतिषी
Astronomer	एस्ट्रोनॉमर	खगोलशास्त्री
Auditor	ऑडिटर	हिसाब निरीक्षक
Auctioneer	आक्शनीयर	नीलामी करने वाला
Author	ऑथर	लेखक, ग्रन्थकार
Baker	बेकर	नानबाई
Banker	बैंकर	साहूकार
Bankrupt	बैंकरप्ट	दिवालिया
Beggar	बेगर	भिखारी
Blacksmith	ब्लैक स्मिथ	लोहार
Book-binder	बुक-बाइण्डर	जिल्दसाज
Book-seller	बुक-सेलर	पुस्तक विक्रेता
Boatman	बोट-मैन	नाविक
Brasier	ब्रेजियर	ठठेरा
Bursar	बर्सर	कोषाधिकारी
Butler	बटलर	भण्डारी
Butcher	बुचर	कसाई
Barrister	बैरिस्टर	अधिवक्ता
Betel-seller	बीटल सेलर	पनवाड़ी
Broker	ब्रोकर	दलाल
Carder	कार्डर	धुनिया
Carpenter	कारपेन्टर	बढ़ई
Carrier	कैरियर	माल ढ़ोने वाला
Cashier	कैशियर	रोकड़िया
Chauffeur	शौफर	कार चालक
Cultivator	कल्टिवेटर	कृषक
Chemist	केमिस्ट	दवाई विक्रेता
Clerk	क्लर्क	मुंशी, लिपिक
Cobbler	कॉबलर	मोची
Coachman	कोचमैन	कोचवान
Cleaner	क्लीनर	साफ करने वाला
Contractor	कॉन्ट्रैक्टर	ठेकेदार
Constable	कांस्टेबल	सिपाही
Conductor	कण्डक्टर	संवाहक
Confectioner	कनफैक्शनर	हलवाई
Cook	कुक	रसोइया
Compounder	कम्पाउण्डर	औषधि बनाने वाला

Word	Pronunciation	Hindi Meaning
Coolie	कुली	कुली
Compositor	कम्पोजीटर	अक्षरों से पाठ्य-सामग्री तैयार करने वाला
Cloth merchant	क्लॉथ मर्चेन्ट	वस्त्र व्यापारी
Carter	कार्टर	गाड़ीवान्
Clergyman	क्लर्जीमैन	पुरोहित
Dancer	डांसर	नर्तकी
Darner	डार्नर	रफूगर
Dentist	डेन्टिस्ट	दन्त चिकित्सक
Doctor	डॉक्टर	चिकित्सक
Draper	ड्रेपर	बजाज
Draftsman	ड्राफ्ट्समैन	नक्शानवीस
Dramatist	ड्रामाटिस्ट	नाटककार
Druggist	ड्रगिस्ट	औषधि-विक्रेता
Dyer	डायर	रंगसाज
Driver	ड्राइवर	यान चालक
Drummer	ड्रमर	ढ़ोलची
Editor	एडिटर	सम्पादक
Enameller	इनेमलर	मीनाकार
Engineer	इन्जीनियर	अभियन्ता
Examiner	एग्जामिनर	परीक्षक
Farmer	फार्मर	किसान
Fisherman	फिशरमैन	मछेरा
Florist	फ्लोरिस्ट	फूल विक्रेता
Gardener	गार्डनर	माली
Gatekeeper	गेटकीपर	दरबान
Glazier	ग्लेजिअर	शीशा जड़ने वाला
Goldsmith	गोल्डस्मिथ	सुनार
Grocer	ग्रोसर	पंसारी
Groom	ग्रूम	सईस
Green-grocer	ग्रीन-ग्रोसर	कुंजड़ा
Gleaner	ग्लीनर	सिल्ला बटोरने वाला
Halwai	हलवाई	हलवाई
Hawker	हॉकर	फेरी वाला
Inkman	इंकमैन	रोशनाई वाला
Inspector	इन्स्पेक्टर	निरीक्षक
Jeweller	ज्वेलर	जौहरी
Juggler	जगलर	मदारी
Landlord	लैण्डलॉर्ड	जमींदार
Lawyer	लॉयर	वकील
Magician	मैजीशियन	जादूगर

Word	Pronunciation	Hindi Meaning
Manager	मैनेजर	प्रबन्धक
Mason	मैसन	राज, राजगीर
Marchant	मर्चेन्ट	सौदागर
Messenger	मेसेन्जर	दूत
Mechanic	मेकेनिक	मिस्त्री
Midwife	मिडवाइफ	दाई
Milkman	मिल्कमैन	ग्वाला
Milkmaid	मिल्कमेड	ग्वालन
Musician	म्यूजीशियन	संगीतकार
Miner	माइनर	खान खोदने वाला
News-agent	न्यूज-एजेण्ट	.समाचार विक्रेता
News-monger	न्यूज-मांगर	खबर फैलाने वाला
Novelist	नॉवेलिस्ट	उपन्यासकार
Nurse	नर्स	दाई, आया
Oilman	ऑयलमैन	तेली
Operator	ऑपरेटर	मशीन चालक
Painter	पेन्टर	रंगसाज
Palmist	पामिस्ट	हाथ देखने वाला
Peon	पीअन	चपरासी
Perfumer	पर्फ्यूमर	गन्धी
Photographer	फोटोग्राफर	छायाकार
Physician	फिजिशियन	वैद्य, चिकित्सक
Pilgrim	पिल्ग्रिम	तीर्थ-यात्री
Poet	पोयट	कवि
Potter	पॉटर	कुम्हार
Postman	पोस्टमैन	डाकिया
Printer	प्रिन्टर	मुद्रक
Priest	प्रीस्ट	पुरोहित, पुजारी
Politician	पॉलिटीशियन	राजनीतिज्ञ
Porter	पोर्टर	कुली, दरबान
Proprietor	प्रोप्राइटर	मालिक
Pedlar	पैडलर	फेरी वाला
Pilot	पायलट	वायुयान-चालक
Pleader	प्लीडर	अधिवक्ता
Publisher	पब्लिशर	प्रकाशक
Principal	प्रिन्सिपल	प्रधानाचार्य
Parcher	पार्चर	भड़भूजा
Procurer	प्रोक्योरर	प्रापक, दलाल
Proctor	प्रोक्टर	अनुशासनाधिकारी
Professor	प्रोफेसर	प्राध्यापक

Word	Pronunciation	Hindi Meaning
Procurator	प्रोक्युरेटर	कोषाधिकारी
Quack	क्वैक	नीम-हकीम
Quaestor	क्वेस्टॉर	दण्डनायक
Quizzer	क्विजर	परीक्षाकर्त्ता
Retailer	रिटेलर	खुदरा व्यापारी
Repairer	रिपेयरर	मरम्मत वाला
Sailor	सेलर	नाविक
Sanitary Inspector	सेनिटरी-इन्स्पेक्टर	सफाई दरोगा
Sculptor	स्कल्पटर	पत्थर काटने वाला
Seedsman	सीड्समैन	बीज-विक्रेता
Shepherd	शेफर्ड	गड़ेरिया
Shoe-maker	शू-मेकर	मोची
Shop-keeper	शॉपकीपर	दुकानदार
Stamp-vendor	स्टाम्प-वेन्डर	टिकट विक्रेता
Surgeon	सर्जन	शल्य चिकित्सक
Sweeper	स्वीपर	सफाईकर्मी
Stationer	स्टेशनर	कागज, कलम विक्रेता
Sorcerer	सोर्सेरर	तान्त्रिक
Tailor	टेलर	दर्जी
Tanner	टैनर	चमड़ा रँगने वाला
Teacher	टीचर	अध्यापक
Treasurer	ट्रेजरर	कोषाध्यक्ष
Turner	टर्नर	खरादिया
Tutor	ट्यूटर	ट्यूशन पढ़ाने वाला
Trader	ट्रेडर	व्यापारी
Tinman	टिनमैन	कलई करने वाला
T.T.E.	टी.टी.ई.	टिकट निरीक्षक
Usurer	यूजरर	सूदखोर
Washerman	वाशरमैन	धोबी
Watchman	वाचमैन	चौकीदार
Water carrier	वाटर कैरियर	महरा
Weaver	वीवर	जुलाहा
Writer	राइटर	लेखक
Watch-maker	वाचमेकर	घड़ीसाज

Important Tools

Word	Pronunciation	Hindi Meaning
Anchor	एन्कर	लंगर
Anvil	एन्विल	निहाई
Auger	ऑगर	बरमा
Awl	ऑल	टंकुआ
Axe	ऐक्स	गेंती, कुल्हाड़ी
Bagging-hook	बैगिंग हुक	दराँती
Balance	बैलेन्स	तराजू
Barshare	बार-शेअर	कस्सी, फाली
Bead-plane	बीड-प्लेन	गोल रन्दा
Bellows	बेलॉज	धौंकनी
Blow-pipe	ब्लो-पाइप	फूँकनी
Clamp	क्लैम्प	काँटा
Cleat	क्लीट	फन्नी
Chisel	चिजेल	छैनी
Colter	कोल्टर	हल की फाल
Compass	कम्पास	कुतुबनुमा
Cone	कोन	शंकु
Dagger	डैगर	छुरा, खंजर
Dibble	डिब्बल	रंभा
Divider	डिवाइडर	परकार
Drill	ड्रिल	बरमी
Fast	फास्ट	मोची का फरमा
File	फाइल	रेती
Fishing rod	फिशिंग रॉड	पकड़ने की डोरी
Gauge	गेज	नापने का यन्त्र
Hammer	हैमर	हथौड़ा
Hand saw	हैण्ड सा	आरी
Hand vice	हैण्ड वाइस	हाथ बाँक
Jack plane	जैक प्लेन	बड़ा रन्दा
Last	लास्ट	जूता बनाने का फर्मा
Lancet	लैन्सेट	नश्तर की छुरी
Lever	लीवर	उत्तोलक
Loom	लूम	करघा
Lathe	लेथ	खराद
Mallet	मैलिट	मुगरी
Needle point	नीडल प्वाइंट	विरंजी
Oar	ओर	डांडा, चप्पू
Oil-mill	ऑयल मिल	कोल्हू
Plough	प्लाऊ	हल

Word	Pronunciation	Hindi Meaning
Plough share	प्लाऊ शेयर	हल की फांल
Plumb line	प्लम्ब लाइन	साहुल
Pruning shear	प्रूनिंग शीअर	दस्ती कैंची
Rasp	रैस्प	मोटी रेती
Razor	रेजर	उस्तरा
Rebate plane	रिबेट प्लेन	पताम रंदा
Rudder	रडर	पतवार
Screw	स्क्रू	पेंच
Spanner	स्पैनर	ढ़िबरी कसने की चाभी
Stone chisel	स्टोन चिजेल	पत्थर तराशने वाली छेनी
Smoothing plane	स्मूथिंग प्लेन	बारीक रंदा
Still	स्टिल	भभका
Stock and dies	स्टॉक एण्ड डायस	वादिया
Tooling plane	टूलिंग प्लेन	धारी रंदा
Trying plane	ट्राइंग प्लेन	छोटा रंदा
Try square	ट्राइ स्कवेअर	गुनिया
Trowel	ट्रॉवल	करनी
Trying angle	ट्राइंग एंगल	गुनिया

Musical Instruments

Word	Pronunciation	Hindi Meaning
Bell	बेल	घण्टी
Bugle	बिगुल	तुरही
Bag pipe	बैग पाइप	मशकबाजा
Banjo	बैन्जो	बैन्जो
Bassoon	बसून	अलगोजाह
Clarion	क्लैरियन	बाँसुरी, तुरही
Clarionet	क्लैरियोनेट	क्लैरिनेट
Cymbal	सिम्बल	झांझ
Conch	कोंच	शंख
Drum	ड्रम	ढ़ोलक, नगाड़ा
Drumnet	ड्रमेट	डुगडुगी
Flute	फ्लूट	बाँसुरी
Guitar	गिटार	सितार
Gong	गाँग	घण्टा
Gourd Flute	गोर्ड फ्लूट	बीन
Harmonium	हारमोनियम	हारमोनियम
Harp	हार्प	वीणा
Horn	हॉर्न	सींग

Word	Pronunciation	Hindi Meaning
Haut boy	हॉट बॉय	शहनाई
Jew's Harp Lute	ज्यूज हार्प ल्यूट	मरचंग
Kettle-drum	केटल-ड्रम	नगाड़ा
Mandolin	मैनडोलिन	एक वाद्य-यन्त्र
Mouth organ	माउथ ऑर्गन	बीन-बाजा
Piano	पियानो	पियानो
Sarod	सरोद	सरोद
Sitar	सितार	सितार
Tabor	टैबर	तबला
Tom-tom	टमटम	ढोलक
Tambourine	टैम्बूरीन	डफ
Trombone	ट्रम्बोन	तुरही
Violin	वायलिन	वीणा
Whistle	व्हिसल	सीटी

Terminology of Warfare

Word	Pronunciation	Hindi Meaning
Aggression	अग्रेशन	आक्रमण
Anti-aircraft gun	एण्टी एअरक्राफ्ट गन	विनाशक
Army	आर्मी	सेना
Arms	आर्म्स	हथियार
Armaments	आमामेन्ट्स	युद्ध के शस्त्र
Ammunition	एम्युनिशन	गोला-बारूद
Armour	आर्मर	कवच
Atom bomb	एटम बम	अणु बम
Atomic warfare	एटॉमिक वारफेअर	परमाणु युद्ध
Attack	अटैक	आक्रमण
Auxiliary force	आग्जिलियरी फोर्स	सहायक सेना
Battle	बैटल	युद्ध
Battlefield	बैटलफील्ड	युद्धक्षेत्र
Belligerent nation	बेलिजेरेन्ट नेशन	लड़ने वाला राष्ट्र
Battle-ship	बैटल शिप	युद्धपोत
Blockade	ब्लॉकेड	नाकाबन्दी
Bombardment	बम्बार्डमेन्ट	बमबारी
Bloodshed	ब्लडशेड	रक्तपात
Bomb	बॉम्ब	बम
Brute force	ब्रूट फोर्स	पाशविक शक्ति
Bullet	बुलेट	गोली
Bunker	बंकर	मोर्चा

Word	Pronunciation	Hindi Meaning
Campaign	कैम्पेन	युद्ध-प्रवृत्ति
Cannon	कैनन	तोप
Cannon Ball	कैनन बाल	तोप के गोले
Cartridge	कारट्रेज	कारतूस
Cavalry	कैवलरी	घुड़सवारी सेना
Cease fire	सीज फायर	युद्ध विराम
Civil war	सिविल वार	गृह युद्ध
Combatants	कम्बैटैंट्स	योद्धा
Commander in chief	कमाण्डर इन चीफ	सेनापति
Conscription	कान्सक्रिप्शन	अनिवार्य भर्ती
Defence	डिफेन्स	सुरक्षा
Defence Ministry	डिफेन्स मिनस्ट्री	रक्षा मन्त्रालय
Defence Service	डिफेन्स सर्विस	रक्षा सेवा
Demobilization	डिमोबिलाइजेशन	सेनाभंग
Destroyer	डेस्ट्रॉयर	विध्वंसक
Enemy	एनिमी	शत्रु
Expedition	एक्सपेडीशन	अभियान
Explosive bomb	एक्सप्लोसिव बॉम्ब	विस्फोटक बम
Field Marshal	फील्ड मार्शल	सैन्य अधिकारी
Fighter plane	फाइटर प्लेन	लड़ाकू जहाज
Fortification	फोर्टीफिकेशन	किलाबन्दी
Gas-mask	गैस-मास्क	गैस नकाब
Guerilla	गुरिल्ला	गुरेला
Gun powder	गन पाउडर	बारूद
Land-force	लैण्ड-फोर्स	स्थल सेना
Machine-gun	मशीनगन	तोप
Magazine-gun	मैगजीन गन	कारतूस वाली बन्दूक
Magazine	मैगजीन	बारूद खाना
Morale	मॉरेल	मनोबल
Mutiny	म्यूटिनी	बगावत, विद्रोह
Navy	नेवी	जल सेना
Operation	ऑपरेशन	सेना की गति
Prisoners of war	प्रिजनर्स ऑफ वार	युद्ध बन्दी
Provisions	प्रोविजन्स	रसद, सामग्री
Recruitment	रिक्रूटमेन्ट	सेना में प्रवेश
Siege	सीज	घेरा
Strategy	स्ट्रेटजी	युद्ध कौशल
Sub-marine	सब-मेरिन	पनडुब्बी
Treaty	ट्रीटी	सन्धि
Trench	ट्रेन्च	खाई

Word	Pronunciation	Hindi Meaning
Troops	ट्रूप्स	सेना की टुकड़ी
Torpedo-boat	टोरपीडो-बोट	गोले वाली नौका
War	वार	युद्ध
War Minister	वार मिनिस्टर	युद्ध मन्त्री

Flowers

Word	Pronunciation	Hindi Meaning
Bud	बड	कली, कोपल
Balsam	बालसम	गुलमेंहदी
Chrysenthemum	क्रिसेन्थेमम	गुल दाउदी
Colera-flower	कोलेरा फ्लावर	नागभिका
Creeper	क्रीपर	लता, बेल
Daisy	डेजी	गुलबहार
Erythrinia	एरीथ्रइनिया	पारिजात
Fir	फर	सनोवर
Hiptage	हिप्टेज	माध्वी पुष्प
Jasmine	जैसमिन	चमेली
Knop	नोप	कली
Lily	लिली	कुमुदिनी
Lotus	लोटस	कमल
Magnolia	मेग्नोलिया	चम्पा
Marigold	मैरीगोल्ड	गेंदा
Mushroom	मशरूम	कुकुरमुत्ता
Motia	मोतिया	मोतिया
Murraya	मरैया	कामिनी
Narcissus	नार्सिसस	नरगिस
Oleander	ओलीन्डर	करवीर, कनेर
Pandanus	पैन्डेनस	केतकी
Poppy	पोपी	पोस्त का फूल
Prickly pear	प्रिकली पियर	नागफनी
Rose	रोज	गुलाब
Stramonium	स्ट्रैमोनियम	धतूरा
Sun flower	सनफ्लॉवर	सूरजमुखी
Touch-me-not	टच-मी-नाट	छुई-मुई

Vegetables

Word	Pronunciation	Hindi Meaning
Amaranthus	एमरान्थस	चौलाई
Arum	ऐरम	अरबी
Bean	बीन	सेम
Bitter gourd	बिटर गॉर्ड	करेला
Brinjal	ब्रिंजल	बैंगन
Cabbage	कैबैज	बन्द गोभी
Carrot	कैरट	गाजर
Cauliflower	कॉलीफ्लॉवर	फूलगोभी
Charantis	चारनटिस	करेला
Chilli	चिली	लाल मिर्च
Citron	सिट्रॉन	गलगल
Clocasia	क्लोकासिया	कचालू
Coriander	कोरिअंडर	धनिया
Cow-pea	काऊ पी	लोबिया
Cucumber	कुकुम्बर	ककड़ी
Fenugreek	फेनूग्रीक	मैथी
Garlic	गार्लिक	लहसुन
Ginger	जिंजर	अदरक
Gourd	गॉर्ड	घीया, कद्दू
Greens	ग्रीन्स	साग
Jack-fruit	जैकफ्रूट	कटहल
Lady finger	लेडी फिंगर	भिण्डी
Lettuce	लेट्यूस	सलाद
Lime	लाइम	नींबू
Luffa	लुफ्फा	घीया तोरी
Mint	मिन्ट	पोदीना
Mushroom	मशरूम	कुकुरमुत्ता
Onion	ओनियन	प्याज
Pea	पी	मटर
Potato	पोटैटो	आलू
Pumpkin	पम्पकिन	लौकी
Radish	रैडिश	मूली
Red pumpkin	रैड पम्पकिन	सीताफल, पेठा
Snake gourd	स्नेक गोर्ड	चिचड़ा
Spinach	स्पाइनैक	पालक
Sweet potato	स्वीट पोटैटो	शकरकन्दी
Tamarind	टैमेरिन्ड	इमली
Tomato	टोमैटो	टमाटर

Word	Pronunciation	Hindi Meaning
Turnip	टर्निप	शलजम
Yam	याम	कचालू

Fruits (Also Dryfruits)

Word	Pronunciation	Hindi Meaning
Almond	आमण्ड	बादाम
Apple	एप्पल	सेब
Apricot	एप्रिकोट	खुबानी
Banana	बनाना	केला
Betel-nut	बीटल-नट	सुपारी
Beet-root	बीट-रूट	चुकन्दर
Berry	बेरी	बेर
Black-berry	ब्लैक-बेरी	जामुन
Carambola	कैरमबोला	कमरख
Cashewnut	कैश्युनट्	काजू
Cherry	चेरी	चेरी
Chest-nut	चेस्ट-नट	अखरोट
Coconut	कोकोनट	नारियल
Currant	कुरांट	दाख
Citron	सइट्रॉन	चकोतरा
Custard apple	कस्टर्ड एप्पल	शरीफा
Date	डेट	खजूर
Fig	फिग	अंजीर
Grape	ग्रेप	अंगूर
Gravia asiatica	ग्रेविया एशियाटिका	फालसा
Ground-nut	ग्राउण्ड-नट	मूँगफली
Guava	गुआवा	अमरूद
Lichi	लीची	लीची
Lilac	लिलैक	बिकाइन
Loquat	लोकाट	लोकाट
Malta	माल्टा	माल्टा
Mango	मैंगो	आम
Melon	मैलन	खरबूजा
Mosambi	मौसम्बी	मौसमी
Musk-melon	मस्क-मेलन	खरबूजा
Mimusops	मिमुसॉप्स	खिरनी
Mulberry	मलबेरी	शहतूत
Okra	ओकरा	एक फल
Olive	अलाइव	जैतून

Word	Pronunciation	Hindi Meaning
Orange	ऑरेन्ज	सन्तरा
Palm	पाम	ताड़ का फल
Peach	पीच	आड़ू
Pear	पीयर	नाशपाती
Papaya	पपाया	पपीता
Pineapple	पाइनएप्पल	अनानास
Pistachio	पिस्टैशियो	पिस्ता
Plum	प्लम	बेर
Pomegranate	पोमग्रेनेट	अनार
Pyrus malus	पाइरस मैलस	बब्बूगोशा
Plantain	प्लैन्टेन	केला
Raisin	रेजिन	किशमिश
Sapodilla	सैपोडिल्ला	चीकू
Sole	सोल	आलू बुखारा
Sour cherry	सोर चेरी	खट्टी चेरी
Sugarcane	शुगरकेन	गन्ना
Water-melon	वाटर-मेलन	तरबूज
Water-nut	वाटर-नट	सिंघाड़ा

Trees and Plants

Word	Pronunciation	Hindi Meaning
Acacia	अकेशिया	बबूल
Apple tree	एप्पल ट्री	सेब का पेड़
Abbizzia labbek	अब्बिजिया लैबेक	सिरस
Bamboo	बम्बू	बाँस
Banyan	बैनयान	बरगद
Betel-nut tree	बीटल-नट ट्री	सुपारी का पेड़
Birch	बर्च	भोजपत्र
Teak	टीक	सागवान
Cactus	कैक्टस	थूहर
Cane	केन	बेंत
Cedar	सीडार	देवदार
Cypress	साइप्रस	सरू
Coco	कोको	नारियल का पेड़
Creeper	क्रीपर	लता, बेल
Conifer	कॉनिफर	झाऊ
Date-palm	डेट-पाम	खजूर का पेड़
Ebony	एबॉनी	आबनूस
Eleocarpus	एलियोकार्पस	रूद्राक्ष

Word	Pronunciation	Hindi Meaning
Fir	फर	देवदार, सनोवर
Flax	फ्लैक्स	सन
Grass	ग्रास	घास
Guava	गुआवा	अमरूद
Grape vine	ग्रेप-वाइन	अंगूर की बेल
Indigo	इन्डिगो	नील
Jack tree	जैक ट्री	कटहल का पेड़
Jute	जूट	पटसन
Mahogany	महोगनी	महोगनी
Mango tree	मैंगो ट्री	आम का पेड़
Oak	ओक	बलूत
Peepal	पीपल	पीपल
Palm tree	पाम ट्री	ताड़ का पेड़
Paddy	पैडी	धान का पौधा
Pine	पाइन	चीड़ का पेड़
Polyalthia	पोलयाल्थिया	अशोक
Sandal	सन्दल	चन्दन
Sal tree	साल ट्री	साल का पेड़
Shrub	श्रब	झाड़ी
Silk cotton	सिल्क कॉटन	सेमल
Stamen	स्टैमेन	जीरा
Sugar cane	शुगर केन	गन्ना
Shishman	शीशम	शीशम

Various Parts of Trees and Plants

Word	Pronunciation	Hindi Meaning
Bark	बार्क	छाल
Branch	ब्रान्च	टहनी, शाखा
Bud	बड	कली
Bulb	बल्ब	कन्द
Bush	बुश	झाड़ी
Bubil	ब्यूबिल	पत्रकन्द
Coir	कॉयर	जटा
Conifer	कॉनिफर	झाऊ
Fibre	फाइबर	रेशा
Flower	फ्लॉवर	फूल
Fruit	फ्रूट	फल
Graft	ग्राफ्ट	कलम

Word	Pronunciation	Hindi Meaning
Germ	जर्म	अंकुर
Gum	गम	गोंद
Juice	जूस	रस
Leaf	लीफ	पत्ता
Pistil	पिस्टिल	गर्भ केसर
Pollen grain	पॉलेन ग्रेन	पराग कण
Pollen tube	पॉलेन ट्यूब	पराग नलिका
Pulp	पल्प	गूदा
Root	रूट	जड़
Root stalk	रूट स्टाक	प्रकन्द
Seed	सीड	बीज
Skin	स्किन	छिलका
Sprout	स्प्राउट	अंकुर
Stamen	स्टैमेन	पुमंग
Stem	स्टेम	धड़
Thorn	थॉर्न	काँटा
Trunk	ट्रंक	तना
Wood	वुड	लकड़ी

Cereals/Grains

Word	Pronunciation	Hindi Meaning
Barley	बार्ले	जौ
Beaten paddy	बीटन पैडी	चिवड़ा
Bran	ब्रान	चोकर
Buck wheat	बक व्हीट	मोथा
Cluster bean	क्लस्टर बीन	ग्वार
Corn	कॉर्न	अनाज, दाना
Castor seed	कास्टर सीड	अरण्डी
Flour	फ्लोर	आटा
Fine flour	फाइन फ्लोर	मैदा
Field pea	फील्ड पी	गोल मटर
Grain	ग्रेन	अनाज
Gram	ग्राम	चना
Great millet	ग्रेट मिलेट	ज्वार
Kidney bean	किडनी बीन	राजमा
Lentil	लेन्टिल	मसूर
Linseed	लिनसीड	अलसी
Maize	मेज	मकई

Word	Pronunciation	Hindi Meaning
Millet	मिलेट	बाजरा, ज्वार
Mustard	मस्टर्ड	सरसों, राई
Oat	ओट	जई
Paddy	पैडी	धान
Pea	पी	मटर
Pigeon pea	पिजन पी	अरहर
Phaseolies mungo	फैसियोलीज मंगो	उड़द
Pearl millet	पर्ल मिलेट	बाजरा
Poppy seed	पॉपी सीड	पोस्त
Pulse	पल्स	दाल
Rice	राइस	चावल
Sago	सागो	साबूदाना
Sesamum	सीसेमम	तिल
Semolina	सैमोलीना	सूजी
Wheat	व्हीट	गेहूँ

Eatables and Potables

Word	Pronunciation	Hindi Meaning
Arrow-root	एरोरूट	अरारोट
Bacon	बैकन	सूअर का मांस
Beef	बीफ	गाय का मांस
Breakfast	ब्रेकफास्ट	कलेवा, नाश्ता
Biscuit	बिसकिट	बिस्कुट
Broth	ब्रॉथ	शोरबा, रसा
Butter	बटर	मक्खन
Bread	ब्रैड	रोटी
Boiled rice	बॉयल्ड राइस	भात
Butter milk	बटर मिल्क	छाछ
Brandy	ब्रैण्डी (ब्राण्डी)	शराब
Betel	बीटेल	पान
Bidi	बीड़ी	बीड़ी
Cake	केक	केक
Cheese	चीज	पनीर
Clarified butter	क्लैरीफाइड बटर	घी
Coffee	कॉफी	कहवा
Comfit	कॉम्फिट	इलायची दाना
Cream	क्रीम	मलाई
Cocoa	कोको	कोको
Cigar	सिगार	चुरट

Word	Pronunciation	Hindi Meaning
Cigarette	सिगरेट	सिगरेट
Curd	कर्ड	दही
Curry	करी	कढ़ी
Chapati	चपाती	रोटी
Condensed milk	कन्डैन्स्ड मिल्क	खोया
Corn-ear	कॉर्न इयर	भुट्टा
Dinner	डिनर	रात का भोजन
Frumenty	फ्रूमेण्टी	खीर, दलिया
Feast	फीस्ट	दावत
Flesh	फ्लेश	कच्चा मांस
Flour	फ्लोर	आटा
Food	फूड	भोजन
Gruel	ग्रूएल	दलिया
Honey	हनी	शहद
Ice	आइस	बर्फ
Ice-cream	आइसक्रीम	कुल्फी
Jam	जैम	मुरब्बा
Loaf	लोफ	पाव रोटी
Lemon juice	लेमन ज्यूस	नींबू का रस
Loaf sugar	लोफ शुगर	शक्कर
Meat	मीट	मांस
Mid-day meal	मिड-डे मील	दोपहर का भोजन
Milk	मिल्क	दूध
Minced meat	मिन्स्ड मीट	कीमा
Mutton	मटन	बकरे का मांस
Meal	मील	भोजन
Molasses	मोलैसेज	शीरा, राब
Oil	ऑयल	तेल
Opium	ओपियम	अफीम
Puffed rice	पफ्ड राइस	मुरमुरा
Pickle	पिकल	अचार
Porridge	पोरिज	दलिया
Pork	पोर्क	सूअर का मांस
Pudding	पुडिंग	दलिया
Parched rice	पार्च्ड राइस	भाप से पके चावल
Snacks	स्नैक्स	जलपान
Sauce	सॉस	चटनी
Soup	सूप	शोरबा
Sugar candy	शुगर कैण्डी	मिश्री
Supper	सपर	रात का भोजन

Word	Pronunciation	Hindi Meaning
Sweet-meat	स्वीटमीट	लड्डू
Syrup	सिरप	शर्बत
Surti	सुर्टी	सुरती
Smoking	स्मोकिंग	धूम्रपान
Tea	टी	चाय
Tiffin	टिफिन	जलपान
Treacle	ट्रीकल	राब, खाण्ड
Whey	व्हे	मट्ठा
Vinegar	विनेगर	सिरका
Wine	वाइन	मदिरा

Spices and Grocery Items

Word	Pronunciation	Hindi Meaning
Aconite	ऐकोनाइट	कुचला
Aloe	अलो	अगरू
Alum	ऐलम	फिटकरी
Arsenic	ऑर्सेनिक	संखिया
Aniseed	एनीसीड	सौंफ
Asafoetida	आसाफीटिडा	हींग
Aflatoon	अफलाटून	गूगल
Alkali	अलकली	सज्जीखार
Acid	एसिड	अम्ल
Basil	बैसिल	तुलसी
Barilla	बरिल्ला	सब्जखार
Belladona	बैलाडोना	धतूरा
Black-pepper	ब्लैक-पैपर	काली मिर्च
Bitumen	बिटूमेन	शिलाजीत
Borax	बोरेक्स	सुहागा
Bonezin	बोनजीन	लोबान
Bamboo camphor	बैम्बू-कैम्फर	बंश लोचन
Caraway	कैरावे	अजवाइन
Camphor	केम्फर	कपूर
Cassia	कैसिया	तेजपात
Catechu	कैटेचू	कत्था
Cinnamon	सिन्नामोन	दाल चीनी
Chirata	चिराता	चिरायता
Clove	क्लोव	लौंग
Cocaine	कोकेन	कोकीन
Coriander seed	कोरिएण्डर सीड	धनिया

Word	Pronunciation	Hindi Meaning
Cardamom	कार्डेमॉम	इलायची
Cumin seed	क्यूमिन सीड	जीरा
Carbonate of soda	कार्बोनेट ऑफ सोडा	पापड़ खार
Cubeb	क्यूबेब	कबाब चीनी
Dry ginger	ड्राई जिंजर	सौंठ
Gall-nut	गॉल नट	माजूफल
Indian madder	इण्डियन मैडर	मजीठ
Hemp	हेम्प	भांग
Hog plums	हॉग प्लम्स	आँवला
Liquorice	लिक्वोराइस	मुलेठी
Litharge	लिथार्जे	सफेदा
Long pepper	लॉंग पैपर	पीपल
Mace	मेस	जावित्री
Mangosteen	मैंगोस्टीन	अमचूर
Menthol	मेन्थॉल	पोदीने का सत
Musk	मस्क	कस्तूरी
Myrobalan	माइरोबालान	हर्र, हरड़, अरहर
Nigella	नाइजेला	कलौंजी
Nux vomica	नक्स वोमीका	कुचला
Nutmeg	नटमेग	जायफल
Nitre	नाइटर	सुरिया खार
Niger	नाइगर	तिल्ली का तेल
Oat	ओट	जई
Origanum	ओरिगैनम	शिकाकाई
Pellitory	पेलिटोरी	अकरकरा
Pepper	पैपर	मिर्च
Pepper root	पैपर रूट	पीपल मूल
Parsley	पारस्ले	अजवायन
Pistil	पिस्टिल	गर्म केसर
Poppy seed	पोपी सीड	खसखस
Phyllanthus emblica	फिलेन्थस एम्बलीका	आँवला
Red pepper	रेड पैपर	लाल मिर्च
Rock salt	रॉक साल्ट	सेंधा नमक
Red powder	रेड पाउडर	अबीर
Ruddle	रडल	गेरू
Saffron	सैफरॉन	केसर
Salt	साल्ट	नमक
Sal-ammoniac	साल-अमोनिआक	नौसादर
Saltpetre	साल्टपीटर	शोरा
Senna	सैना	सनाय

Word	Pronunciation	Hindi Meaning
Soap nut	सोप नट	रीठा
Turmeric	टरमेरिक	इमली
Vinegar	विनेगर	सिरका
Vitriol	विट्रिऑल	कसीसा
Yeast	यीस्ट	खमीर

Building Parts and Buildings

Word	Pronunciation	Hindi Meaning
Arch	आर्च	वृत्तखण्ड
Attic	अटिक	अटारी
Aviary	एवियरी	चिड़ियाखाना
Bar	बार	छड़
Barrack	बैरेक	सेनानिवास
Bath-room	बाथरूम	स्नानगृह
Battlement	बैटलमेन्ट	मुन्डेर
Bedroom	बैडरूम	शयनागार
Booking office	बुकिंग-ऑफिस	टिकटघर
Bracket	ब्रैकेट	कोनिया
Bungalow	बंगलो	बंगला
Building	बिल्डिंग	इमारत
Balcony	बाल्कनी	बरामदा
Brick	ब्रिक	ईंट
Bolt	बोल्ट	चटखनी
Church	चर्च	गिरजाघर
College	कॉलेज	महाविद्यालय
Cement	सीमेण्ट	सीमेण्ट
Courtyard	कोर्टयार्ड	सहन (आँगन)
Cell	सेल	तहखाना
Cornice	कॉर्निस	कॉर्निस
Ceiling	सीलिंग	छत
Cottage	कॉटेज	झोंपड़ी
Chimney	चिमनी	धुआँकश
Cloister	क्लॉयस्टर	मठ
Dais	डायस	मचान
Dome	डोम	गुम्बद
Door	डोर	दरवाजा
Door frame	डोर फ्रेम	चौखट

Word	Pronunciation	Hindi Meaning
Door sill	डोर सिल	देहली
Drain	ड्रेन	नावदान, नाली
Factory	फैक्ट्री	कारखाना
Floor	फ्लोर	फर्श
Fort	फोर्ट	किला
Foundation	फाउण्डेशन	नींव, बुनियाद
Fountain	फाउण्टेन	फव्वारा
Gate	गेट	दरवाजा
Grating	ग्रेटिंग	जाली
Girder	गर्डर	गाटर
Gutter	गटर	परनाला
Granary	ग्रेनरी	खलिहान
Gymnasium	जिम्नेजिअम	जिमशाला
House	हाउस	मकान
Hamlet	हेमलेट	गाँव
Hermitage	हर्मिटेज	साधु कुटी
Hospital	हॉस्पिटल	अस्पताल
Hotel	होटल	होटल
Hinge	हिंज	कब्जा
Hall	हाल	बड़ा कमरा
Hook	हुक	हुक
Hearth	हर्थ	अंगीठी
Inn	इन	सराय
Kitchen	किचन	रसोई
Latch	लैच	चटखनी
Laboratory	लेबोरेट्री	प्रयोगशाला
Latrine	लैटरिन	शौचालय
Lattice	लैटिस	जाली
Lunatic asylum	ल्यूनैटिक एसायलम	पागलखाना
Library	लायब्रेरी	पुस्तकालय
Lime	लाइम	चूना
Ladder	लैडर	सीढ़ी
Mosque	मॉस्क	मस्जिद
Mud	मड	कीचड़
Minaret	मिनारेट	मस्जिद की मीनार
Niche	निच	आला
Nail	नेल	कील

Clothes, Dresses and Wearing Apparels etc

Word	Pronunciation	Hindi Meaning
Alpaca	अलपाका	ऊँट के रोएँ से बना वस्त्र
Banian	बनियान	बनियान
Belt	बेल्ट	बेल्ट
Bodice	बॉडिस	अंगिया
Border	बॉर्डर	किनारा
Brassiere	ब्रेजरी	चोली
Cap	कैप	टोपी
Calico	कैलिको	दरेस
Canvas	कैनवस	किरमिच
Cashmere	कैशमीअर	कश्मीरा
Chester	चैस्टर	बड़ा कोट
Chemise	शैमीज	शमीज
Cloth	क्लॉथ	कपड़ा
Clothes	क्लोद्ज	सिले कपड़े
Cloak gown	क्लोक गाउन	लबादा
Chintz	शिंज	छींट
Coat	कोट	कोट
Collar	कॉलर	कॉलर
Cotton	कॉटन	सूत
Crepe	क्रेप	महीन कपड़ा
Cushion	कुशन	गच्छी गद्दी
Damask	दमश्क	जामदनी
Darn	डार्न	रफू
Diaper	डायपर	पोतड़ा
Deep colour	डीप कलर	गहरा रंग
Flannel	फ्लानेल	फलालैन
Frock	फ्रॉक	फ्राक
Gauge	गॉज	जाली
Gloves	ग्लव्स	दस्ताने
Gown	गाउन	चोगा, लबादा
Handkerchief	हैण्डकरचीफ	रूमाल
Hat	हैट	टोप
Half-pant	हाफ पैन्ट	निक्कर
Hem	हेम	मगजी
Hood	हुड	कनटोप
Jacket	जैकेट	जाकेट
Jersey	जरसी	जर्सी
Jumper	जम्पर	जम्पर
Knicker	निकर	निक्कर

Word	Pronunciation	Hindi Meaning
Lace	लेस	बेल
Laces	लेसेज	तस्मे, फीते
Linen	लिनन	मलमल
Loin cloth	लॉइन क्लॉथ	लंगोटी
Long skirt	लॉंग स्कर्ट	लहँगा
Loop	लूप	घुण्डी
Mat	मैट	चटाई, कपड़ा
Mattress	मैट्रेस	गद्दा, तोशक
Muffler	मफलर	मफलर
Muslin	मस्लिन	मलमल
Napkin	नैपकिन	अंगोछा
Overcoat	ओवरकोट	बड़ा कोट
Pantaloon	पैन्टालून	पतलून
Patch	पैच	पैबन्द
Petticoat	पैटीकोट	पेटीकोट, साया
Prints	प्रिन्ट्स	छपे हुए वस्त्र
Pyjama	पायजामा	पायजामा
Rug	रग	मोटा ऊनी कपड़ा
Saree	सारी	साड़ी
Satin	साटिन	साटन
Scarf	स्कार्फ	दुपट्टा, रूमाल
Serge	सर्ज	सरज
Shawl	शॉल	शाल
Sheet	शीट	चादर
Shirting	शर्टिंग	कमीज का कपड़ा
Skirt	स्कर्ट	घाघरा
Silk	सिल्क	रेशम
Suiting	सूटिंग	सूट का कपड़ा
Sleeves	स्लीव्ज	आस्तीन
Socks	सॉक्स	जुराब
Stockings	स्टॉकिंग्स	लम्बे मोजे
Stays	स्टेज	चोली
Stripped Mule	स्ट्राइप्ड म्यूल	डोरिया
Tape	टेप	फीता
Thread	थ्रैड	धागा
Trimming	ट्रिमिंग	झालर/कतरन
Tunic	ट्यूनिक	अंगरखा
Turban	टर्बन	पगड़ी, साफा
Trouser	ट्राउजर	पायजामा
Underwear	अन्डरवियर	जाँघिया

Word	Pronunciation	Hindi Meaning
Uniform	यूनिफॉर्म	वेशभूषा/वर्दी
Veil	वेल	घूँघट
Velvet	वेल्वेट	मखमल
Wool	वूल	ऊन
Waistcoat	वेस्टकोट	वास्कट
Yarn	यार्न	सूत

Terms Relating to Office Stationery

Word	Pronunciation	Hindi Meaning
Book	बुक	पुस्तक
Blank paper	ब्लैंक पेपर	कोरा कागज
Blue ink	ब्लू इन्क	नीली स्याही
Black board	ब्लैक बोर्ड	श्याम पट
Call bell	कॉल बेल	पुकारने की घण्टी
Carbon paper	कार्बन पेपर	प्रतिलिपि बनाने का कागज
Card	कार्ड	गत्ता
Clip	क्लिप	चिमटी
Copying pencil	कॉपींग पेन्सिल	नकल करने की पेन्सिल
Cork	कॉर्क	काग, डाट
Compass	कम्पास	परकार, पैमाना
Crayon	क्रेयॉन	चाक, पेन्सिल
Counterfoil	काउन्टरफॉइल	आधी रसीद
Chair	चेयर	कुर्सी
Daily paper	डेली पेपर	दैनिक समाचार-पत्र
Dictionary	डिक्शनरी	शब्दकोष
Divider	डिवाइडर	परकार
Drawing paper	ड्रॉइंग पेपर	चित्र बनाने का कागज
Drawing pin	ड्रॉइंग पिन	दबाने की पिन
Damper	डैम्पर	चमकाने वाला
Drawing copy	ड्रॉइंग कॉपी	रेखाचित्र पुस्तिका
Duster	डस्टर	झाड़न
Diary	डायरी	दैनन्दिनी
Easy chair	इजी चेयर	आराम कुर्सी
Eraser	इरेजर	रबड़
Envelope	एन्वेलप	लिफाफा
Exercise book	एक्सरसाइज बुक	कॉपी
Fastener	फासनर	बाँधने वाली डोरी या फीता
Fountain pen	फाउन्टेन पेन	कलम
Foot rule	फूट रूल	फुटा, पैमाना

Word	Pronunciation	Hindi Meaning
Geometry box	ज्योमेट्री बॉक्स	रेखागणित यन्त्र बक्सा
Glue	ग्लू	सरेस, गोंद
Gum	गम	गोंद
Ink	इन्क	स्याही
Inkpot	इन्कपॉट	दवात
Invitation card	इन्विटेशन कार्ड	निमन्त्रण पत्र
Inland letter	इनलैण्ड लेटर	अन्तर्देशीय पत्र
Ink-stand	इन्क स्टैण्ड	स्याहीदान
Ledger	लेजर	लेखाबही
Letter pad	लैटर पैड	पत्र-लेखन पैड
Magazine	मैगजीन	पत्रिका
Mapping pen	मैपिंग पेन	बारीक पेन
Nib	निब	निब
Newspaper	न्यूजपेपर	समाचार-पत्र
Note-book	नोट बुक	छोटी कापी
Office tray	ऑफिस ट्रे	कागज-पत्र रखने की लकड़ी की ट्रे
Paper	पेपर	कागज
Paper-cutter	पेपर-कटर	कागज तराश
Paper-weight	पेपर-वेट	कागज दाब
Pencil	पेन्सिल	पेन्सिल
Packing paper	पैकिंग पेपर	लपेटने का पेपर
Punch	पन्च	छेदनी
Punching machine	पन्चिंग मशीन	छिद्र करने का यन्त्र
Pin	पिन	पिन, सुई
Pin cushion	पिन कुशन	पिन लगाने की गद्दी
Pastel	पेस्टल	चित्र बनाने के रंग
Pencil cutter	पेन्सिल कटर	चाकू
Pen knife	पेन नाइफ	कलम तराश
Protractor	प्रोट्रैक्टर	चाँदा
Register	रजिस्टर	खाता, रजिस्टर
Receipt book	रिसिप्ट बुक	रसीद बही
Red ink	रेड इन्क	लाल स्याही
Ribbon	रिबन	फीता
Rubber	रबर	रबड़
Rubber stamp	रबर स्टैम्प	रबड़ की मोहर
Ruler	रूलर	पैमाना
Seal	सील	मोहर
Sealing wax	सीलिंग वैक्स	लाख
Slate	स्लेट	स्लेट
Stool	स्टूल	तिपाई, स्टूल

Word	Pronunciation	Hindi Meaning
Steel pen	स्टील पेन	लोहे का पेन
Scribbling book	स्क्रिब्लिंग बुक	फुटकर लेखन पुस्तिका
Steel pin	स्टील पिन	लोहे की पिन
Scale	स्केल	फुटा, स्केल
Set-square	सेट स्क्वायर	सेट स्क्वायर
Stencil machine	स्टेन्सिल मशीन	स्टेन्सिल काटने की मशीन
Stencil paper	स्टेन्सिल पेपर	स्टेन्सिल कागज
Tag	टैग	धागा, डोरी
Tracing cloth	ट्रेसिंग क्लॉथ	मोमी कपड़ा
Tracing paper	ट्रेसिंग पेपर	प्रतिरूप उतारने का कागज
Typewriter	टाइपराइटर	टंकण मशीन
Visiting card	विजिटिंग कार्ड	भेंट कार्ड
Waste paper basket	वेस्ट पेपर बास्केट	रद्दी की टोकरी
Wire	वायर	तार
Writing pad	राइटिंग पैड	लेखन पट्टी
Writing paper	राइटिंग पेपर	लिखने का कागज
Weekly paper	वीकली पेपर	साप्ताहिक सामाचार-पत्र
Wrapping paper	रैपिंग पेपर	लपेटने का कागज

Terms Relating to Games & Sports

Word	Pronunciation	Hindi Meaning
Athletics	एथलेटिक्स	व्यायाम
Badminton	बैडमिन्टन	बैडमिन्टन
Badminton court	बैडमिन्टन कोर्ट	बैडमिन्टन खेलने का मैदान
Ball	बॉल	गेंद
Bandy	बन्डी	बर्फ पर खेली जाने वाली हॉकी
Billiards	बिलियर्ड्स	रंगीन गेंदों से खेला जाने वाला खेल
Billiards table	बिलियर्ड्स टेबल	बिलियर्ड्स खेलने की मेज
Basket ball	बास्केट बाल	बास्केट बाल
Bat	बैट	बल्ला
Boxing	बॉक्सिंग	मुक्केबाजी
Hide and seek	हाइड एण्ड सीक	लुका-छिपी
Basket	बास्केट	टोकरी
Boxing ring	बॉक्सिग रिंग	घूँसेबाजी का रिंग
Carrom	कैरम	कैरम का खेल
Carrom board	कैरम बोर्ड	कैरम खेलने का बोर्ड
Chess	चेस	शतरंज
Chess board	चेस बोर्ड	शतरंज की बिसात
Chess pieces	चेस पीसेज	शतरंज के मोहरे

Word	Pronunciation	Hindi Meaning
Cricket	क्रिकेट	क्रिकेट
Cycle race	साइकिल रेस	साइकिल की दौड़
Dice	डाइस	चौपड़
Duck and drake	डक एण्ड ड्रेक	पानी में खेला जाने वाला एक खेल
Discuss throw	डिस्कस थ्रो	गोला फेंक
*Football	फुटबाल	फुटबाल
Golf	गोल्फ	गोल्फ
Golf course	गॉल्फ कोर्स	गोल्फ का मैदान
Horse Race	हॉर्स रेस	घुड़ दौड़
High jump	हाई जम्प	ऊँची कूद
Hunting	हन्टिंग	शिकार
Hockey	हॉकी	हॉकी
Javelin throw	जैवलिन थ्रो	भाला फेंक
Jumping	जम्पिंग	कूदना
Kite-flying	काइट फ्लाइंग	पतंग उड़ाना
Long jump	लाँग जम्प	लम्बी कूद
Marbles	मार्बल्स	गोली/कँचे का खेल
Ping pong	पिंग पाँग	एक प्रकार का टेनिस का खेल
Polo	पोलो	घोड़े पर सवार होकर हॉकी की तरह खेला जाने वाला खेल
Playing cards	प्लेइंग कार्ड्स	ताश का खेल
Race	रेस	दौड़
Racing track	रेसिंग ट्रैक	दौड़ का मैदान
Snake and ladder	स्नेक एण्ड लैडर	साँप-सीढ़ी का खेल
Ski-ing	स्कीइंग	बर्फ पर सन्तुलन बनाकर फिसलने का खेल
Swimming	स्विमिंग	तैराकी
Tennis	टेनिस	टेनिस
Tennis racket	टेनिस रैकेट	टेनिस का बल्ला
Table tennis	टेबल टेनिस	टेबल टेनिस
Lawn tennis	लॉन टेनिस	घास के मैदान पर खेली जाने वाली टेनिस
Volley-ball	वॉली-बाल	वाली-बाल
Pole vault	पोल-वॉल्ट	बल्लीकूद
Weight lifting	वेट लिफ्टिंग	भार उठाना
Wrestling	रैसलिंग	कुश्ती लड़ना
Water polo	वाटर पोलो	पानी में गेंद से खेला जाने वाला खेल

Directions

Word	Pronunciation	Hindi Meaning
East	ईस्ट	पूर्व
West	वेस्ट	पश्चिम
North	नॉर्थ	उत्तर
South	साउथ	दक्षिण
North-East	नॉर्थ-ईस्ट	उत्तर-पूर्व
North-West	नॉर्थ-वेस्ट	उत्तर-पश्चिम
South-West	साउथ वेस्ट	दक्षिण-पश्चिम

Planets in Our Solar System

Planet	Pronunciation	Hindi Meaning
Mars	मार्स	मंगल
Mercury	मर्करी	बुध
Neptune	नेप्च्यून	वरुण
Saturn	सैटर्न	शनि
Earth	अर्थ	पृथ्वी
Jupiter	जुपीटर	बृहस्पति
Uranus	यूरेनस	यूरेनस
Venus	वीनस	शुक्र

Units in Measuring Distance etc

Word	Pronunciation	Hindi Meaning
Gross	ग्रॉस	गुर्स/12 दर्जन/144 इकाई
Dozen	डजन	दर्जन/12 इकाई
Score	स्कोर	कौड़ी/2 इकाई
Quire	क्वायर	दस्ता/24 कागज
Rim	रिम	रिम/4 दर्जन/2 दस्ते/48 कागज
Bundle	बण्डल	बण्डल/2 रिम
Bale/Gattha	बेल/गट्ठा	गट्ठा/1 रिम/5 बण्डल
Inch	इंच	इंच
Foot	फुट	फुट/12 इंच
Yard	यार्ड	गज/3 फुट
Furlong	फरलाँग	फरलाँग/22 गज
Mile	माइल	मील/8 फरलाँग/176 गज
Knot	नॉट	समुद्री मील/68 फुट

Seasons

Word	Pronunciation	Hindi Meaning
Summer	समर	ग्रीष्म
Winter	विन्टर	शरद
Spring	स्प्रिंग	बसन्त
Autumn	ऑटम	पतझड़
Rainy	रेनी	वर्षा
Hemant	हेमन्त	शिशिर

English Months

Month	Pronunciation	Hindi Meaning
January	जैनुअरी	जनवरी
February	फैब्रुअरी	फरवरी
March	मार्च	मार्च
April	एप्रिल	अप्रैल
May	मे	मई
June	जून	जून
July	जुलाई	जुलाई
August	औगस्ट	अगस्त
September	सेप्टेम्बर	सितम्बर
October	ऑक्टोबर	अक्टूबर
November	नोवेम्बर	नवम्बर
December	डैसेम्बर	दिसम्बर

Days

Word	Pronunciation	Hindi Meaning
Sunday	सनडे	रविवार
Monday	मनडे	सोमवार
Tuesday	ट्यूजडे	मंगलवार
Wednesday	वैडनसडे	बुधवार
Thursday	थर्सडे	बृहस्पतिवार
Friday	फ्राइडे	शुक्रवार
Saturday	सैटरडे	शनिवार

Time Measure

Word	Pronunciation	Hindi Meaning
Moment	मोमेन्ट	क्षण, पल
Jiffy	जिफी	पल
Second	सेकेण्ड	सेकिण्ड
Minute	मिनट	मिनट
Hour	ऑवर	घण्टा
Morning	मॉर्निंग	प्रातःकाल
Dawn	डॉन	उषाकाल
Sunrise	सनराइज	सूर्योदय
Noon	नून	दोपहर
Mid-day	मिड-डे	मध्यान्ह
Afternoon	आफ्टरनून	दोपहर बाद
Evening	ईवनिंग	सायंकाल
Dusk	डस्क	गोधूलि बेला
Sun-set	सन-सेट	सूर्यास्त
Quarter	क्वार्टर	चौथाई
Half	हाफ	आधा
Twilight	ट्वाइलाइट	सन्ध्याकाल
Midnight	मिडनाइट	मध्यरात्रि
Fortnight	फोर्टनाइट	पखवाड़ा
Month	मन्थ	महीना
Year	ईयर	वर्ष
Decade	डिकेड	दशक
Century	सेंचुरी	शताब्दी
Millennium	मिलेनियम	हजार वर्ष
Era/ Epoch	इरा/इपोक	युग
Date	डेट	तिथि
Today	टुडे	आज
Tonight	टुनाइट	आज की रात
Yesterday	यस्टर डे	बीता कल
Yester night	यस्टर नाइट	बीते कल की रात
Day before yesterday	डे बिफोर यस्टरडे	परसों बीता हुआ दिन
Tomorrow	टुमॉरो	आने वाला कल
Day after tomorrow	डे आफ्टर टुमॉरो	आने वाला परसों का दिन

Colours

Word	Pronunciation	Hindi Meaning
Azure	एज्योर	आसमानी
Black	ब्लैक	काला
Blue	ब्लू	नीला
Brown	ब्राउन	भूरा
Crimson	क्रिमसन	गहरा लाल
Dusky	डस्की	राख का सा रंग
Golden	गोल्डन	सुनहरा
Grey	ग्रे	सलेटी
Green	ग्रीन	हरा
Indigo	इन्डिगो	नीला
Lemon	लेमन	हल्का पीला
Maroon	मैरून	गहरा सुर्ख
Mauve	मॉव	चमकीला गुलाबी
Orange	ऑरेन्ज	नारंगी
Pale	पेल	हल्का पीला
Pink	पिन्क	हल्का गुलाबी
Purple	पर्पल	बैंगनी
Red	रेड	लाल
Rosy	रोजी	गुलाबी
Saffron	सैफरॉन	केसरिया
Violet	वायोलेट	जामुनी
Vermillion	वर्मिलियन	सिन्दूरी
White	व्हाइट	सफेद
Yellow	येलो	पीला

Medical Terms

Word	Pronunciation	Hindi Meaning
Allopathy	एलोपैथी	अंग्रेजी औषधि पद्धति
Ayurved	आयुर्वेद	भारतीय औषधि पद्धति
Arnica	अर्निका	ज्वरनाशक (होम्योपैथिक औषधि)
Bandage	बैन्डेज	पट्टी
Boric acid	बोरिक एसिड	सेक करने की दवा
Castor oil	कैस्टर ऑयल	रेण्डी का तेल

Word	Pronunciation	Hindi Meaning
Cocaine	कोकैन	सुन्न करने की दवा
Drug	ड्रग	औषधि, दारू, दवाओं का घोल
Dose	डोज	दवा की मात्रा, खुराक
Decoction	डिकोक्शन	काढ़ा
Distilled water	डिस्टिल्ड वाटर	आसुत जल
Diet	डायट	पथ्य, आहार
Emetic	एमेटिक	वमन, उल्टी कराने वाली दवा
Fomentation	फोमेन्टेशन	सेंक, सिकाई
Fumigation	फ्यूमिगेशन	बफारा/धूनी देना
Gargle	गर्गल	कुल्ली/गरारा करने की तरल दवा
Homeopathy	होमियोपैथी	प्राकृतिक तत्वों की छोटी-छोटी मात्रा से की जाने वाली चिकित्सा
Injection	इन्जेक्शन	टीका
Jalap	जैलप	रेचक (दस्तावर) दवा
Lancet	लैन्सेट	नश्तर
Laxative	लैक्सेटिव	जुलाब, विरेचक दवा
Mixture	मिक्सचर	तरल दवाइयों का मिश्रण
Opium	ओपियम	अफीम
Ointment	ऑयन्टमेन्ट	मरहम
Poultice	पुल्टिस	फोड़े को पकाने का लेप
Powder	पाउडर	चूर्ण
Plaster	प्लास्टर	लेप
Potassium Permanganate	पोटैशियम परमैंगनेट	लाल दवा
Purgative	पर्गेटिव	जुलाब
Quinine	क्वीनाइन	कुनैन
Snuff	स्नफ	सूँघनी
Tincture	टिंक्चर	चोट की दवा
Tablet	टैबलेट	गोली
Unani	यूनानी	यूनानी पद्धति
Vaccination	वैक्सीनेशन	रोग प्रतिरोधक टीका

UNIT 15

Foreign Words

Some of the foreign words generally used in our daily life and these words are given below for the convenience of the students. Students are advised to learn these words. These words are seen many times in competitive examination papers also.

A

Ab aeterno (L.)–from eternity.	अनादि काल से
Ab ante (L.)–from before.	पूर्व काल से
Ab antiquo (L.)–from olden time.	प्राचीन काल से
Ab initio (L.)–from the beginning.	आरम्भ से
Ab intra (L.)–from within.	भीतर से
Ab irato (L.)–in a fit of passion.	उद्वेग से, क्रोध से
Abonnement (Fr.)–subscription.	शुल्क, चन्दा
Ab origine (L.)–from the beginning.	आरम्भ से, आदि से
Ad arbitrium (L.)–at pleasure.	इच्छानुसार
Ad extra (L.)–outward.	बाहरी ओर
Ad finem (L.)–to the end.	अन्त तक
Ad infinitum (L.)–up to infinity.	अनन्त तक, अन्तिम सीमा तक
Ad interim (L.)–for the meantime.	बीच के समय के लिए, अन्तरिम
A' discretion (Fr.)–without restriction.	बिना किसी रुकावट के, अबाध
Ad modum (L.)–After the method of.	रीति से, रीति के अनुसार
Ad valorem (L.)–according to value.	मूल्य के अनुसार
Ad verbum (L.)–word for word.	शाब्दिक रूप में, अविकल
Advivum (L.)–to the life.	जीवनपर्यन्त या जीवन भर
Aequanimiter (L.)–calmly.	शान्तिपूर्वक
A' fond (Fr.)–throughly.	पूर्ण रूप से
A' gauche (Fr.)–to the left.	बाईं ओर
Age quod agis (L.)–do with all your power what you do.	जो कुछ करो अपनी पूरी शक्ति लगाकर करो
Alinude (L.)–from another place.	दूसरे स्थान से
Allons ! (Fr.)–come along, let us go !	आओ हम लोग चलें
Alter ego (L.)–one's second self, intimate friend.	द्वितीय आत्मा, परम मित्र
Alter ipse amicus (L.)–a friend is another self.	मित्र दूसरी आत्मा है
A' maximis ad minima (L.)–from the greatest to the smallest.	सबसे बड़े से सबसे छोटे तक

Amicus curiae (L.)–a friend of the law-court.	अदालत का मित्र
Amicus humani generis (L.)–a friend of humanity.	मनुष्य जाति का मित्र
Anglice (L.)–in English.	अंग्रेजी में
Anima mundi (L.)–the soul of the world.	संसार की आत्मा
Animo et Jide (L.)–by courage and faith.	साहस और विश्वास से
Annus mirabilis (L.)–year of wonders.	अद्भुत घटनाओं का वर्ष
Ante bellum (L.)–before the war.	युद्ध के पहले
Ante mer idiem (L.)–before noon.	मध्याह्न (दोपहर) से पहले
Antiquarium (L.)–collection of antiquities.	प्राचीन पदार्थों का संग्रह
A posteriori (L.)–from the effect to the cause.	परिणाम से कारण तक
A' propos (Fr.)–to the point.	आशय तक
Arbitrium (L.)–power of decision.	निर्णय का अधिकार
Arcana imperii (L.)–state secrets.	राज्य के गुप्त भेद

B

Bella, horrida bella (L.)–wars, horrible wars.	युद्ध, भयंकर युद्ध
Bellum lethale (L.)–deadly war.	भयंकर युद्ध, भीषण संग्राम
Biennium (L.)–period of two years.	दो वर्ष का समय
Bona fides (L.)–good faith.	सच्चा हृदय या विश्वास
Bona mobilia (L.)–movable goods.	चल सम्पत्ति

C

Cadeau (Fr.)–a present, a gift.	उपहार, इनाम
Caeca est invidia (L.)–envy is blind.	ईर्ष्या अन्धी होती है
Casus belli (L.)–whatever eg. involves a war.	युद्ध का (आदि) कारण
Caveat actor (L.)–let the doer beware.	करने वालों सचेत या होशियार रहो
Centum (L.)–a hundred.	शत, सौ
Cito (L.)–quickly.	शीघ्रता से
Compos mentis (L.)–of sound mind, sane.	स्थिर चित्तवाला
Consilio et animis (L.)–by wisdom and courage.	बुद्धि तथा साहस द्वारा
Con spirito (It.)–with spirit.	उत्साह से
Contra bonos mores (L.)–against good manners or morals.	सदाचार या नैतिकता के विरुद्ध
Coram populo (L.)–in the presence of the public.	जनता की उपस्थिति में
Coup de hasard (Fr.)–a lucky chance.	सौभाग्य
Crimen falsi (L.)–crime of perjury.	विश्वासघात
Culpa levis (L.)–a slight fault.	छोटा-सा अपराध
Currente calamo (L.)–with a running pen.	घसीट (लिखावट में)

D

Data et accepta (L.)–expenses and receipts.	आय-व्यय
De bon augure (Fr.)–of good omen.	अच्छे शकुन का
De die in diem (L.)–from day-to-day.	दिन-दिन, प्रतिदिन
De facto (L.)–really, in fact, actual.	वस्तुतः, सचमुच, यथार्थ में
Dei gratia (L.)–by the grace of God.	ईश्वर की दया से
De integro (L.)–afresh, anew.	नया, ताजा
De jure (L.)–by right, in law.	अधिकार से, कानूनन
Deo favente (L.)–with God's favour.	ईश्वर की कृपा से
Deo gratias (L.)–thanks to God.	ईश्वर को धन्यवाद
Deus avertat ! (L.)–God forbid !	ईश्वर न करे
Deus det (L.)–God grant !	ईश्वर करे
Dictum de dicto (L.)–hearsay, report.	जनश्रुति, अफवाह
Domine, dirige nos ! (L.)–God, direct us !	ईश्वर हमें मार्ग दिखलावे
Dum spiro, spero (L.)–while I breathe, I hope.	जब तक मैं जीवित हूँ मुझे आशा है, जब तक साँस तब तक आस

E

Editio princeps (L.)–original edition (of a book).	किसी पुस्तक की मूल प्रतिलिपि
Eo nomine (L.)–by that name.	इस नाम का
Erenata (L.)–according to the exigencies of the case.	मामले की आवश्यकतानुसार
Et hoc genus omne, et id grnus ome (L.) –and everything of this or that sort.	और इस या उस प्रकार का प्रत्येक पदार्थ
Et, tu, Brute (L.)–and you too Brutus.	और ब्रूटस् तुम भी
Ex curia (L.)–out of court.	अदालत से बाहर
Ex delicto (L.)–owing to crime.	अपराध के कारण
Ex dono (L.)–as a gift.	उपहार के रूप में
Ex officio (L.)–by virtue of his office.	पदाधिकारेण
Ex parte (L.)–on one side only.	एक ओर से, एकतरफा
Expressis verbis (L.)–in express terms.	स्पष्ट शब्दों में
Ex tacito (L.)–silently.	चुपचाप
Ex utraque parte (L.)–on either side.	दोनों ओर
Ex voto (L.)–according to one's prayer.	प्रार्थना के अनुसार

F

Faber est quisque fortunae suae (L.)–everyone fashions his own fortune.	हर मनुष्य अपना भाग्य स्वयं बनाता है
Facta non verba (L.)–deeds not words.	काम होना चाहिए, केवल शब्द नहीं
Factum est (L.)–it is done.	कार्य हो गया
Fadaise (Fr.)–a silly talk.	मूर्खतापूर्ण बात
Fait accompli (Fr.)–a thing already done.	पहले से किया हुआ काम
Fata obstant (L.)–the Fate opposes it.	भाग्य इसके विरुद्ध है
Fecit (L.)–made or executed.	बनाया हुआ
Fiat justitia, ruat clelum (L.)–let justice be done, though the heavens should fall.	न्याय करो चाहे आकाश ही क्यों न गिर पड़े
Fidu et amore (L.)–by faith and love.	श्रद्धा और प्रेम से
Fidu et amore (L.)–faithful and bold.	विश्वासी तथा साहसी
Fillius nullius (L.)–a bastard.	दोगला

G

Gaillard (Fr.)–lively.	आनन्दपूर्ण, प्रसन्न
Garcon (Fr.)–a boy, bachelor.	लड़का, छोकरा, कुँवारा
Gloria in excelsis (L.)–Glory to God is the highest.	सबसे बड़ी महिमा ईश्वर की है

H

Hoc age (L.)–attend to what you do.	जो करो उस पर ध्यान दो
Hoc anno (L.)–in this year.	इस वर्ष
Hoc loco (L.)–in this place.	इस स्थान में
Hoc tempore (L.)–at this time.	इस समय
Hominis est errare (L.)–to err is human.	दोष मनुष्य से ही होता है

I

Impromptu (L.)–without study.	बिना अध्ययन का
In abstracto (L.)–in the abstract.	भाव रूप में
In camera (L.)–in the private room.	कमरे के भीतर, गुप्त स्थान में
In curia (L.)–in court.	न्यायालय में
In equilibris (L.)–in euilibrium.	बराबरी में, सन्तुलन में
In esse (L.)–in fact.	स्थिति में, वस्तुतः
In extenso (L.)–at full length.	पूरी तरह से
Infra dignitatem (L.)–below one's dignity.	मर्यादा के विरुद्ध

In pace (L.)–in peace.	शान्ति में
In statu quo (L.)–in the former state.	पूर्व अवस्था में
Inter alia (L.)–among other things.	दूसरी वस्तुओं के बीच में
In terrorem (L.)–as a warning.	चेतावनी के रूप में
Inter se (L.)–amongst themselves.	परस्पर, आपस में
In toto (L.)–in the whole, entirely.	पूर्ण रूप से, निपट
Ipso facto (L.)–really.	सत्यता में, वास्तविक रूप में

J

Jure divino (L.)–by divine law.	दैवी नियम से
Jure humano (L.)–by human law.	मनुष्य के बनाए नियम पर

L

Labor ipsev oluptas (L.)–labour itself is pleasure.	परिश्रम ही आनन्द है
Lapsus calami (L.)–a slip of the pen.	लेखनी की भूल
Lapsus linguae (L.)–a slip of the tongue.	बोलने में हुई भूल
Lapsus memoriae (L.)–a slip of the memory.	स्मरण शक्ति की भूल
Lese majeste (Fr.)–high treason.	राजद्रोह
Lingua Franca (It.)–a mixed language spoken by the Europeans.	मिश्रित भाषा जिसको यूरोप के लोग बोलते हैं
Locus standi (L.)–place for standing, right of interfering.	खड़ा होने का स्थान, हस्तक्षेप करने का अधिकार
Lucri causa (L.)–for the sake of gain.	लाभ के लिए
Lusus naturae (L.)–a freak of nature.	प्रकृति की विषमता

M

Magnum bonum (L.)–a great good.	बड़ा उपकार या लाभ
Magnum opus (L.)–a great work.	बड़ा कार्य
Mala fide (L.)–faithlessly, treacherously.	विश्वासघात से
Memento mori (L.)–remember that thou shalt die.	याद रख कि तू मरेगा
Mirabile dictu (L.)–wonderful to tell.	कहने में विलक्षण
Mirabile visu (L.)–wonderful to see.	देखने में विलक्षण

N

Nolens volens (L.)–willing or not willing, whether he will or not	उसकी इच्छा हो अथवा न हो
Noli me tangere (L.)–do not touch me.	मुझे स्पर्श मत करो
Nota bene (L.)–abbr. N B take notice, mark well.	भली-भाँति ध्यान दो
Nulli secundus (L.)–unparalleled, second to none.	अद्वितीय
Nunc est bibendum (L.)–now is the time for drinking.	अब (मदिरा) पीने का समय है

O

Omnia bona bonis (L.)–all things are good to the good.	भले के लिए सब भला होता
Onus probandi (L.)–the burden of proof.	सिद्ध करने का आधार

P

Pari passu (L.)–with equal pace, together.	बराबरी की गति से, एक साथ
Particeps criminis (L.)–an accomplice.	अपराध करने में सहायक
Per annum (L.)–per year.	प्रति वर्ष
Per centum (L.)–by the hundred.	प्रति सैकड़ा
Per diem (L.)–per day, daily.	प्रतिदिन
Per se (L.)–by itself.	स्वयं
Populus vult decipi (L.)–the people wish to be fooled.	लोग मूर्ख बनना चाहते हैं
Post mortem (L.)–after death.	मृत्यु के उपरान्त
Post obitum (L.)–after death.	मृत्यु के बाद
Prima facie (L.)–on the first view.	पहली दृष्टि में
Primo (L.)–in the first place.	पहले पहल
Pro rata (L.)–in proportion.	अनुपात में, यथोचित
Pro tempore (L.)–for the time being temporarily.	इस (वर्तमान) समय के लिए, अस्थायी रूप में

Q

Quid pro quo (L.)–something given or taken as equivalent to another.	दूसरी वस्तु के समान दी या ली गई कोई वस्तु
Qui tacet consentit (L.)–he who keeps silence consents.	चुप रहने से स्वीकृति का अनुमान होता है, मौनं सम्मतिलक्षणम्

R

Res gestae (L.)–exploits.	साहस के कार्य
Resume (Fr.)–a summary or abstract.	संक्षेप, सारांश, तत्त्व

S

Sine die (L.)–without a difinite day, of a meeting adjourned for an indefinite period.	बिना निश्चित दिन के, अनिश्चित काल के लिए स्थगित बैठक के सन्दर्भ में
Sine odium (L.)–without hatred.	बिना घृणा के
Sine qua non (L.)–without which not, an indispensable condition.	जिसके बिना न (हो सके), आवश्यक या अनिवार्य स्थिति
Sponte sua (L.)–of one's own accord.	अपनी इच्छा से, अपने आप
Status quo (L.)–the state or condition in which a thing is existing.	जिस स्थिति या अवस्था में कोई वस्तु हो, वर्तमान स्थिति
Sub judice (L.)–under consideration.	विचाराधीन
Suus cuique mos (L.)–everyone has peculiar habits.	प्रत्येक मनुष्य का स्वभाव अलग-अलग होता है

T

Terra incognita (L.)–an unknown country.	अज्ञात देश
Tu quoque Brute ! (L.)–and thou too Brutus !	और ब्रूटस् तू भी

U

Ultima thule (L.)–the utmost limit.	अन्तिम सीमा
Ultra vires (L.)–beyond one's powers.	किसी की शक्ति-सामर्थ्य के बाहर

V

Vale (L.)–farewell.	विदाई
Veni, vidi, vici (L.)–I came, I saw, I conquered.	मैं आया, मैंने देखा, मैंने जीता
Versus (L.)–abbr.V–against.	विरुद्ध
Vice (L.)–in place of.	बदले में, वास्ते
Vice versa (L.)–the order being reversed, the terms being exchanged.	क्रम बदल दिया गया, शब्द का क्रम उलटा हुआ
Vis-a-vis (Fr.)–opposite, facing.	आमने-सामने
Volente Deo (L.)–God willing.	यदि ईश्वर की इच्छा हो
Vox populi,vox Dei (L.)–the voice of the people is the voice of God.	पंचों का कथन ईश्वर का वाक्य है

X

Xystum (L.)–a shaded walk in a garden.	वृक्षों से आच्छादित बगीचे का मार्ग

Z

Zonam perdidit (L.)–he has lost his wealth, he is in need of money.	उसका धन चला गया, उसे धन की आवश्यकता है

Phobias

Phobias are a kind of situation under which a person starts fearing from certain objects, conditions or circumstances for which there may be a logical ground or there may not be so. This is basically a psychological aspect of one's behaviour that is often not controlled by the brain.

Different Kinds of Phobias

Acrophobia	fear of height
Agoraphobia	fear of open spaces
Ailurophobia	fear of cats
Algophobia	fear of pain
Amathophobia	fear of dust
Amaxophobia	fear of riding in a car
Ambulophobia	fear of walking
Anthrophobia	fear of humans
Aquaphobia	fear of water
Arachnophobia	fear of spiders
Autophobia	fear of solitude
Ballistophobia	fear of missiles
Bibliophobia	fear of books
Blennophobia	fear of slime
Brontophobia	fear of thunder and lightning
Cancerophobia	fear of cancer
Cathisophobia	fear of sitting
Cenophobia	fear of empty spaces
Chrematophobia	fear of money
Claustrophobia	fear of closed spaces
Climacophobia	fear of falling down stairs
Clinophobia	fear of staying in bed
Cyberphobia	fear of computers
Cynophobia	fear of dogs
Ecophobia	fear of home
Eosophobia	fear of dawn
Ergasiophobia	fear of work
Ergophobia	fear of work

Erotophobia	fear of sex
Euphobia	fear of good news
Gamophobia	fear of marriage
Geniophobia	fear of chins
Genophobia	fear of sex
Gerascophobia	fear of growing old
Graphophobia	fear of writing
Gymnophobia	fear of nudity
Heliophobia	fear of sunlight
Herpetophobia	fear of snakes
Homichlophobia	fear of fog
Homophobia	fear of homosexuals
Hydrophobia	fear of water
Hypsophobia	fear of high places
Iatrophobia	fear of going to the doctor
Kenophobia	fear of empty spaces
Ligyrophobia	fear of loud noises
Muriphobia	fear of mice
Nebulaphobia	fear of fog
Necrophobia	fear of corpses
Negrophobia	fear of blacks
Neophobia	fear of novelty
Nosophobia	fear of disease
Ochlophobia	fear of crowds
Pantophobia	fear of everything
Phengophobia	fear of daylight
Phonophobia	fear of noise or of speaking aloud
Photophobia	fear of light
Pogonophobia	fear of beards
Psychrophobia	fear of the cold
Pteronophobia	fear of being tickled by feathers
Pyrophobia	fear of fire
Sciaphobia	fear of shadows
Scotophobia	fear of the dark
Tocophobia	fear of pregnancy or childbirth
Toxicophobia	fear of poisoning
Toxiphobia	fear of poison or being poisoned
Uranophobia	fear of heaven
Xenophobia	fear of foreigners
Zelophobia	fear of jealousy
Zoophobia	fear of animals

UNIT 17

Manias

Manias are primarily a kind of strong urge for anything tangible or intangible beyond the rational level. This generally arises out of intense interest of someone for a thing or for an emotion that lures him the most.

Different Kinds of Mania

Anthomania	obsession with flowers
Aphrodisiomania	abnormal sexual interest
Bibliomania	craze for books or reading
Bruxomania	compulsion for grinding teeth
Choreomania	dancing mania or frenzy
Clinomania	excessive desire to stay in bed
Copromania	obsession with feces
Dacnomania	obsession with killing
Dipsomania	abnormal craving for alcohol
Discomania	obsession for disco music
Doromania	obsession with giving gifts
Dromomania	compulsive longing for travel
Ecdemomania	abnormal compulsion for wandering
Egomania	irrational self-centered attitude or self-worship
Erotomania	abnormally powerful sex drive
Graphomania	obsession with writing
Gynaecomania	abnormal sexual obsession with women
Hippomania	obsession with horses
Hydromania	irrational craving for water
Melomania	craze for music
Methomania	morbid craving for alcohol
Musomania	obsession with music
Nymphomania	excessive or crazed sexual desire
Oenomania	obsession or craze for wine
Oniomania	mania for making purchases
Onomamania	mania for names

Onomatomania	irresistible desire to repeat certain words
Opiomania	craving for opium
Politicomania	mania for politics
Polkamania	craze for polka dancing
Pornomania	obsession with pornography
Potomania	abnormal desire to drink alcohol
Satyromania	abnormally great male sexual desire; satyriasis
Technomania	craze for technology
Theatromania	craze for going to plays
Theomania	belief that one is a God
Timbromania	craze for stamp collecting
Tomomania	irrational predilection for performing surgery
Toxicomania	morbid craving for poisons
Uranomania	obsession with the idea of divinity
Verbomania	craze for words
Xenomania	inordinate attachment to foreign things

UNIT 18

Group of Collective Noun

A

Anthology of poems
Anthology of prose
Archipelago of islands
Argument of architects
Argument of wizards
Argumentation of historians
Armada of ships
Army of ants
Army of caterpillars
Army of eagles
Army of frogs
Army of herrings
Army of soldiers

B

Band of jays
Band of men
Band of musicians
Bank of circuits
Bank of monitors
Bank of swans
Banner of knights
Barrel of monkeys
Bed of flowers
Bed of oysters
Bed of snakes
Bellowing of bullfinches
Belt of asteroids
Bench of bishops
Bench of judges
Bench of magistrates
Boll of flour
Bond of women
Book of wagers
Bouquet of flowers
Bouquet of pheasants (when flushed)
Brace of bucks
Brace of ducks (a pair)

C

Cartload of monkeys
Cast of actors
Cast of falcons
Cast of hawks
Caste of flower-pots
Catch of fish
Cavalcade of horsemen
Cete of badgers
Chain of bobolinks
Chain of islands
Chain of matches
Charm of finches
Charm of fairies
Charm of goldfinches
Charm of hummingbirds
Chatter of budgerigars
Chattering of chicks
Chattering of choughs
Chattering of goldfinches
Chest of drawers
Clutter of spiders
Clutter of starlings
Coalition of cheetahs
Coil of wigeon
Collection of objects
Collective of nouns
Colony of ants
Colony of badgers
Colony of bats
Colony of beavers
Colony of frogs
Company of moles
Convocation of eagles
Convoy of lorries
Convoy of trucks
Copse of trees
Cornucopia of slugs
Corps of giraffes
Cortege of mourners
Cote of doves
Coterie of prairie dogs
Coven of witches
Cover of coots

D

Descent of relatives
Descent of woodpeckers
Desert of lapwings
Destruction of cats (feral)
Dicker of hides
Disguising of tailors
Dissimulation of birds
Diving of teal
Division of soldiers
Doading of Sheldrake's
Dole of doves
Dole of turtles
Dopping of ducks (diving)
Dopping of sheldrakes
Dout of cats (house cats)
Down of hares
Down of rabbits
Down of sheep
Doyft of swine
Draught of butlers
Draught of fish
Dray of squirrels
Drift of bees
Drift of boars (herded)

E

Eleven of cricketers
Eleven of footballers
Embarrassment of riches
Equivocation of politicians
Erst of bees
Exaltation of larks

F

Flight of airplanes
Flight of bees
Flight of birds
Flight of cormorants
Flight of doves
Flight of dragons
Flight of goshawks
Fling of ox birds
Fling of sandpipers
Flink of cows
Float of crocodiles
Flock of birds
Flock of bustards
Flock of camels
Flock of pigeons
Flock of seagulls
Flock of sheep
Flock of swifts
Flock of tourists
Flock of turkeys
Flotilla of boats

G

Gam of whales
Gang of elk
Gang of hoodlums
Gang of labourers
Gang of slaves
Gang of thieves
Garland of sonnets
Gathering of clans
Gatling of woodpeckers
Gaze of raccoons
Generation of vipers
Giggle of girls
Glaring of cats
Gleam of herrings
Glide of flying fish
Glint of goldfish
Glitter of generals
Glory of unicorns
Grist of bees
Group of guinea pigs

H

Herd of horses
Herd of llamas
Herd of moose
Herd of oxen
Herd of pigs
Herd of ponies
Herd of sea horses
Herd of seals
Herd of swans
Herd of swine
Herd of walruses
Herd of whales
Herd of wolves
Herd of wrens
Herd of yaks (conversation)
Herd of zebras (crossing)
Hill of beans
Hill of ruffs
Hive of bees
Holiness of donuts
Horde of gerbils

I

Illusion of painters
Implausibility of guns
Intrusion of cockroaches

K

Kendle of kittens
Kennel of dogs
Kettle of hawks
Kindle of kittens
Kine of cattle
Knab of toads
Knob of seals
Knob of teal
Knob of wigeon

L

Lead of foxes
Leap of lambs
Leap of leopards
Leash of bucks
Leash of deer
Leash of foxes
Leash of greyhounds
Leash of hares
Leash of hawks
Leash of hounds
Leash of rabbits
Lepe of leopards
Litter of cats (kittens)
Litter of cubs
Litter of dogs (puppies)
Litter of kittens
Litter of piglets
Litter of pups
Litter of whelps
Lodge of beavers

M

Mask of raccoons
Mass of priests
Match of nightingales
Melody of harpers
Memory of elephants
Menagerie of animals
Mess of grits
Miller of whores
Mischief of mice
Mischief of rats
Mob of emus
Mob of kangaroos
Mob of meerkats
Mob of sheep (Australian)
Movement of moles
Multiply of husbands
Murder of crows
Murmuration of starlings
Muscle of marines
Muster of peacocks
Muster of soldiers

N

Nest of eggs
Nest of hornets
Nest of machine guns
Nest of mice
Nest of pheasants
Nest of rabbits
Nest of snakes
Nest of vipers
Nest of wasps
Neverthriving of jugglers
Nide of pheasants (on the ground)
Nosegay of flowers
Nuisance of cats (house cats)

O

Observance of hermits
Obstinacy of buffaloes
Orchestra of musicians
Ostentation of peacocks

P

Pile of books
Pile of dung
Pint of mussels
Pit of snakes
Piteousness of doves
Pitying of doves
Pitying of turtle doves
Plump of ducks (flying)
Plump of seals
Plump of waterfowl
Plump of wildfowl
Plump of woodcock
Pocket of hops
Pocket of oranges
Pod of seals
Pod of walruses
Pod of whales
Pod of whiting
Ponder of philosophers
Pontification of preachers
Pontification of priests

Q

Quarrel of sparrows
Quire of newspapers
Quiver of arrows
Quiver of cobras

R

Raft of alligators
Raft of coots
Raft of ducks (while idle in water)
Raft of otter
Raft of penguins (in water)
Raft of puffins (on water)
Raft of widgeon
Rafter of turkeys
Rag of colts
Rainbow of butterflies
Rake of colts
Rake of mules
Rangale of deer
Range of mountains
Rayful of knaves
Rhumba of rattlesnakes

Richesse of martens
Roost of fowls
Roost of pigeons
Rope of onions
Rope of pearls
Rouleau of coins
Rouleau of money

S

School of fish
School of porpoises
School of salmon
School of shark
School of sharks
School of whales
Scold of jays
Scorn of camels
Scourge of mosquitoes
Screech of gulls
Scurry of squirrels
Sea of bishops
Sedge of bitterns
Siege of bitterns
Siege of cranes
Siege of herons
Singular of boars
Sizzle of sausages (snaggle)
Skein of geese (in flight)
Sleuth of bears
Slew of homework
Slither of snakes
Sloth of bears
Smack of jellyfish
Snarl of leopards
Sprinkle of hoses
Stand of flamingo
Stand of plovers
Stand of trees
Staple of zines
Stare of owls
State of princes
Stench of skunks
Stick of (air-dropped) bombs
Stick of paratroopers
Stock of businessmen
Storytelling of crows

T

Team of cattle
Team of ducks (in flight)
Team of footballers
Team of horses
Team of oxen
Team of players
Team of seals
Thought of barons
Threatening of courtiers
Thunder of dragons
Tiding of magpies
Tittering of magpies
Toil of peasants
Tok of capercailzies
Torment of trainers
Totter of giraffes
Tower of giraffes
Trace of hares
Tribe of sparrows
Trimming of finches
Trip of dotterel
Trip of goats
Trip of hares
Troop of dogfish
Troop of horsemen
Troop of horses
Troop of kangaroos
Troop of lions
Troop of monkeys

U & V

Ubiquity of sparrows
Unkindness of ravens
Venue of vultures
Volery of birds

W

Wad of bills
Wad of money
Waddle of penguins (dry land)
Wake of buzzards
Wake of vultures
Warren of rabbits
Warren of wombats
Watch of nightingales
Wealth of information
Wedge of geese (flying in a V)
Wheel of puffins (flying)
Whiteness of swans
Wisdom of owls
Wisp of snipe (in flight)
Wolfpack of submarines
Whoop of gorillas

Y & Z

Yap of chihuahuas
Yoke of cattle (two)
Yoke of oxen (two)
Zeal of zebras
Zap of lasers

Words : Used in British and American English

British English	American English
Biscuits	Cookies
Return ticket	Roundtrip
Lift	Elevator
Cinema	Movies
Trousers	Pants
Holiday	Vacation
Queue	Line
Petrol	Gasoline
Lorry	Truck
Autumn	Fall
Jumper	Sweater
Sweets	Candy
Flat	Apartment
Flatmate	Roommate
Chips	Fries
Rubbish	Garbage
Dustbin	Trashcan
Bonnet	Hood
Keen	Eager
Knackered	Exhausted
Pissed	Drunk
Mad	Crazy
Rubber	Eraser
Timetable	Routine
Torch	Flashlight
Lolly	Sucker
Pushchair	Stroller
Ring	Call

UNIT 20

Traits of People

- **Ambivert**
- **Argumentative** Quarrels in an attempt of convincing others.
- **Adaptable** Fits easily with other people.
- **Courteous** Polite, considerate and respectful.
- **Diligent** One who has a capacity to work hard.
- **Domineering** One who tries to control others with no consideration for their feeling or their opinions.
- **Extrovert** Bold, daring, fun loving, always communicating first and attempting to be a "can do" person.
- **Enthusiastic** One who shows a lot of excitement and eagerness.
- **Frank** Very open and direct in what one says.
- **Introvert** Reserved, shy and responding to communication with some persuasion, also a "can do" person but within closed doors.
- **Inquisitive** One who tries to find out details about other people.
- **Modest** One who does not like to talk one's own quality.
- **Maestro** Master of something.
- **Narrow minded** Unwilling to seriously consider opinions or views that are so different from his own.
- **Proud** One who has a high opinion of own abilities.
- **Systematic** One who does his work in a well planned manner.
- **Shy** One who is nervous in other's company.
- **Stubborn** One who is not willing to change his mind.
- **Submissive** One who is always willing to yield to other's authority.
- **Tactful** One who is careful not to upset others.

UNIT 21

Cries of Animals and Birds

Apes	Gibber	Hens	Cackle and cluck
Asses	Bray	Horses	Neigh and whinny
Bees	Hum	Hyenas	Laugh
Beetles	Drone	Jays	Chatter
Bears	Growl	Kittens	Mew
Bitterns	Boom	Lambs	Baa and bleat
Blackbirds	Whistle	Larks	Sing
Bulls	Bellow	Linnets	Chuckle
Canaries	Sing or quaver	Lions	Roar
Cats	Mew, purr, swear, and caterwaul	Magpies	Chatter
		Mice	Squeak and squeal
Calves	Bleat and blear	Monkeys	Chatter and gibber
Chaffinches	Chirp or pink	Owls	Hoot and screech
Chickens	Pip	Oxen	Low and bellow
Cicadae	Sing	Parrots	Talk
Cocks	Crow	Peacocks	Scream
Cows	Moo or low	Pigeons	Coo
Crows	Caw	Pigs	Grunt, squeak, and Squeal
Cuckoo	Cry		
Deer	Bell	Ravens	Croak
Dogs	Bark, bay, howl, and yelp	Redstarts	Whistle
		Rooks	Caw
Doves	Coo	Screech-owls	Screech or shriek
Ducks	Quack	Sheep	Baa or bleat
Eagles	Scream	Snakes	Hiss
Falcons	Chant	Sparrows	Chirp or yelp
Flies	Buzz	Stags	Bellow and call
Foxes	Bark and yelp	Swallows	Twitter
Frogs	Croak	Swans	Cry
Geese	Cackle and hiss	Thrushes	Whistle
Grasshoppers	Chirp and pitter	Tigers	Growl
Guineafowls	Cry "come back"	Turkey-cocks	Gobble
Guineapigs	Squeak	Vultures	Scream
Hares	Squeak	Whitethroats	Chirr
Hawks	Scream	Wolves	Howl

UNIT 22

Collocation

A collocation is a combination of words that should be commonly used together.

Collocations starting with the verb 'do'

- Do me a favour
- Do the cooking
- Do the housework
- Do the shopping

Collocations with the verb 'have'

- Have a good time
- Have a bath
- Have a drink
- Have a haircut
- Have a holiday

Collocations with the verb 'break'

- Break the law
- Break a leg
- Break a promise
- Break a record

Collocations with the verb 'take'

- Take a break
- Take a chance
- Take a look
- Take a rest
- Take a seat

Collocations with the verb 'make'

- Make a difference
- Make a mess
- Make a mistake
- Make a noise
- Make an effort

Collocations with the verb 'catch'

- Catch the bus
- Catch a ball
- Catch a cold
- Catch a thief
- Catch fire

Collocations with the verb 'pay'

- Pay respect
- Pay a fine
- Pay attention
- Pay by credit card
- Pay cash

Collocations with the verb 'keep'

- Keep the change
- Keep a promise
- Keep a secret
- Keep an appointment
- Keep calm

Collocations with the verb 'go'

- Go bald
- Go abroad
- Go astray
- Go bad
- Go bankrupt
- Go blind
- Go crazy
- Go fishing

Collocations with the verb 'come'

- Come under attack
- Come close
- Come direct
- Come early
- Come first
- Come into view
- Come last
- Come late
- Come on time

Collocations with the verb 'get'

- Get the sack
- Get a life
- Get a job
- Get a shock
- Get angry
- Get divorced
- Get drunk
- Get frightened

Collocations related to time

- Bang on time
- Dead on time
- Free time
- From dawn till dusk
- Great deal of time
- Early/late 15th century
- Make time for
- Next few days
- Past few weeks

Collocations related to business English

- Annual turnover
- Keep in mind
- Break off negotiations
- Close a deal
- Close a meeting
- Come to the point
- Dismiss an offer
- Draw a conclusion

Collocations with the verb 'save'

- Save yourself the trouble
- Save electricity
- Save energy
- Save money
- Save someone a seat

UNIT 23

Words with their Roots and their Meaning

Roots (Prefix and Suffix)	Meaning of Roots	Words with Root
a, ac, ad, af, ag, al, an, ap, as, at	*to, toward, near, in addition to, by*	aside, accompany, adjust, aggression, allocate, annihilate, affix, associate, attend, adverb
a-, an-	*not, without*	apolitical, atheist, anarchy, anonymous, apathy, aphasia, anemia
ab, abs	*away from, off*	absolve, abrupt, absent
-able, -ible	*Adjective: worth, ability*	solvable, incredible
acer, acid, acri	*bitter, sour, sharp*	acerbic, acidity, acrid, acrimony
act, ag	*do, act, drive*	active, react, agent, active, agitate
acu	*sharp*	acute, acupuncture, accurate
-acy, -cy	*Noun: state or quality*	privacy, infancy, adequacy, intimacy, supremacy
-ade	*act, product, sweet drink*	blockade, lemonade
aer, aero	*air, atmosphere, aviation*	aerial, aerosol, aerodrome
ag, agi, ig, act	*do, move, go*	agent, agenda, agitate, navigate, ambiguous, action
-age	*Noun: activity, or result of action*	courage, suffrage, shrinkage, tonnage
agri, agro	*pertaining to fields or soil*	agriculture, agroindustry
-al	*Noun: action, result of action*	referral, disavowal, disposal, festival
-al, -ial, -ical	*Adjective: quality, relation*	structural, territorial, categorical
alb, albo	*white, without pigment*	albino, albite
ali, allo, alter	*other*	alias, alibi, alien, alloy, alter, ego, altruism
alt	*high, deep*	altimeter, altitude
am, ami, amor	*love, like, liking*	amorous, amiable, amicable, enamoured
ambi	*both*	ambidextrous
ambul	*to walk*	ambulatory, amble, ambulance, somnambulist

Roots (Prefix and Suffix)	Meaning of Roots	Words with Root
-an	*Noun: person*	artisan, guardian, historian, magician
ana, ano	*up, back, again, anew*	anode, anagram, anagenetic
anthrop	*man*	anthropology, misanthrope, philanthropy
anti, ant	*against, opposite*	antisocial, antiseptic, antithesis, antibody, antinomies, antifreeze, antipathy
anti, antico	*old*	antique, antiquated, antiquity
apo, ap, aph	*away from, detached, formed*	apology, apocalypse, aphagia
aqu	*water*	aqueous
-ar, -ary	*Adjective: resembling, related to*	spectacular, unitary
arch	*chief, first, rule*	archangel, architect, archaic, monarchy, matriarchy, patriarchy, Archeozoic era
-ard, -art	*Noun: characterised*	braggart, drunkard, wizard
aster, astr	*star*	aster, asterisk, asteroid, astronomy, astronaut
bar	*weight, pressure*	barometer
be	*on, around, over, about, excessively, make, cause, name, affect*	berate, bedeck, bespeak, belittle, beleaguer
belli	*war*	rebellion, belligerent, casus belli, bellicose
bene	*good, well, gentle*	benefactor, beneficial, benevolent, benediction, beneficiary, benefit
bi, bine	*two*	biped, bifurcate, biweekly, bivalve, biannual
bibl, bibli, biblio	*book*	bibliophile, bibliography, Bible
bio, bi	*life*	biography, biology, biometricsm, biome, biosphere
brev	*short*	abbreviate, brevity, brief
cat, cata, cath	*down, with*	catalogue, category, catheter
caus, caut	*burn, heat*	caustic, cauldron, cauterize
cause, cuse, cus	*cause, motive*	because, excuse, accusation
ceas, ced, cede, ceed, cess	*to go, to yield, move, go, surrender*	succeed, proceed, precede, recede, secession, exceed, succession
cent	*hundred*	centennial, century, centipede
cit	*call, start*	incite, citation, cite
civ	*citizen*	civic, civil, civilian, civilisation
clam, claim	*cry out*	exclamation, clamor, proclamation, reclamation, acclaim
clin	*lean, bend*	decline, aclinic, inclination

Roots (Prefix and Suffix)	Meaning of Roots	Words with Root
clud, clus, claus	*to close, shut*	include, exclude, clause, claustrophobia, enclose, exclusive, reclusive, conclude
co, cog, col, coll, con, com, cor	*with, together*	cohesiveness, cognate, collaborate, convene, commitment, compress, contemporary, converge, compact, confluence, convenient, concatenate, conjoin, combine, correct
cour, cur, curr, curs	*run, course*	occur, excursion, discourse, courier, course
crat, cracy	*rule*	autocrat, aristocrat, theocracy, technocracy
crit	*separate, choose*	critical, criterion, hypocrite
cur, curs	*run*	current, concurrent, concur, incur, recur, occur, courier, precursor, cursive
cura	*care*	curator, curative, manicure
cycl, cyclo	*wheel, circle, circular*	Cyclops, unicycle, bicycle, cyclone, cyclic
de-	*from, down, away, to do the opposite, reverse, against*	detach, deploy, derange, decrease, deodorize, devoid, deflate, degenerate
dec, deca	*ten, ten times*	decimal, decade, decalogue, decimate, decathlon
dec, dign	*suitable*	decent, decorate, dignity
dei, div	*God*	divinity, divine, deity, divination, deify
dem, demo	*people, populace, population*	democracy, demography, demagogue, epidemic
dent, dont	*tooth*	dental, denture, orthodontist, periodontal
derm	*skin, covering*	hypodermic, dermatology, epidermis, taxidermy
di-, dy-	*two, twice, double*	divide, diverge, diglycerides
dia	*through, across, between*	diameter, diagonal, dialogue dialect, dialectic, diagnosis, diachronic
dic, dict, dit	*say, speak*	dictation, dictionary, dictate, dictator, dictaphone, edict, predict, verdict, contradict, benediction
dis, dif	*not, opposite of, reverse, separate, deprive of, away*	dismiss, differ, disallow, disperse, dissuade, divide, disconnect, disproportion, disrespect, distemper, disarray
dit	*give*	credit, audit
doc, doct	*teach, prove*	docile, doctor, doctrine, document, dogma, indoctrinate
domin	*master, that which is under control*	dominate, dominion, predominant, domain
don	*give*	donate, condone
dorm	*sleep*	dormant, dormitory

Roots (Prefix and Suffix)	Meaning of Roots	Words with Root
dox	*thought, opinion, praise*	orthodox, heterodox, paradox, doxology
-drome	*run, step*	syndrome, aerodrome, velodrome
duc, duct	*to lead, pull*	produce, abduct, product, transducer, viaduct, aqueduct, induct, deduct, reduce, induce
-ed	*Verb: past tense*	dressed, faded, patted, closed, introduced
-ed	*Adjective: having the quality or characteristics of*	winged, moneyed, dogged, tired
-en	*Verb: to cause to become*	lengthen, moisten, sharpen
-en	*Adjective: material*	golden, woolen, silken
en-, em-	*put into, make, provide with, surround with*	enamor, embolden, enslave, empower, entangle
-ence, -ency	*Noun: action or process, quality or state*	reference, emergency, dependence, eminence, latency
end-	*inside, within*	endorse, endocardial, endergonic, endoskeleton, endoscope, endogenous
epi-	*upon, close to, over, after, altered*	epicenter, epicarp, epilogue, epigone, epidiorite
equi-	*equal*	equidistant, equilateral, equilibrium, equinox, equation, equator
-er, -ier	*Adjective: comparative*	better, brighter, sooner, hotter, happier
-er, -or	*Noun: person or thing that does something*	flyer, reporter, player, member, fryer, collector, concentrator
-er, -or	*Verb: action*	ponder, dishonor, clamor
erg	*work, effect*	energy, erg, allergy, ergometer, ergograph, ergophobia
-ery	*collective qualities, art, practice, trade, collection, state, condition*	snobbery, bakery, geenery, gallery, slavery
-es, -ies	*Noun: plural of most nouns ending in -ch, -s, -sh, -o and -z and some in -f and -y*	passes, glasses, ladies, heroes
-es, -ies	*Verb: third person singular present indicative of verbs that end in -ch, -s, -sh, - and some in -y*	blesses, hushes, fizzes, defies
-ess	*female*	actress, goddess, poetess
-est, -iest	*Adjective or Adverb: superlative*	latest, strongest, luckiest, lyingest
ev-, et-	*time, age*	medieval, eternal
ex-	*out of, away from, lacking, former*	exit, exhale, exclusive, exceed, explosion, ex-mayor

Roots (Prefix and Suffix)	Meaning of Roots	Words with Root
exter-, extra-, extro-	*outside of, beyond*	external, extrinsic, extraordinary, extrapolate, extraneous, extrovert
fid, fide, feder	*faith, trust*	confidante, fidelity, confident, infidelity, infidel, federal, confederacy
fig	*shape, form*	figurem, effigy, figure, figment
fila, fili	*thread*	filigree, filament, filter, filet, filibuster
fin	*end, ended, finished*	final, finite, finish, confine, fine, refine, define, finale
fix	*repair, attach*	fix, fixation, fixture, affix, prefix, suffix
flex, flect	*bend*	flex, reflex, flexible, flexor, inflexibility, reflect, deflect, circumflex
flict	*strike*	affliction, conflict, inflict
flu, fluc, fluv, flux	*flow*	influence, fluid, flue, flush, fluently, fluctuate, reflux, influx
-fold	*Adverb: in a manner of, marked by*	fourfold
for, fore	*before*	forecast, fortune, foresee
forc, fort	*strength, strong*	effort, fort, forte, fortifiable, fortify, forte, fortitude
form	*shape, resemble*	form, format, conform, formulate, perform, formal, formula
fract, frag, frai	*break*	fracture, infraction, fragile, fraction, refract, frail
fuge	*flee*	subterfuge, refuge, centrifuge
-ful	*Noun: an amount or quantity that fills*	mouthful
-ful	*Adjective: having, giving, marked by*	fanciful
fuse	*pour*	confuse, transfuse
-fy	*make, form into*	falsify, dandify
gam	*marriage*	bigamy, monogamy, polygamy
gastr, gastro	*stomach*	gastric, gastronomic, gastritis, gastropod
gen	*kind*	generous
gen	*birth, race, produce*	genesis, genetics, eugenics, genealogy, generate, genetic, antigen, pathogene
geo	*earth*	geometry, geography, geocentric, geology
germ	*vital part*	germination, germ, germane
gest	*carry, bear*	congest, gestation
giga	*billion*	gigabyte, gigaflop
gin	*careful*	gingerly
gloss, glot	*tongue*	glossary, polyglot, epiglottis

Roots (Prefix and Suffix)	Meaning of Roots	Words with Root
glu, glo	*lump, bond, glue*	glue, agglutinate, conglomerate
graph, gram, graf	*write, written, draw*	graph, graphic, autograph, photography, graphite, telegram, polygraph, grammar, biography, lithograph, graphic
grat	*pleasing*	congratulate, gratuity, grateful, ingrate
her, here, hes	*stick*	adhere, cohere, cohesion, inherent, hereditary, hesitate
hetero	*other, different*	heterodox, heterogeneous, heterosexual, heterodyne
hex, ses, sex	*six*	hexagon, hexameter, sestet, sextuplets
homo	*same*	homogenise, homosexual, homonym, homophone
hum, human	*earth, ground, man*	humus, exhume, humane
hydr, hydra, hydro	*water*	dehydrate, hydrant, hydraulic, hydraulics, hydrogen, hydrophobia
hyper	*over, above*	hyperactive, hypertensive, hyperbolic, hypersensitive, hyperventilate, hyperkinetic
hypn	*sleep*	hypnosis, hypnotherapy
-ia	*Noun: names, diseases*	phobia
-ian, an	*Noun: related to, one that is*	pedestrian, human
-iatry	*Noun: art of healing*	psychiatry
-ic	*Adjective: quality, relation*	generic
-ic, ics	*Noun: related to the arts and sciences*	arithmetic, economics
-ice	*Noun: act*	malice
-ify	*Verb: cause*	specify
ignis	*fire*	ignite, igneous, ignition
-ile	*Adjective: having the qualities of*	projectile
in, im	*into, on, near, towards*	instead, import
in, im, il, ir	*not*	illegible, irresolute, inaction, inviolate, innocuous, intractable, innocent, impregnable, impossible, imposter
infra	*beneath*	infrared, infrastructure
-ing	*Noun: material made for, activity, result of an activity*	flooring, swimming, building
-ing	*Verb: present participle*	depicting
-ing	*Adjective: activity*	cohering

Roots (Prefix and Suffix)	Meaning of Roots	Words with Root
inter	*between, among*	international, intercept, interject, intermission, internal, intermittent,
intra	*within, during, between layers, underneath*	intramural, intranet, intranatal
intro	*into, within, inward*	interoffice, introvert, introspection, introduce
-ion	*Noun: condition or action*	abduction
-ish	*Adjective: having the character of*	newish
-ism	*Noun: doctrine, belief, action or conduct*	formalism
-ist	*Noun: person or member*	podiatrist
-ite	*Noun: state or quality*	graphite
-ity, ty	*Noun: state or quality*	lucidity, novelty
-ive	*Noun: condition*	native
-ive, -ative, -itive	*Adjective: having the quality of*	festive, cooperative, sensitive
-ize	*Verb: cause*	fantasize
jac, ject	*throw*	reject, eject, project, trajectory, interject, dejected, inject, ejaculate, adjacent
join, junct	*join*	adjoining, enjoin, juncture, conjunction, injunction, conjunction
judice	*judge*	prejudice
jug, junct, just	*to join*	junction, adjust, conjugal
juven	*young*	juvenile, rejuvenate
labor	*work*	laborious, belabor
lau, lav, lot, lut	*wash*	launder, lavatory, lotion, ablution, dilute
lect, leg, lig	*choose, gather, select, read*	collect, legible, eligible
leg	*law*	legal, legislate, legislature, legitimise
-less	*Adjective: without, missing*	motiveless
levi	*light*	alleviate, levitate, levity
lex, leag, leg	*law*	legal, college, league
liber, liver	*free*	liberty, liberal, liberalise, deliverance
lide	*strike*	collide, nuclide
liter	*letters*	literary, literature, literal, alliteration, obliterate
macr-, macer	*lean*	emaciated, meager
magn	*great*	magnify, magnificent, magnanimous, magnate, magnitude, magnum
main	*strength, foremost*	mainstream, mainsail, domain, remain

Roots (Prefix and Suffix)	Meaning of Roots	Words with Root
mal	*bad, badly*	malformation, maladjusted, dismal, malady, malcontent,malfunction, malfeasance, maleficent
man, manu	*hand, make, do*	manual, manage, manufacture, manacle, manicure, manifest, maneuver, emancipate, management
mand	*command*	mandatory, remand, mandate
mania	*madness*	mania, maniac, kleptomania, pyromania
mar, mari, mer	*sea, pool*	marine, marsh, maritime, mermaid
matri	*mother*	matrimony, maternal, matriarchate, matron
medi	*half, middle, between, halfway*	mediate, medieval, Mediterranean, mediocre, medium
mega	*great, million*	megaphone, megaton, megaflop, megalomaniac, megabyte, megalopolis
mem	*recall, remember*	memo, commemoration, memento, memoir, memorable
ment	*mind*	mental, mention
-ment	*Noun: condition or result*	document
meso	*middle*	mesomorph, mesoamerica, mesosphere
meta	*beyond, change*	metaphor, metamorphosis, metabolism, metahistorical, metainformation
meter	*measure*	meter, voltammeter, barometer, thermometer
metr	*admeasure, apportion*	metrics, asymmetric, parametric, telemetry
micro	*small, millionth*	microscope, microfilm, microcard, microwave, micrometer, microvolt
migra	*wander*	migrate, emigrant, immigrate
mill, kilo	*thousand*	millennium, kilobyte, kiloton
milli	*thousandth*	millisecond, milligram, millivolt
min	*little, small*	minute, minor, minuscule
mis	*wrong, bad, badly*	misconduct, misinform, misinterpret, mispronounce, misnomer, mistake, misogynist
mit, miss	*send*	emit, remit, submit, admit, commit, permit, transmit, omit, intermittent, mission, missile
mob, mov, mot	*move*	motion, remove, mobile, motor
mon	*warn, remind*	monument, admonition, monitor, premonition
mono	*one*	monopoly, monotype, monologue, mononucleosis, monorail, monotheist,

Roots (Prefix and Suffix)	Meaning of Roots	Words with Root
mor, mort	*mortal, death*	mortal, immortal, mortality, mortician, mortuary
morph	*shape, form*	amorphous, dimorphic, metamorphosis, morphology, polymorphic, morpheme, amorphous
-ness	*Noun: state, condition, quality*	kindness
neur	*nerve*	neuritis, neuropathic, neurologist, neural, neurotic
nom	*law, order*	autonomy, astronomy, gastronomy, economy
oct	*eight*	octopus, octagon, octogenarian, octave
oligo	*few, little*	oligocene, oligosaccharide, oligotrophic, oligarchy
omni	*all, every*	omnipotent, omniscient, omnipresent, omnivorous
onym	*name*	anonymous, pseudonym, antonym, synonym
oper	*work*	operate, cooperate, opus
-or	*Noun: condition or activity*	valor, honor, humor, minor
ortho	*straight, correct*	orthodox, orthodontist, orthopedic, unorthodox
-ory	*Noun: place for, serves for*	territory, rectory
-ous, -eous, -ose, -ious	*Adjective: having the quality of, relating to*	adventurous, courageous, verbose, fractious
over	*excessive, above*	overwork, overall, overwork
pac	*peace*	pacifist, pacify, pacific ocean
pair, pare	*arrange, assemblage, two*	repair, impair, compare, prepare
paleo	*old*	paleozoic, paleolithic, paleomagnetism, paleopsychology
pan	*all*	Pan-American, pan-African, panacea, pandemonium (place of all the demons),
para	*beside*	paradox, paraprofessional, paramedic, paraphrase, parachute
pat, pass, path	*feel, suffer*	patient, passion, sympathy, pathology
pater, patr	*father*	paternity, patriarch, patriot, patron, patronise
path, pathy	*feeling, suffering*	pathos, sympathy, antipathy, apathy, telepathy
ped, pod	*foot*	pedal, impede, pedestrian, centipede, tripod, podiatry, antipode, podium

Roots (Prefix and Suffix)	Meaning of Roots	Words with Root
pedo	*child*	orthopedic, pedagogue, pediatrics
pel, puls	*drive, push, urge*	compel, dispel, expel, repel, propel, pulse, impulse, pulsate, compulsory, expulsion, repulsive
pend, pens, pond	*hang, weigh*	pendant, pendulum, suspend, appendage, pensive, append
per	*through, intensive*	persecute, permit, perspire, perforate, persuade
peri	*around*	periscope, perimeter, perigee, periodontal
phage	*eat*	macrophage, bacteriophage
phan, phas, phen, fan, phant, fant	*show, make visible*	phantom, fantasy
phe	*speak*	blaspheme, cipher, phenomenon, philosopher
phil	*love*	philosopher, philanthropy, philharmonic, bibliophile
phlegma	*inflammation*	phlegm, phlegmatic
phobia, phobos	*fear*	phobia, claustrophobia, acrophobia, aquaphobia, ergophobia, homophobia
phon	*sound*	telephone, phonics, phonograph, phonetic, homophone, microphone, symphony, euphonious
phot, photo	*light*	photograph, photoelectric, photogenic, photosynthesis, photon
pico	*trillionth*	picofarad, picocurie, picovolt
pict	*paint, show, draw*	picture, depict
plac, plais	*please*	placid, placebo, placate, complacent
pli, ply	*fold*	reply, implicate, ply
plore	*cry out, wail*	implore, exploration, deploring
plu, plur, plus	*more*	plural, pluralist, plus
pneuma, pneumon	*breath*	pneumatic, pneumonia,
pod	*foot, feet*	podiatry, tripod
poli	*city*	metropolis, police, politics, Indianapolis, megalopolis, acropolis
poly	*many*	polytheist, polygon, polygamy, polymorphous
pon, pos, pound	*place, put*	postpone, component, opponent, proponent, expose, impose, deposit, posture, position, expound, impound
pop	*people*	population, populous, popular

Roots (Prefix and Suffix)	Meaning of Roots	Words with Root
port	*carry*	porter, portable, transport, report, export, import, support, transportation
portion	*part, share*	portion, proportion
post	*after, behind*	postpone, postdate
pot	*power*	potential, potentate, impotent
pre, pur	*before*	precede
prehendere	*seize, grasp*	apprehend, comprehend, comprehensive, prehensile
prin, prim, prime	*first*	primacy, prima donna, primitive, primary, primal, primeval, prince, principal
pro	*for, foward*	propel
proto	*first*	prototype, protocol, protagonist, protozoan, proterozoic, protoindustrial
psych	*mind, soul*	psyche, psychiatry, psychology, psychosis
punct	*point, dot*	punctual, punctuation, puncture, acupuncture, punctuation
pute	*think*	dispute, computer
quat, quad	*four*	quadrangle, quadruplets
quint, penta	*five*	quintet, quintuplets, pentagon, pentane, pentameter
quip	*ship*	equip, equipment
quir, quis, quest, quer	*seek, ask*	query, inquire, exquisite, quest
re	*back, again*	report, realign, retract, revise, regain
reg, recti	*straighten*	regiment, regular, rectify, correct, direct, rectangle
retro	*backwards*	retrorocket, retrospect, retrogression, retroactive
ri, ridi, risi	*laughter*	deride, ridicule, ridiculous, derision, risible
rog, roga	*ask*	prerogative, interrogation, derogatory
rupt	*break*	rupture, interrupt, abrupt, disrupt, ruptible
serv	*save, serve, keep*	servant, service, subservient, servitude, preserve, conserve, reservation, deserve, conservation, observe
-ship	*Noun: status, condition*	relationship, friendship
sign, signi	*sign, mark, seal*	signal, signature, design, insignia, significant
simil, simul	*like, resembling*	similar, assimilate, simulate, simulacrum, simultaneous
sist, sta, stit	*stand, withstand, make up*	assist, insist, persist, circumstance, stamina, status, state, static, stable, stationary, substitute

Roots (Prefix and Suffix)	Meaning of Roots	Words with Root
soci	*to join, companions*	sociable, society
sol, solus	*alone*	solo, soliloquy, solitaire, solitude, solitary, isolate
solv, solu, solut	*loosen, explain*	solvent, solve, absolve, resolve, soluble, solution, resolution, resolute, dissolute, absolution
somn	*sleep*	insomnia, somnambulist
soph	*wise*	sophomore (wise fool), philosophy, sophisticated
spec, spect, spi, spic	*look, see*	specimen, specific, spectator, spectacle, aspect, speculate, inspect, respect, prospect, retrospective, introspective, expect, conspicuous
sper	*render favourable*	prosper
sphere	*ball, sphere*	sphere, stratosphere, hemisphere, spheroid
spir	*breath*	spirit, conspire, inspire, aspire, expire, perspire, respiration
stand, stant, stab, stat, stan, sti, sta, st, stead	*stand*	stature, establish, stance
-ster	*person*	mobster, monster
strain, strict, string, stige	*bind, pull, draw tight*	stringent, strict, restrict, constrict, restrain, boa constrictor
stru, struct, stroy, stry	*build*	construe, structure, construct, instruct, obstruct, destruction, destroy, industry, ministry
sub, suc, suf, sup, sur, sus	*under, below, from, secretly, instead of*	sustain, survive, support, suffice, succeed, submerge, submarine, substandard, subnormal, subvert
tain, ten, tent, tin	*hold, keep, have*	retain, continue, content, tenacious
tect, teg	*cover*	detect, protect, tegular, tegument
tele	*distance, far, from afar*	telephone, telegraph, telegram, telescope, television, telephoto, telecast, telepathy
tem, tempo	*time*	tempo, temporary, extemporaneously, contemporary, pro tem, temporal
ten, tin, tain	*hold*	tenacious, tenant, tenure, untenable, detention, retentive, content, pertinent, continent, obstinate, contain, abstain, pertain, detain
tend, tent, tens	*stretch, strain*	tendency, extend, intend, contend, pretend, superintend, tender, extent, tension, pretense

Roots (Prefix and Suffix)	Meaning of Roots	Words with Root
tera	*trillion*	terabyte, teraflop
term	*end, boundary, limit*	exterminate, terminal
terr, terra	*earth*	terrain, terrarium, territory, terrestrial
test	*to bear witness*	testament, detest, testimony, attest, testify
the, theo	*God, a God*	monotheism, polytheism, atheism, theology
therm	*heat*	thermometer, theorem, thermal, thermos bottle, thermostat, hypothermia
thesis, thet	*place, put*	antithesis, hypothesis, synthesis, epithet
tire	*draw, pull*	attire, retire, entire
tom	*cut*	atom (not cutable), appendectomy, tonsillectomy, dichotomy, anatomy
tor, tors, tort	*twist*	torture, retort, extort, distort, contort, torsion, tortuous, torturous
tox	*poison*	toxic, intoxicate, antitoxin
tract, tra, trai, treat	*drag, draw, pull*	attract, tractor, traction, extract, retract, protract, detract, subtract, contract, intractable
trans	*across, beyond, change*	transform, transoceanic, transmit, transportation, transducer
tri	*three*	tripod, triangle, trinity, trilateral
trib	*pay, bestow*	tribute, contribute, attribute, retribution, tributary
tribute	*give*	contribute, distribute, tributary
turbo	*disturb*	turbulent, disturb, turbid, turmoil
typ	*print*	type, prototype, typical, typography, typewriter, typology, typify
ultima	*last*	ultimate, ultimatum
umber, umbraticum	*shadow*	umbra, penumbra, (take) umbrage, adumbrate
un	*not, against, opposite*	unceasing, unequal
uni	*one*	uniform, unilateral, universal, unity, unanimous, unite, unison, unicorn
-ure	*Noun: act, condition, process, function*	exposure, conjecture, measure
vac	*empty*	vacate, vacuum, evacuate, vacation, vacant, vacuous
vade	*go*	evade, invader
vale, vali, valu	*strength, worth*	equivalent; valiant, validity, evaluate, value, valor
veh, vect	*to carry*	vector, vehicle, convection, vehement

Roots (Prefix and Suffix)	Meaning of Roots	Words with Root
ven, vent	*come*	convene, intervene, venue, convenient, avenue, circumvent, invent, convent, venture, event, advent, prevent
ver, veri	*true*	very, aver, verdict, verity, verify, verisimilitude
verb, verv	*word*	verify, veracity, verbalise, verve
vert, vers	*turn, change*	convert, revert, advertise, versatile, vertigo, invert, reversion, extravert, introvert, diversion, introvert, convertible, reverse, controversy
vi	*way*	viable, vibrate, vibrant
vic, vicis	*change, substitute*	vicarious, vicar, vicissitude
vict, vinc	*conquer*	victor, evict, convict, convince, invincible
vid, vis	*see*	video, evident, provide, providence, visible, revise, supervise, vista, visit, vision, review, indivisible
viv, vita, vivi	*alive, life*	revive, survive, vivid, vivacious, vitality, vivisection, vital, vitamins, revitalise
voc, voke	*call*	vocation, avocation, convocation, invocation, evoke, provoke, revoke, advocate, provocative, vocal
vol	*will*	malevolent, benevolent, volunteer, volition
volcan	*fire*	volcano, vulcanize, Vulcan
volv, volt, vol	*turn about, roll*	revolve, voluble, voluminous, convolution, revolt, evolution
vor	*eat greedily*	voracious, carnivorous, herbivorous, omnivorous, devour
-ward	*Adverb: in a direction or manner*	homeward
-wise	*Adverb: in the manner of, with regard to*	timewise, clockwise, bitwise
with	*against*	withhold, without, withdraw, forthwith
-y	*Noun: state, condition, result of an activity*	society, victory
-y	*Adjective: marked by, having*	hungry, angry, smeary, teary
zo	*animal*	zoo (zoological garden), zoology, zodiac, protozoan